MEDJUGORJE
DAY BY DAY

MEDJUGORJE DAY BY DAY

A Daily Meditation Book Based on the
Messages of Our Lady of Medjugorje

REV. RICHARD J. BEYER

AVE MARIA PRESS
Notre Dame, Indiana 46556

First printing, January 1993
Seventh printing, August 2004
77,000 copies in print

© 1993 by Ave Maria Press, Inc., P.O. Box 428, Notre Dame, IN 46556

www.avemariapress.com

International Standard Book Number: 0-87793-494-0

Library of Congress Catalog Card Number: 92-74779

Cover and text design by Elizabeth J. French

Photo on p. 194 courtesy of St. James' Church, Medjugorje. All other photos are by the author.

Printed and bound in the United States of America.

Acknowledgments

Scripture quotations are from the *New Revised Standard Version Bible*, copyright © 1989 by the Division of Christian Education of the National Council of Churches of Christ in the United States of America. Used by permission.

The English translation of *Te Deum* (Oct 13), copyright by the International Consultation on English Texts.

Excerpts from "The Church Today" (May 19 and Dec 20) and "The Laity" (Dec 21) are from *The Documents of Vatican II*, edited by Walter M. Abbott, copyright © 1966 by the America Press, New York.

"Instructions to Prayer Groups" (Jan 26), "The Rosary of Jesus" (Feb 9), "Petition to God" (Apr 2), "Prayer to Give Oneself to Mary" (Apr 3), "Our Lady's Commentary on the Our Father" (Sep 5-7), "Consecration to the Heart of Mary" (Nov 24), and "Consecration to the Heart of Jesus" (Nov 25) were translated by the priests of the St. James parish church in Medjugorje. Used with their permission.

The various prayers, reflections, and sermons by Fr. Slavko Barbaric are used with his permission.

"There Comes a Time" by Josephine Cordaro (May 8) is reprinted from the Irish newsletter *The Medjugorje Echo*. Used with the general permission of the publication.

Excerpts from "A Dedication of a Prayer Time" (Oct 24) and "Sacred Heart Psalm" (Oct 26) are from *Prayers for a Planetary Pilgrim*, copyright © 1989 by Edward Hays, Forest of Peace Books, Easton, KS. Used by permission.

English translations of "Prayer for a Faithful and Upright Heart" (Jan 28) and "Prayer in Praise of the Mother of God" (Aug 20), "Prayer on Independence Day" (Jul 4), and "Novena to Our Guardian Angel" (Oct 2) are from *The New St. Joseph Peoples' Prayer Book*, edited by Francis Evans, 1980, Catholic Book Publishing Co., New York. Used by permission.

"Prayer to St. Michael the Archangel" (Sep 29) by Noel O'Donoghue is from *Prayers for Our Times*, edited by John

*Dedicated
to Our Lady
The Queen of Peace
and
to my mother
Catherine E. Beyer
with love*

Preface

In compiling this book it was my intention to meet several requests of Our Lady of Medjugorje.

The first concerns the messages she has given over these past years. In February of 1989 she said, in part:

Dear children, during this time multiply your prayers and go deeper into the messages that I have given. . . .

And again, on Christmas Day in 1989:

Therefore, little children, read everyday the messages I gave you and transform them into life. . . .

For this reason I have begun each day's reflection with one of Our Lady's messages. Since many were originally given on a particular feast day or during a special liturgical season, such as Advent, I have matched these messages to the corresponding day of the church calendar. A message given on the Feast of the Annunciation, for instance, is found on the very day of the feast, March 25th. This helps to enhance the meaning and impact of the messages.

As a second request, Our Lady has asked that sacred scripture also become a daily part of our lives. In June of 1983 she said:

Read what has been written about Jesus. Meditate on it and convey it to others.

And in October of 1984:

Dear children, today I call you to read the Bible every day in your homes, and let it be in a visible place. . . .

Again, to Jelena's prayer group she said, "Read the gospels, and you will understand everything." In answer to this request, I have chosen a passage from scripture that corresponds to the Virgin's message for the day. In a message on love, for example, I have used St. Paul's sermon on love in 1 Corinthians 13:1-13. I might also say that I have had little difficulty in correlating sacred scripture to Our Lady's messages, which speaks highly of their biblical roots.

As a third element, I have added a reflection after the two readings which normally ties them together and may include a personal thought or experience, an explanation of a church teaching touched upon, or the insight of another writer, theologian, or poet that I felt would be valuable to the reader.

And last, I have closed each day's reflection with an application that seeks to ground it in day-to-day life.

This is a pastoral book that I hope will draw Medjugorje into the fabric of the reader's daily life. It is the fruit of many trips to Medjugorje and a sabbatical which allowed me to live there for extended periods. It is my prayer that it will be spiritually helpful to all who use it.

I would like to express my special thanks to Miss Betty Felder for her help and encouragement in the writing of this book. She continues in her ministry as nurse-in-residence at Medjugorje, where she has remained even during the fiercest days of the Yugoslavian civil war.

I also extend my deep appreciation to the following friends for their support and assistance: Fr. Slavko Barbaric, Marija Pavlovic, and Kennedi and Marija Kozina—all from Medjugorje; and from the United States: The Most Reverend Gerald O'Keefe, Bishop of Davenport, Iowa: Mr. Carl Stahler, Jr., Dennis and Patricia Weber, Mr. Robert Hamma of Ave Maria Press, and Mr. Steve Beyer.

Statue of Our Lady in front of St. James Church

A Brief History of the Events at Medjugorje

On June 24, 1981, two teen-age girls went for a walk in the rocky hills above their village in western Yugoslavia. Suddenly, one of them saw in the distance the luminous silhouette of a young woman. "Mirjana, look! It's Our Lady!" Ivanka said. But her companion, without bothering to look, replied, "Come on! Why would Our Lady appear to us!?"

Returning to the village, they spoke of their experience and were later joined at the hill by four friends, who also saw the apparition. But that night at their homes no one believed their story.

The next day four members of the original group, along with two friends who had not been with them the previous day, went to the hill (Mt. Podbrdo) at the same time, about 6:30 p.m. These six constituted the group of visionaries from that time on. They are:

Ivanka Ivankovic, then 15, born April 21, 1966;

Mirjana Dragicevic, then 16, born March 18, 1965;

Vicka Ivankovic, then 16, born July 3, 1964;

Ivan Dragicevic, then 16, born May 25, 1965;

Marija Pavlovic, then 15, born April 1, 1965;

and Jakov Colo, then 10 years old, born June 3, 1971.

On the second day they saw the apparition close-up for the first time. The woman appeared young, nineteen or twenty, and was "beautiful beyond anything in this world," they later said. She wore a silver-gray gown and a white veil, with a circle of twelve stars around her head. Her hair was dark and her eyes light blue. She looked at them with extraordinary affection. For the first time she spoke, identifying herself as the Blessed Virgin Mary.

Thus began the longest series of Marian apparitions in church history, from 1981 until the present day. The six visionaries began to experience daily appearances of the Virgin. She said she had come to bring peace and reconciliation to a world that was intent on destroying itself. This was the time of the nuclear arms race, Communist expansionism, the Iron Curtain and the Berlin Wall. Yugoslavia itself was under the heel of a communist dictatorship. Even in the West, the moral fabric of society continued to unravel: "Darkness reigns over the entire earth," the Virgin said; "faith is being extinguished."

Later on the second day of the apparitions, one of the seers, Marija Pavlovic, saw the Madonna crying, carrying a wooden cross. "Peace, peace, peace!" she said. "Be reconciled! Only peace!" Wishing to be known in Medjugorje as the "Queen of Peace," she sought to rally the faithful in prayer and penance for the cause of peace, for mankind's cooperation was essential.

In the course of her messages, the Blessed Mother gave the specific means to achieve her plan. These are the core messages of Medjugorje: *prayer, conversion, penance, peace,* and *fasting.* They were given essentially within the first five days of the apparitions, and the following years have served to underline their importance.

Tied in to the urgent tone of the messages are ten secrets regarding the destiny of the world. They will be revealed in due course, three days before each of them is fulfilled. Several have to do with threats hanging over the world, the consequence of the collective sin of mankind. Two of the seers have received all ten secrets and no longer have daily apparitions; the other four have received nine.

The appearances of the Mother of God in Medjugorje have been accompanied by a number of miracles, including physical healings (now numbered at 360), reports of the sun dancing or spinning in the sky, rosary links and medals that apparently change from silver to gold, and other phenomena. But the most frequently reported miracles are those of the spirit—deep conversions, the grace of inner peace, the indwelling of a new hope and a deeper love. "This is a time of grace the world has not known since ancient times," the Madonna said.

Just as Christ worked miracles during his earthly life to authenticate his teaching and ministry, so Our Lady of Medjugorje seems to be using them to validate her presence and messages, which, as always, direct us to her Son. "I do nothing on my own," she once said, "but only the will of God." This is an essential aspect of the apparitions—*that they are the initiative of God and that Mary is the intermediary he has chosen to use:* "I am the servant of the Lord—let it be done to me as you say" (Lk 1:38).

A unique happening in the annals of Marian apparitions took place at Medjugorje a year and one-half after the event started. Without ceasing to appear to the original visionaries, the Blessed Virgin began manifesting herself in a completely new way to two young girls, Jelena Vasilj, then ten years old (born May 14, 1972), and Marijana Vasilj (no relation), also ten (born October 5, 1972). They receive what is termed "locutions," in which they hear the distinct voice of Our Lady and see her inwardly "with the heart." She appears to be using them for a deeper work of the Holy Spirit, speaking to them of holiness and the spiritual life. In May of 1983, the Virgin began giving Jelena teachings on spirituality, which she was to write down and eventually convey to the church. The locutions especially emphasize prayer: "She said that prayer is everything and without prayer we can do nothing," Jelena states. Through Marijana and Jelena, the Blessed Mother is issuing a special call to personal holiness.

The Madonna also told Jelena to form a prayer group within the parish which the Virgin would lead herself through the two locutionists. Comprised mainly of young people, the group of fifty-six meets weekly and adheres to a set of spiritual guidelines given by the Virgin. Others throughout the world were encouraged to follow this program.

The Blessed Mother also leads a prayer group through Ivan and Marija, two of the original visionaries. It meets in the evening at the site of the first apparition on Mt. Podbrdo, and at times on Mt. Krizevac. After singing songs and praying the rosary, the Virgin occasionally appears to the two seers and prays with them, sometimes giving a special message and blessing those present. In the last few years the group has invited pilgrims that happen to be in Medjugorje to join them.

The major event in the village, of course, is the daily apparition of the Blessed Virgin to the visionaries at 6:40 in the evening. Normally several of the seers gather in a room in the north tower of the church, but the Madonna will appear to them wherever they happen to be—at home, overseas, together or separately. For some time she gave Marija a special message for the world each Thursday; it is now given on the 25th of each month.

Preceding the nightly apparition, the villagers and visiting pilgrims gather at St. James Church to pray the Joyful and Sorrowful Mysteries of the rosary. After the apparition, the Eucharist is celebrated. This in turn is followed by a blessing of religious articles, a healing service, and usually the Glorious Mysteries. The apparitions, then, are set closely within the life of the church, and the seers have benefited from the support and guidance of the local Franciscan friars, three of whom should be especially noted.

Fr. Jozo Zovko was the pastor at Medjugorje when the apparitions began. Because of his defense of the visionaries and courageous preaching, he was imprisoned by the Communist government for a year and one-half on a charge of "fostering sedition." He now resides in a parish about twenty-five minutes from Medjugorje, but continues to minister to the many pilgrims who come from all over the world. His spiritual gifts and holiness are now legendary and he has been gifted with apparitions of the Madonna although he rarely discusses the fact.

Fr. Tomislav Pervan, a scripture scholar, became pastor at St. James in August of 1982. He also endured the government's antagonism, yet his quiet perseverance and leadership have won him great respect among the clergy and people of Medjugorje and beyond. He has served as spiritual director to Jelena and Marijana, the locutionists, and their prayer group, and has since founded a religious community dedicated solely to living the messages of the Queen of Peace.

Fr. Slavko Barbaric has served at St. James almost from the beginning. A scholar and trained psychologist, he has written extensively on the events and messages. Through the visionaries, he was asked by the Blessed Virgin to remain indefinitely to officially record the messages and events as they transpire. He is spiritual guide to the seers and also directs retreats at St. James.

There are three special sites in Medjugorje that are associated with the apparitions and have become the primary places of pilgrimage. The first is Mt. Podbrdo, or the Hill of Apparitions, where Our Lady first appeared, until the Communist authorities forbade its use. It is here that the Madonna has promised to leave a permanent miraculous sign, visible to all, as an impetus to conversion and to authenticate the apparitions.

The second pilgrimage site is Mt. Krizevac, or Cross Mountain, on which stands a fifteen-ton concrete cross which was erected by the people of the area in 1933, to commemorate the nineteen-hundredth anniversary of Christ's crucifixion and resurrection. The Blessed Virgin refers to Mt. Krizevac many times in her messages and has appeared there a number of times to Ivan and Marija during their prayer group meetings. Many other miraculous phenomena have occurred on the mountain.

The third site is that of St. James Church itself, where the spiritual life of the village is centered. It is here that the Madonna continues to appear to the seers. Providentially, the namesake of the church, the apostle James, is the patron saint of pilgrims.

The Catholic church has withheld judgment of the Medjugorje events until the official investigating commission reports its findings, probably not before the apparitions end. Pope John Paul II has watched the unfolding of events with great interest, and has privately affirmed the spiritual fruits of Medjugorje. In answer to a question by a delegation of Italian bishops in 1986, the Pontiff said, "Let the people go to Medjugorje if they pray, fast, do penance, confess, and convert" (the Virgin's five core messages).

From all accounts, and in looking at the new world around us since 1981, Medjugorje has ushered in a new age of peace. It is the fountainhead of a number of apparition sites around the world, including San Nicolas, Argentina; Damascus, Syria; Escorial, Spain; Kibeho, Rwanda (Africa); Cairo, Egypt; and Oliveto Citra, Italy. It is a time of grace that the world has rarely seen, nor will ever see again: "These are my last apparitions on earth," the Madonna told the visionaries. They herald a rebirth of faith among all the children of God.

For Further Reading:

Craig, Mary, *Spark From Heaven*, Ave Maria Press, Notre Dame, Indiana, 1988.

Laurentin, Fr. Rene, and Ljudevit, Rupcic, *Is the Virgin Mary Appearing at Medjugorje?* Gaithersburg, Maryland, 1984.

Laurentin, Fr. Rene, *The Apparitions of the Blessed Virgin Mary Today*, Veritas Publications, Dublin, Ireland, 1990.

Pelletier, Fr. Joseph A., *The Queen of Peace Visits Medjugorje*, Assumption Publications, Worcester, Massachusetts, 1985.

Key to the Messages

The messages of Our Lady in Medjugorje in this book are newly translated. Each is coded in brackets at the end of the passsage, referring to its source and date (for example: WM 11-27-86). Please note that all the weekly and monthly messages end with the phrase: "Thank you for responding to my call." Due to space limitations this has not always been included. The key to the abbreviations is as follows:

WM—Weekly Message. One of the weekly messages of the Blessed Virgin to the world, given between March 1, 1984 and January 8, 1987.

MM—Monthly Message. The monthly messages of the Virgin, given from January 25, 1987 until the present.

VPG—Visionary's Prayer Group. Given to Ivan and/or Marija in the context of a prayer group meeting, often on the Hill of Apparitions or Mt. Krizevac.

LJM—Locution to Jelena or Marijana. Messages given to the two girls to whom Our Lady speaks through inner locutions or "within the heart."

FY—First Years. Messages given during the first years of the apparitions, before the weekly messages began.

SM—Special Message. Messages not included in the foregoing categories.

JANUARY 1

Solemnity of Mary, Mother of God

In October of 1981, the Blessed Virgin gave the following message:

> *I am the Mother of God and the Queen of Peace (FY 10-12-81).*

And on New Year's Day in 1987, she said:

> *Dear children, today, the first day of the New Year, I invite all of you to live the messages which I give you. You know, dear children, that because of you, I have stayed here this long in order to teach you to walk on the road to holiness.*
>
> *Therefore, dear children, pray constantly, and live all the messages which I give you. I do it with a great love for God—and for you (WM 1-1-87).*

Living anew the messages during the New Year speaks of fresh beginnings. From Paul's letter to the Colossians:

> You have stripped off the old self with its practices and have clothed yourselves with the new self, which is being renewed in knowledge according to the image of its creator (Col 3:9-10).

And from 2 Corinthians:

> So if anyone is in Christ, there is a new creation: everything old has passed away; see, everything has become new (2 Cor 5:17).

Reflection: It's appropriate that on this New Year's Day, Our Lady calls us to live her messages anew, for she knows they are the key to the spiritual gifts we so desire—an abiding peace and happiness, a spirit of love.

Living the messages of prayer, peace, penance, and fasting means, as St. Paul says today, to be formed anew in the image of the Creator over time. It means a new perspective, a new attitude toward life and death, where, as Revelation says, "He shall wipe every tear from their eyes," and make all things new.

On this feast of Mary, the Mother of God, let us recommit ourselves to her messages and her plan of salvation, which she is giving us, as she says today, "with great love toward God." In the words of the poet Joseph Krauskoph:

Dawns another year,
Open it aright;
Thou shalt have no fear
In its fading light.

Application: Today, offer Our Lady a special prayer of commitment to living her messages in this new year. If you have difficulty in living some particular message, ask for the special grace you need to practice it in the year ahead.

This is also the World Day of Prayer for Peace. Offer a rosary for this special intention which Mary emphasizes so much in Medjugorje.

JANUARY 2

Become my heralds

In this message dated January 2, 1989, the Madonna calls us to be her heralds:

My dear children, for this year I especially want to tell you: pray! I, your mother, love you. I want to help you—and I need your assistance too. I want you to become, dear children, my heralds and my sons who will bring peace, love, and conversion to others. I want you to be a sign for others.

In this new year I want to give you peace; I want to give you love and harmony. Abandon all your problems and difficulties to my care. Live my messages. Pray, pray! (VPG 1-29-89).

And in Matthew's gospel, Christ sends out the twelve apostles to be his heralds:

These twelve Jesus sent out with the following instructions. . . . "As you go, proclaim the good news, 'The kingdom of heaven has come near.' Cure the sick, raise the dead, cleanse the lepers, cast out demons. You received without payment; give without payment" (Mt 10:5-8).

Reflection: "As far as we can discern," wrote the psychiatrist Carl Jung, "the sole purpose of human existence is to kindle a light in the darkness of mere being." Both Christ and Our Lady call us today to kindle that light, to be heralds of God's love and peace.

This is a vital and repeated theme in both scripture and the Medjugorje messages. In the Madonna's weekly message of May 8, 1986, she says:

Dear children, you are the ones responsible for the messages . . . you are the vessels which convey the gifts. . . .Each one of you shall be responsible according to your own abilities (WM 5-8-86).

We have been charged with a special responsibility by Our Lady, one that can bring her peace to many hearts. At the same time, we are enriched by the grace she mediates to be confident and joyous in helping with her great work.

Application: This week, share the story of Medjugorje with a friend, coworker, or fellow parishioner. Could you give a presentation in your parish? Is it possible to form a Medjugorje prayer group? Could you lend someone a book or video on the apparitions?

JANUARY 3

Persevere in fasting

Our Lady has a special request for us in the new year:

Pray as much as possible and fast. You must persevere in prayer and fasting. I wish that the new year be spent in prayer and penance. Persevere in prayer and in sacrifice, for I will protect you and always hear your prayers (FY 12-31-82).

Fasting was an ancient practice among the Israelites. The following passage from the Book of Ezra dates from 500 B.C.:

Then I proclaimed a fast there, at the river Ahava, that we might deny ourselves before our God, to seek from him a safe journey for ourselves, our children, and all our possessions (Ezr 8:21).

Reflection: Fasting is perhaps the most difficult teaching from Medjugorje, but its fruits are so astonishing that it deserves our special attention. Consider the following:

Through fasting and prayer, one can stop wars, one can suspend the laws of nature (FY 7-21-82).

Pray and fast that the kingdom of God may appear in your midst. . . (FY 3-14-84).

Dear children, today I call on you to begin fasting with your heart. . . (WM 9-20-84).

Live the message of fasting, for by it you will achieve God's plans in Medjugorje. . . (WM 9-26-85).

Pray and fast, for I wish to purify your hearts complete-ly. I wish to make you happy (LJM 2-14-84).

We will look at fasting again later in the year, but for now, it is important for us to recognize it as one of the primary messages of Our Lady of Medjugorje, a message that brings extraordinary gifts of grace to all who practice it.

Application: Today, make a decision to fast next Friday. It is perfectly all right to begin small—perhaps by skipping one meal, foregoing a favorite food, or drinking tea instead of coffee; the important thing is to make a start. Don't forget to offer your fast for one of your prayer intentions.

JANUARY 4

St. Elizabeth Ann Seton

The Blessed Mother sees our happiness as the best way to attract others to the faith. She said to Jelena's prayer group:

When you convey my messages, be on your guard that they are not lost. Convey my messages with humility, so that in seeing your happiness, others will desire to share it.

Do not carry my messages lightly, to simply scatter before people (LJM 7-85).

In his letter to the Romans, Paul also stresses the great importance of those who carry the message of faith:

"Everyone who calls on the name of the Lord shall be saved."

But how are they to call on one in whom they have not believed? And how are they to believe in one of whom they have never heard? And how are they to hear without someone to proclaim him? And how are they to proclaim him unless they are sent? As it is written, "How beautiful are the feet of those who bring good news!" (Rom 10:13-15).

Reflection: The American saint, Elizabeth Ann Seton, exemplified the qualities of discipleship we see in our readings today: courage in carrying the message of faith, a joyfulness that attracted others, and the zeal to bear a great harvest for the Lord. Upon the death of her husband, by whom she had five children, Elizabeth became a convert to Catholicism, and in 1809 established an order of teaching sisters. She founded a great number of Catholic schools and is now honored as the patroness of Catholic education in America.

In her short life (she died on this day at the age of 46), she had a profound effect on American Catholicism which is still felt to this day.

Application: In her honor, let us offer the Anima Christi (Body of Christ) written by Elizabeth Ann Seton:

Soul of Jesus, sanctify me; blood of Jesus, wash me; passion of Jesus, comfort me; wounds of Jesus, hide me; heart of Jesus, receive me; Spirit of Jesus, enliven me; goodness of Jesus, pardon me; beauty of Jesus, draw me; humility of Jesus, humble me; peace of Jesus, pacify me; love of Jesus, inflame me; kingdom of Jesus, come to me; grace of Jesus, replenish me; mercy of Jesus, pity me; sanctity of Jesus, sanctify me; purity of Jesus, purify me.

Live each new day with love

Of love and peace, Our Lady said to Jelena:

> *Dear children! I want you to live each new day with love and peace. I want you to be the carrier of peace and love. People need so much those graces of peace and love, but they have lost them because they don't pray!*
>
> *Create in your hearts a permanent prayer, because only thus will you be able to be prepared vessels. Through prayer your Father will build you into the vessels he wants. For this abandon yourselves completely to him! (LJM 7-11-87).*

And to Marija in 1985:

> *I have given you my love, so that you may give it to others (FY 9-85).*

In Romans, Paul echoes this call to love:

> Let love be genuine; hate what is evil, hold fast to what is good; love one another with mutual affection; outdo one another in showing honor. Do not lag in zeal, be ardent in spirit, serve the Lord (Rom 12:9-11).

Reflection: With the Blessed Mother, St. Paul also emphasizes the law of love, which supersedes even civil and religious laws. Sometimes we can excuse our indifference to others simply because we have no legal obligation to help them. We even can justify harming them if our actions are technically legal.

But Jesus and his Mother do not leave loopholes in their call to love. Whenever love requires it, we are asked to go beyond human legal requirements and imitate their loving kindness.

Application: Today, reflect on this thought by St. Catherine of Siena: "The reason why God's servants love others so much is that they see how much Christ loves them, and it is one of the properties of love to love what is loved by the person we love. . . ."

JANUARY 6

Life will flow from your hearts

The following locution was received by Jelena Vasilj for her prayer group:

> *If you pray, a source of life will flow from your hearts. If you pray with strength, if you pray with faith, you will receive graces from this source, and your group will be strengthened (LJM 10-24-83).*

Jesus speaks of group prayer in the following passage from scripture:

> Again, truly I tell you, if two of you agree on earth about everything you ask, it will be done for you by my Father in heaven. For where two or three are gathered in my name, I am there among them (Mt 18:19-20).

Reflection: In Medjugorje Our Lady has made a point of encouraging group prayer, and has founded two prayer groups herself—one led by Ivan and Marija, the other by the two young locutionists, Jelena and Mirjana Vasilj.

Concerning such groups, Ivan has said, "The Gospa would like prayer groups throughout the world. Through prayer we come to know God, and there is much power in group prayer."

With regard to the organization of such groups, Ivan emphasizes the importance of a dedicated and reliable leader. "Also," he says, "the prayer group should have a definite goal. The members should have a reason to meet and pray and fast." The goal of his own group is to help the Blessed Virgin to achieve God's plans, no less than the conversion of the world. "We do this," he says, "through living the messages and encouraging others to live them."

Application: Have you considered joining a prayer group in your local area, or perhaps starting one if none exist? You could count on an array of blessings from the Mother of God in doing so.

JANUARY 7

Deepen your faith

The Blessed Mother speaks today of deepening our faith:

For you who have the faith, this time constitutes a great opportunity for you to be converted, and to deepen your faith (LJM 12-15-82).

And Jesus speaks of the great power of faith:

He said to them, "Because of your little faith. For truly I tell you, if you have faith the size of a mustard seed, you will say to this mountain, move from here to there, and it will move; and nothing will be impossible for you" (Mt 17:20).

Reflection: There is a story of the poet Coleridge who one day listened to a visitor's vehement argument against religious education of the young. His acquaintance had concluded with a statement of his determination not to prejudice his children toward any faith or religion, but to let them make up their own minds when they reached maturity. Coleridge made no immediate comment, but shortly afterwards asked this same visitor if he would like to see his garden. Receiving a positive response, he led his guest to a strip of lawn that was overgrown with weeds.

"Why, this is no garden. It's nothing but a weed patch," said his guest.

"Oh," replied Coleridge, "that's because it hasn't come to its maturity yet. The weeds, you see, have taken the opportunity to grow, and I thought it would be unfair of me to prejudice the soil toward roses and strawberries."

Clearly one of the responsibilities of faith is to pass it on to the next generation. If we believe it to be the most precious of gifts, as Jesus and his Mother teach us today, then we will be anxious to share it with others, especially those closest to us.

Application: In your own life, who was most instrumental in handing on the faith to you? In prayer, reflect on the ways that you in turn can pass on your faith to others.

JANUARY 8

A transfigured body

Today Our Lady speaks of the kingdom of heaven in answer to questions by the visionaries:

We go to heaven in full conscience: that which we have now. At the moment of death, we are conscious of the separation of the body and the soul. It is false to teach people that we are reborn many times and that we pass to different bodies. One is born only once.

The body, drawn from the earth decomposes after death. It never comes back to life again. Man receives a transfigured body (FY 7-24-82).

When speaking of heaven, Jesus liked to use analogies such as the following:

The kingdom of heaven is like treasure hidden in a field, which someone found and hid; then in his joy he goes and sells all that he has and buys that field. Again, the kingdom of heaven is like a merchant in search of fine pearls; on finding one pearl of great value, he went and sold all that he had and bought it (Mt 13:44-46).

Reflection: The visionary Mirjana describes the vision of heaven the Virgin gave her in this way:

The first thing I noticed were the faces of the people there; they were radiating a type of inner light which showed how immensely happy they were. . . . The trees, the meadows, the sky are totally different from anything we know on the earth. And the light is much more brilliant. Heaven is beautiful beyond any possible comparison with anything I know of on the earth.

Mirjana goes on to speak of the people there, concluding with, "They have everything. They need or want nothing. They are totally full."

Vicka, another of the visionaries who were shown heaven, describes it as, "a vast space, and it has a brilliant light which does not leave it. It is a life which we do not know here on earth. . . . People in heaven know the absolute fullness of a created being."

And a last note on heaven by little Jakov: "If I thought about it too much, I would die of loneliness."

Application: Reflect on the following today: "See, this kingdom of God is now found within us. The grace of the Holy Spirit shines forth and warms us, and, overflowing with many varied scents into the air around us, regales our senses with heavenly delight, as it fills our hearts with joy inexpressible" (Seraphim of Sarov).

JANUARY 9

They do not repent

In response to a question by Mirjana as to how God could send anyone to hell, Our Lady responded:

Men who go to hell no longer want to receive any benefit from God. They do not repent nor do they cease to blaspheme. They make up their minds to live in hell and do not contemplate leaving it (SM 1-10-83).

In the parable of Lazarus and the rich man, Jesus also alludes to the reality of hell:

The poor man died and was carried away by the angels to be with Abraham. The rich man also died and was buried. In Hades, where he was being tormented, he looked up and saw Abraham far away with Lazarus by his side (Lk 16:22-23).

Reflection: The word "hell" was translated from the word "Gehenna," which was named after the Hinnom Valley, where in times past children had been sacrificed by fire to the pagan gods. It was a term that evoked horror.

Concerning hell, which the Madonna had shown her, Vicka relates:

In the center of this place is a great fire, like an ocean of raging flames. We could see people before they went into the fire, and then we could see them coming out of the fire. Before they go in, they look like normal people. The more they are against God's will, the deeper they enter into the fire, and the deeper they go, the more they rage against him. When they come out of the fire, they don't have a human shape anymore; they are more like grotesque animals, but unlike anything on earth. It's as if they were never human beings before.

Vicka echoes the Blessed Virgin when she says, of those choosing hell, that "they deny God, even when it is time to die. And they continue to deny him, after they are dead. It is their choice. It is their will that they go to hell. They choose hell."

Application: We can choose one of two paths in our lives: to become ever more humane, compassionate, and loving, or become ever more inhumane, cruel, animal-like. In prayer today, tell the Lord again of your choice for him; ask him for the help and grace you will need to achieve perfect love, or heaven.

JANUARY 10

I wish to give everything

Today the Blessed Mother speaks of her fondest desire:

Dear children, I would like for the whole world to be my child, but it does not want it. I wish to give everything for the world. For that, pray! (LJM 3-82).

Jesus also wishes the whole world to be his child:

Then little children were being brought to him in order that he might lay his hands on them and pray. The disciples spoke sternly to those who brought them; but Jesus said, "Let the little children come to me, and do not stop them; for it is to such as these that the kingdom of heaven belongs." And he laid his hands on them and went on his way (Mt 19:13-15).

Reflection: All of the Madonna's messages to the world begin with the endearing, "Dear children," for that is what we are in her eyes, and in the eyes of her Son. The visionary Mirjana once said that, "The Gospa led us to understand that she is our real mother. Later, as time went on and we began to be comfortable with her, we were able to speak to her as our mother about our problems and all our desires."

Ivanka, another of the seers, affirmed that the Virgin, "loves every person on earth. We are all her children." She adds that, "I know from my years with the Blessed Mother how very much she, as our mother, loves each one of us."

Jakov also speaks of this love: "It is beyond our comprehension now," he says, "to understand how very much she loves each person on the earth." He says that many neglect their heavenly Mother because they don't know they have one, and yet, "the Blessed Mother is not neglecting any one of her children. She is faithful to God. She loves and nurtures and prays for each of her children on earth, whether they know it or not."

Application: Close your eyes and with your imagination, picture yourself as a child again—in the presence of the Blessed Mother, perhaps sitting on her knee or holding her hand. Imagine what you would say to her. What would she say to you? This also is a form of prayer.

JANUARY 11

Be converted

Concerning the urgency of conversion, Our Lady said in a locution to Jelena:

Hurry to be converted. Do not wait for the great sign. For the unbelievers, it will then be too late to be converted. For you who have the faith, this time constitutes a great opportunity for you to be converted, and to deepen your faith (LJM after 12-15-82).

Jesus also speaks of the pressing need for conversion:

The people of Nineveh will rise up at the judgment with this generation and condemn it, because they repented at the proclamation of Jonah, and see, something greater than Jonah is here! (Mt 12:41).

Reflection: In the ancient ruins of Pompeii, there was found a petrified woman who, instead of trying to flee from the city, had spent her time in gathering up her jewels. In one of the houses was found the skeleton of a man who, for the sake of a few coins, a small plate and a saucepan of silver, had remained in his house until the street was half-filled with volcanic matter, then was trying to escape from the window.

Because life (and death) is built around priorities, both Christ and his Mother press us to put God and the spiritual first in our lives. This boils down to the various decisions we make every day. Deciding for God, or conversion, is an ongoing process. Little decisions build on one another, for good or bad. That is why Our Lady says to, "hurry to be converted . . . to deepen your faith," for it is a gradual process, rarely occurring overnight.

Application: In the decisions and choices you make today, try to be aware of the Lord's presence and what would please him.

JANUARY 12

Advance against Satan

The Blessed Mother never mentions Satan without identifying the means to defeat him:

> *Dear children, today I call you especially now to advance against Satan by means of prayer. Satan wants to work still more now that you know he is at work. Dear children, put on the armor for battle and with the rosary in your hand, defeat him! (WM 8-8-85).*

Jesus also speaks of defeating the Evil One:

> Or how can one enter a strong man's house and plunder his property, without first tying up the strong man? Then indeed the house can be plundered. Whoever is not with me is against me, and whoever does not gather with me scatters (Mt 12:29-30).

Reflection: Binding Satan is always a matter of faith and prayer, yet it also helps to be aware of his strategies, such as the following:

Five Ploys of Satan

Doubt	Tempts us to question God's Word and his goodness, forgiveness, and love
Discouragement	Tempts us to focus intently on our problems rather than entrusting them to God's care

Diversion	Tempts us to see the wrong things as attractive so that we will want them more than the right things
Defeat	Tempts us to feel like a failure so that we don't even try
Delay	Tempts us to procrastinate so that things never get done

Application: Reflect on these ploys of Satan, and if you find that he has darkened your life on any of these counts, lift up the situation to Our Lady in prayer. Recall her advice on binding the evil one: "Put on the armor of battle. With the rosary in your hand, defeat him!"

JANUARY 13

Hold on in your suffering

Our Lady speaks today of perseverance and suffering as especially touching the heart of her Son:

Thanks to all of you who have come here, so numerous during this year, in spite of snow, ice and bad weather, to pray to Jesus. Continue, hold on in your suffering.

You know well that when a friend asks you for something, you give it to him. It is thus with Jesus. When you pray without ceasing and you come in spite of your tiredness, he will give you all that you ask from him. For that pray. Suffering leads us to the heart of Christ (LJM 12-1-83).

In this passage from 1 Peter, suffering is presented as a positive and redemptive force when linked to the passion of Christ:

For it is a credit to you if, being aware of God, you endure pain while suffering unjustly. If you endure when you are beaten for doing wrong, what credit is that? But if you endure when you do right and suffer for it, you have God's approval. For to this you have called, because Christ also suffered for you, leaving you an example, so that you should follow in his steps (1 Pt 2:19-21).

Reflection: During the First World War, a village behind the lines in the Somme Valley had been repeatedly shelled, and there were many civilian casualties. The church too had been damaged, but it was the largest building available for an emergency hospital. The altar was turned into an improvised operating table.

One of the casualties brought in by stretcher was a young soldier who belonged to the village and was home on leave. He was badly wounded and his leg would have to come off at once. "You'll have to be brave," said the doctor, "I'm afraid this is going to be painful. We've got no anesthetic; it was all destroyed when the hospital was hit."

The young man looked at the "surgical altar," and pointed with his head towards the large crucifix over it. "I'll be all right on the altar," he said. "So long as I can look at him, I'll manage."

With Jesus Christ, all things are bearable, and even acquire a redemptive value when linked to his cross. For the Christian there is no empty pain; it is transformed with Christ's into a path to salvation.

Application: Offer a prayer to the Lord today giving him any annoyances, discomfort, or pain you may experience. Try to make this a daily offering.

JANUARY 14

Pray and believe firmly

With regard to what we can do for the sick, the Virgin said:

> *Pray! Pray and believe firmly. Say the prayers which have already been requested. [Seven Our Fathers, Hail Marys, Glory Bes and the Creed.] Do more penance (FY 4-25-82).*

Healing the sick was a major part of Christ's ministry on earth:

> When Jesus entered Peter's house, he saw his mother-in-law lying in bed with a fever; he touched her hand, and the fever left her, and she got up and began to serve him. That evening they brought to him many who were possessed with demons; and he cast out the spirits with a word, and cured all who were sick (Mt 8:14-16).

Reflection: Rather than speak of the sick, let us today simply pray for them as Our Lady asks. The following prayer was given to Jelena, the locutionist, by the Madonna. She said that it was the most beautiful prayer that could be offered for those who are ill.

Application: Today, offer the following Prayer for the Sick:

O my God,
behold your sick child before you.
Heed his special request,
that which he feels is most important for him.
May you, my Lord, entrust to his heart
  these words:
"The health of the soul, too, is vital."

Lord, may your will be done in him;
if you choose his healing, may he be cured;
if you choose another blessing,
may he bear his cross with love.

I also pray to you
for all who intercede for him.
Purify our hearts
that we may worthily convey
your holy mercy.

Protect your child, relieve his pain,
that your will may be done in him,
and that your presence and love
may be revealed through him.
Grant him the grace
to bear his cross with courage. Amen.

JANUARY 15

Until you are filled with joy

In this rare locution, Jesus himself speaks to Jelena of joy:

*I am joyful, but my joy is not complete until you are
filled with joy. You are not yet filled with joy because
you are not yet at the stage of understanding my
immense love (LJM 10-86).*

And from the prophet Isaiah, words of joy:

I will greatly rejoice in the Lord,
my whole being shall exult in my God;
for he has clothed me with the garments of
   salvation,
he has covered me with the robe of righteousness,
as a bridegroom decks himself with a garland,
and as a bride adorns herself with her jewels.

—Isaiah 61:10

Reflection: The great Austrian composer, Franz Josef Haydn, once said, "When I think upon my God, my heart is so full of joy that the notes dance and leap from my pen; and since God has given me a cheerful heart, it will be pardoned me that I serve him with a cheerful spirit."

Joy is the echo of God's love within us. To the degree that we can comprehend his love, through prayer, the deeper our joy will be. Marija Pavlovic, one of the Medjugorje visionaries, says that, "God's love is very great, and in his love he has created us. We are the fruit of his love. God has given us a special gift; he wants to love us more than himself . . . . He created us to respond to his love."

Application: Reflect on the following today: "The supreme happiness of life is the conviction of being loved for yourself, or more correctly, of being loved of yourself" (Victor Hugo).

JANUARY 16

Have confidence in me

In answer to the visionaries doubts as to whether they would be strong enough to endure, the Virgin said:

You will be able to, my angels. Do not fear. You will be able to endure everything. You must believe and have confidence in me (FY 6-29-81).

Jesus also prepared his disciples for persecution:

See, I am sending you out like sheep into the midst of wolves; so be wise as serpents and innocent as doves. Beware of them, for they will hand you over to councils and flog you in their synagogues; and you will be dragged before governors and kings because of me, as a testimony to them and the Gentiles. You will be hated by all because of my name. But the one who endures to the end will be saved (Mt 10:16-18; 22).

Reflection: Today both Christ and Our Lady speak of endurance in the midst of persecution, not only for the individual, but for the church as a whole. Almost every nation on earth has a record of Catholics who suffered and died in the name of the Christian religion. Elizabethan England, for example, saw the ruthless persecution of Catholics who took enormous risks to practice their faith. The issues were clear—a kingdom or state determined to crush the Catholic religion as something manifestly opposed to its goals, and a threat to its principles.

In more recent times, Nazi Germany also recognized the threat presented by the church, as is attested by the presence of over 2,000 priests in Dachau alone. During the Cold War, Eastern Europe and the Soviet Union had an appalling number of Catholics and Christians who suffered severely for their faith, and usually the issues were as clearly defined as before: they represented a threat to a state determined to exterminate their ways and attitudes.

But the persecutions have never succeeded, although today they are more subtle and so, more dangerous. They take the form of a gradual wearing away of Christian values and beliefs by constant exposure to a hedonistic and materialistic culture through the mass media, the cinema, the arts, and even the courts.

Application: Persecution is not always overt; do not be robbed of your faith through stealth. Stay close to Our Lady, live her messages. Remember her encouraging words today, "You will be able to endure everything. You must believe and have confidence in me."

Read Matthew 6:24-34

Our Lady directs us to Matthew's gospel today:

Each Thursday, read again the passage of Matthew 6:24-34, before the most Blessed Sacrament, or if it is not possible to come to church, do it with your family (LJM 3-1-84).

Reflection: Let us prayerfully reflect on that passage, which will also serve as our reflection today:

No one can serve two masters; for a slave will either hate the one and love the other, or be devoted to the one and despise the other. You cannot serve God and wealth.

Therefore I tell you, do not worry about your life, what you will eat or what you will drink, or about your body, what you will wear. Is not life more than food, and the body more than clothing? Look at the birds of the air; they neither sow nor reap nor gather into barns, and yet your heavenly Father feeds them. Are you not of more value than they? And can any of you by worrying add a single hour to your span of life?

And why do you worry about clothing? Consider the lilies of the field, how they grow; they neither toil nor spin, yet I tell you, even Solomon in all his glory was not clothed like one of these. But if God so clothes the grass of the field, which is alive today and tomorrow is thrown into the oven, will he not much more clothe you—you of little faith?

Therefore do not worry, saying, "What will we eat?" or "What will we drink?" or "What will we wear?" For it is the Gentiles who strive for all these things; and indeed your heavenly Father knows that you need all these things. But strive first for the kingdom of God and his righteousness, and all these things will be given to you as well.

So do not worry about tomorrow, for tomorrow will bring worries of its own. Today's trouble is enough for today (Mt 6:24-34).

Application: Heeding Our Lady's advice today, place a book mark in your Bible at Matthew 6:24. Reflect on this passage on Thursdays for the next several weeks.

JANUARY 18

Put into practice the messages

In her monthly message of August, 1990, Our Lady said:

Dear children, today I desire to invite you to take with seriousness and put into practice the messages which I am giving you. You know, little children, that I am with you, that I desire to lead you along the same path to heaven which is beautiful for those who discover it in prayer.

Therefore, little children, do not forget that these messages which I am giving you have to be put into your everyday life in order that you might be able to say: "There, I have taken the messages and tried to live them." Dear children, I am protecting you before the heavenly Father by my own prayers (MM 8-25-90).

In the following passage from scripture, Jesus also calls us to "live the messages" of the gospel:

As for what was sown among thorns, this is the one who hears the word, but the cares of the world and the lure of wealth choke the word, and it yields nothing. But as for what was sown on good soil, this is it, who indeed bears fruit and yields, in one case a hundred fold, in another sixty, and in another thirty (Mt 13:22-23).

Reflection: Both Christ and Our Lady urge us today to live the message of the gospel (of which the Medjugorje messages are a reflection). They remind us that it is one thing to hear the message, another to act on it. This was the topic of a sermon given in Medjugorje by Fr. Slavko Barbaric in December of 1985:

> We would be misguided to say, "I will convert tomorrow," or "I will forgive tomorrow," or "I will be reconciled tomorrow." Confession is asked of me today, not tomorrow. And so the messages have this meaning: to be committed and awake to God in faith, in our work, in prayer, in belief, in abandoning ourselves to him so that we are open and ready each day to meet him if he should call us to himself.

> To live the messages also means to live in the Lord's peace, to have safe harbor in turbulent times, and a firm hope in the future, all in the here and now.

Application: Are there parts of the gospel message that you have failed to live? Identify one area that you can work on this week.

JANUARY 19

Believe and pray

Our Lady once spoke to Mirjana of faith and healing:

> *Have them believe and pray; I cannot help him who does not pray and does not sacrifice. . . . The more you believe firmly, the more you pray and fast for the same inten-*

tion, the greater is the grace and the mercy of God (FY 8-18-82).

Jesus also viewed faith as a prerequisite to healing:

When he entered Capernaum, a centurion came to him, appealing to him and saying, "Lord, my servant is lying at home paralyzed, in terrible distress." And [Jesus] said to him, "I will come and cure him." The centurion answered, "Lord, I am not worthy to have you come under my roof; but only speak the word, and my servant will be healed."

When Jesus heard him, he was amazed and said to those who followed him, "Truly I tell you, in no one in Israel have I found such faith."

And to the centurion Jesus said, "Go; let it be done for you according to your faith." And the servant was healed in that hour (Mt 8:5-8, 10, 13).

Reflection: Both Our Lady of Medjugorje and St. Matthew draw a strong parallel between faith and healing. Mary asks the sick "to believe and pray; I cannot help him who does not pray and does not sacrifice." And Matthew reports that, "Jesus said to the officer, 'Go home, and what you believe will be done for you.'"

An expectant faith, a deep trust in the power of God, can work miracles in our lives, spiritually as well as physically. In the words of the American religious writer Harry Emerson Fosdick, "It is illness and fear that freeze life; it is faith that thaws it out, releases it, sets it free."

Application: Today, pray simply for a deeper and more vibrant faith. Also, commend the sick to Christ and his Mother.

Remain steadfast

Today the visionaries are asked to motivate people to prayer and conversion:

> *I know that many will not believe you, and that many who have an impassioned faith will grow cold. But you must remain steadfast and motivate people to pray, to do penance, and to convert. In this way you will be happier in the end (FY 1983).*

In Luke's gospel, John the Baptist also urges the people to put their faith into action:

> And the crowds asked him, "What then should we do?" In reply he said to them, "Whoever has two coats must share with anyone who has none; and whoever has food must do likewise" (Lk 3:10-11).

Reflection: Faith is never a strictly private affair. As we see from our readings, it is meant to affect others, to draw them to faith, prayer, and works of love. In this vein, an anonymous poet once wrote:

Faith is not merely praying
Upon our knees at night;
Faith is not merely straying
Through darkness into light;
Faith is not merely waiting
For glory that may be.
Faith is the brave endeavor,
The splendid enterprise,
The strength to serve, whatever
Conditions may arise.

Application: Today, reflect on whether your faith touches the lives of others.

Do not worry about material things

Today Our Lady speaks of one of the pitfalls of modern life:

> Dear children, you are so preoccupied with material things that you lose everything that God wants to give you. Pray then, dear children, for the gifts of the Holy Spirit. They are necessary so that you can give witness to my presence here, and to all that I give you.
>
> Dear children, abandon yourselves to me so that I can guide you always. Do not worry about material things (WM 4-17-86).

Jesus, too, called attention to the danger of material goods which can distort our sense of priorities:

> He replied, "I have kept all these since my youth." When Jesus heard this, he said to him, "There is still one thing lacking. Sell all that you own and distribute the money to the poor, and you will have treasure in heaven; then come, follow me." But when he said this, he became sad; for he was very rich (Lk 18:21-23).

Reflection: Satan provides us with an array of addictions and diversions that promise security, but simply divert us from God's kingdom. Material things are not necessarily evil in themselves, but when our lives are centered around them, they work to destroy the soul. The mystical poet Angelus Silesius wrote, "Be sure, as long as worldly fancies you pursue, you are a hollow man—a pauper lives in you." A pauper, rather than God.

Today Jesus and his Mother warn us of worldly addictions, and Our Lady gives us the remedy in her message: "Pray for the gifts of the Holy Spirit . . . abandon yourselves to me so that I can guide you always."

Application: Walk through your house today noting your possessions. Is there anything there you cannot live without? In prayer, offer all these things to the Blessed Mother.

JANUARY 22

Know that I love you

Today Our Lady blesses us with love:

Know that I love you. Know that you are mine. For no one do I wish to do more than what I wish to do for you.

Come to me, all of you. Stay close to me so that I can be your mother always. Come, for I wish to have all of you (LJM 2-25-85).

St. John speaks of God's love in this famous passage:

God abides in those who confess that Jesus is the Son of God, and they abide in God. So we have known and believe the love that God has for us.

God is love, and those who abide in love abide in God, and God abides in them. Love has been perfected among us in this: that we may have boldness on the day of judgment, because as he is, so are we in this world (1 Jn 4:15-17).

Reflection: "Come to me, all of you," Mary beckons us today, inviting us to feel their protective love. This is the motivation of our faith, our hope, our service to others. St. John even capsulized the divine nature in saying simply: "God is love."

It was the startling experience of this love, during a dark period of my life, that drew me to the priesthood. My whole understanding of God, faith, of life itself, was changed profoundly. I saw love as the center of everything, and it was then that I decided on the goal of my life: *to serve love*. This was my conversion, the opening to a new life.

Having been reared a Catholic, it seemed to me that the priesthood was a natural way to live out this goal. Then came the seminary, the books, theology, and training. But the first thing was love.

Application: In prayer, relive an experience of God's love. Reflect on the following:

> The longest way to God, the indirect,
> lies through the intellect.
> The shortest way lies through the heart.
> Here is my journey's end, and here its start.
> —Angelus Silesius

JANUARY 23

Believe in his cure

In the first week of the apparitions, the parents of a deaf and mute child asked the visionaries to intercede on behalf of the boy. The seers asked the Virgin to cure the child so that people would believe them. She responded:

> *Have them firmly believe in his cure. Go in the peace of God (FY 6-29-81).*

Little Daniel Setka was cured later that same evening.

In the gospels, Christ also focused on faith as the foundation of healing:

> Then suddenly a woman who had been suffering from hemorrhages for twelve years came up behind him and touched the fringe of his cloak, for

she said to herself, "If I only touch his cloak, I will be made well." Jesus turned, and seeing her he said, "Take heart daughter; your faith has made you well." And instantly the woman was made well (Mt 9:20-22).

Reflection: The power of faith is limitless: it heals, consoles, and strengthens. But the opposite is also true. Once when Jesus was visiting Nazareth, he could work no miracles there because the people's lack of faith distressed him so.

How to deepen our faith? Cardinal Newman once said: "It is love that makes faith, not faith love." And Our Lady gives this answer: "Faith will not know how to be alive without prayer. Therefore, pray!" (10-10-81).

The healing of the handicapped child in Medjugorje, the cure of the hemorrhaging woman in Matthew's gospel, were both dependent on faith. May our own healing of body, mind, or spirit also be the fruit of our expectant faith.

Application: Pray today for a deeper faith; ask for healing if you are in need. Assist someone who is sick through your presence or prayers.

JANUARY 24

St. Francis de Sales

The Blessed Mother speaks of holiness today:

> Dear children, today I again call you to pray with your whole heart and to change your life day by day. I especially ask you, dear children, to live in holiness through your prayer and sacrifices. I desire that each of you who have been to this fountain of grace shall come to paradise one day and present to me a special gift— that of your holiness.

> *Therefore, dear children, pray and change your life that it may become holy. I will always be close to you (WM 11-13-86).*

St. Paul's letter to the Ephesians also deals with holiness:

> You were taught to put away your former way of life, your old self, corrupt and deluded by its lusts, and to be renewed in the spirit of your minds, and to clothe yourselves with the new self, created according to the likeness of God in true righteousness and holiness (Eph 4:22-24).

Reflection: St. Francis de Sales exemplified holiness in his life, which was characterized by a supreme trust in God. Born at Savoy in 1567, he worked tirelessly to restore Catholicism to his country after the Reformation. Later, as Bishop of Geneva, he became renowned for his compassion to his people and priests. Because of his insightful writings he was later proclaimed a Doctor of the Church.

The following excerpt from his classic work, *The Devout Life*, deals with trust, that mark of holiness which Our Lady and St. Paul speak of today:

> In all your affairs, rely wholly on God's providence. . . . Imitate little children, who with one hand hold fast to their father, and with the other hand gather strawberries or blackberries along the hedges. So too, as you gather and handle the goods of this world with one hand, you must with the other always hold fast the hand of your heavenly Father, turning yourself toward him from time to time to see if your actions or occupations be pleasing to him.
>
> Above all things, take heed that you never leave his hand or think to gather more or to gain some advantage. For should he forsake you, you will

not be able to go a step further without falling to the ground.

Application: Today, through the intercession of St. Francis, pray for a deep trust in God that banishes all fear and doubt.

JANUARY 25

The Conversion of St. Paul

Speaking of conversion, the Blessed Mother said:

Dear children, today I call you again to complete conversion, which is difficult for those who have not chosen God. I am inviting you, dear children, to convert fully to God.

God can give you everything that you seek from him. But you seek only when sicknesses, problems, and difficulties come to you, and you think that God is far from you and is not listening and does not hear your prayers.

No, dear children, that is not the truth. When you are far from God, you cannot receive graces, because you do not seek them with a firm faith. Day by day, I am praying for you, and I want to draw you ever more near to God. I cannot, if you do not desire it. Therefore, dear children, put your life in God's hands. I bless you all (MM 1-25-88).

From the Acts of the Apostles, the story of Paul's conversion:

Now as he was going along and approaching Damascus, suddenly a light from heaven flashed around him. He fell to the ground and heard a voice saying to him, "Saul, Saul, why do you persecute me?" He asked, "Who are you, Lord?"

The reply came, "I am Jesus, whom you are persecuting. But get up and enter the city, and you will be told what you are to do."

The men who were traveling with him stood speechless because they heard the voice but saw no one. Saul got up from the ground, and though his eyes were open, he could see nothing; so they led him by the hand and brought him into Damascus (Acts 9:4-8).

Reflection: Conversion can be spectacular and instantaneous, like St. Paul's, or a gradual coming to faith, which may be the most common experience. Both are gifts of grace bestowed by a loving God on all who have opened their hearts to him. But it is important to realize that our subsequent spiritual journey is itself a lifelong conversion process through which we draw closer to God.

Conversion is not easy. Friends and family members may resist the changes they see in us, for they are unfamiliar. They may send out messages or signals, some given subconsciously, for us to "change back" to our old selves. We should resist such pressures, confident in the help of our Mother. The essential thing is to nourish this process by an abiding openness to God's grace, like living plants open to the sunshine, and by living Our Lady's messages with conviction.

Application: Today pray the "Petition to God" (see April 2) for your ongoing conversion and that of your family and friends.

Make a commitment

Today Our Lady asks for our commitment so that her plans in Medjugorje will succeed:

Dear children, I would like this to be a time of decision for you. Make a commitment to follow me, follow me! I wish to do so much, but I cannot do anything without you; your resolve is too weak.

So pray during this time, dear children. Only through prayer can you receive the strength of commitment that you need. I am here to help you, my children (VPG 8-19-88).

In Mark's gospel, Jesus also asks for a decision:

As Jesus passed along the Sea of Galilee, he saw Simon and his brother Andrew casting a net into the sea—for they were fishermen. And Jesus said to them, "Follow me and I will make you fish for people." And immediately they left their nets and followed him (Mk 1:16-18).

Reflection: Discipleship, or commitment, is foundational to our Christian faith; both Mary in her messages, and Jesus in the gospels, speak of the necessity of deciding completely for God.

And this decision, which we are asked to renew periodically in prayer, surfaces naturally from the grace of God in our hearts. "Happy are they," writes Dietrich Bonhoeffer, "who know that discipleship simply means the life that springs from grace, and that grace simply means discipleship."

Application: In prayer today, ask Christ and the Blessed Mother to strengthen your commitment in following them with enthusiasm and courage.

JANUARY 27

Let prayer illuminate your life

The Blessed Mother speaks of her favorite subject today:

> *Dear children, today I call you to prayer. By means of prayer, little children, you will find joy and peace. Through prayer you will be richer in the mercy of God. Therefore, little children, let prayer illuminate your entire life.*
>
> *Especially, I call you to pray that those who are far from God may be converted. Then our own hearts will be richer because God will reign in the hearts of all. And so, little children, pray, pray, pray! Let prayer reign throughout the whole world (MM 8-25-89).*

In this passage from Matthew's gospel, Jesus bears out the importance of prayer, and also its great power:

> In the morning, when he returned to the city, he was hungry. And seeing a fig tree by the side of the road, he went to it and found nothing at all on it but leaves. Then he said to it, "May no fruit ever come from you again!" And the fig tree withered at once.
>
> When the disciples saw it, they were amazed, saying, "How did the fig tree wither at once?" Jesus answered them, "Truly I tell you, if you have faith and do not doubt, not only will you do what has been done to the fig tree, but even if you say to this mountain, 'Be lifted up and thrown into the

sea,' it will be done. Whatever you ask for in prayer with faith, you will receive" (Mt 21:18-22).

Reflection: Prayer is by far the most common subject of Our Lady's messages in Medjugorje, as well as a primary teaching of Christ in the gospels. It is the root of joy and peace, as Mary reminds us today, and its power is unbounded, as Jesus teaches his disciples in the gospel. Of prayer with the heart, John Bunyan wrote, "When thou prayest, rather let thy heart be without words, than thy words without heart."

So much has been written about prayer that for now we might simply underline the words of Mary's message today: prayer begets true joy and peace. This is the peace the world cannot give; this is the joy that abides deep within the heart. There is no other way to obtain these gifts, not money, cars, homes, nor any of the world's allurements. There is only one way, a very simple way: our hearts opened to God in quiet prayer, in quiet communion with the divine Lord.

Application: Give your fears and anxieties over to Our Lady today in prayer. Remain with her until you feel at peace.

JANUARY 28

St. Thomas Aquinas

The following is the Gospa's message for April, 1990:

Dear children, today I call you to seriously accept and live the messages I have given you. I am with you and I wish to draw each of you ever closer to my heart.

But to accomplish this, little children, I need you to pray and always seek the will of God in your everyday life. I wish that each of you discover the way of holiness and grow in it until eternity.

I will pray and intercede for you before God that you can understand my presence here for the great gift that it is—a gift from God to both of us (MM 4-25-90).

The ultimate purpose of the messages, of course, is to transform us into the image of Christ, that his peace may prevail:

> Now the Lord is the Spirit, and where the Spirit of the Lord is, there is freedom. And all of us, with unveiled faces, seeing the glory of the Lord as though reflected in a mirror, are being transformed into the same image from one degree of glory to another; for this comes from the Lord, the Spirit (2 Cor 3:17-18).

Reflection: Through his many scholarly books on theology, St. Thomas Aquinas' goal, like that of the Blessed Virgin, was to draw the individual closer to Christ so that he could be transformed into his image and likeness. He spent great effort in examining the characteristics of the divine nature and showing how we might acquire them. His composition of the following prayer reveals those virtues which he considered most important.

Application: As Our Lady recommends, let us offer this Prayer for a Faithful and Upright Heart from the heart.

> O Lord my God,
> help me to be obedient without reserve,
> poor without servility,
> chaste without compromise,
> humble without pretense,
> joyful without depravity,
> serious without affectation,
> active without frivolity,
> submissive without bitterness,

truthful without duplicity,
fruitful in good works without presumption,
quick to revive my neighbor without haughtiness,
and quick to edify others by word and example
without simulation.

Grant me, O Lord, an ever-watchful heart
that no alien thought can lure away from you;
a noble heart
that no base love can sully;
an upright heart
that no perverse intention can lead astray;
an invincible heart
that no distress can overcome;
an unfettered heart
that no impetuous desires can enchain.

O Lord my God,
also bestow upon me
understanding to know you,
zeal to seek you,
wisdom to find you,
a life that is pleasing to you,
unshakable perseverance,
and a hope that will one day take hold of you.

May I do penance here below
and patiently bear your chastisements.
May I also receive the benefits of your grace,
in order to taste your heavenly joys
and contemplate your glory. Amen.

JANUARY 29

Through fasting

In the second year of the apparitions, the Blessed Virgin
gave the following message on fasting:

The best fast is on bread and water. Through fasting and prayer, one can stop wars, one can suspend the laws of nature. Charity cannot replace fasting. Those who are not able to fast can sometimes replace it with prayer, works of love, and confession; but everyone, except the sick, must fast (FY 7-21-82).

Fasting was a common practice in the early church. In this passage, Paul and Barnabas fast and pray for the new church leaders:

> And after they had appointed elders for them in each church, with prayer and fasting they entrusted them to the Lord in whom they had come to believe (Acts 14:23).

Reflection: In *The Canterbury Tales*, Chaucer wrote,

> Who will pray, he must fast and be clean,
> And fat his soul, and make his body lean.

Fasting is a difficult teaching, for it entails sacrifice and self-denial. And yet Our Lord and his Mother would not ask it of us unless it were vitally important, as Mary says, to "the salvation of the world," to the fulfillment of her plans in Medjugorje. And as she has told us many times, those plans are totally dependent on our prayers and sacrifices.

If we feel trepidation at the prospect of fasting, it is best simply to confide this to Our Lady and ask for the special graces we need to live this message. We can be sure that she will answer this prayer without delay, for she urgently needs our help.

Application: Asking boldly for Mary's help, make a decision to fast this Friday. Be sure to offer this sacrifice for one of your prayer intentions, or those of Our Lady, since fasting greatly amplifies the power of prayer, even to working the miraculous.

JANUARY 30

Surrender yourselves to God

In this weekly message, Our Lady speaks of surrender:

> *Dear children, I invite you to decide completely for God. I beseech you, dear children, to surrender yourselves totally, and then you will be able to live everything I have been telling you. Truly, it will not be difficult for you to surrender yourselves to God in this way (WM 1-2-86).*

Surrender to God presupposes faith and trust, which Jesus asks of Nicodemus—and us:

> Very truly, I tell you, we speak of what we know and testify to what we have seen: yet you do not receive our testimony. If I have told you about earthly things and you do not believe, how can you believe if I tell you about heavenly things? (Jn 3:11-12).

Reflection: Surrender to God means trusting him enough to carry our problems, worries, relationships, and joys. It means falling backwards into his arms, like the game a child might play with his parents. This trust usually comes by degrees rather than all at once, but it still requires an element of risk. Are we getting better in taking a risk on God?

Application: Today, offer the following Prayer of Abandonment; you may wish to pray it each day this week as a special gift of yourself to the Lord.

Father, I abandon myself into your hands;
do with me what you will.
Whatever you may do, I thank you;
I am ready for all, I accept all.
Let only your will be done in me,

and in all your creatures.
I wish no more than this, O Lord.
Into your hands I commend my soul;
I offer it to you with all the love of my heart,
for I love you, Lord,
and so need to give myself,
to surrender myself into your hands,
without reserve, and with boundless confidence
For you are my Father.

—Charles de Foucauld

JANUARY 31

Go to confession

In the first months of the apparitions, the following was given to Vicka and Jakov:

Pray, pray! It is necessary to believe firmly, to go to confession regularly, and also to receive Holy Communion. It is the only salvation (FY 2-10-82).

The confession of sins was an ancient practice in Israel. It was also a major element in John the Baptist's evangelization:

Now John wore clothing of camel's hair with a leather belt around his waist, and his food was locusts and wild honey. Then the people of Jerusalem and all Judea were going out to him, and all the region along the Jordan, and they were baptized by him in the river Jordan, confessing their sins (Mt 3:4-6).

Reflection: Confession is the gateway to salvation. It removes the obstacles of sin that we have erected that keep God at a distance. With this guilt and shame dissipated, we can encounter the Lord anew and experience more fully his mercy and love.

In addition, confession creates in us a grateful heart, for we know in faith that God holds nothing against us. We begin a new life, as if we were newly baptized. Last, the power and grace of this sacrament uplifts and strengthens us for the future. It is so powerful, in fact, that Our Lady has said that it will be the remedy for the church of the West, which she had once said was lost. What a gift we have received!

Application: Consulting your parish bulletin, note the times when confessions are heard at your local church. On your calendar, choose a time each month when you can receive the sacrament.

Pilgrims' trail up Mt. Krizevac

Pray for the Holy Spirit

Today Our Lady speaks of the Holy Spirit:

Dear children, during these days of the Pentecost novena, pray for the outpouring of the Holy Spirit on your families and on your parish.

You will never regret prayer. God will give you the gifts by which you will glorify him until the end of your life on earth (WM 6-2-84).

And in Galatians, Paul speaks of the Spirit's gifts:

Live by the Spirit, I say, and do not gratify the desires of the flesh. For what the flesh desires is opposed to the Spirit, and what the Spirit desires is opposed to the flesh; for these are opposed to each other, to prevent you from doing what you want. But if you are led by the Spirit, you are not subject to the law (Gal 5:16-18).

Reflection: Echoing the Blessed Mother and St. Paul, Pope Leo XIII once wrote: "Each one of us greatly needs the protection and help of the Holy Spirit. The more one is lacking in wisdom, weak in strength, borne down with trouble, prone to sin, the more he ought to fly to him who is the never-ceasing fount of light, strength, consolation, and holiness."

With this encouragement, let us offer this prayer for the seven gifts of the Holy Spirit:

O Lord Jesus Christ, who, before ascending into heaven, did promise to send the Holy Spirit to finish your work in the souls of your apostles and disciples—deign to grant the same Holy Spirit to me, to perfect in my soul the work of your grace and your love.

Grant me the Spirit of Wisdom, that I may not be attached to the perishable things of this world, but aspire only after the things that are eternal.

The Spirit of Understanding, to enlighten my mind with the light of Your divine truth.

The Spirit of Counsel, that I may ever choose the surest way of pleasing God and gaining heaven.

The Spirit of Fortitude, that I may bear my cross with you, and that I may overcome with courage all the obstacles that oppose my salvation.

The Spirit of Knowledge, that I may know God and know myself, and grow perfect in the science of the saints.

The Spirit of Piety, that I may find the service of God sweet and amiable.

The Spirit of Fear, that I may be filled with a loving reverence toward God and may avoid anything that may displease him.

Mark me, dear Lord, with the sign of your true disciples, and animate me in all things with your Spirit. Amen.

Application: Add to your daily prayers a petition for the gifts of the Holy Spirit, as Our Lady encourages us today.

FEBRUARY 2

The Presentation of the Lord

On this feast of the Presentation, Our Lady seeks to present *us* to God:

Dear children, again today, I invite you to abandon yourself completely to me. Only then, in turn, can I present each of you to God. Dear children, you know that I love you immeasurably, and I wish each of you to

*be mine. But God gives everyone freedom, which I
lovingly respect, and to which I humbly submit.*

*Dear children, I wish that God's plan regarding this
parish be realized. But, if you do not pray, you will not
be able to recognize my love, nor God's plan for this
parish, and for each of you.*

*Pray that Satan does not entice you with his pride
and deceptive strength. I am with you and want you to
believe that I love you (MM 11-25-87).*

From St. Luke, the story of the Presentation:

When the time came for their purification according to the law of Moses, they brought him up to
Jerusalem to present him to the Lord, and they
offered a sacrifice according to what is stated in
the law of the Lord, "a pair of turtledoves or two
young pigeons."

Now there was a man in Jerusalem whose name
was Simeon.... Guided by the Spirit, Simeon came
into the temple; and when the parents brought in
the child Jesus, to do for him what was customary
under the law, Simeon took him in his arms and
praised God, saying,

"Master, now you are dismissing your servant
in peace, according to your word; for my eyes have
seen your salvation, which you have prepared in
the presence of all peoples, a light for revelation to
the Gentiles and for glory to your people Israel"
(Lk 2:22-32).

Reflection: From a sermon by St. Sophronius, the
seventh century bishop: "Rejoicing with old Simeon
with the Christ child in his arms, let us sing a hymn of
thanksgiving to God, the Father of Light, who sent the
true Light to dispel the darkness and to give us all a
share in his splendor." This is a day of joy, for the Lord

was presented to God in the temple, and by extension, presented to his people Israel and to all humankind. The Son of God is among us!

As a baby, Jesus was of course small and vulnerable when he was presented by Mary and Joseph. In the same way, we are called to become open and vulnerable in order to present ourselves to the Lord. The Blessed Virgin urges us to give up our false security in material things so that, like a child, we become dependent on our parent, on God, for our safety and security to let go and let God.

In such a way, Our Lady can then ask us "to decide to surrender again everything completely to me. . . . Only that way will I be able to present each of you to God."

Application: So that Mary can present us to the Lord, let us now present and dedicate ourselves to her through the prayer of consecration she gave to Jelena, found on November 24.

FEBRUARY 3

Begin working on your hearts

The Blessed Virgin speaks of our hearts today:

> *Dear children, there is a time for everything. Today I call you to begin working on your hearts. Now that all the work in the fields is over, you have found time to clean even the most neglected places—but you have left your hearts aside. I ask you now to work with love in cleansing the recesses of your own hearts (WM 10-17-85).*

Jesus also affirms the need to cleanse our hearts:

> Do you not see that whatever goes into the mouth enters the stomach, and goes out into the sewer?

But what comes out of the mouth proceeds from the heart, and this is what defiles. For out of the heart comes evil intentions, murder, adultery, fornication, theft, false witness, slander. These are what defile a person... (Mt 15:17-20).

Reflection: Four hundred years before Christ, Socrates wrote, "I pray thee, O God, that I may be beautiful within." The urgings of Christ and the Blessed Mother that we cleanse our hearts is due in part to their being the dwelling places of God himself. In this vein the psychiatrist Carl Jung wrote, "Too few people have experienced the divine image as the innermost possession of their own souls. Christ only meets them from without, never within the heart."

The great mystics of the church would agree with this. In the sixteenth century St. John of the Cross affirmed that, "In the center of the soul is God." His contemporary, St. Teresa of Avila, based her spiritual masterpiece *The Way of Perfection* on the same truth—the spiritual life was primarily a journey inward to discover the presence of God within one's own soul.

It is this priceless treasure, the gift of God within, that urges us to faith, to prayer, the sacraments, and to love—the *means* by which we cleanse our hearts for the indwelling Spirit of God.

Application: In prayer today, reflect on the following: "The gift of the Holy Spirit closes the last gap between the life of God and ours .... When we allow the love of God to move in us, we can no longer distinguish ours and his; he becomes us, he lives us" (Austin Farrer).

FEBRUARY 4

Love all with my love

A message from the Madonna on love:

> *Dear children, I am calling you to a complete surrender to God. Pray, little children, that Satan does not sway you like branches in the wind. Be strong in God. I desire that through you the whole world may get to know the God of joy. Neither be anxious nor worried. God will help you and show you the way. I want you to love all with my love, both the good and the bad. Only that way will love conquer the world (MM 5-25-88).*

Christ gives us an example of indiscriminate love in this scene from Luke's gospel:

> After this he went out and saw a tax collector named Levi, sitting at the tax booth; and he said to him, "Follow me." And he got up, left everything, and followed him.
>
> Then Levi gave a great banquet for him in his house; and there was a large crowd of tax collectors and others sitting at the table with them. The Pharisees and their scribes were complaining to his disciples, saying, "Why do you eat and drink with tax collectors and sinners?" Jesus answered, "Those who are well have no need of a physician, but those who are sick; I have come to call not the righteous but sinners to repentance" (Lk 5:27-32).

Reflection: The visit to Matthew's home hurt Jesus' reputation, yet Matthew's soul was obviously worth the price, and more. God values and loves all of us, whether saint or sinner, beyond our comprehension. And he asks us in turn to reach out in love to others, especially the sinful and the hurting, that he might heal them through our touch.

In the words of an anonymous poet:

Love has a hem to its garment
That touches the very dust;
It can reach the stains of the streets and lanes,
And because it can, it must.

This is also the core of Our Lady's message today: "I want you to love all men with my love, both the good and the bad. Only that way will love conquer the world . . . ."

Application: Let us pray with Dietrich Bonhoeffer, who wrote these words while in a Nazi concentration camp: "Give me such love for you, O Lord, and for all men, as will blot out all hatred and bitterness."

FEBRUARY 5

Charity cannot replace fasting

Today Our Lady speaks of something very important to her:

The best fast is on bread and water. Through fasting and prayer, one can stop wars, one can suspend the laws of nature. Charity cannot replace fasting. Those who are not able to fast can sometimes replace it with prayer, charity, and a confession; but everyone, except the sick, must fast (FY 7-21-82).

In Matthew's gospel, Jesus answers a question on fasting:

Then the disciples of John came to him, saying, "Why do we and the Pharisees fast often, but your disciples do not fast?" And Jesus said to them,

"The wedding guests cannot mourn as long as the bridegroom is with them, can they? But the days will come when the bridegroom will no longer be with them, and then they will fast" (Mt 9:14-15).

Reflection: As we await the second coming of the bridegroom, we are now in that perilous time when it is proper to fast. Since the seers of Medjugorje have been advised on fasting by Our Lady, it would be wise to hear their views.

When asked the purpose of fasting, Vicka responded:

Through fasting we purify our hearts. In order to have a pure heart, we need the grace that comes from fasting. And when we totally cleanse our hearts, we are able to realize the Blessed Mother's plan, and what she is expecting from us.

Concerning problems we may encounter in fasting, Vicka advises:

The first time is always the most difficult. When we try to fast, Satan tries hard to distract us, to make us think, "Well, I could eat a little something extra." We have to pray hard this first time, really hard. When we pray and when we fast, Satan can do nothing to us. The second time will be easier, and the third time even easier. Then it will become natural.

Application: Make a commitment in prayer to fast this Wednesday and/or Friday. If it is your first time, be sure to set aside extra time for prayer to ward off diversions by the Evil One.

Pray especially for the young

On Mt. Podbrdo, the Blessed Mother speaks of families and young people to Ivan's prayer group and visiting pilgrims:

Dear children, I would like to tell you tonight to pray especially for the young. I would like to recommend to my priests that they create and organize groups where young people can be taught and given good advice for their lives. You, dear children, who are here tonight, must be messengers of peace to others, especially to young people (VPG 9-9-88).

In Ephesians, Paul also speaks of children and parents:

Children, obey our parents in the Lord, for this is right. "Honor your father and mother"—this is the first commandment with a promise: "so that it may be well with you and you may live long on the earth" (Eph 6:1-3).

Reflection: These are troubled times for the family, for so many factors in our culture mitigate against it. Thus Our Lady is tireless in her request for family prayer, knowing that when her Son is invited into a family, his grace, protection, and love immediately surround and support it.

Application: Call the family together this week for prayer, even if it is only an extended prayer time at the evening meal. Suggest that each member voice a prayer intention, and then all join in the Our Father, Hail Mary, and Glory Be.

Families need to pray today

Speaking of the family to Ivan's prayer group, Our Lady said:

> *Dear children, tonight your Mother wishes to call you, as I have before, to renew prayer in the family. Dear children, families need to pray today. It is my wish, dear children, that you would live my messages through family prayer (VPG 1-1-90).*

St. Paul also speaks of the family, specifically, of husbands and wives:

> "For this reason a man will leave his father and mother and be joined to his wife, and the two will become one flesh." This is a great mystery, and I am applying it to Christ and the church. Each of you, however, should love his wife as himself, and a wife should respect her husband (Eph 5:31-33).

Reflection: There has never been a time when the institution of marriage has been threatened more. With a divorce rate of over 50%, a culture that denigrates commitment, and a prevailing atmosphere of narcissism, the support beams of marriage appear to have fallen away. But Our Lady gives us a simple yet profound remedy in family prayer. When the presence and grace of Christ touch a marriage, it is protected and nurtured by the hand of God himself, and is no longer dependent on solely human factors.

Application: If you are married, take the initiative to talk with your spouse about a prayer time together. You can begin, perhaps, by offering the following Marriage Prayer:

Lord Jesus, grant that we may have a true and understanding love for each other. Grant that we may both be filled with faith and trust. Give us the grace to live with each other in peace and harmony.

May we always bear with one another's weaknesses and grow from each other's strengths. Help us to forgive one another's failings, and grant us patience, kindness, cheerfulness, and the spirit of placing the well-being of one another ahead of self.

May the love that brought us together grow and mature with each passing year. Bring us both ever closer to you through our love for each other. Let our love grow to perfection. Amen.

FEBRUARY 8

Help peace to reign

The Mother of God speaks of peace today:

Dear children, today I call you to pray especially for peace. Dear children, without peace you cannot truly experience the birth of Jesus in your daily lives.

Therefore, pray to the Lord of Peace that he will protect you with his mantle, and that he may help you understand how important it is to have a great peace in your hearts. Having this, you will be able to spread the peace of your hearts throughout the world.

I am always with you and intercede to God for you. Pray, for Satan wants to destroy my plans for peace. Be reconciled with each other and, by your lives, help peace to reign over the entire earth (MM 12-25-90).

Isaiah prophesies of peace in this well-known passage:

He shall judge between the nations,
and shall arbitrate for many peoples;

they shall beat their swords into plowshares,
and their spears into pruning hooks;
Nation shall not lift up sword against nation,
neither shall they learn war any more.

—Isaiah 2:4

Reflection: One of the key messages of Medjugorje is that peace begins in the individual heart, and then spreads to the family, the workplace, the local community, and then to the world. Years before the Medjugorje apparitions, Pope Paul VI spoke of peace in words that could easily have come from Our Lady:

Peace demands a mentality and a spirit which, before turning to others, must first permeate him who wishes to bring peace. Peace is first and foremost personal before it is social. And it is precisely this spirit of peace which it is the duty of every true follower of Christ to cultivate.

The fall of the Berlin Wall, the liberation of Eastern Europe, the demise of Communism in Russia—all were miracles of peace wrought by the Mother of God and her children which began with peace in a few individual hearts.

Application: Today, pray simply for peace of mind, heart, and soul.

FEBRUARY 9

The rosary in your hands

Today the Mother of God speaks of love and the rosary:

May the love of God always be within you, for without it you cannot be fully converted. Let the rosary in your hands make you think of Jesus (LJM 6-1-84).

After Christ's resurrection, his Mother and the apostles often met in prayer in the legendary upper room:

> When they had entered the city, they went to the room upstairs where they were staying . . . . All these were constantly devoting themselves to prayer, together with certain women, including Mary the mother of Jesus, as well as his brothers (Acts 1:13-14).

Reflection: Not surprisingly, sacred scripture places the same emphasis on prayer as Our Lady does in her messages at Medjugorje.

Her message today to, "Let the rosary in your hands make you think of *Jesus*," calls to mind the special "Rosary of Jesus" that she asked Jelena and her prayer group to offer. Dictated to her by the Virgin, each of the seven mysteries has the following format: 1) Announcement of the mystery; 2) Announcement of the prayer intention; 3) Quiet reflection on the mystery and then a spontaneous prayer from the heart; 4) Five Our Fathers; 5) and last, the phrase: "O Jesus, be our strength and protection." The following are the mysteries and prayer intentions:

The Apostles' Creed

FIRST MYSTERY: The birth of Christ

Prayer intention: for peace in the world

SECOND MYSTERY: The compassion and love of Jesus for the poor and afflicted

Prayer intention: For the Holy Father and the bishops

THIRD MYSTERY: The trust of Jesus for his Father and the performance of his will

Prayer intention: For priests, religious, and all who are consecrated to God in a special way

FOURTH MYSTERY: Jesus willingly came to earth, suffered and died, because of his great love for us

Prayer intention: For families, parents, and their children

FIFTH MYSTERY: Jesus gave his life as a sacrifice for us

Prayer intention: That we too will be capable of offering our lives for others

SIXTH MYSTERY: The resurrection of Jesus—his victory over Satan and death

Prayer intention: For the elimination of all sin in our lives so that Jesus may relive in our hearts.

SEVENTH MYSTERY: The Ascension of Jesus to heaven

Prayer intention: For the triumph of God's will, and that we may always be open to his will in our own lives

CONCLUSION: Jesus sends forth the Holy Spirit

Prayer intention: That the Spirit may descend upon us

Seven Glory Bes

Verse or refrain from a suitable hymn.

Application: Pray the "Rosary of Jesus" for the next several days to familiarize yourself with it.

Love your enemies

Our Lady speaks of a profound love today:

> *Love your enemies. Banish from your heart all hatred, bitterness, and judgmentalism. Instead, pray for your enemies and call a divine blessing upon them (LJM 6-16-83).*

The Virgin's message is an echo of Christ's words:

> But I say to you that listen, love your enemies, do good to those who hate you, bless those who curse you, pray for those who abuse you. If anyone strikes you on the cheek, offer the other also; and from anyone who takes away your coat, do not withhold even your shirt (Lk 6:27-29).

Reflection: This great love, which encompasses even our enemies, is a direct reflection of divine love. But rather than commenting on it, perhaps it would be more effective simply to see it in action, as others have practiced it in their own lives. The following story is from Ernest Gordon's account of life and death in a Japanese P.O.W. camp on the River Kwai:

> Farther on, we were shunted onto a siding for a lengthy stay. We found ourselves on the same track with several carloads of Japanese wounded. They were on their own and without medical care. No longer fit for action, they had been packed into railway trucks which were being returned to Bangkok. Whenever one of them died *en route*, he was thrown off into the jungle. The ones who survived to reach Bangkok would presumably receive some form of medical treatment there. But they were given none on the way.

Without a word, most of the officers in my section unbuckled their packs, took out part of their ration and a rag or two, and with water canteens in their hands, went over to the Japanese train to help them. Our guards tried to prevent us, bawling, "No goodka! No goodka!" But we ignored them and knelt by the side of the enemy to give them food and water, to clean and bind their wounds, to smile and say a kind word. Grateful cries of "Aragatto!" (thank you) followed us when we left.

An allied officer from another section of the train had been taking it all in. "What bloody fools you all are!" he said to me. "Don't you realize that those are the enemy?"

Application: In prayer today, let us do what Our Lady asks: "Pray for your enemies and call a divine blessing upon them."

FEBRUARY 11

Feast of Our Lady of Lourdes

Today Our Lady speaks of consecration:

Dear children, today I invite you again to consecrate your life to me in love, so that I can guide you lovingly. It is a very special love that I bear for you, dear children, and it is my desire to lead all of you to heaven, near to God. Understand that this life lasts only a short time in comparison with that of heaven.

That is why, dear children, again today, decide in favor of God. Only in this way can I show you how dear you are to me, and how much I desire that all of you be saved, to be with me in heaven (WM 11-27-86).

From Exodus, the miracle of water from the rock:

> But the people thirsted there for water; and the people complained against Moses and said, "Why did you bring us out of Egypt, to kill us and our children and our livestock with thirst?"

> So Moses cried out to the Lord, "What shall I do with this people? They are almost ready to stone me." The Lord said to Moses, "Go on ahead of the people, and take some of the elders of Israel with you; take in your hand the staff with which you struck the Nile, and go. I will be standing there in front of you on the rock at Horeb. Strike the rock and the water will come out of it, so that the people may drink." Moses did so, in the sight of the elders of Israel (Ex 17:3-6).

From a letter by St. Bernadette Soubirous, 1861:

> The third time I went, the lady spoke to me and asked me to come every day for fifteen days. She also told me to drink from the stream. . . . She indicated a little trickle of water close by. I went back each day for fifteen days and each time . . . the lady appeared and told me to look for a stream and wash in it. . . .

Reflection: As with Moses and the Israelites in the desert, miraculous water flowed from the grotto at Lourdes as a sign of God's healing power and love.

In response to this life-giving love, we are called, like St. Bernadette, to consecrate our lives to the Blessed Mother so that, as she says, "I can guide you with love."

In love we can see with new eyes that, "this life lasts briefly compared to the one in heaven," and so Our Lady urges us to prioritize our lives, putting God in first place. "Decide again for God," she says, which will enable her to guide us to peace and eternal life.

The water in the desert and the healing waters at Lourdes both invite us to drink generously of God's grace and love. Only a prayer and an open heart are necessary.

Application: In our own words, let us tell the Lord, as Mary asks, that we decide again for him. And since Our Lady says to "consecrate your life to me with love," let us do just that using the Prayer of Consecration she gave to us, found on November 24.

FEBRUARY 12

A time of temptation

To Ivan's prayer group in 1988:

> *Dear children, I am your Mother and I warn you this time is a time of temptation. Satan is trying to find emptiness in you, so he can enter and destroy you. Do not surrender! I will pray with you. Do not pray just with your lips, but pray with the heart. In this way prayer will obtain victory! (VPG 7-4-88).*

In Matthew's gospel, the powers of evil retreat when confronted by the Son of God:

> When he came to the other side, to the country of the Gadarenes, two demoniacs coming out of the tombs met him. They were so fierce that no one could pass that way. Suddenly they shouted, "What have you to do with us, Son of God? Have you come here to torment us before the time?"
>
> Now a large herd of swine was feeding at some distance from them. The demons begged him, "If you cast us out, send us into the herd of swine."

And he said to them, "Go!" So they came out and entered the swine; and suddenly the whole herd rushed down the steep bank into the sea and perished in the water (Mt 8:28-32).

Reflection: Our Lady always seeks to protect us from harm, and so naturally warns us of approaching danger. Thus she reveals Satan to us, although he would much rather remain hidden. "Satan is trying to find emptiness in you," she says, "so he can enter and destroy you. *Do not surrender!*"

The gospel writers also reveal to us the Evil One and his cruelty, but show us as well his powerlessness when confronted by the Son of God. This eternal victory of Christ over evil is also our victory. When calling on his name in time of temptation, the enemy is immediately routed.

It is tapping into this power of Christ through prayer that is our chief weapon against Satan. This is why the Gospa urges us not to pray in a rote fashion, "but pray with the heart. In this way prayer will obtain victory!"

Application: For the next few days, offer the Prayer to St. Michael, perhaps forming a daily habit:

St. Michael the Archangel, defend us in the day of battle; be our safeguard against the wickedness and snares of the devil. May God rebuke him, we humbly pray, and may thou, O prince of the heavenly host, by the power of God, cast into hell, Satan and all the other evil spirits, who prowl through the world, seeking the ruin of souls. Amen.

Devote your prayers to me

From a monthly message in 1988:

Dear children, again I call you to prayer and complete surrender to God. You know that I love you, and have come here out of love so that I could show you the way to peace—and to salvation for your souls. Do not let Satan corrupt you—obey me in this. Satan is very strong and therefore I ask you to devote your prayers to me, so that those who are under his influence may be saved.

Witness by your lives. Sacrifice your lives for the salvation of the world. Know that I am with you and am grateful to you; in heaven you will receive the Father's reward, as he has promised.

And so, dear children, do not be afraid. If you pray, Satan cannot harm you in the least, for you are God's children and he watches over you. Pray, and let the rosary always be in your hands as a sign to Satan that you belong to me (MM 3-25-88).

In Matthew's gospel, Jesus also calls us to prayer. Note that the Our Father contains a prayer against Satan as well: "and lead us not into temptation, but deliver us from evil." In Matthew, this petition is expressed in these words: "And do not bring us to the time of trial, but deliver us from the evil one" (Mt 6:13).

Reflection: At times we may notice that our prayer has become too self-centered. This is an opportunity to again focus on others, on "we" rather than "I," which is the spirit of the Lord's Prayer. In this vein, Charles Thompson writes:

You can not pray the Lord's Prayer,

and even once say "I."
You can not pray the Lord's Prayer
and even once say "My."
Nor can you pray the Lord's Prayer,
and not pray for another;
for when you ask for daily bread,
you must include your brother.
For others are included
in each and every plea:
from the beginning to the end of it,
it does not once say "Me."

Application: Review the focus of your prayer today. Is it weighted more to yourself or to others? How can you correct the imbalance?

FEBRUARY 14

St. Valentine's Day

On this Valentine's Day, the Blessed Mother asks for our hearts:

> *Dear children, today I invite you to offer me your hearts so that I can change them to be like my own. You ask yourselves why you are not able to satisfy my requests? You are not able to because you have not entrusted your hearts to me, so that I can change them. You give me words, but you do not act. So then, do all that I tell you. Only in that way can I be with you (WM 5-15-86).*

Reflection: On this feast of St. Valentine, Our Lady asks for our hearts, "so I can change them to be like my own." Once we give them, they are filled with God's own life and love; indeed, they are made eternal:

> See what love the Father has given us, that we should be called children of God; and that is what we are. The reason the world does not know us is

that it did not know him. Beloved, we are God's children now; what we will be has not yet been revealed. What we do know is this: when he is revealed, we will be like him, for we will see him as he is (1 Jn 3:1-2).

This is the great inheritance of love, a gift beyond imagining—to share in the very life of God.

This is also the reason Our Lady asks for our hearts today, that she can begin to transform them into the image of her Son's. We can then begin to live the life of heaven while on earth, embracing others with the divine love that has been given to us. As St. Teresa of Avila wrote:

O soul in God hidden from sin,
What more desires for thee remain,
Save but to love, and love again,
And all on flame with love within,
Love on, and turn to love again?

Application: In prayer today, simply ask the Lord to deepen his love within your heart.

FEBRUARY 15

A year for youth

The Blessed Mother speaks of youth today:

Dear children, from today I would like you to begin a special "year for youth." Pray for young people during this year; talk with them. Today our young people find themselves in a very difficult situation, and so I ask you to help each other. . . . Pray, dear children (VPG 8-15-88).

In his first letter to Timothy, St. Paul encourages his young friend:

Let no one despise your youth, but set the believers an example in speech and conduct, in love, in faith, in purity (1 Tm 4:12).

Reflection: Both Our Lady and St. Paul emphasize the special role of young people in the church. Paul's friend Timothy was a young leader in the early church at Ephesus, of whom the apostle wrote: "I have no one like him who will be genuinely concerned for your welfare. All of them are seeking their own interests, not those of Jesus Christ."

In Timothy's assignment at Ephesus, Paul knew that it would be easy for older Christians to question his leadership because of his youth, but he earned their respect by setting an example in his teaching, life, love, and faith. Regardless of age, the Lord uses us in his great plan of salvation. Clearly the zeal and enthusiasm of youth are not only treasures of the church, but also its bright future.

Application: Let us simply heed the Madonna's advice today: "Pray for young people; talk with them."

FEBRUARY 16

How strong my love is

Today Our Lady speaks of our need to recognize her love:

> *Dear children, today I wish to give you my love. You do not realize, dear children, how strong my love is or how to accept it. I wish to show it to you in many ways, dear children, but you do recognize it. You do not listen to my words with your hearts, and thus you do not comprehend my love. Dear children, accept me into your life and then you will be able to accept all that I tell you and all that I am calling you to (WM 5-22-86).*

In Psalm 19, the author sees creation as an expression of God's love:

The heavens are telling the glory of God;
and the firmament proclaims his handiwork.
Day to day pours forth speech,
and night to night declares knowledge.
There is no speech, nor are there words;
their voice is not heard;
Yet their voices go out to all the earth,
and their words to the end of the world.

—Psalm 19:1-4

Reflection: Today the Blessed Mother says that she attempts to show us her love in various ways, but often we do not recognize it. The same is true of God's love; we seem to need "new eyes" to look about and see his gifts around us. One of the ways he shows us this love is in creation, as our psalm reveals: "The heavens declare the glory of God." Indeed, some people have actually come to faith by seeing the Lord in nature, in the beauty of the created world. The following verses speak of this insight:

Who sees his lord
Within every creature
Deathlessly dwelling
Amidst the mortal:
That man sees truly. . . .

—The Bhagavad-Gita

Application: This week, try to spend some time outdoors, perhaps taking a walk in the park, or just around the neighborhood. Try to be conscious of God's presence in his creation, aware that this also is prayer.

Mass is the greatest prayer to God

Today Our Lady emphasizes the importance of preparing for Mass:

The Mass is the greatest prayer to God. You will never be able to comprehend its importance. That is why you must be perfect and humble at Mass, and should prepare yourselves beforehand (FY 1983).

The word "eucharist" translates into "thanksgiving," which is the spirit of Psalm 116:

What shall I return to the Lord
for all his bounty to me?
I will lift up the cup of salvation
and call on the name of the Lord.

—Psalm 116:12-13

Reflection: In reflecting on the eucharist today, as the readings indicate, it would be appropriate to hear as well from one of the visionaries on its importance to our spiritual lives. Several years ago, Vicka said:

Before going to holy Mass, focus intently on who you will be receiving. During Mass, open your heart to Jesus. See him with the "eyes" of your heart. We see and experience and live with Jesus through faith. That's why, during Mass, our faith must be very strong. The stronger our faith, the better prepared we are to welcome him in the holy eucharist.

We must not only listen during Mass, we must really experience all the holy words of the Mass with love. That's why, toward the end of Mass when you are receiving Jesus alive, if your heart is open, he is truly with you. When the Mass ends and you leave the church, you will be filled with unspeakable joy!

Application: When attending your next Mass, arrive early so you can prepare. Think of Christ, as Vicka recommends, and give him any worries or problems that might distract you from the eucharist. Review the day's readings from the Sunday missalette, or if attending a daily Mass, use a weekday missal for this purpose (available at religious goods stores).

FEBRUARY 18

On the way to holiness

Speaking of holiness, the Blessed Mother says:

> *Dear children, you know that I wish to lead you on the way of holiness, but I cannot compel you to be saints by force. I wish that each of you help me, and yourself, by your small sacrifices. Then I will be able to guide and help you to grow in holiness day by day (WM 10-9-86).*

St. Peter speaks of holiness as well:

> Like obedient children, do not be conformed to the desires that you formerly had in ignorance. Instead, as he who called you is holy, be holy yourselves in all your conduct; for it is written, "You shall be holy, for I am holy" (1 Pt 1:14-16).

Reflection: Holiness means to be devoted or dedicated to God, to be set aside for his special purpose, and set apart from sin and its influence. We are set apart and different, not blending in with the crowd, yet not being different just for the sake of being different. What distinguishes us are the qualities of God in our lives; our focus and priorities are his.

Growth in these qualities and priorities usually occurs a bit at a time, for holiness is a process. Patience as well as commitment is called for. In the words of Andrew Bonar:

A holy Christian life is made up of a
number of small things:
  Little words, not eloquent sermons;
  Little deeds, not miracles of battle
  Or one great, heroic deed of martyrdom;
The little constant sunbeam,
not the lightning.

The avoidance of little evils,
  Little inconsistencies, little weaknesses,
  Little follies and indiscretions,
  And little indulgences of the flesh make up
The beauty of a holy life.

Application: Reflect today on the following: "The greatest thing for us is the perfection of our own soul; and the saints teach us that this perfection consists in doing our ordinary actions well" (Archbishop Ullathorne).

FEBRUARY 19

I forgive easily

Of prayer and forgiveness, the Blessed Mother said:

Dear children, I, your Mother, love you, and so I urge you to pray. I am tireless, dear children, and I call you even when you are far from my heart. I am a Mother, and although I feel pain for each one who goes astray, I forgive easily and am happy for every child who returns to me (WM 11-14-85).

As Our Lady forgives with joy, so her Son enjoins each of us to do the same:

Then Peter came and said to him, "Lord, if another member of the church sins against me, how often should I forgive? As many as seven times?" Jesus said to him, "Not seven times, but, I tell you, seventy-seven times" (Mt 18:21-22).

Reflection: Once, the Duke of Wellington was about to pronounce the death sentence on a confirmed deserter. Deeply moved, the great general said, "I am extremely sorry to pass this severe sentence, but we have tried everything, and all the discipline and penalties have failed to improve this man, who is otherwise a brave and good soldier."

Then he gave the man's comrades an opportunity to speak for him. "Please, your excellency," said one of the men, "there is one thing you have never tried. You have not tried forgiving him." Surprisingly, the general did forgive him, and it worked. The soldier never again deserted.

It might be added here that the other benefit of forgiveness is that, once we have experienced it ourselves, we seem to naturally turn around and forgive others. The effect is, as Our Lady knows so well, peace.

Application: Pray for forgiveness today and for the grace to forgive another for some hurt in your heart.

FEBRUARY 20

Open yourselves to the Holy Spirit

Regarding the Holy Spirit, Our Lady once said:

Dear children, this is a time of grace. Open yourselves to the Holy Spirit that he may make you strong. Your Mother, dear children, calls you especially to prayer and sacrifice during this time (VPG 6-1-90).

In Galatians, Paul speaks of the fruits of the Holy Spirit:

> By contrast, the fruit of the Spirit is love, joy, peace, patience, kindness, generosity, faithfulness, gentleness, and self-control. There is no law against such things. And those who belong to Christ Jesus have crucified the flesh with its passions and desires. If we live by the Spirit, let us also be guided by the Spirit (Gal 5:22-25).

Reflection: Isaac Hecker, the founder of the Paulists, once wrote: "The whole future of the human race depends on bringing the individual soul more completely and perfectly under the sway of the Holy Spirit." This Spirit is always at work within us, gently transforming us into the likeness of Christ and imbuing us with the divine gifts of peace, kindness, faithfulness, and the other virtues of which Paul speaks today.

These traits are not the reward of our own spiritual achievements—the most we can do is open ourselves radically to God—but are pure gifts from the Holy Spirit. Pope Leo XIII wrote, "Whatever we are, that we are by the divine goodness; and this goodness is especially attributed to the Holy Spirit." But because our God possesses infinite generosity and love, he will fill with the Spirit any emptiness within us, if it has been emptied for him.

Application: "Every time we say, 'I believe in the Holy Spirit,'" writes J. B. Phillips, "we mean that we believe there is a living God able and willing to enter human personality and change it." Today, pray for the gifts of the Holy Spirit, as Our Lady urges us, for she has said, "When you have the Holy Spirit, you have everything."

It is up to you to choose

In answer to a question by the visionaries about their futures, the Blessed Virgin responded:

I would like all of you to become priests and religious, but only if you desire it. You are free. It is up to you to choose. . . (FY 12-8-81).

Vocations are also the theme from this passage from Matthew's gospel:

When he saw the crowds, he had compassion for them, because they were harassed and helpless, like sheep without a shepherd. Then he said to his disciples, "The harvest is plentiful, but the laborers are few; therefore ask the Lord of the harvest to send our laborers into his harvest" (Mt 9:36-38).

Reflection: There are two conditions on which vocations to the priesthood and religious life hinge. The first, as Christ tells us today, is prayer. Through prayer an individual discerns the call of God, and through prayer God's people help to plant the seeds of vocations.

Second, the environment and support of a Christian family nourishes these budding vocations. I have a friend from a farming family who was working in a field one day with his father. In the course of their conversation on Ken's future, his father said, "Have you ever thought of the priesthood?" That's all it took. These seven words contained approval and encouragement for such a career, which is what Ken needed to think seriously about it. Today he is pastor of a parish in his home state of Iowa.

I believe my own vocation was inspired by my parent's example of faith as well as a large measure of God's grace. I was also blessed to have as role models several fine Benedictine friars from my home parish. Prayer, family, example, and grace: the essentials needed to bring in the workers of the harvest.

Application: How can you encourage a vocation within your own family? Have you ever broached the subject with a friend or acquaintance who might be a promising candidate? The following Prayer for Vocations is a response to Christ's request that we pray for more laborers. Try to pray it often:

Lord, you told us that, "The harvest is great but the laborers are few. Pray, therefore, that the Lord of the harvest send laborers to his field." We ask you to strengthen us as we follow the vocation to which you have called us. We pray particularly for those called to serve as priests, sisters, brothers and deacons: those whom you have called, those you are calling now, those you will call in the future.

Grant them the grace to be open and responsive to your urgent call. We ask this through Christ, our Lord. Amen.

FEBRUARY 22

The Chair of Peter

In the first weeks of the apparitions, the Blessed Virgin kissed an image of the Pope and said:

He is your father, the spiritual father of all. It is necessary to pray for him (FY 11-8-81).

And in March of 1982, smiling at two large pictures of the Pope that had been brought by a woman from

Osijek, Our Lady said: "He is your father, my angels" (FY 3-2-82).

In Matthew's gospel, Jesus responds to Peter's faith in these words:

> And I tell you, you are Peter, and on this rock I will build my church, and the gates of Hades will not prevail against it. I will give you the keys of the kingdom of heaven, and whatever you bind on earth shall be bound in heaven, and whatever you loose on earth will be loosed in heaven (Mt 16:18-19).

Reflection: On the cross, Jesus gave us his mother to be our own. In a like manner, in today's message, Mary in turn points to the Holy Father and gives him to us as "the spiritual father of all."

The Chair of Peter is a gift from God who never leaves us without a shepherd to guide and teach us. It has been the charge of the Popes through the ages to hand down the body of faith which Christ gave to his apostles and followers, to preserve it in its integrity for future generations. Through the calm and turbulence of 2000 years, that legacy of faith has now come down to us and to the present Pope, who in turn will teach and preserve it.

No other institution of any kind has so survived the ages, a sign of the Spirit's presence with the church, once called "Mother" to signify its mission of nourishing God's children. As Christians and Catholics, we give thanks today for this priceless legacy and for the successor of Peter who is "father of all."

Application: Our Lady says of the Pope in her message, "He is your father . . . it is necessary to pray for him." Let us then offer a rosary for the Holy Father today, and remember him in prayer for the rest of the week.

Pray, pray, pray!

Our Lady's monthly message for October, 1991 (in the midst of the Yugoslavian civil war), was startling in its brevity. It was simply: "Pray, pray, pray!"

In St. John's gospel, Jesus weeps out of love for his friend Lazarus:

> When Jesus saw her weeping, and the Jews who came with her also weeping, he was greatly disturbed in spirit and deeply moved. He said, "Where have you laid him?" They said to him, "Lord, come and see." Jesus began to weep. So the Jews said, "See how he loved him!" (Jn 11:33-36).

Reflection: Today we have two brief but powerful messages from Jesus and the Blessed Mother: prayer and love. It is these qualities that mark the following love letter from Jesus (quoted from the Apostleship of Prayer):

Dear Friend,

How are you? I just had to send a note to tell you how much I love you and care about you.

I saw you yesterday as you were talking with your friends. I waited all day, hoping you would want to talk with me also. As evening drew near, I gave you a sunset to close your day and a cool breeze to rest you—and I waited. You never came. Oh, yes, it hurts me—but I still love you because I am your friend.

I saw you fall asleep last night and longed to touch your brow, so I spilled moonlight upon your pillow and face. Again I waited, wanting to rush down so we could talk. I have so many gifts for you! You awakened late and rushed off to work. My tears were in the rain.

Today you looked so sad—so all alone. It makes my heart ache because I understand. My friends let me down and hurt me many times, too, but I love you.

Oh, if you would only listen to me. I love you! I try to tell you in the blue sky and in the quiet green grass. I whisper it in the leaves on the trees and breathe it in the colors of flowers. I shout it to you in mountain streams and give the birds love songs to sing. I clothe you with warm sunshine and perfume the air with nature scents. My love for you is deeper than the ocean and bigger than the biggest want or need in your head. Oh, if you only knew how much I want to walk and talk with you. We could spend an eternity together in heaven.

I know how hard it is on this earth; I really know! And I want to help you. I want you to meet my Father. He wants to help you, too. My Father is that way, you know.

Just call me, ask me, talk with me! Oh, please don't forget me. I have so much to share with you!

All right, I won't bother you any further. You are free to choose me. It's your decision. I have chosen you, and because of this I will wait, because I love you!

Your friend,
Jesus

Application: Today, simply speak to the Lord with your heart.

Even the smallest prayers

Today the Blessed Mother speaks of prayer from the heart:

Dear children, today I call you to pray with the heart. Throughout this season of grace, I wish each of you to be united with Jesus. But without unceasing prayer, you cannot experience the great and beautiful graces which God is offering you.

Therefore, little children, at all times fill your hearts with even the smallest prayers. I am with you and I keep watch unceasingly over every heart which is given to me (MM 2-25-89).

St. James advises:

If any of you is lacking in wisdom, ask God, who gives to all generously and ungrudgingly, and it will be given you. But ask in faith, never doubting, for the one who doubts is like a wave of the sea, driven and tossed by the wind (Jas 1:5-6).

Reflection: James emphasizes that our prayer should be confident and hopeful, for God will deny nothing that is good to his children. And the Blessed Virgin stresses the importance of "even the smallest prayers," for they too are an encounter with her divine Son.

The following is a special "small prayer" for inner peace which seeks the intercession of St. Thérèse, the Little Flower:

Lord Jesus, inspired by the example of St. Thérèse, I place all my trust in your Sacred Heart, and surrender myself to your will. Come into my life, drive away my fears, stop my restless strivings, and show me new ways of pleasing you. Teach me to discern the good in others, and to love them with an affectionate smile, a gentle touch, a patient ear, and an affirming word.

St. Thérèse, pray that I may become alive again with awe, the appreciation of truth, and the courage to oppose evil. Remind me always that I am created for happiness, for the joy of living in the presence of God. St. Thérèse, pray that I, and all God's people, may have the inner peace that comes from confidence, surrender, and affirmation. Amen.

Application: While reflecting on this prayer, you may wish to copy it on a small piece of paper and tuck it into your wallet or purse for use in troubled or anxious times.

FEBRUARY 25

Shine for others

The Blessed Virgin calls us to be a light for others:

Thank you for the things you have renounced during Lent. Most of all, renounce sin. Be a light so you can shine for others. Encourage them to pray, fast, and do penance. Give your love to others (VPG 2-22-88).

Ephesians also calls us to light:

For once you were darkness, but now in the Lord you are light. Live as children of light—for the fruit of the light is found in all that is good and right and true.

Try to find out what is pleasing to the Lord. Take no part in the unfruitful works of darkness, but instead expose them. For it is shameful even to mention what such people do secretly; but everything exposed by the light becomes visible, for everything that becomes visible is light. Therefore it says, "Sleeper, awake! Rise from the dead, and Christ will shine on you" (Eph 5:8-14).

Reflection: The most celebrated lighthouse of antiquity was the one erected by Ptolemy Soter on the island of Pharos, opposite Alexandria. The historian Josephus says it could be seen at a distance of forty-two miles. It was one of the seven wonders of the ancient world.

A holy life produces the deepest impression on others. Lighthouses blow no horns; they only shine. And so Our Lady urges us today to, "Be light, shine for others," and St. Paul asks that we, "Live as children of light." How? By living the messages of the Blessed Mother, the basic gospel message. For there are two ways of spreading light: to be the candle, or the mirror that reflects it.

Application: For meditation today: "To reflect God in all that is, both here and now, my heart must be a mirror empty, bright and clear" (Angelus Silesius).

FEBRUARY 26

Come to Mass

Today Our Lady speaks of love and the eucharist:

Dear children, I wish to tell you that this is a special time for you and the parish. During the summer, you said that you had a great deal of work. But the work in the fields is now finished, and so I call you now to work on yourselves! Come to Mass, for the time is now provided.

Dear children, there are many who come to Mass, even in the worst weather, because they love me and want to prove their love. Now I call you to show me your love by coming to Mass. The Lord will reward you abundantly (WM 11-21-85).

St. Paul also speaks of the eucharist:

For I received from the Lord what I also handed on to you, that the Lord Jesus on the night when he was betrayed took a loaf of bread, and when he had given thanks, he broke it and said, "This is my body that is for you. Do this in remembrance of me." In the same way, he took the cup also, after supper, saying, "This cup is the new covenant in my blood. Do this, as often as you drink it, in remembrance of me." For as often as you eat this bread and drink this cup, you proclaim the Lord's death until he comes (1 Cor 11:23-26).

Reflection: The Mass has come down to us as the greatest gift God could give his people: the gift of himself. Once Vicka, one of the visionaries of Medjugorje, was asked to identify the most important thing in her life. She responded:

The Blessed Mother has led me to understand that the center of my life is the eucharist, which is Jesus, who is God. In the Mass, we are receiving Jesus, who is alive. In this sacrament we are really receiving Jesus, his own body and blood. We must be prepared to receive Christ alive. We must do this consciously, knowing what it means to receive him alive. Then we can experience Jesus' real presence within us and around us.

Vicka's reverence for the eucharist extends to the point that, when once asked if she had to choose between an apparition of the Gospa or receiving holy communion, she responded that she would choose the eucharist, for that was the gift of God himself.

Application: How does your devotion to the eucharist compare to that of Vicka's? Given the great importance of this gift, could you participate in it more frequently?

FEBRUARY 27

Ask then, for all that you need

The following message was given to Marija while she was in America in November, 1988:

I invite you to pray and to give yourselves completely to God. I will give you strength and help you whenever you are in need; ask then, for all that you need, for I will intercede for you in God's presence (SM 11-23-88).

While trusting Our Lady to give us all that we need, we will find at the same time that our trust in God will grow ever stronger:

The Lord is a stronghold for the oppressed,
  a stronghold in times of trouble.
And those who know your name put their trust
  in you,
for you, O Lord, have not forsaken those who
  seek you.

—Psalm 9:9-10

Reflection: The Lord never forsakes those who seek and trust him; nor can Our Lady, who is forever faithful as her Son. Although loss or suffering may wound us deeply, our God is as close as a whispered prayer. We can trust him to heal us.

This is the spirit of trust that John Cardinal Newman expressed in the following prayer:

God has created me to do him some definite service; he has committed some work to me which he has not committed to another. I have my mission—I may never know it in this life, but I shall be told it in the next.

I am a link in a chain, a bond of connection between persons. He has not created me for naught. I shall do good. I shall do his work. I shall be an angel of peace, a preacher of truth in my own place *while not intending it*—if I do but keep his commandments.

Whatever, wherever I am, I can never be thrown away. If I am in sickness, my sickness may serve him; in perplexity, my perplexity may serve him; if I am in sorrow, my sorrow may serve him. He does nothing in vain. He knows what he is about. He may take away my friends, he may throw me among strangers, he may make me feel desolate, make my spirits sink, hide my future from me—still he knows what he is about. Therefore *I will trust him.*

Application: Simply reflect on Cardinal Newman's prayer once more today. You may wish to offer it especially in anxious or troubled times.

FEBRUARY 28

Experience this peace

Our Lady speaks of peace in this monthly message:

Dear children, today I thank you and I want to invite you all to God's peace. I want each of you to experience, in your heart, this peace which only God can give. I bless you with God's blessing and beseech you to live, dear children, in the way I have shown you.

I love you, dear children, which is why I do not count the number of times I have called you—and continue to call you.

I thank you for all you have done according to my wishes. Help me, please, that I may present you to God and guide you to salvation (MM 6-25-87).

And in John's gospel, Christ gives his peace to his disciples:

But the Advocate, the Holy Spirit, whom the Father will send in my name, will teach you everything, and remind you of all that I have said to you. *Peace I leave with you; my peace I give to you.* I do not give to you as the world gives. Do not let your hearts be troubled, and do not let them be afraid (Jn 14:26-27).

Reflection: The effect of the Holy Spirit's work in our lives is often a deep and lasting peace. Unlike the world's peace, which is only the absence of conflict, this peace lives in us as a confident assurance in all circumstances. With Christ's peace, we have no need to fear the past, present, or future.

Application: Reflect today on this line from the philosopher Baruch Spinoza: "Peace is not an absence of war; it is a virtue, a state of mind, a disposition for benevolence, confidence, and justice."

Mt. Krizevac

The winds of March

Regarding a very strong wind blowing, which the parishioners noticed on the way to church, Our Lady said:

> *The wind is my sign. I will come in the wind. When the wind blows, know that I am with you. You have learned that the cross represents Christ; it is a sign of him. It is the same for the crucifix you have in your home. For me, it is not the same. When it is cold, you come to church; you want to offer everything to God. I am, then, with you. I am with you in the wind. Do not be afraid (LJM 2-15-84).*

Sacred scripture also speaks of another heavenly presence in the wind:

> When the day of Pentecost had come, they were all together in one place. And suddenly from heaven there came a sound like the rush of a violent wind, and it filled the entire house where they were sitting. Divided tongues, as of fire, appeared among them, and a tongue rested on each of them. All of them were filled with the Holy Spirit and began to speak in other languages, as the Spirit gave them ability (Acts 2:1-4).

Reflection: The wind can be strong or calm, a soft breeze or a mighty storm; it can come from the south or north; it can be warm or cold.

In the same way, life itself can sometimes be turbulent or serene, happy or sad. There are tragic as well as joyful episodes.

But there is peace in knowing our Mother is with us in the wind, in all of life's changes and turnings. In the power of the Holy Spirit she says to us simply, "I am with you . . . do not be afraid."

Application: In prayer today, confide your problems and joys to Our Lady of Peace. Try to leave them in her hands all day, and call on her name if you encounter anxiety or uncertainty.

MARCH 2

Thank you for each sacrifice

During Lent of 1986, Our Lady gave the following message:

> *Dear children, today I invite you to live this Lent with your small sacrifices. Thank you for each sacrifice which you have already presented to me. Dear children, continue to live in this way and, with your love, help me to present your offerings to God, who will reward you (WM 3-13-86).*

St. Paul also speaks of sacrifice:

> Do not neglect to do good and to share what you have, for such sacrifices are pleasing to God (Heb 13:16).

Reflection: "Live this Lent," Our Lady says today, "with your small sacrifices." The Gospa knows well that God lovingly receives our sacrifices and uses them to draw us closer to him, and to aid in no less than the salvation of mankind.

Sacrifice is the truest sign of love, for on the external level we gain nothing for ourselves, but direct our action outward for the benefit of another. For instance, we can speak many words of concern for the mentally handicapped, but it is quite a different thing to sacrifice several hours a week to help out at a local center, especially if we find it a demanding experience. In much the same way, our sacrifice of giving up, say, alcohol or coffee for Lent, is a concrete action of love for God that goes beyond mere words. A sacrifice made with love, as Mary urges us, is even redemptive in the hands of God, for it becomes joined to the greatest love-sacrifice of all, that of Christ on the cross.

In addition, sacrifices such as fasting amplify the power of prayer many fold. For again, it is a concrete expression of love—more than words—that directly touches the heart of God.

Thus Our Lady's message, "live this Lent with your small sacrifices," refers to a living love for God that is proved by more than words. It says to him, "See that I love you by my sacrifices, by my self-denial. I am serious. I love you even when it hurts, just as you loved me."

Application: St. Thérèse, the Little Flower, once prayed and fasted for the conversion of a murderer on death row, who was also an atheist. On the day of his execution, at the gallows, he astonished everyone by reaching for the chaplain's crucifix and kissing it. How aware are you of the great power you possess in prayer with sacrifice? For what intention can it be offered this week?

MARCH 3

People resume their bad habits

The Blessed Mother was in tears when she gave this message to the visionaries:

So many people who have been here, and have started to pray, to be converted, to fast, and to do penance, quickly forget when they return home, and resume their bad habits (SM 4-24-84).

Our Lady's implicit call to repentance is echoed by the prophet Joel:

Put on sackcloth and lament, you priests;
wail, you ministers of the altar.
Come, pass the night in sackcloth,
you ministers of my God!
Grain offering and drink offering
are withheld from the house of your God.

Sanctify a fast,
call a solemn assembly.
Gather the elders
and all the inhabitants of the land
to the house of the Lord your God,
and cry out to the Lord.

—Joel 1:13-14

Reflection: Lent is a time for renewal and repentance, for turning back to God with our whole heart. Although we may have stepped backwards in our spiritual journey, now is the time to rearrange our priorities, to recommit ourselves to the Lord. Of this renewal, Pope Paul VI wrote:

We must aim above all at an inner renewal, a liberation from the mere following of conventions, a new departure in our way of thinking. More than anything else, we must lament our shortcomings before God, and the community of our brethren. We must renew the self-understanding each must have of himself or herself as a child of God, as a Christian, as a member of the Church.

May our Lenten renewal reward us with a deeper share of God's love and peace at the feast of Easter.

Application: Remembering Our Lady in tears, reflect on how you can deepen your spiritual life during these remaining days of Lent.

MARCH 4

Jesus gives himself to you!

The Virgin speaks to Jelena of the joy of salvation:

> *How can you not be happy? Jesus gives himself to you! I wish to fill the souls of all. But I am sad this evening, for many have not prepared themselves for Easter. Thus Jesus will not be able to unite himself to their souls on that great day (LJM 4-14-84).*

Paul explains salvation as a pure gift of Christ:

> But God, who is rich in mercy, out of the great love with which he loved us even when we were dead through our trespasses, made us alive together with Christ—by grace you have been saved—and raised us up with him and seated us with him in the heavenly places in Christ Jesus, so that in the ages to come he might show the immeasurable riches of his grace in kindness toward us in Christ Jesus. For by grace you have been saved through faith, and this is not your own doing; it is the gift of God (Eph 2:4-8).

Reflection: St. Paul emphasizes that we do not need to live any longer under sin's power. The penalty of sin and its power over us were destroyed by Christ on the cross. Through him we stand acquitted, "not guilty," before God (cf. Rom 3:21-22).

Our Lady urges us to accept and rejoice in this gift of salvation. When someone gives you a gift, do you say,

"That's very nice, now how much do I owe you?" No, the appropriate response is, "Thank you." Yet some of us, even after we've been given the gift of salvation, feel obligated to try to work or earn our own way to God. But because salvation and even faith are pure gifts, our response can only be one of gratitude, praise, and joy.

Application: Have we ever accepted, deep down, the gift of salvation? Today, pray that you may experience the awesome impact of this greatest of gifts, as Our Lady urges.

MARCH 5

Make a special decision for prayer

The Mother of Jesus urges us to pray as a defense against evil. To Ivan's prayer group:

> *Dear children, your Mother warns you tonight that Satan is active in a special way these days. Do not allow emptiness inside of you, but fill this emptiness with prayer. Dear children, prayer is the best medicine these days to defend yourselves against evil. And so, dear children, make a special decision for prayer during Lent. Tonight I expect you to pray the Glorious Mysteries when you return home (VPG 2-19-90).*

Fittingly, Psalm 54 is entitled, "Confident Prayer in Great Peril":

> But surely, God is my helper;
> the Lord is the upholder of my life.
> He will repay my enemies for their evil.
> In your faithfulness, put an end to them.
>
> With a freewill offering I will sacrifice to you;
> I will give thanks to your name, O Lord, for it
> is good.

For he has delivered me from every trouble,
and my eye has looked in triumph on
    my enemies.

—Psalm 54:4-7

Reflection: As Our Lady tells us today, prayer is our chief weapon against evil. It is of such importance that she once told Jelena, the locutionist, "I have nothing else to tell you, but pray, pray, pray."

In a sermon on prayer, Fr. Tomislav Vlasic, formerly assigned to Medjugorje, made the analogy that, "Just as we find ourselves talking to a friend for hours on end, so it is just as natural to talk with Jesus Christ." On problems in prayer, he suggests that, "If we are distracted or absent-minded in prayer, it may be that we are too far from God, too devoted to the world, and have not given enough time to seeking him in prayer."

He adds: "I therefore invite you to a continuous deepening of prayer. The Holy Spirit will enlighten you each step of the way and Satan will be completely disarmed."

Application: Let's simply heed the Virgin's advice today: "Don't allow emptiness inside of you; fill this emptiness with prayer . . . it is the best medicine to defend yourselves against evil."

MARCH 6

Be converted!

The season of Lent has always been a time of repentance, conversion, and penance—a time for turning back to the Lord, renouncing sin, and beginning anew. This is the call of Our Lady today:

Be converted! It will be too late when the sign comes. Beforehand, several warnings will be given to the world. Have people hurry to be converted. I need your prayers and your penance.

My heart is burning with love for you. It suffices for you to be converted. To ask questions is unimportant. Be converted. Hurry to proclaim it. Tell everyone that it is my wish, and that I do not cease repeating it. Be converted, be converted. It is not difficult for me to suffer for you. I beg you, be converted.

I will pray to my Son to spare you the punishment. Be converted without delay. You do not know the plans of God; you will not be able to know them. You will not know what God will send, nor what he will do. I ask you only to be converted. That is what I wish.

Be converted! Be ready for everything, but be converted. That is all I wish to say to you. Renounce everything else. All that is part of conversion. Good bye, and may peace be with you (LJM 4-25-83).

Our Lady's message is echoed in the Acts of the Apostles:

> In this way God fulfilled what he had foretold through all the prophets, that his Messiah would suffer. Repent therefore, and turn to God so that your sins may be wiped out, so that times of refreshing may come from the presence of the Lord, and that he may send the Messiah appointed for you, that is, Jesus (Acts 3:18-20).

Reflection: During this Lenten season, let us take the Blessed Mother seriously and seek conversion in renewed prayer, penance, and works of love. This will bring us great joy at Easter and a confirmation of the Gospa's words today: "My heart is burning with love for you."

Application: During Lent, set aside extra time for prayer and works of charity. Be active in the special Lenten devotions of your local parish. Go the extra mile for Our Lord and Our Lady.

MARCH 7

Prepare through renunciation

During Lent of 1988, Our Lady said to Ivan's prayer group:

Prepare yourself for the time of Lent by renouncing something. During Lent I will need your help for the accomplishment and fulfillment of all my plans (VPG 2-1-88).

Ezekiel also asks us to renounce something—the spirit of sin:

But if the wicked turn away from all their sins that they have committed and keep all my statutes and do what is lawful and right, they shall surely live; they shall not die. None of the transgressions that they have committed shall be remembered against him; for the righteousness that they have done they shall live (Ez 18:21-22).

Reflection: The concept of renunciation or penance often has a negative connotation; to give up something for Lent or Advent seems to be an imposition that no one welcomes. And yet the actual effect of penance is to set us spiritually free; we develop a greater desire for God and a growing freedom from material things—and thus peace begins to take root in our hearts. When we begin to live this interior freedom from exterior things, we begin to grow rapidly in the spiritual life.

Fr. Slavko Barbaric, spiritual director to the visionaries, has written:

> Once you embrace God, you let go of other things, because there is no room for them anymore. So the core issue is not giving up luxury or wealth; you have found something better when you have found God. God leaves no room in your life for other things.

For instance, a candidate for the Olympic swimming team will need to "renounce" smoking if he is to realize his dream of competing for the gold medal. When Our Lady asks a penance or sacrifice from us, it is so that we can win in the spiritual life, with its attendant gift of inner peace. The issue is one of liberation or freedom from material appetites that shackle us from embracing God more and more with our hearts.

Application: Let us heed the Gospa's request today by renouncing (giving up) something special so that we can grow spiritually.

MARCH 8

Give this love to others

The Blessed Mother speaks of love to the prayer group on Mt. Podbrdo:

> *Dear children, tonight your Mother is happy to see so many of you. I desire, dear children, that from today you begin to live a different life. Your Mother gives you her love and asks that you give this love to others so that we can all live the Easter message. When you return to your homes, conclude the day with prayer (VPG 3-24-89).*

Of love, St. Peter writes:

Above all, maintain constant love for one another,
for love covers a multitude of sins (1 Pt 4:8).

Reflection: The message of love of neighbor reaches far back in our Judeo-Christian roots. The rabbi Hillel was a renowned scribe in Jerusalem about the time of Christ's birth; he seems to have died about A.D. 10 at an advanced age. He was called "the Great" or "the Elder," and his interpretations of the Law were more generous than others. He is said to have been the grandfather of Gamaliel (Acts 22:3) who taught St. Paul. Jesus must have heard often of Hillel, and could possibly have spoken with him as a youth during the three days he remained in the Temple.

Here is one of the tales Our Lord probably heard. A certain Gentile came to Shammai (Shammai was the leader of the more strict school of interpretation) and said that he would like to become a convert, but could not stay long in Jerusalem. "Can you teach me the whole Torah while I am standing on one foot?" Shammai sent him away angrily. So the Gentile went to Hillel with the same question. Hillel admitted him as a convert, and said, "Whatever is hateful to thee, do not do to thy fellow man. This is the whole Torah, all the rest is commentary. Now go and study."

Application: For reflection today:

Love seeketh not itself to please,
nor for itself have any care,
but for another gives its ease,
and builds a heaven in hell's despair
(William Blake).

You can give up a number of things

To the visionaries during the first year of the apparitions:

If you are experiencing difficulties or if you need something, come to me. If you do not have the strength to fast on bread and water, you can give up a number of things. It would be a good thing to give up television, because after some programs you are distracted and unable to pray. You can give up alcohol, cigarettes, and other pleasures. You yourselves know what you have to do.

(The Gospa then kneels down, and with hands extended, prays to Christ.) My beloved Son, I beseech you to be willing to forgive the world its great sin through which it offends you (FY 12-8-81).

St. John also speaks of the world and sin:

Do not love the world or the things in the world. The love of the Father is not in those who love the world; for all that is in the world—the desire of the flesh, the desire of the eyes, the pride in riches—comes not from the Father but from the world. And the world and its desire are passing away, but those who do the will of God live forever (1 Jn 2:15-17).

Reflection: Worldliness is not limited to external behavior, but also affects us internally, within the heart. It seems to be characterized by any of three attitudes: a preoccupation with gratifying physical desires; craving and accumulating material things; or an obsession with one's status or importance.

By contrast, God calls us to restraint, a spirit of generosity, and to loving service. To achieve these virtues—and their fruit of inner peace—Our Lady asks us to surmount our worldliness through acts of sacrifice. During Lent especially, we are encouraged to practice some form of self-denial as a gesture of love for God and to strengthen our spiritual lives.

Application: If you have not already done so, choose a special sacrifice for the remainder of Lent, as the Gospa asks.

MARCH 10

Conquer some fault each day

During Lent of 1985, Our Lady said to Jelena:

I give you some advice: I would like you to try to conquer some fault each day. If your fault is to get angry at everything, try each day to get angry less. If your fault is not to be able to study, try to study. If your fault is not to be able to obey, or if you cannot stand those who do not please you, try on a given day to speak with them. If your fault is not to be able to stand an arrogant person, you should try to approach that person. If you desire that person to be humble, be humble yourself. Show that humility is worth more than pride.

Thus, each day, try to go beyond, and to reject every vice from your heart. Find out which are the vices that you most need to reject. During this Lent, you should try and truly desire to spend it in love. Strive as much as possible (LJM 2-20-85).

In his first letter, Peter also speaks of rejecting vices:

You have already spent enough time in doing what the Gentiles like to do, living in licentiousness, passions, drunkenness, revels, carousing, and lawless idolatry.... The end of all things is near; therefore be serious and discipline yourselves for the sake of your prayers (1 Pt 4:3, 7).

———————

Reflection: Philip Henry, a fifteenth-century English writer, once wrote that, "Sins are like circles in the water when a stone is thrown into it; one produces another. When anger was in Cain's heart, murder was not far off." Recognizing our sins and the vices that produce them is not a pleasant task, yet it is the doorway to peace and holiness. The sacrament of confession is especially helpful in this.

In our examination of conscience we can go one step further to identify the roots of our sins. For example, the sin of lying may be founded in pride; sexual misconduct rooted in selfishness. Once we identify these roots, we can then take action to modify and eventually eliminate them from our lives, as Our Lady asks today: "Each day try to go beyond, to reject every vice from your heart."

Application: When you prepare for your next confession, actually write down your sins and, next to them, the vice from which they come. During the sacrament itself, present both to your priest so that the Lord can begin his healing work within you.

MARCH 11

Confession will be the remedy

Regarding questions on confession, the Blessed Virgin answered:

One must invite people to go to confession each month, especially the first Saturday. Here I have not spoken about it yet. I have invited some people to frequent confession. I will give you yet some concrete messages for our time. Be patient because the time has not yet come. Do what I have told you. They are numerous who do not observe it. Monthly confession will be a remedy for the church in the West. One must convey this message to the West (SM 8-6-82).

Psalm 32 speaks of confession and its fruit:

Then I acknowledged my sin to you,
and I did not hide my iniquity;
I said, "I will confess my transgressions to
    the Lord,"
and you forgave the guilt of my sin.

Therefore let all who are faithful
offer prayer to you;
at a time of distress, the rush of mighty waters
shall not reach them.

—Psalm 32:5-6

Reflection: A soldier asked a holy monk if God accepted repentance. He said, "Tell me, if your cloak is torn, do you throw it away?" The soldier replied, "No, I mend it and use it again." The old man said to him, "If you are so careful about your cloak, will not God be equally careful about his people?"

To experience the joy of forgiveness is a great gift of God, but it requires that we let go of our guilt and truly believe that the Lord has actually forgiven us. This can be difficult when a sin has taken deep root and grown over many years, or if it is very serious or causes deep shame. Then we are in need of a special grace that will convince us of God's infinite mercy that remits all sin of whatever depth or kind. This grace puts us in mind of the staggering price Jesus paid for our souls through his Passion and death, an almost impossible love that absorbs all sin, hurt, shame, and injury.

Therefore not to accept the Lord's forgiveness is to belittle or even ignore his Passion and cross, to say to him in effect: "I don't believe you. Your love isn't great enough to forgive *this* sin, to wash away *my* guilt. And so I refuse you." This is a self-inflicted exile that Satan always has a hand in.

Clearly it is much better to pray for the grace to realize God's forgiveness deep within ourselves, that we may be healed and set free.

Application: As we see, the sacrament of confession is a great gift. If you haven't done so already, mark your calendar for your Lenten confession. Can you also schedule a regular day each month when you can receive the sacrament, as Our Lady asks today?

MARCH 12

Only peace

On the third day of the apparitions, as Marija was descending Podbrdo, she was drawn to the side of the path where she again saw the Blessed Virgin. Weeping, and carrying a wooden cross, the Madonna said:

> *Peace, Peace, Peace! Be reconciled! Only Peace. Make your peace with God and among yourselves. For that, it is necessary to believe, to pray, to fast, and to go to confession (FY 6-26-81).*

In Isaiah, there is also anguish in the absence of peace:

> Listen! the valiant cry in the streets;
> the envoys of peace weep bitterly.
> The highways are deserted,
> travelers have quit the road.
> The treaty is broken,
> its oaths are despised,
> its obligation is disregarded.
> The land mourns and languishes;

Lebanon is confounded and withers away;
Sharon is like a desert;
and Bashan and Carmel shake off their leaves.
—Isaiah 33:7-9

Reflection: Our Lady's words today comprise her first and most powerful message on peace. Weeping and carrying a cross symbolizing man's sin, enmity and strife, she pleads for reconciliation. And she immediately gives us the means: faith, prayer, fasting, and confession.

Given on the third day of the apparitions, the Virgin in effect summarizes her messages for all the years ahead. We can only surmise the gravity of the world's situation which has required her to stay with us so long.

In Colossians, Paul also tells us to let peace reign in our hearts. Our hearts are the center of conflict, for there feelings and desires clash—our fears and hopes, our distrust and trust, our jealousy and love. How can we deal with these constant conflicts and live as God wants? Both Paul and the Blessed Mother ask that we decide between conflicting elements by using the rule of peace: which choice will promote peace in our souls and among our neighbors?

Application: Referring back to the Virgin's message, are we promoting peace through the means she gives us? Today, how can you be a peacemaker within your family, your workplace, your parish?

MARCH 13

Special message for Lent

During Lent of 1989, Ivan reported the following message to his prayer group:

Our Lady wants this from us during Lent:

1) Review and live her messages.

2) Read the Bible more.

3) Pray more and offer all for the intentions of Our Lady.

4) Make more sacrifices.

Our Lady will be with us and will accompany us. She gave a special blessing (VPG 2-6-89).

In his letter to the Colossians, Paul also urges the people to seek "the things above":

So if you have been raised with Christ, seek the things that are above, where Christ is seated at the right hand of God. Set your minds on things that are above, not on things that are on earth, for you have died, and your life is hidden with Christ in God. When Christ who is your life is revealed, then you also will be revealed with him in glory (Col 3:1-4).

Reflection: Seeking "the things that are above" could be defined as striving to put heaven's priorities into daily practice, or to concentrate on the eternal rather than the temporal. It is to view life from the Lord's perspective and to seek what he desires. This is also the antidote to materialism, for we view material goods as God does.

The more we see life around us as God sees it, the more we live in harmony with him and experience his peace. This is also the reason for Mary's requests today; to pray, to live her messages, to read the scriptures, and to make sacrifices, are all intended to focus us on "the things above" and bring us into harmony with God.

Application: Let us simply apply to our lives the very specific advice the Gospa gives us in her message today.

MARCH 14

Satan is trying to destroy

Regarding Satan, the Blessed Mother said to Ivan's prayer group:

Dear children, during this Lent Satan is trying by every means to destroy in you what we have started. I warn you as a mother, let prayer be your weapon against him (VPG 3-14-88).

In his first letter, Peter also warns of Satan:

Discipline yourselves, keep alert. Like a roaring lion your adversary the Devil prowls around, looking for someone to devour. Resist him, steadfast in your faith, for you know that your brothers and sisters in all the world are undergoing the same kinds of suffering (1 Pt 5:8-9).

Reflection: The Madonna of Medjugorje continues to emphasize the reality and danger of Satan, for just as a physician cannot treat an illness without a diagnosis, so we cannot fight the Evil One without first acknowledging his existence and power.

In a sermon in Medjugorje on this subject, Fr. Tomislav Vlasic, at one time the spiritual director to the visionaries, said:

Recently Our Lady's messages have been warning us of Satan's presence and we in Medjugorje have actually been experiencing this. It is not an academic question for us, but the actual experience of Satan's presence and attacks. . . . But

Our Lady has taught us how to face this problem, how to fight it. She always points out the weapons we can use against the Evil One: prayer, penance, and an active spiritual life. . . .

Through Our Lady, we have discovered Satan's presence hidden in civilization, which has denied his existence, just as it has denied the presence of God. Satan exists, he is real. But we have the weapons to fight him.

Application: Simply take to heart the Madonna's message today: "I warn you as a mother, let prayer be your weapon against Satan."

MARCH 15

Read the Bible

The Queen of Peace speaks of scripture to the prayer group:

I ask you again to multiply your prayers to prepare yourself for Easter. Also, read the Bible, especially those passages that speak of the Passion of Jesus. Prepare yourself to look at Jesus "eye to eye." Tonight when you go home, pray in front of the cross in thanksgiving for all the graces you have received (VPG 3-17-89).

In Hebrews, Paul speaks of the power of scripture:

Indeed, the word of God is living and active, sharper than any two-edged sword, piercing until it divides soul from spirit, joints from marrow; it is able to judge the thoughts and intentions of the heart (Heb 4:12).

Reflection: The American poet Timothy Dwight once said: "The Bible is a window in this prison-world, through which we may look into eternity." And yet it cannot enlighten or reveal God's will to us unless we read and reflect upon it, which Our Lady calls us to do today.

In Hebrews, Paul speaks of scripture as living, life-changing, and dynamic. God's word reveals who we are and the purpose of life. It penetrates the core of our moral and spiritual life; it helps us to discern what is within us, both good and bad.

As the message of scripture becomes a part of us, it will affect our lifestyle, character, and decisions. It will begin to shape our lives.

Application: Continue to make sacred scripture a part of your daily life. As Our Lady requests of us for Lent, begin to read the narratives of Christ's Passion, beginning today with Matthew 26:36—27:61. The others are Mark 14:32—15:47; Luke 22:39—23:56; and John 18:1—19:42.

MARCH 16

Many live in sin

The visionaries say that the Virgin is usually happy when she appears to them, but in giving today's message she was in tears:

> *There are so many men who live in sin. Here there are likewise among you some people who have offended my heart. Pray and fast for them (LJM 3-21-84).*

Reflection: Although sin is a tragic reality of our world, as the Gospa reminds us today, so is the limitless mercy and forgiveness of God, who has reconciled us to himself through the Cross. As St. John writes:

My little children, I am writing these things to you so that you may not sin. But if anyone does sin, we have an advocate with the Father, Jesus Christ the righteous; and he is the atoning sacrifice for our sins, and not for ours only but also for the sins of the whole world (1 Jn 2:1-2).

The grace of God's forgiveness is freely given to all who acknowledge their sin with a repentant heart; indeed, the church gives us the season of Lent for this very purpose. From Psalm 51, the Prayer of Repentance:

Have mercy on me, O God, in your goodness;
in the greatness of your compassion wipe out
    my offense.
Thoroughly wash me from my guilt
and of my sin cleanse me.

For I acknowledge my offense,
and my sin is before me always:
"Against you only have I sinned,
and done what is evil in your sight"
That you may be justified in your sentence,
vindicated when you condemn.

A clean heart create for me, O God,
and a steadfast spirit renew within me.

—Psalm 51:1-6; 12 *(NAB)*

Repentance always touches the heart of God, and he embraces us with tender forgiveness. The Blessed Mother not only calls us personally to repentance today, but also asks us to pray and fast for the many souls who are hardened in sin. In fact, throughout her many messages this is a major theme. In engaging in this ministry of prayer for the conversion of sinners, we are going that extra mile in living Our Lady's messages.

Application: Today offer the Sorrowful Mysteries for the conversion of sinners, and perhaps your fasting or other sacrifice on Friday.

St. Patrick's Day

Today Our Lady speaks to us of reflecting the light of Christ:

> *Dear children, I invite you to decide whether or not you want to live the messages which I give you. I wish that you live and actively convey my messages to others.*
>
> *In a very particular way, dear children, I wish that all of you become a reflection of Jesus, and bear witness to this unfaithful world. I desire that you become a light to all, that all of you will testify to the light.*
>
> *Dear children, you are not called to darkness, but to light. So be a light, by the way you live your life (WM 6-6-86).*

———————————

In the gospel of Matthew, we see Christ giving an identical message, in different words, to his followers:

> You are the light of the world. A city built on a hill cannot be hid. No one after lighting a lamp puts it under the bushel basket, but on the lampstand, it gives light to all the house. In the same way, let your light shine before others, so that they may see your good works and give glory to your Father in heaven (Mt 5:14-16).

———————————

Reflection: St. Patrick was a light of love and hope to the people of Ireland, a missionary of rare courage and holiness. In the same way, we are to be a light to others, "the reflection of Jesus," Our Lady says, "which will enlighten this unfaithful world walking in darkness."

Perhaps we spread the messages of Medjugorje most effectively by living them. Others are attracted to the peace and love they perceive in us and wish to share in it themselves. This is a "ministry of attraction" which the Blessed Virgin has charged us with: "I wish all of you to be light for everyone, and that you give witness to the light."

Example is powerful. There is a saying that "faith is caught, not taught," which was undoubtedly the case in the early church. Despite the constant persecution and murder of Christians, the new faith grew at an amazing pace. The reason? People wanted the hope and love they saw in the lives of Jesus' followers, and would risk everything to possess it.

The writer Thoreau once said, "If you would convince a man that he does wrong, do right. Men will believe what they see. Let them see." On this Feast of St. Patrick, a shining light to the Irish, the Virgin calls us as well to "live the light with your own life."

Application: In prayer today, reflect on the following: If your country was occupied by an enemy force and all Christians were tried and imprisoned, would the courts find any evidence to convict you? How might your faith shine forth more courageously?

MARCH 18

Be thankful in front of the cross

Our Lady reminds us of her message of March 13th, and speaks of gratitude:

> *Dear children, remember the four things you have to do during Lent. Tonight when you go home, I ask you to be thankful in front of the cross for all that you feel you should be grateful for; thank Jesus for what you have. My Son will hear you (VPG 2-13-89).*

Second Corinthians also speaks of gratitude:

> Yes, everything is for your sake, so that grace, as
> it extends to more and more people, may increase
> thanksgiving, to the glory of God (2 Cor 4:15).

Reflection: The Virgin speaks many times of gratitude in her messages, for it is a form of love of God. Poets and writers have searched for words beautiful enough to express their thanks for such great gifts, but none have succeeded so well as St. Francis of Assisi. May his Canticle of the Sun be our own hymn of thanksgiving today:

O most high, almighty Lord God,
To You belong praise, glory, honor and all
   blessings.
Praise to my Lord God with all his creatures,
And especially our brother the sun, who brings
   us the day and who brings us the light;

Fair is he who shines with such great splendor;
O Lord, he signifies You to us!

Praise to my Lord for our sister the moon and
   for the stars,
Which he has set clear and lovely in heaven.

Praise to my Lord for our brother the wind,
   for air and clouds, calms and all weather
By which You sustain life in all creatures.

Praise to my Lord for all those who pardon
   one another for his love's sake,
And who endure weakness and tribulation;

Blessed are they who peaceably shall endure;
For You, O God, shall give them a crown!

Praise to my Lord for our sister, the death
   of the body from which no man escapes.
Woe to him who dies in mortal sin!

Blessed are they who are found walking in

Your most holy will,
For the second death shall have no power
  to do them harm.

Praise and bless the Lord and give him thanks,
And serve him with great humility.

Application: Offer one decade of your rosary today simply in thanksgiving to God for all his gifts. In addition, review Our Lady's message of March 13th, as she has requested today.

MARCH 19

St. Joseph, Husband of Mary

As St. Joseph is the patron of workers, it is appropriate today that we hear Our Lady's special message on this topic:

Dear children, always pray before your work and end it with prayer. If you do that, God will bless you and your work. These last days, you have prayed little and worked very much. Pray more. In prayer, you will find rest (WM 7-5-84).

In his second letter to the Thessalonians, St. Paul also takes up the theme of work:

For you yourselves know how you ought to imitate us; we were not idle when we were with you, and we did not eat anyone's bread without paying for it; but with toil and labor we worked night and day, so that we might not burden any of you. This was not because we do not have that right, but in order to give you an example to imitate. For even when we were with you, we gave you this command: Anyone unwilling to work should not eat (2 Thes 3:7-10).

Reflection: Today we honor St. Joseph, the great guardian and protector of God's greatest treasures, namely, his divine Son, and Mary, our Mother. St. Bernadine of Siena, a Franciscan of the fifteenth century, once wrote, "In Joseph the Old Testament finds its fitting close. He brought the noble line of patriarchs and prophets to its promised fulfillment. What God had offered as a promise to them, he held in his arms."

Joseph is also the patron saint of workers, which is the subject of our readings today. He taught the skills of carpentry to Jesus, who gave labor an intrinsic dignity. From the Vatican II document "The Church Today": "We hold that by offering his labor to God, a man becomes associated with the redemptive work of Jesus Christ, who conferred an eminent dignity on labor when, at Nazareth, he worked with his own hands." In the words of Kahlil Gibran, "work is love made visible"; today we celebrate this love in the person of St. Joseph.

Application: In her message, Our Lady calls us to "always pray before your work, and end your work with prayer." Today let us do exactly that, beginning a practice that will hopefully evolve into a habit.

MARCH 20

Pray before the crucifix

On this day in 1989, the Blessed Virgin said to the prayer group:

From tonight I ask you to pray even more. Meditate on the wounds of Jesus. Pray as much as you can in front of the crucifix (VPG 3-20-89).

1 Corinthians also speaks of the cross:

> For the message about the cross is foolishness to those who are perishing, but to us who are being saved it is the power of God. . . . For Jews demand signs and Greeks desire wisdom, but we proclaim Christ crucified, a stumbling block to Jews and foolishness to Gentiles, but to those who are the called, both Jews and Greeks, Christ the power of God and the wisdom of God. For God's foolishness is wiser than human wisdom, and God's weakness is stronger than human strength (1 Cor 1:18; 22-25).

———————

Reflection: Once Our Lady said to the seers, "If you knew how much I loved you, you would weep for joy." In much the same way, prayer before a crucifix can bring the same tears, for it is the greatest evidence of God's love in the universe.

This is the reason why Mary asks us to contemplate the wounds of Christ, for they speak so clearly of his love. Christ's entire life, and especially his passion, were one unequaled act of divine love. He would go to any extreme to win us back; he would endure any suffering to save us; he would give anything, even his life. It is hard to fathom such an all-consuming love, but the more we ponder it, the more we realize its astonishing depth. This is Mary's wish.

On the surface, the Lord's crucifixion was an abhorrent and terrifying event—a man tortured to death by degrees. But what motivated Jesus to endure the unthinkable, his intense love for us, is the key to understanding what the world calls "the folly of the cross." Yet believers know that the cross is the inscrutable wisdom of God, the wisdom of Love seeking its surest proof, its fullest expression for the sake of the beloved.

The mystery of the cross, for truly it is a mystery of the deepest currents of love, can only be comprehended through prayer, and then only by degrees. Hence Our Lady's request today.

Application: Spend time in prayer today before a crucifix, contemplating the wounds of Christ and the love they signify for you.

MARCH 21

Give up something dear

The Blessed Mother speaks of sacrifice today:

Thursday (day of the Eucharist), may each one find his way to fast; he who smokes, may abstain from smoking; he who drinks alcohol, have him not drink. Have each one give up something which is dear to him. May these recommendations be conveyed to the parish (SM 3-1-84).

———————————

From the prophet Isaiah:
Seek the Lord while he may be found,
call upon him while he is near;
let the wicked forsake their way,
and the unrighteous their thoughts;
let them return to the Lord, that he may have
    mercy on them,
and to our God, for he will abundantly pardon.
—Isaiah 55:6-7

———————————

Reflection: The concept of sacrifice and repentance reaches far back into the Old Testament. In the ancient rites of animal sacrifice, a person who had sinned brought an unblemished animal to the Temple priest. The individual then placed his hand on the head of the animal while it was killed, symbolizing his identification with the animal as his substitute. He symbolically transferred his sins to the animal, and thus his sins were taken away (atonement). Finally the animal was burned on the altar, signifying the person's complete dedication to God.

But the Lord required more than a sacrifice. He also asked the sinner to be truly repentant of his sins. The outward symbol (the sacrifice) and the inner change (repentance) were to work together in seeking the forgiveness of God.

In our own day, sacrifices such as Our Lady recommends (foregoing alcohol, television, smoking, etc.) also serve as outward signs of repentance, but they also speak of dedication and reverence for the Lord, for they involve the whole person, soul and body. Words of love are easy, but backing them up with sacrifice adds credibility and power to our prayer. Acts of self-denial also keep us focused on the Lord and help build character, in that we learn not to jump at every stray impulse. Involved here are some forgotten truths, brought to light again by the Blessed Virgin.

Application: Our Lady is very specific in her message today. Let us simply heed her advice.

MARCH 22

I have been appealing for renewal

The Madonna is firm in her call to Lenten renewal and prayer:

> *Dear children, day after day I have been appealing to you for renewal and prayer in the parish, but you are not responding. Today I am calling you for the last time. This is the season of Lent, and you as a parish should, out of love, be moved to live my messages. If you do not, I do not wish to continue giving them. God is permit-*

ting me that. Thank you for responding to my call (WM 2-21-85).

Psalm 38 is a repentant call to God:

> For I am ready to fall,
> and my pain is ever with me.
> I confess my iniquity;
> I am sorry for my sin.
> Those who are my foes without cause are mighty,
> and many are those who hate me wrongfully.
> Those who render me evil for good
> are my adversaries because I follow after good.
> Do not forsake me, O Lord;
> O my God, do not be far from me;
> make haste to help me,
> O Lord, my salvation.

> —Psalm 38:17-22

Reflection: Both Our Lady and the psalmist today call us to repentance, to acknowledge our sin, neglect, or indifference in the sight of God.

Because we have a tendency to sin or to be spiritually lethargic, repentance is the true measure of spiritual sensitivity. It means asking the Lord to forgive us and then abandoning our sinful or lethargic ways. But we cannot do this sincerely unless we are truly sorry for our misdeeds and then commit ourselves to positive action.

This is the Virgin's wish today, that we take to heart her call to renewal and prayer. It is a serious matter for all of us.

Application: Review your spiritual life today. Has Lent been a time of prayer and renewal for you? If not, make a fresh start today.

Renounce those things which are hurting you

During Lent of 1990 Our Lady spoke of attachments:

> *Dear children, I invite you to surrender to God. In this season of Lent, I ask you to especially renounce those things to which you are attached but which are hurting you and your spiritual life. Therefore, little children, decide completely for God, and do not allow Satan into your life through those things that hurt both you and your spiritual life.*
>
> *Little children, God is offering himself totally to you, but you can discover and recognize him only in prayer. Therefore, make a decision for prayer! (MM 2-25-90).*

St. Paul also warns of worldly attachments:

> Brothers and sisters, join in imitating me, and observe those who live according to the example you have in us. For many live as enemies of the cross of Christ; I have often told you of them, and now I tell you even with tears. Their end is destruction; their god is the belly; and their glory is in their shame; their minds are set on earthly things. But our citizenship is in heaven, and it is from there that we are expecting a Savior, the Lord Jesus Christ (Phil 3:17-20).

Reflection: St. Paul criticizes the self-indulgent Christians of his day, for although they claim allegiance to Christ, they ignore his model of servanthood and sacrifice. They seem to satisfy their own desires even before thinking about the needs of others; to their detriment, they are "set upon the things of this world."

Our Lady of Medjugorje points to the same danger: "I ask you to especially renounce," she says, "those things to which you are attached, but which are hurting you and your spiritual life."

Application: Today, take the time to identify those attachments or addictions that hurt you spiritually. They could include alcohol, drugs, shopping, television, status seeking, power games, manipulation of others, and materialism in many forms. After you identify your own harmful attachments, isolate one and consciously work on moderating or even eliminating it for one week. At the same time, pray to the Blessed Mother for the special grace you will need; she will generously provide it.

MARCH 24

The Vigil of the Annunciation

On this vigil in 1985 Our Lady said:

> *Today I invite all of you to confession, even if you have already gone a few days ago. I wish that you would live my feast in your hearts. You are not able to, if you do not abandon yourselves completely to the Lord. It is for this reason that I call all of you to reconciliation with the Lord (FY 3-24-85).*

This reconciliation to God is possible because of the redeeming sacrifice of Christ on Calvary:

> For in [Christ] all the fullness of God was pleased to dwell, and through him God was pleased to reconcile to himself all things, whether on earth or in heaven, by making peace through the blood of his cross. And you who were once estranged and hostile in mind, doing evil deeds, he has now

reconciled in his fleshly body through death, so as to present you holy and blameless and irreproachable before him. . . (Col 1:19-22).

Reflection: On this vigil of the Annunciation, Our Lady says that, "I wish that you would live my feast in your hearts." This may sound puzzling until we reflect on the core message of the Annunciation, which is Mary's complete abandonment to God's will, signified by her unequivocal yes to all he asked of her. Thus the Blessed Mother wishes us to experience this same surrender to God in our own hearts, this same yes to God that consecrates us entirely to him. Thus her feast day, her yes, is experienced within us.

The fruit of this abandonment in our lives is a profound trust and confidence in the Lord, the same trust that Mary possessed. She longs to share it with us.

The one obstacle is sin, and so it follows that Our Lady would end her message by saying, "Therefore, I call all of you to reconciliation with God." Our reading from St. Paul resounds with the same advice. Mary invites everyone to confession, where our sins are forgiven and can no longer separate us from God. We can therefore abandon ourselves to the Lord like trusting children, joining our yes to God with that of hers.

Application: If you have not received the sacrament of reconciliation within the last month, make a firm commitment to do so this week, as Our Lady urges in her message today.

The Annunciation of Our Lord

On this feast day in 1986, Our Lady gave the following message:

Today, before God, I say my "Fiat" for all of you. I repeat it: I say my "Yes" for all of you. Dear children, pray, so that the kingdom of love may come into the whole world. How mankind would be happy if love reigned (VPG 3-25-86).

It's also appropriate that we reflect on the Annunciation as found in sacred scripture:

In the sixth month the angel Gabriel was sent by God to a town in Galilee called Nazareth, to a virgin engaged to a man whose name was Joseph, of the house of David. The virgin's name was Mary.

And he came to her and said, "Greetings, favored one! The Lord is with you." But she was much perplexed by his words and pondered what sort of greeting this might be.

The angel said to her, "Do not be afraid, Mary, for you have found favor with God. And now, you will conceive in your womb and bear a son, and you will name him Jesus."

Mary said to the angel, "How can this be, since I am a virgin?" The angel said to her, "The Holy Spirit will come upon you, and the power of the Most High will overshadow you; therefore the child to be born will be holy; he will be called Son of God."

Then Mary said, "Here am I, the servant of the Lord; let it be with me according to your word."

Then the angel departed from her (Lk 1:26-31, 34-35, 38).

Reflection: Today Our Lady says her *fiat* for all of us; she says yes to God for our sakes. Our very redemption through Christ was dependent on Mary's consent to bring the Son of God into the world. The new Eve brought salvation, not sin, as her legacy to mankind.

Now it is our turn to say yes to God by consecrating our lives to him and living out our baptismal promises. We also pray, "that the kingdom of love may come to the whole world," which means that all might open their hearts to God and experience deep conversion.

Let us close with the words the Blessed Virgin gave to the visionaries on this feast day in 1985: "Through my joy and the joy of this people, I say to all of you this evening, I love you and I wish you well."

Application: In prayer today, say yes to God's will for you in all things, in imitation of the Mother of Christ and in honor of her feast.

MARCH 26

See how he was martyred

Asked by the visionaries why she showed them heaven, Our Lady responded: "*I did so that you could see the happiness which awaits those who love God.*" During the same apparition, Jesus appears to the seers with injuries covering his body, wearing a crown of thorns. The Virgin says:

> *Do not be afraid. It is my Son. See how he was martyred. But despite it all, he was joyful and endured all with patience.*

(Then Jesus himself says:) See how I was wounded and martyred! But in spite of all, I have won the victory. My angels, you also be persevering in your faith and pray that you may overcome every obstacle (FY 11-2-81).

In his letter to the Romans, Paul speaks of Christ's blood as the price of our redemption and forgiveness:

> For there is no distinction, since all have sinned and fall short of the glory of God; they are now justified by his grace as a gift, through the redemption that is in Christ Jesus, whom God put forward as a sacrifice of atonement by his blood, effective through faith. . . (Rom 3:22-25).

Reflection: Paul speaks of the Passion and death of Christ as effecting two great miracles: redemption and forgiveness. Originally, the term redemption indicated the price paid to gain freedom for a slave (Lv 25:47-54). Through his death, Jesus paid the price to release us from slavery to sin. Forgiveness was granted in ancient Israel on the basis of the shedding of animals' blood in sacrifice (Lv 17:11). Now we are forgiven on the basis of the shedding of Jesus' blood, for he died as the perfect and final sacrifice.

The mystery of redemption holds the secret of unimaginable love, which can be penetrated only through prayer. Thus Jesus says today: "Persevere in your faith—and pray. . . ."

Application: Today, holding a crucifix in your hands, reflect on the love of Christ as expressed in his redemptive Passion and death.

Honor the wounds of my Son

Today the Gospa gives a Lenten message on the passion of Christ:

> *Dear children, in a special way this evening, I am calling you during Lent to honor the wounds of my Son, which he received from the sins of this parish. Unite yourselves with my prayers for the parish so that his sufferings may be bearable (WM 3-22-84).*

In the prophet Isaiah we find the image of the suffering servant:

Surely he has borne our infirmities
and carried our diseases;
yet we accounted him stricken,
struck down by God, and afflicted.
But he was wounded for our transgressions,
crushed for our iniquities;
upon him was the punishment that made
  us whole,
and by his bruises we are healed.
All we like sheep have gone astray;
we have all turned to our own way,
and the Lord has laid on him
the iniquity of us all.

—Isaiah 53:4-6

Reflection: Both the Blessed Virgin and Isaiah speak of the Savior who suffered for our sins: "By his wounds are we healed," the prophet writes. No one in Isaiah's day would have dreamed that God would choose to save the world through a suffering servant, rather than a messianic king. The idea was contrary to human pride and logic. True, the Israelites offered animals as sacrifices for their sins. But a human being? The Messiah himself?

He was the Lamb of God, the sinless servant who offered himself in sacrifice for the sins of mankind; the Anointed One who suffered in place of the guilty.

How can we fathom such love? Today the Virgin tells us it is through prayer: "Honor the wounds of my Son. . . . Unite yourselves with my prayers." The Holy Spirit will give us insight into these deep currents of love which can be understood in no other way.

Application: From *The Imitation of Christ*: "Take comfort in the passion of Christ, and dwell willingly in his sacred wounds. Endure with Christ, suffer for him, if you wish to reign with him."

Today, with a crucifix in your hands, offer the Lord's Prayer in honor of each of the Savior's wounds, concluding with your own prayer of dedication.

MARCH 28

Encounter the living God

Our Lady speaks of encountering the Lord today:

Dear children, today I wish to call you to prayer so that you may encounter the living God. He offers and gives himself to you, asking only that you freely answer his call.

Therefore, little children, set aside a special time each day when you can pray in peace and humility, meeting with God the Creator. I am with you and intercede to God for you. Be alert that your prayer truly be a joyful encounter with God (MM 11-25-88).

In this passage, Paul gives us an example of intercessory prayer:

For this reason, since the day we heard of it, we have not ceased praying for you and asking that you may be filled with the knowledge of God's will in all spiritual wisdom and understanding. . . (Col 1:9).

Reflection: As Our Lady stresses today, prayer is the most essential component of our lives, for it is a direct encounter with the living God.

Elsewhere, the Madonna asks that we pray for a number of her intentions (peace, conversion of sinners, the sick, etc.), as well as our own. As this array of prayer intentions can sometimes be difficult to remember or fit into one day, the following suggestions may help.

First, you may wish to write down on an index card the intentions you wish to pray for every day. Place the card in your wallet or purse (or in a prayerbook you use each day). Consult it as you pray the rosary, offering one decade for each intention; this will allow you to pray for five to fifteen intentions each day.

Second, just as a priest normally has an intention for each Mass he offers, so you too can offer the Masses you attend for one or more special intentions. The same can be done for other prayer forms which the church offers us, such as the Stations of the Cross, litanies, and of course novenas.

Another form is conversational prayer with God. Here we simply speak to the Lord about our prayer intention, describing it and lifting it up, so to speak, for him to see and bless. But the most beautiful form of prayer may be that of sheer praise and gratitude, with the Lord himself searching our hearts for our special needs and intentions.

Application: If advisable, write down your prayer intentions today. Remember that they can be prayed for in a variety of ways. It is our faithfulness that is most important.

MARCH 29

Wipe the tears from my face

The following message from the Queen of Peace is her lengthiest—and one of the most important. Along with a short passage from scripture, it will serve as our reading and reflection for this Lenten day.

My dear children! I came to you in order to lead you to purity of soul and then to God. But how did you receive me? At first with disbelief, fearful and suspicious of the children I had chosen. Later on, most of you received me in your hearts and began to live your Mother's messages. But that did not last for long.

Whenever I come to you my Son comes with me, but so does Satan. You unwittingly permitted him to influence you and now he drives you on. It is up to you to recognize when your behavior is displeasing to God, but you often stifle the thought.

Do not give in, dear children. Wipe from my face the tears that I shed when I see you acting like this. Rouse yourselves. Take the time to meet God in your church. Come into your Father's house. Take time for family prayer so you can receive God's grace. Remember your deceased; give them joy by offering a Mass for them.

Do not be scornful of those who beg you for a piece of bread. Do not turn them away from your overladen tables. Help them and God will help you. Perhaps this is the way in which God will hear you and bestow upon you blessings in thanksgiving.

You have forgotten all this, my children, under Satan's influence. Be wary! Pray with me! Do not deceive yourselves in thinking, "I am good, but my brother next door is not." You would be wrong. Your Mother loves you and so I warn you.

People do not know the secrets, my children, but when they learn of them it will be too late. Return to prayer! Nothing is more important. I wish the Lord would permit me to enlighten you a little more about the secrets, but the graces you have already received are great enough.

Think how much you have offended him. What have you given him of yourself? When was the last time you gave up something for the Lord? I do not want to reprimand you further, but to call you once again to prayer, fasting, and penance. If you wish to obtain a special grace from God by fasting, then let no one know you are fasting. If you wish to obtain a certain grace from God through a gift to the poor, then keep your almsgiving a secret between you and the Lord.

Listen to me, my children! Meditate on my message in prayer (SM 1-28-87).

And from the Acts of the Apostles, this quote from Isaiah echoes Our Lady's words:

For this people's heart has grown dull, and their ears are hard of hearing, and they have shut their eyes; so that they might not look with their eyes, and listen with their ears, and understand with their heart and turn—and I would heal them (Acts 28:27).

Application: Simply heed the Gospa's advice in the last sentence of her message today: "Meditate on my message in prayer."

Reflect on Jesus' Passion

The Blessed Virgin speaks of the cross and prayer today:

Dear children, here is my second message for Lent. Renew your prayer before the cross. Dear children, I offer you special graces and Jesus offers you the extraordinary merits of the cross. Accept them and live! Reflect on Jesus' passion. Unite your life to his (WM 2-20-86).

Scripture and Reflection: In view of Our Lady's message today, it might be well for us to simply meditate on the Passion of her Son, rather than engage in commentary. St. Thomas á Kempis emphasized this as well when he wrote, "Take comfort in the Passion of Christ, and dwell willingly in his sacred wounds. Endure with Christ, suffer for him, if you wish to reign with him."

As you meditate on the passion narrative of St. Mark, read the lines unhurriedly, and pause in silent prayer if a phrase or word strikes you, for this is the Holy Spirit at work.

Then the soldiers led him into the courtyard of the palace (that is, the governor's headquarters); and they called together the whole cohort. And they clothed him in a purple cloak; and after twisting some thorns into a crown, they put it on him. And they began saluting him, "Hail, King of the Jews!" They struck his head with a reed, spat upon him, and knelt down in homage to him. After mocking him, they stripped him of the purple cloak and put his own clothes on him. Then they led him out to crucify him.

. . . Then they brought Jesus to the place called Golgotha (which means the place of a skull). And they offered him wine mixed with myrrh; but he did not take it. And they crucified him, and divided his clothes among them, casting lots to decide what each should take.

. . . When it was noon, darkness came over the whole land until three in the afternoon. At three o'clock Jesus cried out with a loud voice, "Eloi, Eloi, lema sabachthani?" which means, "My God, my God, why have you forsaken me?"

When some of the bystanders heard it, they said, "Listen, he is calling for Elijah." And someone ran, filled a sponge with sour wine, put it on a stick, and gave it to him to drink, saying, "Wait, let us see whether Elijah will come to take him down." Then Jesus gave a loud cry and breathed his last. And the curtain of the temple was torn in two, from top to bottom. Now when the centurion, who stood facing him, saw that in this way he breathed his last, he said, "Truly this man was God's Son!" (Mk 15:16-20, 22-24, 33-39).

Application: Today, spend five minutes in meditation before the cross.

MARCH 31

Open your hearts to the Holy Spirit

The Holy Spirit is the topic of Our Lady's message today:

Dear children, during these days I call you to especially open your hearts to the Holy Spirit, who is working through you. Open your hearts and surrender your lives to Jesus so that he can work through your hearts and strengthen you in faith (WM 5-23-85).

And from Acts:

> But you will receive power when the Holy Spirit has come upon you; and you will be my witnesses in Jerusalem, in all Judea and Samaria, and to the ends of the earth (Acts 1:8).

Reflection: Jesus wishes to give us the power of the Holy Spirit, and the Blessed Mother asks us to be open to receive his power. With faith and openness, then, let us pray to the Spirit using The Sequence of the Holy Spirit, one of the loveliest prayer-poems of the church:

> Holy Spirit, Lord of light,
> from the clear celestial height
> Thy pure beaming radiance give.
> Come, thou Father of the poor,
> Come, with treasures which endure;
> Come, thou light of all that live!
>
> Thou, of all consolers best,
> Thou, the soul's delightful guest,
> Dost refreshing peace bestow;
> Thou in toil art comfort sweet;
> Pleasant coolness in the heat;
> Solace in the midst of woe.
>
> Light immortal, light divine,
> Visit thou these hearts of thine,
> and our inmost being fill:
> If thou take thy grace away,
> Nothing pure in man will stay;
> All his good is turned to ill.
>
> Heal our wounds, our strength renew;
> On our dryness pour thy dew;
> Wash the stains of guilt away;
> Bend the stubborn heart and will;
> Melt the frozen, warm the chill;
> Guide the steps that go astray.

Thou, on us who evermore
Thee confess and thee adore,
With thy sevenfold gifts descend:
Give us comfort when we die;
Give us life with thee on high;
Give us joys that never end.

Application: Make it a habit to pray to the Holy Spirit each day, as the Virgin asks of us.

May you be the joy of mankind

The Blessed Virgin speaks of joy today:

> *Dear children, persevere in prayer so that your hearts may be filled with joy. Dear children, may you be the hope and joy of mankind. But you can only achieve this through prayer. Pray, pray! (VPG 5-3-86).*

In his prayer to the Father, Jesus speaks of conveying his joy to his disciples:

> While I was with them, I protected them in your name that you have given me. I guarded them, and not one of them was lost except the one destined to be lost, so that the scripture might be fulfilled. But now I am coming to you, and I speak these things in the world so that they may have my joy made complete in themselves (Jn 17:12-13).

Reflection: Joy is a unique quality of the Christian life. It seems to be born of trust in God's love for us and for all aspects of our lives. Fr. Slavko Barbaric, spiritual director to the visionaries, recently gave a sermon on Our Lady's messages of prayer and joy. Here, in part, is what he said:

> Normally, after meeting someone, you need time to get to know him, tell him about yourself, exchange views, and so forth. However, if our prayer only consists of an occasional "hello" to someone who only occupies a corner of our lives, then we probably aren't going to experience great joy.
>
> The problem is that we all want joy but we're not willing to follow the path that leads to its source: prayer from the heart. That is why Our Lady asks

us so urgently to, "pray, pray!" It is the means to happiness.

Application: Today the Mother of God asks that we make our hearts "joyful through the means of prayer." To this end, try to extend and deepen your prayer so that you will more fully experience that joy.

APRIL 2

Pray to understand the Father's love

Our Lady speaks of understanding the will of the Father and his love:

O children! Remember that the only way you can be always with me, and know the will of the Father, is to pray. That is why I call you again today. Do not let my calls go unheeded. Above all else, continue to pray, for then you will understand the Father's will and his love for you (LJM 5-16-87).

In Matthew's gospel, Christ also speaks of the Father and his promised reward to those who pray:

And whenever you pray, do not be like the hypocrites; for they love to stand and pray in the synagogues and at the street corners, so that they may be seen by others. Truly I tell you, they have received their reward. But whenever you pray, go into your room and shut the door and pray to your Father in secret; and then your Father, who sees in secret, will reward you (Mt 6:5-6).

Reflection: Prayer to God the Father is powerful, for among other things, "you will understand the Father's will and his love for you," as Mary tells us today.

Humble prayer, "in secret," as Jesus advises in our gospel reading, is always heard by the Father and swiftly answered.

The following "Petition to God" was dictated to Jelena, one of the Medjugorje locutionists, by the Blessed Mother. It was distributed throughout the church by the priests at Medjugorje. Let us offer it in response to the Virgin's message today:

O God, our hearts are deeply obscured, despite our bond to your heart. Our hearts are rent between you and Satan; between good and evil; enlighten and unify them with your grace. Do not permit two loves to exist in us, or two faiths; grant that we may never be torn between lying and sincerity, love and hatred, honesty and dishonesty, humility and pride.

Help us to raise our hearts to you like those of children. May you renew and fill our hearts with peace; may the longing for peace grow within us. May your holy will and love dwell in us that we may truly desire to be your children. Remember our past devotion and help us to again receive your Spirit.

With open hearts we seek that your will be done in us. With open souls we seek your tender mercy. May your mercy strengthen us to recognize our sins which make us impure. Lord God, we wish to be your children, humble and devout, sincere and cherished, as you desire us to be.

And may you, brother Jesus, intercede with the Father, that he may bless us with his goodness and inspire us to respond with goodness. Help us, Lord Jesus, to comprehend the Father's infinite love and manifold gifts, that we may never fail to please him with works of love and peace. Amen.

Application: Offer this Petition to God once more today, perhaps this evening. May it be a prayer from your heart.

APRIL 3

Abandon yourselves to me

Our Lady speaks of the fruits of abandonment today:

> *If you would abandon yourselves to me, you would not even feel the passage from this life to the next. You would begin to live the life of heaven on earth (LJM 1986).*

From the cross, when Jesus entrusted his Mother to his apostle John, she was given to all of us as well:

> When Jesus saw his mother and the disciple whom he loved standing beside her, he said to his mother, "Woman, here is your son." Then he said to the disciple, "Here is your mother." And from that hour the disciple took her into his own home (Jn 19:26-27).

Reflection: Just as Mary was given to us by Jesus, so we in turn are called to give ourselves to the Blessed Mother. Let us do just that, using the "Prayer to Give Oneself to Mary, Mother of Goodness, Love, and Mercy," dictated to Jelena in 1984:

> O my Mother,
> Mother of goodness, love, and mercy,
> I love you so much, and I now offer myself to you.
> Save me through your goodness,
> your love, and your mercy.
> I wish to be yours.
> Deep is my love for you,

and I place myself under your protection.
Grant to my heart, Mother Mary,
a share of your own goodness,
that I may someday join you in heaven.
In your great love, grant
that I may have the grace to love all people
as you loved your Son, Jesus Christ.
Grant me the grace to be so merciful
that it may touch your own heart.
I now offer myself completely to you
and ask you to accompany me at each step,
for you are full of grace.
May I never forget your love and grace;
but should I ever lose sight of it,
I shall call upon you
and you will help me find it again. Amen.

Application: Since the church has reserved Saturday as Our Lady's special day of the week, you may wish to offer her this prayer of dedication on that day.

APRIL 4

You will encounter God

In her monthly message for October, 1989, Our Lady said:

> *Dear children, today I am also inviting you to prayer. I am always calling you, but you are still far away. Therefore, from today, seriously commit yourselves to dedicating time to God. I am with you and I wish to teach you to pray with the heart. In prayer with the heart, you will encounter God. Therefore, dear children, pray, pray, pray (MM 10-25-89).*

The conditions of quiet and solitude are needed to pray with the heart. In the gospels, Jesus often withdrew to a place of quiet:

> The apostles gathered around Jesus, and told him all that they had done and taught. He said to them, "Come away to a deserted place all by yourselves and rest a while." For many were coming and going, and they had no time even to eat (Mk 6:30-31).

Reflection: Ohiyesa, a Santee Dakota Indian, once said:

> In the life of the Indian there is only one inevitable duty—the duty of prayer—the daily recognition of the unseen and the eternal. He sees no need for setting apart one day in seven as a holy day, since to him all days are God's.

In the past, some of us have suffered from a mentality that tended to reject anything beyond ourselves. Whatever was unseen or eternal remained invisible to us. We were skeptical, scientific, task-oriented, self-centered, unreflective. It was like racing down a country highway at top speed, hardly tuned in to the rich vitality of life that surrounded us. When we stopped the car and explored the terrain, we could suddenly smell the grasses, hear birds singing, perhaps see a whole community in an anthill, or watch a darting squirrel.

Quiet prayer or meditation is not something we create on our own. It is largely a matter of shifting our attention, of being open to the spiritual, to the gentle urgings of the Holy Spirit deep within us. We don't need to force it. We need only to quiet ourselves and listen.

Application: Today, make an effort to live moment to moment with the Spirit of God. Try to spend some time in a quiet place.

I call you to surrender

Today the Blessed Mother speaks of both surrender and joy:

> *Dear children, I call you today to complete surrender to God—to great joy and peace which only God can give. I am with you and I intercede for you every day before God (MM 3-25-89).*

Christ also speaks of the rewards of abandoning oneself to God:

> Peter began to say to him, "Look, we have left everything and followed you." Jesus said, "Truly I tell you, there is no one who has left house or brothers or sisters or mother or father or children or fields, for my sake and for the sake of the gospel, who will not receive a hundred-fold. . ." (Mk 10:28-30).

Reflection: Following Christ, surrendering ourselves to his care, is accompanied by beautiful gifts of the Holy Spirit, chief among them being inner peace. Yet it is a seeming paradox that in abandoning ourselves, placing ourselves totally at God's disposal, we should at the same time experience a profound freedom of spirit. But this is because all our cares, worries, and problems are no longer ours, but the Lord's. We become like trusting children again, confident and safe in the hands of our Father.

Application: Mindful of Our Lady's message today, surrender yourself again to the Lord, using this prayer composed by St. Teresa of Avila:

Lord, grant that I may always allow myself to be guided by you, always follow your plans, and perfectly accomplish your will.

Grant that in all things, great and small, today and all the days of my life, I may do whatever you require of me. Help me to respond to the slightest prompting of your grace, so that I may be a trustworthy instrument for your honor.

May your will be done in time and in eternity— by me, in me, and through me. Amen.

APRIL 6

You are all my children

Today Our Lady speaks of our equality in God's sight. In the context of the cure of an Orthodox child, she said:

> *Tell this priest, tell everyone, that it is you who are divided on earth. The Muslims and the Orthodox, for the same reason as Catholics, are equal before my Son and I. You are all my children.*
>
> *Clearly, all religions are not equal, but all men are equal before God, as St. Paul says. It does not suffice to belong to the Catholic church to be saved; it is also necessary to respect the commandments of God while following your conscience (FY 1985).*

In John's gospel, Christ also speaks of our oneness with God and with each other:

> The glory that you have given me I have given them, so that they may be one, as we are one, I in them and you in me, that they may become completely one, so that the world may know that you have sent me and have loved them even as you have loved me (Jn 17:22-23).

Reflection: Mindful of this call from Christ and his Mother that we be one, united in God's Spirit, let us offer the following prayer for our unity:

Lord Jesus Christ, at your Last Supper you prayed to the Father that all should be one. Send your Holy Spirit upon all who bear your name and seek to serve you. Strengthen our faith in you, and lead us to love one another in humility. May we who have been reborn in one baptism be united in one faith under one shepherd. Amen.

Application: Keeping an eye on the religion section of your local newspaper, watch for the next ecumenical liturgy or service project in your community. Support it by your presence and prayer.

APRIL 7

St. John Baptist de la Salle

In the midst of the civil war in Yugoslavia, the Blessed Mother gave this message to the world in the spring of 1992:

Dear children, today I also call you to prayer. Only by prayer and fasting can war be stopped. Therefore, my dear little children, pray, and by your life give witness that you are mine and that you belong to me, for Satan wants during these turbulent days to seduce as many souls as possible.

Therefore, I call you to decide for God, for he will protect you and show you what you should do and which path to take (MM 4-25-92).

The Virgin's call to show the world that we belong to her are an echo of the words of Christ in Luke's gospel:

> No one after lighting a lamp hides it under a jar,
> or puts it under a bed, but puts it on a lampstand,
> so that those who enter may see the light (Lk 8:16).

Reflection: Example is a teacher's greatest tool of instruction, a fact well understood by St. John Baptist de la Salle, the founder of a teaching order, the Brothers of the Christian Schools. Born in 1651 of a wealthy and noble family, John was both scholarly and devout, beginning his studies for the priesthood while still in his teens. Ordained at twenty-seven, his empathy for the poor and uneducated led him to devote his life to their care.

He was also a great innovator. Individual instruction was replaced by instruction in class; he insisted on silence and order in the classroom, and instructions were given in the native language rather than Latin. He once wrote to his friars:

> You should not doubt that you have been given the grace to teach [children], to instruct them in the gospel, and to form them in religion. This is a great gift from God. . . . Let your students be moved by your untiring care for them and feel as though God were encouraging them through you.
> . . .

Application: "I call you to decide for God," the Virgin says today, "for he will protect you and show you what you should do and which path to take." In the spirit of St. John, make this commitment to God again in prayer today.

APRIL 8

The Holy Spirit is working in a special way

Today Our Lady urges us to seek the Holy Spirit in prayer:

> *Dear children, if only you knew how many graces God is giving you. You do not want to move ahead in these days when the Holy Spirit is working in a special way. Your hearts are turned to earthly things and they preoccupy you. Turn your hearts to prayer and ask that the Holy Spirit be poured forth upon you (WM 5-9-85).*

The prophet Joel speaks of the Spirit poured out upon mankind:

> Then afterward
> I will pour out my spirit on all flesh;
> your sons and your daughters shall prophesy,
> your old men shall dream dreams,
> and your young men shall see visions.
> Even on the male and female slaves,
> in those days, I will pour out my spirit.
> —Joel 2:28-29

Reflection: Rather than speak of God's Spirit, let us today pray to the Advocate as the Virgin recommends, using the following "Daily Prayer to the Holy Spirit:"

> Come Holy Spirit, fill my heart with your holy gifts. Let my weakness be penetrated with your strength this very day, that I may fulfill all my duties conscientiously, and that I may do what is right and just.

Let my love be such that I may offend no one, nor hurt their feelings. May my generosity pardon any wrong done to me.

Assist me, O Holy Spirit, in all my trials of life; enlighten me in your ways, advise me in my doubts, strengthen me in my weakness, help me in all my needs, protect me in temptations, and console me in afflictions.

Graciously hear me, O Holy Spirit, and pour your light into my heart, my soul, and my mind. Help me to live a holy life and to grow in goodness and grace. Amen.

Application: Focus your prayer today on the Holy Spirit, asking for the special graces only he can bestow.

APRIL 9

I call you to humility

The Blessed Mother speaks of humility in this message from 1985:

> *Dear children, today I call you to humility. These days all of you have felt a great joy because of all the people who have come here, and to whom you spoke with love about your experiences. With humility and an open heart, continue to speak with all those who are coming (WM 6-27-85).*

In this great act of humility, the Creator is baptized by the created:

> Then Jesus came from Galilee to John at the Jordan, to be baptized by him. John would have prevented him, saying, "I need to be baptized by you, and yet you come to me?" But Jesus answered him, "Let it be so now; for it is proper for us in this

way to fulfill all righteousness." Then he consented (Mt 3:13-15).

Reflection: Humility is not to be confused with humiliation, which is really degradation. Humility is simply seeing ourselves as God sees us, weak and prone to sin, yet made in his likeness and image. Apart from God we are nothing, yet with him we are the heirs of the kingdom.

This spirit of humility can be gleaned in remarks Florence Nightingale once made about her career:

> If I could give you information on my life, it would be to show how a woman of very ordinary ability has been led by God, in strange and unaccustomed paths, to do in his service what he has done for her. And if I could tell you all, you would see how God has done all, and I nothing. I have worked hard, very hard that is all, and I have never refused God anything.

Thoreau wrote that, "Humility like darkness reveals the heavenly lights." We are called as well to recognize and proclaim that light as it shines in our own lives.

Application: Today, begin to live Our Lady's message on humility, realizing that it is a virtue that rests upon the knowledge of God and of oneself.

APRIL 10

Begin changing your family life

The family is the topic of Our Lady's message today:

> *Dear children, today I call you to begin changing your family life. May it be like a harmonious flower which I can present to Jesus. Dear children, I ask each family to actively pray, for one day the fruit of family prayer will*

be clearly seen. Then I will give you all to Jesus, like the petals of many flowers, in fulfillment of God's plan (WM 5-1-86).

In this passage from Ephesians, Paul urges us to seek wisdom and to rejoice in the name of Jesus Christ:

Be careful then how you live, not as unwise people but as wise, making the most of time, because the days are evil. So do not be foolish, but understand what the will of the Lord is.

Do not get drunk with wine, for that is debauchery; but be filled with the Spirit, as you sing psalms and hymns and spiritual songs among yourselves, singing and making melody to the Lord in your hearts, giving thanks to God the Father at all times and for everything in the name of our Lord Jesus Christ (Eph 5:15-20).

Reflection: Truly our joy resides in Jesus Christ, as Paul tells the Ephesians, and as Our Lady tells the families of the world. Clearly it is in the family that Christ is born into the hearts of children and where the torch of faith is passed from one generation to the next.

And so the Blessed Mother urges that, "Every family be active in prayer," for this makes all the difference.

Application: In response to the Virgin's message today, offer the following prayer for your family:

Lord Jesus, I implore you to grant your special graces to our family. May our home be a shrine of peace, purity, love, labor, and faith. I ask you, dear Jesus, to protect and bless all of us, absent and present, living and dead.

O Mary, loving Mother of Jesus, and our Mother, pray for our family, for all the families of the world. Guard the cradle of the newborn, the schools of the young, and their vocations.

Blessed St. Joseph, holy guardian of Jesus and Mary, assist us by your prayers in all the necessities of life. Ask of Jesus that special grace which he granted to you, to watch over our home and the pillow of the sick and the dying, so that with Mary and with you, heaven may find our family unbroken in the Sacred Heart of Jesus. Amen.

APRIL 11

I love you immeasurably

Our Lady speaks of love today:

Dear children, I thank you for the love which you have shown me. You know, dear children, that I love you immeasurably, and that I pray to the Lord daily that he may help you to realize more fully the love which I bear you. That is why, dear children, pray, pray, pray (WM 8-21-86).

Paul also speaks of love:

For now we see in a mirror, dimly, but then we will see face to face. Now I know only in part; then I will know fully, even as I have been fully known. And now faith, hope and love abide, these three; and the greatest of these is love (1 Cor 13:12-13).

Reflection: Clearly love is the very essence of God's nature and the motivating force of our faith. We could spend our lives attempting to fathom its depth.

For centuries, writers and poets have sought to express God's love in their verse. In modern times, one beautiful passage was written by Major Malcolm Boyle, who was killed in action after the landing on D-day in June, 1944. He had written the following lines in his Bible:

> If I should never see the moon again
> Rising red gold across the harvest field,
> Or feel the stinging of soft April rain,
> As the brown earth her hidden treasures yield.
>
> If I should never taste the salt sea spray
> As the ship beats her course against the breeze,
> Or smell the dog-rose and the new mown hay,
> Or moss and primrose beneath the tree.
>
> If I should never hear the thrushes wake
> Long before the sunrise in the glimmering dawn
> Or watch the huge Atlantic rollers break
> Against the rugged cliffs in baffling scorn.
>
> If I have said goodbye to stream and wood,
> To the wide ocean and the green clad hill,
> I know that he who made this world so good
> Has somewhere made a heaven better still.
>
> This I bear witness with my latest breath
> Knowing the love of God,
> I fear not death.

Application: Let us pray especially today to more fully comprehend the love of God.

APRIL 12

Devote yourselves to prayer

The Blessed Mother speaks of her favorite subject today:

Dear children, today I call you to renew family prayer in your homes. Now that the work in the fields is over, devote yourselves to prayer. Let prayer take first place in your families (WM 11-1-84).

In Psalm 3, David speaks of attaining God's safety through prayer:

But you, O Lord, are a shield around me,
my glory, and the one who lifts up my head.
I cry aloud to the Lord,
and he answers me from his holy hill.
I lie down and sleep;
I wake again, for the Lord sustains me.
—Psalm 3:3-5

Reflection: One of the gifts that often accompanies deep prayer is serenity, a sense of being safe in the hands of God. In this spirit St. Teresa of Avila wrote:

Let nothing disturb you,
Nothing frighten you;
All things are passing;
God never changes;
Patient endurance
Attains to all things;
Who God possesses
In nothing is wanting;
Alone God suffices.

In view of this peace, it would not seem difficult to live the Madonna's call to devote ourselves to prayer. And the fruit of prayer, of course, is serenity.

Application: Try to remain in quiet prayer today until you feel the peace of God within your heart.

Continually give thanks

The Blessed Mother speaks of joy and thanksgiving today:

> Dear children, today I invite you all to rejoice in the life which God has given you. Little children, rejoice in God the Creator for he has created you so wonderfully.
>
> In your prayer, ask that your life be one of joyful thanksgiving, which flows from your heart like a river of joy. Little children, continually give thanks for all that you possess, for even the little gifts, which God has given you. In this way, a joyful blessing will always come down from God upon your life (MM 8-25-88).

Psalm 92 also rings with the spirit of joy and thanksgiving:

> It is good to give thanks to the Lord,
> to sing praise to your name, O Most High;
> to declare your steadfast love in the morning,
> and your faithfulness by night,
> to the music of the lute and the harp,
> to the melody of the lyre.
> For you, O Lord, have made me glad by
> your work;
> at the works of your hands I sing for joy.
>
> —Psalm 92:1-4

Reflection: A spirit of gratitude and joy always accompanies our spiritual journey to God. In quiet moments of prayer we can recognize the beautiful array of gifts the Lord has bestowed on us. The following verses by an anonymous poet were written in that spirit:

> Today upon a bus, I saw a lovely maid
> with golden hair;

I envied her—she seemed so gay—and
    wished I were as fair.
When suddenly she rose to leave, I saw
    her hobble down the aisle;
She had one foot and wore a crutch, but
    as she passed, a smile. . . .
Oh, God, forgive me when I whine;
I'm blessed, indeed! The world is mine. . . .

With feet to take me where I'd go,
With eyes to see the sunset's glow,
With ears to hear what I would know,
Oh, God, forgive me when I whine;
I'm blessed indeed! The world is mine.

Application: Today, simply spend several minutes reflecting on God's gifts and expressing your gratitude for them.

APRIL 14

I need your prayers

The Mother of God speaks to us of prayer today:

Dear children, today I again call you to prayer. I need your prayers so that God can be glorified through all of you. Dear children, I beseech you to hear your Mother's message and live it, for I call you only out of love so that I can help you (WM 1-16-86).

The psalmist lifts up his soul to God in prayer:

Give ear to my words, O Lord;
give heed to my sighing.
Listen to the sound of my cry,
my King and my God,
for to you I pray.

—Psalm 5:1-2

Reflection: The Lord answers all prayers, and yet he may not give us precisely what we ask for, if it would be harmful to us. A child, for instance, may wish to play with matches, but out of love his parent would give him a toy instead.

This loving concern of God is expressed in these lines by an unknown author:

I asked God for strength that I might achieve;
I was made weak that I might learn humbly
   to obey.
I asked for help that I might do greater things;
I was given infirmity that I might do better things.
I asked for riches that I might be happy;
I was given poverty that I might be wise.
I asked for all things that I might enjoy life;
I was given life that I might enjoy all things.
I was given nothing that I asked for;
But everything that I had hoped for.
Despite myself, my prayers were answered;
I am among men most richly blessed.

Application: In prayer today, ask the Lord for what you need, but not for what you want.

APRIL 15

Long for peace

The Mother of God calls us to be peacemakers:

Dear children, I call you to help others through your spirit of peace, that they may see this in you and begin to long for peace within themselves.

Because you are at peace, dear children, you cannot understand the absence of it. That is why I call you, through your life and your prayer, to help destroy every evil among men, and to unmask Satan's deceptions.

Pray, so that truth may prevail in your hearts (WM 9-25-86).

The prophet Micah speaks of the Messiah bringing peace:

> And he shall stand and feed his flock
> in the strength of the Lord,
> in the majesty of the name of the Lord his God.
> And they shall live secure, for now he shall
>   be great
> to the ends of the earth;
> and he shall be the one of peace.

> —Micah 5:4-5

Reflection: In her messages at Medjugorje, Our Lady rarely speaks of peace out of context. Rather, she shows us that it is the fruit of faith, conversion, and love.

The church, too, when speaking of the broader level of peace among nations, also traces the roots of this peace back to love, which includes generosity, mutual respect, and a spirit of brotherhood. From a teaching of the Second Vatican Council:

> Peace cannot be obtained on earth unless personal values are safeguarded and men freely and trustingly share with one another the riches of their inner spirits and their talents.

> A firm determination to respect other men and peoples and their dignity, as well as the studied practice of brotherhood, are absolutely necessary for the establishment of peace. Hence peace is likewise the fruit of love, which goes beyond what justice can provide (*The Church Today*, 78).

Application: Reflect today on these words of Pope Paul VI on peace: "If we wish to have true peace, we must give it a soul. The soul of peace is love."

I want to thank everyone

Today Our Lady thanks the youth of the world:

> Dear children, I want to thank everyone for all you have
> done for me, especially the youth. Dear children, I ask
> you to enter fully into prayer, for it is in prayer that you
> will come to know God's plans (WM 11-28-85).

And from the Old Testament, the advice of a sage:

> Rejoice, young man, while you are young, and let
> your heart cheer you in the days of your youth.
> Follow the inclination of your heart and the desire
> of your eyes, but know that for all these things
> God will bring you into judgment (Eccl 11:9).

Reflection: The Blessed Mother has a special place in
her heart for the young. Interestingly, most of her apparitions have been to children and youth, including
those of Medjugorje.

Perhaps she chooses the young because they are
open, innocent, and full of wonder. Yet we are all called
to these qualities, as the following verses relate:

> Youth is not a time of life . . . it is a state of mind.
> Nobody grows old by merely living a number of
> years; people grow old only by deserting their
> ideals. Years wrinkle the skin, but to give up en-
> thusiasm wrinkles the soul. Worry, doubt, self-dis-
> trust, fear, and despair . . . these are the long, long
> years that bow the head and turn the growing
> spirit back to dust.
>
> Whether seventy or sixteen, there is in every
> being's heart the love of wonder, the sweet amaze-
> ment of the stars and the starlike things and
> thoughts, the undaunted challenge of events, the

unfailing childlike appetite for what is next, and the joy of the game of life.

You are as young as your faith, as old as your doubt; as young as your self-confidence, as old as your fear; as young as your hope, as old as your despair.

Application: Today, simply reflect on this line from Sir J. Stevens: "Every man has in himself a continent of undiscovered character. Happy is he who acts the Columbus to his own soul."

APRIL 17

Receive the sacrament of reconciliation

The Blessed Mother speaks of the sacrament of reconciliation and forgiveness today:

I am happy because you have begun to receive the sacrament of reconciliation on a monthly basis. This is good for the whole world. Continue to persevere in prayer. This is the path that leads to my Son (FY 10-1-82).

The joy of forgiveness is celebrated in Psalm 32:

Happy are those whose transgression is forgiven, whose sin is covered.
Happy are those to whom the Lord imputes no iniquity,
and in whose spirit there is no deceit.

—Psalm 32:1-2

Reflection: Both of our readings celebrate forgiveness today, that love of God which heals and renews our souls. We too are called to forgive one another in imitation of Christ, and this too, takes great love.

Rabbi Leo Beck, a German scholar who took the leadership of German Jews in Hitler's time, testified by his own life to the love and forgiveness of God. He was five times arrested, and finally sent to a concentration camp, where he served on the convicts' committee of management. According to the English educator F. H. Drinkwater, on the very day he was to have been shot, the Russian troops arrived. Beck could have escaped at once, but stayed behind to argue with the Russians, to persuade them to spare the lives of the German camp guards. The Russians decided that the camp guards should be handed over to the inmates. Beck then argued with the inmates and managed to persuade them not to take the vengeance that they were thirsting for.

Application: St. Augustine wrote:

> There are many kinds of alms, the giving of which helps us to obtain pardon for our sins; but none is greater than that by which we forgive from our heart a sin that some one has committed against us.

Today, call to mind those who may have sinned against you; prayerfully lift them up to Christ, forgiving them in his name.

APRIL 18

They will be cured

In answer to the visionaries' questions about the sick, Our Lady responded:

> *Have a strong faith, pray, and fast and they will be cured. Be confident and rest in joy. Go in the peace of God. Be patient and pray for their cure. Goodbye, my angels (FY 11-26-81).*

In John's gospel, Christ also answered questions about the sick and disabled:

> As he walked along, he saw a man blind from birth. His disciples asked him, "Rabbi, who sinned, this man or his parents, that he was born blind?" Jesus answered, "Neither this man nor his parents sinned; he was born blind so that God's works might be revealed in him" (Jn 9:1-3).

Reflection: A common belief in Jewish culture was that calamity or suffering was the result of some great sin. But Christ used this man's suffering to teach about faith and to glorify God.

We live in a fallen world where good behavior is not always rewarded and bad behavior not always punished. Therefore, innocent people sometimes suffer. This is part of the mystery of evil which distorts and corrupts that which was originally good. But regardless of the reasons for suffering, Jesus has the power to renew and heal us.

When you suffer from a disease, tragedy, or handicap, remember that it is not a punishment or rebuke from God, just as the suffering of Jesus was not inflicted by the Father, but by the sin and evil of the world. One positive response is to pray for the Lord's help and strength in dealing with your trial, and to link it to the passion and cross of Christ, which will give your suffering a redemptive value—a sharing in the saving work of Christ and the Blessed Mother. This is how the visionary Vicka coped with her own illness at the advice of the Gospa.

Application: There is a Latin proverb that, "In time of illness the soul collects itself anew." Today, pray for the strength you will need for any future hardship, and pray especially for those who are bearing trials now.

APRIL 19

May Jesus rise in your families

The spirit of the resurrection colors Our Lady's message today:

> *Pray a great deal tomorrow (Easter). May Jesus truly rise in your families. Where there is war, let there be peace. May you become new people.*
>
> *My children, I thank you. Continue to bring about the Resurrection of Jesus in all men (LJM 2-21-84).*

And in Matthew's gospel, the account of the resurrection:

> And suddenly there was a great earthquake; for an angel of the Lord, descending from heaven, came and rolled back the stone and sat on it. His appearance was like lightning, and his clothing white as snow. For fear of him the guards shook and became like dead men. But the angel said to the women, "Do not be afraid; I know that you are looking for Jesus who was crucified. He is not here; for he has been raised, as he said. Come, see the place where he lay. Then go quickly and tell his disciples, 'He has been raised from the dead, and indeed he is going ahead of you to Galilee; there you will see him.' This is my message for you" (Mt 28:2-7).

Reflection: The Chinese princess Tou Wan, who died about 104 B.C., was buried in a jade suit. Her husband, who had died nine years earlier, was given a similar suit. The pair were laid to rest in vast tombs hollowed out of a rocky hillside.

In 1969, when their tombs were discovered, they created a sensation because of the staggering wealth of the 2,800 funeral offerings. Most spectacular of all were the jade suits, each made up of more than 2,000 tiny plates of thin jade, sewn together with gold thread. Nobles of the period believed gold and jade would stand the ravages of time, and so confer immortality.

St. John Chrysostom wrote, "After the royal throne comes death; but after the dunghill comes the kingdom of Heaven." Despite failure, mankind has been undeterred in its attempts to conquer death. But the message of Our Lady and St. Matthew is one of genuine hope and shining promise: "Do not fear. You are eternal, like the stars of heaven. You are the heirs of God." We have no need, then, of jade garments, for we have the promise of Jesus Christ.

Application: Today, while praying the first Glorious Mystery of the rosary, reflect on the gift of eternal life.

APRIL 20

May love flow from your heart

In this message from November of 1991, the Blessed Mother calls us to a special love:

> *Dear children, this time I am also inviting you to prayer. Pray that you might be able to comprehend what God wishes to tell you through my presence here and the messages that I am giving you.*
>
> *I want to draw you ever closer to Jesus and to his wounded heart, that you might be able to understand the immeasurable love which gave itself for each one of you.*

Therefore, dear children, pray that a fountain of love may flow from your heart to every person, both to those who hate you and even those who despise you. In this way, through Jesus' love, you will be able to overcome all the misery in this world of sorrows, which is without hope for those who do not know Jesus.

Thank you for all your sacrifices and prayers. Pray so that I might be able to help you still more. Your prayers are necessary to me (MM 11-25-91).

In the first book of Samuel, Saul develops a tragic hatred for young David:

> The next day an evil spirit . . . rushed upon Saul, and he raved within his house, while David was playing the lyre, as he did day by day. Saul had his spear in his hand; and Saul threw the spear, for he thought, "I will pin David to the wall." But David eluded him twice (1 Sm 18:10-11).

Reflection: It has been said that hatred is never anything but fear; if we feared no one, we would hate no one. When we experience God within, we seem naturally generous with others. But there are times when we focus on what is wrong with them, and how they ought to change. This can be a form of hate. If we are searching for what we have power to change—in our families, in our friendships, in the world—we would be wise to pray for the charity to set aside our fears and controlling behavior.

Do we bear ill will toward someone today? When we are honest with ourselves, do we feel a sense of fear in relation to that person? What are we really afraid of? Perhaps the same person fears us. When we turn to the Lord of Peace with our fear, the hatred melts with no further effort. Then we are truly in touch with the Spirit that sets us free.

Application: Praying for God's strength to face our fears today, let us be cautious of not sending them outward as hatred.

APRIL 21

Heed the call to fasting

In a weekly message in September of 1985 the Madonna said:

> *Dear children, thank you for all your prayers. And thank you for all your sacrifices. I wish to tell you, dear children, to renew the messages which I am giving you.*
>
> *Heed the call to fasting because by fasting you will ensure that the total plan of God here in Medjugorje will be fulfilled. This will give me great joy (WM 9-26-85).*

And from Paul's letter to the Romans:

> Those who observe the day, observe it in honor of the Lord. Also, those who eat, eat in honor of the Lord, since they give thanks to God; while those who abstain, abstain in honor of the Lord and give thanks to God (Rom 14:6).

Reflection: Today, let us consider one of the fruits of fasting, purification of the heart, in which we begin to perceive reality with new eyes. We begin to see clearly all that we have, what we actually need, and what we do not need. A pure heart frees us from the compulsion of needing and wanting more and more, while being blind to what we already have.

Thus fasting changes our perception; we begin to see, for instance, that most material things are not really very important. We are pilgrims only passing through this world in need of only a little. There are many who would be happy with only a roof over their heads and enough food for the day; if they were in our shoes they would be ecstatic. And yet, in our plenty, we are often discontented and unhappy.

The reason for the discontent lies in the fact that we do not see the essential anymore, we have become blind, convinced that what we have is inadequate. Thus many Christians become nailed to this world and cannot move. This is why fasting is so important; its graces free us from the world's shackles and widens our horizon. We see with new eyes.

Application: Have you begun to notice a change in your attitude toward your possessions? On your next fast day, pray especially for new eyes to truly see.

APRIL 22

They have not listened

In today's message, there is an urgent tone to Our Lady's words:

> *My Son suffers very much because men do not want to be reconciled. They have not listened to me. Be converted. Be reconciled (FY 10-15-83).*

The Book of Joel also speaks of conversion, of turning back to God:

> Yet even now, says the Lord,
> return to me with all your heart,
> with fasting, with weeping, and with mourning;
> rend your hearts and not your clothing.
> Return to the Lord, your God,
> for he is gracious and merciful,
> slow to anger, and abounding in steadfast love,
> and relents from punishing (Jl 2:12-13).

Reflection: As we see, conversion is emphasized by both scripture and the Blessed Virgin in her message today. For Fr. Tomislav Pervan, the former pastor at Medjugorje, conversion means, "to accept Jesus with all our life, completely, with all our being—to make him the most important person in our lives. That is what he wants—that he be most important in our lives."

Fr. Pervan comments that conversion is "to accept Jesus completely and to follow him totally . . . to choose his way even if that way is not always easy. And if it is difficult, to fear not: 'I am with you always, to the end of time,' he has said."

Application: In your prayer today, give yourself again to Christ and Our Lady. Ask that they deepen your ongoing conversion.

APRIL 23

Stop slandering

The Mother of God warns us of gossip today:

> *Dear children, this evening I beseech you to stop slandering—and to pray for unity, for my Son and I have a special plan for this parish (WM 4-12-84).*

In some of the strongest language in scripture, James also condemns slander and gossip:

> How great a forest is set ablaze by a small fire! And the tongue is a fire. The tongue is placed among our members as a world of iniquity: it stains the whole body, sets on fire the cycle of nature, and is itself set on fire by hell. For every species of beast and bird, reptile and sea creature, can be tamed and has been tamed by the human species, but no

one can tame the tongue—a restless evil, full of
deadly poison (Jas 3:5-8).

Reflection: Aesop, the philosopher of the fables, was
asked one day what the most useful thing in the world
was. "The tongue," he replied. And what, they asked,
is the most harmful thing in the world? "The tongue,"
he replied once more.

The slanderous tongue can do terrible damage. Satan
can use it for division, for pitting one person against
another, which is why Mary beseeches us "to stop
slandering . . . pray for unity." St. James alerts us that
we may never have perfect control of our tongues in
this life, yet we can still learn enough control to reduce
the damage they can inflict. Clearly it is better to fight
a fire than to go about setting new ones.

Application: Washington Irving once said, "A sharp
tongue is the only edge tool that grows sharper with
constant use." Today, offer a prayer to the Holy Spirit
that he will grant you the grace to control what you say,
mindful of Christ's law of love.

APRIL 24

No one can serve two masters

Today Our Lady reminds us that we must choose between two masters:

> *Read each Thursday the passage from the Gospel of
> Matthew in which it says, "No one can serve two
> masters . . . you cannot serve God and money" (FY
> 8-5-86).*

The following is the passage that the Blessed Mother
refers to:

> No one can serve two masters; for a slave will either hate the one and love the other, or be devoted to the one and despise the other. You cannot serve both God and money (Mt 6:24).

Reflection: Peter Fontaine tells the story of a young man who found a silver dollar. From that time on he never raised his eyes from the ground when he walked. In the next thirty years he accumulated $3.50 in silver, 37 pennies, 18,478 buttons, 14,369 pins, a hunch back, a miserly character, and a very rotten disposition. He lost the beauty and glory of the sunshine, the smiles of friends, the gorgeous colors and beauty of flowers and trees, blue skies, and all there is which makes life worthwhile.

> So keep your head up, your eyes towards the stars. You may miss finding a few pennies, but you will find all the beautiful things that make the living of life a glorious adventure.

In the end, we can serve only one master, as both Christ and his Mother remind us today. In our consumer society, it is easy to become obsessed by money and the things it will buy. This is the danger, the materialistic trap, that we are warned of today, for as Paul says in his letter to Timothy, "For the love of money is a root of all kinds of evil, and in their eagerness to be rich some have wandered away from the faith and pierced themselves with many pains" (1 Tm 6:10).

Application: Today, prayerfully reflect on whether God or money occupies more of your time and thoughts.

St. Mark, Evangelist

On this feast of St. Mark, author of the second gospel, it would be appropriate to review several of Our Lady's messages on sacred scripture. The following was given to Jelena in 1987:

Light won't reign in the world until people accept Jesus, until they live his words, which is the word of the gospel (LJM 7-30-87).

And to the visionaries in 1983:

Read what has been written about Jesus. Meditate on it and convey it to others (FY 6-2-83).

The Madonna rarely uses the word "must," but she does so in this message:

Every family must pray family prayers and read the Bible (Excerpt from weekly message of 2-14-85).

In Peter's second letter, he identifies the divine source of sacred scripture:

First of all you must understand this, that no prophecy of scripture is a matter of one's own interpretation, because no prophecy ever came by human will, but men and women moved by the Holy Spirit spoke from God (2 Pt 1:20-21).

Reflection: St. Mark was a disciple of St. Paul and the author of the gospel which bears his name. Tradition holds that he also founded the Church at Alexandria in Egypt and was martyred there in the latter part of the first century.

On the importance of scripture, the renaissance theologian Erasmus wrote:

These writings bring back to you the living image of that most holy mind, the very Christ himself speaking, healing, dying, rising, in fact so entirely present, that you would see less of him if you beheld him with your own eyes.

St. Jerome, one of the greatest scholars of the church, taught that, "To be ignorant of scripture is not to know Christ." Like the eucharist, sacred scripture nourishes our hearts and souls, drawing us ever closer to Christ and his Mother. It is, as Our Lady insists, an indispensable part of our lives.

Application: One of the most beautiful and fruitful forms of prayer is scriptural prayer. Simply choose a passage from the Bible and read it slowly and meditatively, pausing to reflect on any phrase that strikes you in a special way (this is the Holy Spirit directing your attention). Spend a few minutes each day in this prayer, in response to the Virgin's message: "Read what has been written about Jesus. Meditate on it. . . ."

APRIL 26

Love even those from whom evil comes

Today the Mother of God calls us to love not only our neighbor, but our enemies as well:

> *Dear children, I call you to the love of neighbor and love even for those from whom evil comes to you. In loving this way, you will be able to discern the intentions of hearts. Pray and love, dear children! By love you can do even that which you think is impossible (WM 11-7-85).*

This call of Our Lady in Medjugorje is an echo of Christ's words in the gospel of Matthew:

You have heard that it was said, "You shall love your neighbor and hate your enemy." But I say to you, love your enemies and pray for those who persecute you, so that you may be children of your Father in heaven; for he makes his sun rise on the evil and on the good, and sends rain on the righteous and on the unrighteous.

For if you love those who love you, what reward do you have? Do not even the tax collectors do the same? And if you greet only your brothers and sisters, what more are you doing than others? Do not even the Gentiles do the same? (Mt 5:43-47).

Reflection: "Love will conquer hate," wrote Gandhi, who was familiar with Christ's words in the gospel today. Gandhi based his life on that premise, and was empowered to transform his native land. Love never fails, for it is the greatest power in the universe, the essence of God.

Application: In the program of Alcoholics Anonymous, it's recognized that hatreds or resentments will soon drive a sober member back to drinking. The remedy: pray for the offender each day for fourteen days, and the grace of God will melt the hatred. "He will do for us," says the *Big Book* of A.A., "what we cannot do for ourselves." Try this remedy, similar to the one Our Lady recommends in her message today, when the need arises.

APRIL 27

Say yes to Jesus now!

In a message to Jelena, the locutionist, on commitment, Our Lady said:

> *Dear children, it is truly a great thing when God calls men. Think how sad it would be to let those*

opportunities pass without taking advantage of them. So do not wait for tomorrow or the day after. Say "yes!" to Jesus now! And may your "yes!" be forever (LJM 5-16-87).

When Christ called his disciples, their "yes" was immediate:

As he walked by the Sea of Galilee, he saw two brothers, Simon, who is called Peter, and Andrew his brother, casting a net into the sea—for they were fishermen. And he said to them, "Follow me, and I will make you fishers of men." Immediately they left their nets and followed him (Mt 4:18-20).

Reflection: An anonymous writer once wrote, "There are two words used a great deal by Jesus in the gospels. One is 'come' and the other is 'go.' It's no use coming unless you go, and it's no use going unless you come. Christ call us, as he did his apostles, to make a commitment, a lifetime decision, for him. And at the right time, we are then sent forth to draw others to him through our word and example. First 'come,' then 'go.'" This is precisely the message of Our Lady today.

Application: In your prayer this day, using your own words, commit yourself completely to Christ and his Mother.

APRIL 28

Overcome every temptation

The Blessed Mother warns of temptations today:

Dear children, you know that I promised you an oasis of peace, but you don't realize that beside the oasis stands the desert, where Satan is lurking and wants to tempt each one of you. Dear children, only through

*prayer can you overcome every temptation of Satan
where you are in your life. I am with you, but I cannot
take away your freedom (WM 8-7-86).*

In Matthew's gospel, Jesus encounters the temptations
of Satan:

> Again, the devil took him to a very high moun-
> tain and showed him all the kingdoms of the
> world and their splendor; and he said to him,
> "All these I will give you, if you will fall down
> and worship me." Jesus said to him, "Away
> with you, Satan! for it is written, 'Worship the
> Lord your God, and serve only him.'" Then the
> devil left him, and suddenly angels came and
> waited on him (Mt 4:8-11).

Reflection: To be sure, if Christ was subject to temptation, we likewise will have our share. And yet, according to the Shepherd of Hermas, an early church writer:
"The devil cannot lord it over those who are servants
of God with their whole heart and who place their
hope in him. The devil can wrestle with, but not overcome them."

In today's message, Our Lady teaches that only by
prayer can we overcome the influence of Satan in our
lives. "To realize God's presence," writes Francois
Fenelon, "is the one sovereign remedy against
temptation." And yet God can even use Satan's wiles
for his own ends. As the ancient Hawaiians believed
that the strength and valor of the enemy he killed
passed into himself, so we gain the strength of the
temptations we resist.

Application: Reflect on the following today: "Inconstan-
cy of mind, and small confidence in God, is the beginning
of all evil temptations" (St. Thomas á Kempis).

St. Catherine of Siena

Today the Blessed Mother speaks of divine mercy:

Pray especially on Sunday that the great sign, a gift from God, may come. Pray with fervor and perseverance that God may have mercy on his great children. Go in peace, my angels. May the blessing of God accompany you. Amen. Goodbye (FY 9-6-81).

And from Mary's Magnificat in Luke's gospel:

By the tender mercy of our God,
the dawn from on high will break upon us,
to give light to those who sit in darkness
and the shadow of death,
to guide our feet into the way of peace.

—Luke 1:78-79

Reflection: Of mercy, St. Catherine of Siena once prayed: "O Lord, by reason of your immeasurable love I beg, with all my strength, that you freely extend your mercy to all your lowly creatures." God's unbounded mercy was one of the great motivations of the ministry and work of St. Catherine. A remarkable woman of faith, she was not only a great scholar and reformer of religious life, but also brought peace and concord to the feuding city-states of Italy in the fourteenth century. Her many writings include *The Dialogue on Divine Providence*, from which the following is excerpted:

Eternal God, eternal Trinity, you have made the Blood of Christ immeasurably precious through his sharing in your divine nature. You are a mystery as deep as the sea; the more I search, the more I find, and the more I find the more I search for you.

I can never be satisfied; what I receive will ever leave me desiring more. When you fill my soul I have an even greater hunger and I grow more famished for your light. I desire above all else to see you, the true light, as you really are.

Application: Today, simply offer this little prayer to the Father, also written by St. Catherine:

O tender Father, you gave me more, much more than I ever thought to ask for. I realize that our human desires can never really match what you long to give us.

Thank you, and thank you again, O Father, for having granted my petitions, and even that which I never realized I needed. Amen.

APRIL 30

Everything is God's gift

Speaking of gratitude, the Blessed Mother once said:

Dear children, I am calling you to complete surrender to God. Place all that you possess in the hands of God. Only then can you have true joy in your heart.

Little children, rejoice in all that you have and give thanks to God, for everything is God's gift to you. In this way your life will be one of thanksgiving and you shall discover God in everything, even in the smallest flower (MM 4-25-89).

In his letter to the Colossians, Paul also speaks of gratitude:

As you therefore have received Christ Jesus the Lord, continue to live your lives in him, rooted and built up in him and established in the faith, just as you were taught, abounding in thanksgiving (Col 2:6-7).

Reflection: Gratitude is a universal language and characterizes the spirituality of most religions. Today let us take a look at gratitude as expressed in the Koran, the holy book of Islam:

God is he who created the heavens and the earth and sent down water from the clouds, then brought forth with it the fruits as a sustenance for you. . . .

And he has made subservient to you the sun and the moon pursuing their courses, and he has made subservient to you the night and the day. And he gives you all that you ask him, and if you count God's favors, you will not be able to number them; surely man is very unjust, very ungrateful.

Application: Today, call to mind several reasons in your own life to be grateful to God. Offer a spontaneous prayer of thanksgiving for these gifts.

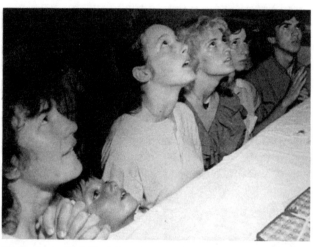

Early photo (1981) of the six visionaries during an apparition
(l. to r.: Vicka, Jakov, Ivanka, Marijana, Marija and Ivan)

MAY 1

May, the Month of Our Lady

Referring to the month of May, Our Lady said:

May this month be for you the month of the rosary and reading your Bible. . . (VPG 5-9-88).

Reflection: The month of May means that spring is here, and all of nature seems to rejoice; budding flowers and trees, green grass and sunshine, usher in a season of soft colors and new life.

This is Mary's month, of May crownings, processions, the rosary and, as she says today, a time for reading sacred scripture.

As Catholics, we are aware that the Bible is the inspired word of God, that his presence and truth are found within its pages. In somewhat the same way, nature reveals the image and beauty of God. St. Paul writes, "Since the creation of the world, invisible realities, God's eternal power and divinity, have become visible, recognized through the things he has made" (Rom 1:20).

As spring unfolds, may we discover anew God's presence in creation, and with the psalmist sing his praise:

You visit the earth and water it,
you greatly enrich it;
the river of God is full of water;
you provide the people with grain,
for so you have prepared it.
You water its furrows abundantly,
settling its ridges,
softening it with showers,
and blessing its growth.
The pastures of the wilderness overflow,

the hills gird themselves with joy,
the meadows clothe themselves with flocks,
the valleys deck themselves with grain,
they shout and sing together for joy.
—Psalm 65:9-10, 12-13

Application: In celebration of this month dedicated to Our Lady, set aside in your home a May altar, placing on it an image of the Blessed Mother, some spring flowers, a candle, and a rosary. As a family, light the candle each day and offer Our Lady some special prayers, such as the rosary, the litany of Mary, or another prayer for the special intentions of the Queen of Peace.

MAY 2

Pray the rosary

Today the Gospa speaks of prayer and the rosary:

Dear children, your prayer has helped my plans to be fulfilled. Pray continually for their complete fulfillment. I beseech the families of the parish to pray the rosary (WM 9-27-84).

Prayer is also on Paul's mind in his letter to Philemon:

When I remember you in my prayers, I always thank my God because I hear of your love for all the saints and your faith toward the Lord Jesus. I pray that the sharing of your faith may become effective when you perceive all the good that we may do for Christ (Phlm 1:4-6).

Reflection: In reflecting on the mysteries of the rosary each day, we are gradually changed into the likeness of Christ. Just as people who have been married for a long time sometimes acquire each other's characteristics, so we acquire the mind and heart of Jesus Christ as we meditate on his life through the rosary.

"The Hail Marys of the rosary," writes Fr. Albert Shamon, "are like background music while you are watching Our Lord's life. Background music helps us when reading and working. We don't pay much attention to the music, but it helps us."

Application: Today, pray the rosary slowly and meditatively; if you have any literature with the mysteries depicted, use it as a visual aid in staying focused.

MAY 3

Thank you for adoring

To the young locutionist, Jelena, the Mother of God once spoke of eucharistic adoration:

> *Thank you for adoring my Son in the sacred host. That touches me very much. I ask you to pray, for I desire to see you happy (1-26-84).*

St. Matthew relates one of the first acts of adoration of Jesus Christ:

> When they had heard the king, they set out; and there, ahead of them, went the star that they had seen at its rising, until it stopped over the place where the child was. When they saw that the star had stopped, they were overwhelmed with joy. On entering the house, they saw the child with Mary his mother; and they knelt down and adored him. Then, opening their treasure chests, they offered him gifts of gold, frankincense, and myrrh (Mt 2:9-11).

Reflection: Like the Magi, we too have been called to adore the Lord of heaven and earth, not in a manger in Bethlehem, but in the Most Blessed Sacrament. Indeed, several of the reported miracles in Medjugorje have been related to eucharistic adoration: the alleged image of Christ sometimes seen at the tabernacle in St. James Church; the disk or host which at times covers the sun, allowing one to look into it for long periods (now commonly known as the "miracle of the sun," which I have witnessed myself); and the visible rays of grace which some see emanate from the tabernacle at St. James and the adoration chapel.

These phenomena seem to be gifts from the Blessed Virgin to strengthen our faith in the true presence of Christ in the eucharist—God's most precious gift to his church. Like the Magi, we too cannot approach the Divine without offering gifts of thanksgiving; and for us, these are our unfailing love and fidelity.

Application: Think of the last time you worshipped Christ in the Blessed Sacrament of your home church. If it has been a while, when can you do it next? Can you visit the Lord on a regular basis?

MAY 4

Follow the way of holiness

In this monthly message, the Gospa urges us to holiness:

Dear children, I beseech you to follow the way of holiness from this day onward. I love you and therefore I wish you to be holy. Do not let Satan block you on this path.

Dear children, pray and accept all that God is offering you on a way which is bitter. But at the same time, God

*will reveal every sweetness to those who travel this
path; he will gladly answer whenever you call on him.
Do not attach importance to petty things, but long for
heaven (MM 7-25-87).*

Paul echoes this call to holiness:

> Pursue peace with everyone, and the holiness
> without which no one will see the Lord (Heb
> 12:14).

Reflection: Both Paul and Our Lady call us to holiness
today, to become more and more the reflection of Christ.
Referring to this transformation, the philosopher Blaise
Pascal wrote, "The serene, silent beauty of a holy life is
the most powerful influence in the world, next to the
might of God."

The Blessed Mother provides the means to holiness
in her message today: prayer, acceptance of God's
grace, refusing to give importance to the petty things in
life, and last, keeping the goal of heaven in sight. She
urges us on in our journey, promising that, "God will
reveal every sweetness to those who travel this path;
and he will gladly answer whenever you call on him."

Application: Today, try to put into practice this advice
from Cardinal Manning: "Holiness consists not in
doing uncommon things, but in doing all common
things with an uncommon fervor."

MAY 5

The great love God has for you

The Madonna speaks of love today:

> *Dear children, today I call you to a complete surrender
> to God. You are not conscious, dear children, of the great*

love God has for you. This is why he has allowed me to be with you, to teach and help you to find the way to peace. But you cannot find it if you do not pray.

Therefore, dear children, forsake everything and consecrate your time to God, for then he will bestow gifts upon you and bless you.

Little children, do not forget that your life is fleeting like a spring flower, which today is wondrously beautiful, but tomorrow has vanished. Therefore, pray in such a way that your prayer, as well as your surrender to God, may become like a road sign. In this way your witness will not only have value for yourself, but also for others—and for all eternity (MM 3-25-88).

In his great love for us, God will deny us nothing which is good:

Ask, and it will be given you; search, and you will find; knock, and the door will be opened for you. For everyone who asks, receives, and everyone who searches, finds, and for everyone who knocks, the door will be opened.

Is there anyone among you who, if your child asks for bread, will give him a stone? Or if the child asks for a fish, would you give a snake? If you then, who are sinful, know how to give good gifts to your children, how much more will your Father in heaven give good things to those who ask him! (Mt 7:7-11).

Reflection: The heart of God overflows with a kindness and generosity beyond our understanding, which is the core of Our Lady's message today: "You dear children, are not conscious of the great love God has for you." Because of this, he can deny us nothing that is good, if we but seek it in prayer: "Ask, and it will be given you; seek, and you will find."

Like a father giving bread to his son, God's power and gifts are available to all his children. The key is prayer; as the Gospa says, "consecrate your time to God, and then he will bestow gifts upon you and bless you."

Application: Today, offer the rosary for the intention that God provide for all your needs, and that you may more deeply understand his love.

MAY 6

Now they are receiving the sacrament

In the fourth week of the apparitions, Our Lady said:

> *Praised be Jesus Christ. A good number of people have been converted, and among them some who had not gone to confession in forty-five years—yet now they are receiving the sacrament. Go in the peace of God (FY 7-22-81).*

Speaking also of confession and forgiveness, St. James wrote:

> The prayer of faith will save the sick, and the Lord will raise them up; and anyone who has committed sins will be forgiven. Therefore, confess your sins to one another (Jas 5:15-16).

Reflection: One of the beautiful effects of confession is that, as we joyfully accept the Lord's forgiveness, we are then moved to forgive others in turn. The following story illustrates this.

A Catholic doctor in Scotland was very lenient with his poor patients, and when he found that it was difficult for them to pay his fees, he wrote in red ink across the record of their indebtedness the one word—"Forgiven." This was such a frequent occurrence that his case book had few pages where the red letters did not appear.

After his death, his executors thought the doctor's estate would be greatly benefited if some of the "forgiven" debts could be collected. After unsuccessful attempts at collection from the poor patients, the executors went to court to recover the amounts. But when the judge examined the case book and saw the word "forgiven" cancelling the entry, he said, "There is no court in the land that could enforce payment of these accounts marked 'forgiven,'" and he dismissed the case.

Application: Today, call to mind those people toward whom you feel anger or resentment. In thanksgiving to the Lord who has forgiven your own sins, lift up these people to God in prayer, forgiving them in his name.

MAY 7

Live my messages

Our Lady speaks of priorities today:

Dear children, today I am calling you to accept and live my messages. Dear children, I love you and have especially chosen this parish, more dear to me than others, where I have gladly remained after the Almighty sent me.

Therefore, I call on you to accept me, dear children, so that everything will go well in your lives. Listen to my messages (WM 3-21-85).

In Matthew's gospel, Christ also speaks of priorities:

Therefore do not worry, saying, "What shall we eat?" or "What will we drink?" or "What will we wear?" For it is the Gentiles who strive for all these things; and indeed your heavenly Father knows that you need all these things. So strive first for the kingdom of God and his righteousness, and all these things will be given to you as well (Mt 6:31-33).

Reflection: Mom was left behind when a nervous husband rushed to the hospital recently in Tulsa, Oklahoma. The father had called police to ask for help in getting his expectant wife to the hospital in a hurry. A patrol car was dispatched to meet the emergency. But after speeding through the city, with police clearing the way, the overanxious husband suddenly discovered that he had left his wife at home. Together with the officer he wheeled around and hastened back to the starting point, picked up his wife and resumed the flight to the hospital.

In the rush of daily living it is easy to get excited about incidentals and to overlook essentials. This is why the Madonna urges that we first live her messages before all else—that we put first things first. It is the same message of Christ in the gospels: "Seek first his kingdom and his justice, and all these things will be given to you besides."

Application: Today, take a few minutes to reflect on the priorities in your life. Your use of time for various activities is a good measure.

MAY 8

Prayer leads to happiness

During a locution in 1984, Our Lady said the following to Jelena:

When you pray, pray with a purpose. Prayer is a conversation with God. To pray means to listen to the

Lord; after it all things become clear. Prayer leads to happiness (LJM 4-20-84).

The psalmist praises God for hearing his prayers:

> I sought the Lord, and he answered me,
> and delivered me from all my fears.
> Look to him, and be radiant;
> so your faces may never be ashamed.
>
> —Psalm 34:4-5

Reflection: There are times when prayer comes with special grace and peace, "when rapture floods the soul with pure delight." As the poet writes:

> There comes a time when we must briefly pause,
> And drink with quiet tranquil grace,
> Sheer beauty blessed with subtle cause,
> Within a fragrant restful place.

> When breathes the essence of God's lingering
>   creation,
> When rapture floods the soul with pure delight,
> Then nature's worth reflects a flowing revelation,
> As the blooming spirit gathers deep insight.

> So let us welcome every sparkling stream,
> Or touch a rose or feel the comfort of the sun,
> Content to wander through life's passing dream,
> To greet shared joy, love's gift to everyone.
> Then comes the time to climb life's lofty mountain,
> Where flows the grace of God's eternal fountain.
>
> —Josephine Cordaro

Application: Today, give yourself time and space to pray, attentive to the quiet stirrings of the Holy Spirit within.

Do not slander

The Gospa asks us today to guard our tongues:

Understand that the church is God's palace, the place in which I gather you and wish to show you the way to God. Come and pray! Do not stare at others or slander them, but rather, let your life be a testimony to the way of holiness (MM 4-25-88).

St. James also warns us of slander:

Do not speak evil against one another, brothers and sisters. Whoever speaks evil against another or judges another, speaks evil against the law and judges the law; but if you judge the law, you are not a doer of the law but a judge. There is one lawgiver and one judge who is able to save and to destroy. So who, then, are you to judge your neighbor? (Jas 4:11-12).

Reflection: Housewreckers in Alexandria, Louisiana, found out too late that they were tearing down the wrong house. The men had removed half the roof, all of the front porch, and most of the upstairs of the two-story frame building when the owner happened to drive by.

He rushed in and halted the workmen. The foreman checked with headquarters and found that an embarrassing mistake had been made. He and his fellow workers should have been tearing down a house two blocks away!

In our speech, we have a tendency to be too hasty in a destructive way before getting the full facts. There is an old English proverb that, "A fool's tongue is always long enough to cut his own throat." Thus Our Lady calls us in our speed to seek every opportunity to "build," rather than "tear down"—to highlight what is good in others, not what is bad.

Application: Today, reflect on the words of Jesus: "The good person brings good out of the treasure of his heart; the evil person brings evil things out of the evil stored in his heart. For it is out of the store of the heart that the mouth speaks" (Lk 6:45).

MAY 10

Celebrate the eucharist

Our Lady speaks today of cherishing the Mass:

> *You do not celebrate the eucharist as you should. If you knew what graces and what gifts you receive, you would prepare yourselves for it for at least an hour every day. . . (FY 85).*

In chapter six of John's gospel, Christ speaks of the eucharist:

> So Jesus said to them, "Very truly, I tell you, unless you eat the flesh of the Son of Man and drink his blood, you have no life in you. Those who eat my flesh and drink my blood have eternal life, and I will raise them up on the last day; for my flesh is true food and my blood is true drink" (Jn 6:53-55).

Reflection: The western church has often taken the Mass for granted; we have been spared the persecutions that once tormented Eastern Europe and the former Soviet Union under Communism. The following story may help us change our perspective:

In 1956, news came through about one of Stalin's forced-labor camps in Siberia, by way of a Dr. Joseph

Scholmer, who had been a prisoner there. He said that four bishops, 700 priests, and 900 monks and nuns had been deported from Lithuania, as well as many lay Catholics. They worked in mines 600 feet below the ground, and Mass was often said down there by some priest dressed in his usual overalls.

The altar-hosts came by mail from Lithuania, allowed through as "Lithuanian bread," and the wine was from the Crimea. The miners had made a tiny silver chalice only one and one-quarter inches high. At Easter over 400 of the Lithuanian miners received their Easter communion hidden in tins of cigarettes which were being distributed. Each host, wrapped in a small piece of linen, was hidden under a top layer of cigarettes, and broken up for four communicants.

Application: Have you ever complained about attending Mass because of the weather, distance, or other reasons? Today, pray especially for a greater love for the sacrament.

MAY 11

Do not worry

Today the Blessed Virgin asks us not to worry:

> Pray! It may seem strange to you that I always speak of prayer, and yet I say: pray! Why do you hesitate? In sacred scripture you have heard the advice, "Do not worry about tomorrow; each day will have its own worries." Then do not worry about the other days as well. Be content with prayer. I, your Mother, will take care of the rest (LJM 2-29-84).

Jesus too asks us not to be anxious:

> He said to his disciples, "Therefore I tell you, do not worry about your life, what you will eat, or

about your body, what you will wear. For life is more than food, and the body more than clothing. Consider the ravens: they neither sow nor reap, they have neither storehouse nor barn, and yet God feeds them. Of how much more value are you than the birds!

"And can any of you by worrying add a single hour to your span of life? If then you are not able to do so small a thing as that, why do you worry about the rest?" (Lk 12:22-26).

Reflection: "Worry" is from an Anglo-Saxon word which means "harm," and is another form of the word "wolf." It bites and tears like a wolf mangling a sheep. Worry can paralyze helpful activity, obscure our vision, and distract us from prayer.

And so Our Lady echoes the words of Christ that we surrender our problems and worries to God. "Your Father," Jesus says, "knows all that you need. Seek first his Kingdom, and all these things will be given to you as well" (Lk 12:31).

Application: Today, surrender your cares and worries to the Lord so that his peace may take root in your heart.

MAY 12

The cross was in God's plan

Referring to the cross on Mt. Krizevac, Our Lady said:

Dear children, the cross was in God's plan when you built it. During these days especially, go up on the mountain and pray at the foot of the cross. I need your prayers (WM 8-30-84).

Of the cross, Our Lord said:

> He called the crowd with his disciples, and said to them, "If any want to become my followers, let them deny themselves and take up their cross and follow me. For those who want to save their life will lose it, and those who lose their life for my sake, and the sake of the gospel, will save it" (Mk 8:34-35).

Reflection: In one of the Nazi concentration camps of the Second World War, a Polish priest named Fr. Maximillian Kolbe was interred for publishing writings unfavorable to the Third Reich. On one occasion, several prisoners escaped from the compound and the camp commandant, to punish the prisoners, ordered ten of them to die through starvation.

Among the condemned prisoners was a young man who was known to have a wife and children. When the prisoners' numbers were called out, Fr. Kolbe stepped forward and insisted on taking the young man's place. Incarcerated in the death cell, he helped his companions prepare for death. Through the long days, the guards did not hear the usual sounds of pleading and anguish, but the subdued sounds of hymns and prayers. Fr. Kolbe was the last to die, and because he had taken so long, they injected him with poison.

After his death, a picture of Christ on the cross was found scratched with his nails on the wall of his death cell.

Application: In prayer today, reflect on the words of Christ: "Unless a grain of wheat falls to the earth and dies, it remains only a single grain; but if it dies, it bears much fruit" (Jn 12:24).

Carry peace to others

Today Our Lady gives a message of peace:

O children! I want you to live each new day with love and peace. I wish that you carry peace and love to others. People need these graces of love and peace so much, yet they lose them because they do not pray.

Create a permanent prayer in your hearts, for only then can you become vessels of the Lord. Through prayer your Father will mold you into the vessels he desires. Abandon yourselves to him so that he can do this (LJM 7-11-87).

In his first letter, Peter also speaks of peace:

Finally, all of you, have unity of spirit, sympathy, love for one another, a tender heart, and a humble mind. Do not repay evil for evil or abuse for abuse; but, on the contrary, repay with a peaceful blessing. It is for this that you were called—that you might inherit a blessing (1 Pt 3:8-9).

Reflection: The Blessed Virgin has often said in Medjugorje that peace must begin within the individual heart and spread outward from there. This is the message of a little story about a father who came home from work hoping to find some rest and quiet. But his young daughter kept pestering him. To keep her quiet, he cut out a map of the world from a newspaper and cut it up into pieces of different sizes. He then told her that he would give her a bar of chocolate when she had "put the world together." He hoped this would give him an hour of peace.

Five minutes later she came back telling him that the map was finished and was laid out on the floor. The father was surprised and asked, "How did you get it together so quickly?" "That was easy," she said, "I just turned the pieces over, and on the other side, I saw the picture of a man. When the man was put together right, the world was right."

Application: Today, pray for peace within your own heart, for only then can it spread outward.

MAY 14

God rules over all religions

The Mother of God speaks of ecumenism, or brotherhood, today. In answer to the question, "Are all religions good?" she responded:

All religions are similar before God. God rules over them just like a sovereign over his kingdom. In the world, all religions are not the same because people have not complied with the commandments of God. They reject and disparage them (FY 10-1-81).

In this same spirit, St. Paul calls us to be ambassadors of reconciliation among God's people:

All this is from God, who reconciled us to himself through Christ, and has given us the ministry of reconciliation; that is, in Christ, God was reconciling the world to himself, not counting their trespasses against them, and entrusting the message of reconciliation to us. So we are ambassadors for Christ, since God is making his appeal through us. . . (2 Cor 5:18-20).

Reflection: Both Our Lady and St. Paul call us to reconciliation with each other, both as individuals and as groups. Today the Gospa tells us that, "All religions are similar before God," although not the same. Her desire is that our common brotherhood unite all faiths, each respecting the other.

This is the spirit that underlies the story of the Grand Rabbi of Lyons, who was a Jewish chaplain to the French during World War I. One day, a wounded man staggered into a trench and told the Rabbi that a Roman Catholic was on the point of death in no man's land, and was begging that his priest should come to him with a crucifix.

The priest could not quickly be found. The Jew rapidly improvised a cross, ran out with it into no man's land, and was seen to hold it before the dying man's eyes. Almost immediately, he was shot by a sniper. The bodies of the Catholic and the Jew were found together.

Application: Today, pray especially for the unity of all God's children. If you ever have the opportunity to go to an ecumenical service (often held on special holidays), make a special effort to attend in response to Our Lady's message today.

MAY 15

Give them light

Today the Blessed Virgin calls us to light:

Dear children, you have all experienced light and darkness during your lives. God gives every person the power to recognize good and evil. I am calling you to light, which you must carry to all who are in darkness. From day to day, people who are in darkness come into your homes. You, dear children, must give them the light (WM 3-14-85).

As we see in John's gospel, Jesus himself is the light:

> Jesus said to them, "The light is with you a little longer. Walk while you have the light, so that the darkness may not overtake you. If you walk in the darkness, you do not know where you are going. While you have the light, believe in the light, so that you may become children of light" (Jn 12:35-36).

––––––––––––––

Reflection: There is a famous cave, some sixty miles from Auckland in New Zealand. It is known as the cave of the glowworms. You reach it in a boat which is pulled by a wire for silence. As you glide down the stream, you suddenly come across a soft light gleaming in the distance; then you enter a magic world. From the top of the cave, thousands of threads hang down from the glowing insects. So great is the light that it is possible to read a book there. But if there is the slightest noise, the bright light dies out, just as if a switch had been turned off.

The light of one committed Christian can illuminate not only his family, but also the parish and community in which he lives. Most of us have known someone like this; their kindness, unselfishness, and love have had a special effect on our lives. If you multiply such an individual several million times, you have a power which can enlighten an entire world. This is the reason why Our Lady came to Medjugorje, and why we have been asked to live her messages.

Application: Carry the light of faith and peace to all you meet today. May your example draw them closer to Christ.

Your first priority

The Blessed Mother reiterates her most important message:

Dear children, today I invite all of you to prayer. Without prayer, dear children, you will not be able to conceive of either God or myself, nor understand the graces which I am giving you. Therefore, I ask you to begin and end your day in prayer.

Dear children, I wish to lead you day after day toward prayer—as much as possible—but you will never grow if you do not want to. And so I exhort you, dear children, to make prayer your first priority (WM 7-3-86).

In Mark's gospel, Christ also calls us to prayer:

Jesus answered them, "Have faith in God. Truly I tell you, if you say to this mountain, 'Be taken up and thrown into the sea,' and if you do not doubt in your heart, but believe that what you say will come to pass, it will be done for you. So I tell you, whatever you ask for in prayer, believe that you have received it, and it will be yours" (Mk 11:22-24).

Reflection: The great mystic, Julian of Norwich, tells us that Christ showed himself to her in different ways. One was as an infant, born of the Blessed Virgin. Another was in his Passion, as he was dying on the cross. Another time, she saw him as if in a point, that is, his presence as Creator in everything, upholding it.

Once he showed himself as if on a pilgrimage, with himself in front leading all his people to heaven. At other times, he was pictured reigning as king. But the way he showed himself to her most often was as king reigning in the soul. "There he has fixed his resting place and his royal city: and out of this worshipful throne he shall never rise, nor forever move his dwelling place from there."

Sometimes we forget that the Lord is both within and without. Our prayer life can often be deepened with the realization that the divine presence abides in our very heart and soul. St. Teresa of Avila spoke of the spiritual journey as a journey inward to the deepest recesses of the soul, where God would be discovered in majesty. "Too few people," wrote Carl Jung, "have experienced the divine image as the innermost possession of their own souls. Christ only meets them from without, never from within, the soul."

Application: You are a living tabernacle of the divine presence. Today, direct your prayers to the God within.

MAY 17

Materialism is leading you into slavery

During Ivanka's apparition on her birthday in 1989, the Blessed Mother said:

> *Pray, for you are in great danger and temptation; the world and materialism are leading you into slavery. Satan is in the midst of this. I so want to help each of you in prayer. And I am interceding with my Son for you (SM 6-25-89).*

In Luke's gospel, Christ also warns us of materialism and possessiveness:

And he said to them, "Take care! Be on your guard against all kinds of greed; for one's life does not consist in the abundance of possessions."

Then he told them a parable: "The land of a rich man produced abundantly. And he thought to himself, 'What should I do, for I have no place to store my crops?' Then he said, 'I will do this: I will pull down my barns and build larger ones, and there I will store all my grain and my goods. And I will say . . . You have ample goods laid up for many years; relax, eat, drink, be merry.'

"But God said to him, 'You fool! This very night your life is being demanded of you. And the things you have prepared, whose will they be?' So it is with those who store up treasures for themselves but are not rich toward God" (Lk 12:15-21).

Reflection: On the triple doorway of the cathedral of Milan, there are three inscriptions spanning the towering arches. Over one is carved a beautiful wreath of roses, and underneath is the inscription, "All that pleases is but for a moment." Over the other is sculptured a cross, and these are the words beneath: "All that troubles is but for a moment." But underneath the great central entrance in the main aisle is the legend, "That only is important which is eternal."

This is the heart of Our Lady's message today. She urges us to focus our lives on what is truly important, and not on the material, which passes away. It is the gospel message reworded:

Therefore I tell you, do not worry about your life, what you will eat; or about your body, what you will wear. . . . Provide purses for yourselves that will not wear out, a treasure in heaven that will not be exhausted. . . . For where your treasure is, there your heart will be also (Lk 12:22, 33-34).

Application: Today, think of your most precious possessions; how much of your time do they occupy? Do your priorities need rearranging?

MAY 18

Read the sacred scriptures

Today the Blessed Mother urges that we read the Bible:

Dear children, on this great day which you have given me, I wish to bless all of you and say: these days that I am with you are days of grace.

I want to teach you and help you walk in the way of holiness. There are many people who do not want to understand my messages nor to seriously accept what I am saying. Therefore I call you to witness to my presence here through your lives—through your day-to-day living.

If you pray, God will help you discern the true reason for my coming. And so, little children, pray and read the sacred scriptures so that through the graces that have accompanied my coming, you can discern the messages in sacred scripture for you.

St. Paul also emphasizes the importance and power of scripture:

For I am not ashamed of the gospel; it is the power of God for salvation to everyone who has faith, to the Jew first and also to the Greek. In it the righteousness of God is revealed... (Rom 1:16-17).

Reflection: Mark Twain once wrote that, "Most people are bothered by those passages in scripture which they cannot understand; but as for me, I always noticed that the passages in scripture which trouble me most are those that I do understand."

The scriptures are indeed challenging, being much more than poetry and parables; they provide a whole new way of living based on our redemption through Jesus Christ. That is why the Blessed Mother urges us to read the Bible daily, for it reveals her Son to us in greater and greater depth. Thus St. Jerome could say: "To be ignorant of the scriptures is not to know Christ." And since he is the way, the truth, and the life, it is essential that we know him intimately.

Application: Today, take several minutes to reflect on the Parable of the Sower as found in Luke 8:4-15.

MAY 19

Put God first in your families

In December of 1991, the Blessed Mother spoke of love and the family:

Dear children, today in a special way I bring the infant Jesus to you, that he may bless you with peace and love. Dear children, do not forget that this is a grace which many people do not understand or accept.

Therefore, all of you who have said that you are mine and seek my help, give your entire self. First, be an example in your own families and give them your love. Since you say that Christmas is a family feast, then, dear children, put God first in your families; then he can give you peace and protect you not only from war, but also from Satan's attacks during peacetime.

When God is with you, you have everything. But when you do not want him, you are miserable and lost, for you do not know whose side you are on. And so, dear children, decide for God and then you will have everything (MM 12-25-91).

In Matthew's gospel, Jesus also spoke of the family, specifically, of marital fidelity and oneness:

> He answered, "Have you not read that the one who made them at the beginning 'made them male and female,' and said, 'For this reason a man shall leave his father and mother and be joined to his wife, and the two shall become one flesh?' So they are no longer two, but one flesh. Therefore what God has joined together, let no one separate" (Mt 19:4-6).

Reflection: "Success in marriage," wrote B. R. Brickner, "is more than finding the right person: it is a matter of being the right person."

The sacrament of marriage received special treatment from the fathers of Vatican II; some of the thoughts expressed were quite beautiful, including the following:

> Authentic married love is caught up into divine love, and is governed and enriched by Christ's redeeming love. . . .
>
> Such love, merging the human with the divine, leads the spouses to a free and mutual gift of themselves, a gift proving itself by gentle affection and by deed. Such love pervades the whole of their lives. Indeed, by its generous activity, it grows better and grows greater. . . .
>
> Sealed by mutual faithfulness and hallowed above all by Christ's sacrament, this love remains steadfastly true in body and in mind, in bright days or dark. . . (*The Church Today*, 48-49).

Application: Today, pray especially for married couples and, if you are married, for your spouse. This evening, offer a prayer together for God's continued blessings on your family.

MAY 20

Testify with your lives

In May of 1991, Our Lady called us to live her messages as an example to others:

Dear children, to those who have heard my message of peace, I ask that you take it seriously and live it lovingly in your life. There are many who think they are doing a lot by simply talking about the messages, but are not actually living them. Dear children, I invite you to life, to change all the negativism in you to the positive.

Dear children, I am with you and I want to help each of you to live so as to testify with your lives to the Good News. I am here, dear children, to help you and to lead you to heaven; the joy of heaven can be lived even now on earth (MM 5-25-91).

Paul urges us as well to be examples of the Christian faith:

Show yourself in all respects a model of good works, and in your teaching show integrity, gravity, and sound speech that cannot be censured; then any opponent will be put to shame, having nothing evil to say of us (Ti 2:7-8).

Reflection: Our readings today reflect an ancient truth of Christianity—that it is normally by example, not words, that the faith spreads. In this vein, the nineteenth-century English novelist Charles Kingsley once wrote:

One good man—one man who does not put on his religion once a week with his Sunday suit, but wears it for his working dress, and lets the thought of God grow into him, and through and through him, till everything he says and does becomes religious—that man is worth a thousand sermons. He is a living gospel—he is the image of God.

Application: In her message today, the Madonna states that, "I want to help each of you to live so as to testify with your lives to the Good News." Ask Our Lady's help today in doing just that.

MAY 21

Change your hearts

The Mother of God speaks of conversion today:

> *Dear children, today I ask you to begin working on your hearts as you have been working in the fields. Work and change your hearts so that the new Spirit of God can dwell in them (WM 4-25-85).*

Christ speaks of conversion as a "new birth" through water and the Spirit:

> Jesus answered him, "Very truly, I tell you, no one can see the kingdom of God without being born from above."
>
> Nicodemus said to him, "How can anyone be born after having grown old? Can one enter a second time into the mother's womb and be born?" Jesus answered, "Very truly, I tell you, no one can enter the kingdom of God without being born of water and the Spirit. What is born of the flesh is flesh, and what is born of the Spirit is spirit" (Jn 3:3-6).

Reflection: What did Nicodemus know about the kingdom? From scripture he knew it would be ruled by God, it would be restored on earth, and it would incorporate God's people. Christ revealed to this devout pharisee that the kingdom would come to the whole world, not just to the Jews, and that Nicodemus would not be a part of it unless he was personally born again.

This was a revolutionary concept; the kingdom was personal, not national or ethnic, and its entrance requirements were *conversion* and *spiritual rebirth*.

Christ also taught that God's kingdom had already begun in the hearts of believers through the presence of the Holy Spirit. It will be fully realized when he returns again and abolishes evil forever.

Application: Today Our Lady calls us to: "Work and change your hearts so that the new Spirit of God can dwell in them." Let us pray for the insight and grace to do just that.

MAY 22

Consecrate yourselves to the cross

The Virgin speaks of the cross today:

Pray before the cross, for special graces come from it. Consecrate yourselves to the cross and do not blaspheme either Jesus or the cross (SM 6-20-86).

And from Luke's gospel, Christ gives his life for us upon the cross:

It was now about noon, and darkness came over the whole land until three in the afternoon, while the sun's light failed; and the curtain of the temple was torn in two. Then Jesus, crying with a loud voice, said, "Father, into your hands I commend my spirit." Having said this, he breathed his last (Lk 23:44-46).

Reflection: Darkness covered the whole land for three hours at midday. All nature seemed to mourn over the stark tragedy of the death of the Son of God. In the midst of this darkness, the curtain in the Temple, separating the holy of holies from the holy place, was torn in two, an event which symbolized the meaning of the cross.

The Temple had three parts: the courtyard area; the holy place, where only priests could enter; and the holy of holies, where the high priest alone could enter once a year to atone for the sins of the people.

It was in the holy of holies that the Ark of the Covenant, the symbol of God's presence, rested. The curtain that split was the one that closed off the holy of holies from view. At Christ's death, the barrier between God and man was torn apart. Now all people are able to approach God directly through Christ.

Application: Our Lady asks us to, "Pray before the cross . . . consecrate yourselves to the cross." Today, with a crucifix in your hands, make this consecration.

MAY 23

The hour of Satan

Our Lady gives us a somber message today:

The hour has come when the demon is authorized to act with all his force and power. The present hour is the hour of Satan (FY 84-85).

As we see in scripture, evil often attacks those dearest to the Lord:

When Herod saw that he had been tricked by the wise men, he was infuriated, and he sent [for] and killed all the children in and around Bethlehem who were two years old or under, according to the time that he had learned from the wise men (Mt 2:16).

Reflection: "This is the hour of Satan," Our Lady warns us. Certainly he has held sway over the last century, which can claim two devastating world wars, the Nazi holocaust, the agonizing rise and spread of Communism, and the wars in Korea, Asia, and the Middle East, to mention only several. It has been the bloodiest century of mankind's history, despite its scientific and material progress.

The hour of Satan also speaks of his relentless attacks on the individual, including the explosion of addictive diseases, thoughtless materialism, an unprecedented crime rate, AIDS, a skyrocketing divorce rate, and an array of other tragedies.

The Blessed Mother wants us to know what we are battling, that Satan attacks the weakest link in both society and the individual, and that his ultimate goal is simply destruction. But she also gives us the weapons to fight the Evil One: conversion, faith, and prayer, the sacraments, and the rosary. To be forewarned is to be forearmed.

Application: The power of Satan has peaked. Since our chief weapon in his demise is prayer, let us add this to our daily prayer intentions, beginning today.

MAY 24

Give time to the rosary

Our Lady speaks of a favorite subject today:

I urge you to ask everyone to pray the rosary. With the rosary you will overcome all the troubles which Satan is trying to inflict on the Catholic church. Let all priests pray the rosary. Give time to the rosary (SM 6-25-85).

St. Paul also speaks of prayer in his letter to the Romans:

Likewise the Spirit helps us in our weakness; for we do not know how to pray as we ought, but that very Spirit intercedes with sighs too deep for words. And God, who searches hearts, knows what the Spirit is saying, for the Spirit intercedes for the saints according to the will of God (Rom 8:26-27).

Reflection: Fr. Albert Shamon tells a unique story of the rosary, revolving around Dr. Carlos Finlay, the Cuban physician who discovered that yellow fever and malaria were carried by the mosquito. Returning home one night, exhausted after a long day's work, he remembered that he had not yet said his rosary, which was a daily devotion for him. So he began to pray, sleepy though he was, but he was distracted by a buzzing mosquito flying persistently around his head.

At that moment, as if inspired by the Virgin, the idea occurred to him that it may be the mosquito which transmits yellow fever and malaria. He began to experiment with this theory and proved that it was indeed correct, ending a century of research into the cause of these dreaded diseases.

Application: Today, simply take the advice of Our Lady to heart: "I urge you to ask everyone to pray the rosary. . . . Give time to the rosary."

MAY 25

A springtime message

The Madonna speaks today of nature, of love, and of surrender to God:

Dear children, I am calling you to open to God. You see, little children, how nature is opening herself and is giving life and fruit. In the same way, I am calling you to a life with God and complete surrender to him.

Little children, I am with you, and unceasingly I desire to lead you to the joy of life. I desire that each of you discover the joy and the love which is found only in God, and which only God can give.

God wants nothing else from you but your surrender. Therefore, little children, decide seriously for God because everything passes away. God alone does not.

Pray that you may discover the greatness and the joy of life which God is giving you (MM 5-25-89).

The author of Psalm 104 also speaks of the fruits of nature and the joy of life, so lovingly bestowed by the Father:

You make springs gush forth in the valleys;
they flow between the hills,
giving drink to every wild animal;
the wild asses quench their thirst.

O Lord, how manifold are your works!
In wisdom you have made them all;
the earth is full of your creatures.

When you send forth your spirit, they are created;
and you renew the face of the ground.

—Psalm 104:10-11; 24, 30

Reflection: In this springtime message of Our Lady, she outlines a three-stage journey that she hopes we will make. We begin with "an openness to God," as she says, and so are able to receive the grace and strength we need to actually begin living as followers of Christ. Second, having experienced the power of the Lord in our lives, we are drawn to surrender ourselves more and more to him. And third, in this new relationship of trusting surrender, we gradually discover through prayer "the greatness and the joy of life which God is giving [us]."

How appropriate that the Blessed Virgin chose the springtime to speak of new life in Christ: "You see, little children, how nature is opening herself and is giving life and fruit. In the same way I am calling you to open to God . . . that I may lead you into the joy of life. . . ." May the song of nature inspire us to a greater openness to God, that we too may sing for joy.

Application: Try to spend some quiet time outdoors today to experience the beauty of God in nature—part of the "joy of life" of which the Virgin speaks.

MAY 26

St. Philip Neri

During a locution to Jelena, the Madonna gave this advice:

Dear children, open your hearts and let Jesus guide you. For many people it seems to be hard, but it is really so easy! You don't have to be afraid because you know that

*Jesus will never leave you, and you know that he leads
you to salvation (LJM 8-11-86).*

The psalmist also speaks of God's guidance:

Then he led out his people like sheep,
and guided them in the wilderness like a flock.
He led them in safety, so that they were not afraid;
but the sea overwhelmed their enemies.
With upright heart he tended them,
and guided them with skillful hand.

—Psalm 78:52-53, 72

Reflection: Since his early youth, St. Philip Neri allowed Christ to guide him with a free hand. Love of others, simplicity of life,and joyous service to God would accurately describe his life and spirit. A priest and friend of the young, Philip also had a great love for the sick and the poor, sharing their lot in order to be close to them in the streets of Rome.

His street ministry also included the unemployed, the homeless, the shopkeepers, and especially wayward young people. He worked to help them improve themselves materially and to appreciate the spiritual as well. After a busy day on the streets, he very often spent the night in prayer.

His spirit of joyful service inspired the priests who joined him in the Congregation of the Oratory, which he founded in 1564. His eye was always on Christ, who he said guided each step of his life. He once wrote:

If you wish for something apart from Christ, you do not know what you are wishing for. If you long for something apart from Christ, you do not know what you are longing for. If you work apart from Christ, you do not know what you are doing.

Application: "Open your hearts," Our Lady says today, "and let Jesus guide you. . . . You don't have to be afraid because you know that Jesus will never leave you." In prayer today, let us open our hearts as the Virgin requests, asking for Christ's guidance during the next twenty-four hours.

MAY 27

Especially you, the youngest

The following was given to Ivan's prayer group on Mt. Podbrdo in July of 1990:

Dear children, tonight your Mother would like to invite you again to prayer. Especially you, the youngest, who will be here in large numbers during these days. I call you to prayer.

Pray, pray, pray, and renew your hearts so you can accept all that I tell you in my messages. Thank you, dear children, for you make me happy by your prayers (VPG 7-30-90).

St. John also affirms the young:

I write to you, children,
because you know the Father.
I write to you, fathers,
because you know him who is from the beginning.
I write to you, young people,
because you are strong
and the word of God abides in you,
and you have overcome the evil one.

—1 John 2:14

Reflection: Two fifteen-year-old boys alarmed on-lookers in Norfolk, Virginia, who watched them drift down the forty-foot-deep Elizabeth River on a makeshift raft. It was a 3x6 foot mortar box used by brickmasons. The Coast Guard finally rescued them as they were floating toward the open ocean in their unseaworthy craft.

Young people are blessed with a daring and adventurous spirit. But it is important that their enthusiasm and resourcefulness be wisely directed. At the same time, great care must be taken not to suppress their spirit and potential.

The Lord himself encouraged his apostles to "launch out into the deep" as fishers of men. But at the same time he made sure they were rooted in divine truth and love. Through prayer and example, we can help young people to be daring in faith and in living the messages of Our Lady.

Application: In prayer today, call to mind the young people of your own family as well as others that you know. Commend them to the Blessed Mother that she may renew their hearts and help them to live her messages. Also today, be especially conscious of your example of faith to the young people around you.

MAY 28

Live love

Our Lady speaks of love today:

Dear children, I wish to thank you for all your sacrifices and I also call you to the greatest sacrifice, the sacrifice of love. Without love, you will be unable to accept either me or my Son. Without love, you will not be able to convey your experiences to others. Therefore, dear children, live love within your hearts (WM 3-27-86).

And from St. John's first letter, a famous passage on love:

> Beloved, let us love one another, because love is from God. Whoever does not love does not know God, for God is love. God's love was revealed among us in this way: God sent his only Son into the world so that we might live through him.
>
> In this is love, not that we loved God, but that he loved us and sent his Son to be the atoning sacrifice for our sins. Beloved, since God loved us so much, we also ought to love one another. No one has ever seen God; if we love one another, God lives in us, and his love is perfected in us (1 Jn 4:7-12).

Reflection: Love can do the impossible. The *New York Times* once ran a story of a crippled woman leaving her crutches and running up a flight of stairs to rescue her three-year-old daughter, when fire threatened to trap the child in an upstairs bedroom. The mother, injured in a car crash two years previously, had been unable to walk without crutches ever since the accident. Realizing that the life of her little daughter was at stake, she momentarily forgot her own physical handicap. She rushed to the upper floor, grabbed the sleeping child and carried her to safety.

For most of us, there are times when our capacity to love is obstructed by self-concern, worry, or a flagging faith. In such a case, the Blessed Mother recommends that we surrender these obstacles to her Son and, through prayer, seek the gift of divine love with a sincere heart.

Application: Today, reflect prayerfully on John's full discourse on love (1 Jn 4:7-21), and then ask the Lord to instill this love within your heart.

MAY 29

Witness to this peace

The Blessed Mother speaks of peace today:

> *Dear children, God has permitted me, in union with him, to found this oasis of peace. I call you to protect it. Through their indifference, some people destroy prayer and peace. And so I beseech you, witness to this peace by your lives, that it may be preserved (WM 6-26-86).*

And in Isaiah, the Lord promises a covenant of peace:

> For the mountains may depart,
> and the hills be removed,
> but my steadfast love shall not depart from you,
> and my covenant of peace shall not be removed,
> says the Lord, who has compassion on you.
>
> —Isaiah 54:10

Reflection: Sometimes a story of men living peace is more valuable than words about peace. F. H. Drinkwater tells such a story, set in Italy during World War II.

In the mountain village of Giazza, north of Verona, German paratroopers were going to execute some villagers, presumably for showing resistance. The parish priest, Fr. Domenico Mercante, offered himself as a hostage. The German accepted his offer, and decided to shoot him. When the time came, one of the firing-party refused to obey orders. "I can't shoot a priest," he said.

He was placed at the priest's side, and both were shot together. The soldier's name is unknown.

Fifteen years later, the Bishop of Verona unveiled a simple white monument commemorating the two heroes. The German embassy in Rome was represented, and the Italian Minister of Justice gave an address. He said, "The example of a priest and a soldier dying by the same rifle fire, in order that not only the written law but the unwritten law too should be respected, provides an example of great moral value. It gives rise to the hope that the cause of peace may find its strongest protection in the conscience of humble but heroic spirits."

Application: Jesus and Our Lady both call us to live peace and pray for peace. Today, pray especially for peace, and strive to be a peacemaker this week within your family, at your workplace, and among your friends.

MAY 30

Memorial Day

In December of 1990, the Blessed Mother spoke of peace:

Dear children, today I invite you to pray especially for peace. Dear children, without peace you cannot experience the birth of the infant Jesus either today nor in your daily lives.

Therefore, pray to the Lord of Peace that he may protect you with his mantle and help you to comprehend the great importance of having peace in your hearts. In this way you will be able to spread peace in hearts around the whole world. I am with you and intercede for you before God.

Pray, for Satan wants to destroy my plans for peace. Be reconciled with one another and, through your lives, help peace to reign over the whole earth (MM 12-25-90).

The psalmist voices a prayer for peace:

Show us your steadfast love, O Lord,
and grant us your salvation.
Let me hear what God the Lord will speak,
for he will speak peace to his people,
to his faithful, to those who turn to him in
their hearts.

—Psalm 85:7-8

Reflection: On this Memorial Day, it is appropriate that we have heard Our Lady speak again of peace, for this is the cause for which so many of our countrymen have given their lives. Their courage and sacrifice have led us closer to that time when, as Isaiah says, "nation shall not lift up sword against nation, neither shall they learn war any more."

Application: In memory and in appreciation of all those who gave their lives for freedom, democracy and peace, let us offer the following prayer today:

Lord Jesus Christ, today we honor the memory of those men and women who have given their lives for America in the cause of freedom. They have worked, fought, and died for the heritage of freedom, brotherhood, and peace that they have passed on to us.

In scripture you said to us: "Greater love than this no man has: that he lay down his life for his friends." We recall that you yourself gave up your life for all people in the cause of true freedom—to save us from sin and selfishness.

As we remember our honored dead, teach us to appreciate the virtue of patriotism—a true and Christian love of country. May we love this Land of the Free and seek to make it a land of goodness, refuge, and equality for all Americans. We place our nation unreservedly in your hands, for in you we hope and trust. Amen.

MAY 31

Feast of the Visitation

As she bore Jesus in her womb when visiting Elizabeth, so Our Lady wishes to bear us to her Son:

Dear children, I am with you even if you are not conscious of it. I want to protect you from everything that Satan offers you, and through which he wants to destroy you. As I bore Jesus in my womb, so also, dear children, do I wish to bear you into holiness.

God wants to save you and sends you messages through men, nature, and so many things, which can only help you to understand that you must change the direction of your life.

Therefore, little children, understand the greatness of the gift which God is giving you through me, so that I may protect you with my mantle and lead you to the joy of life (MM 3-25-90).

And from Luke's gospel, the story of the Visitation:

In those days Mary set out and went with haste to a Judean town in the hill country, where she entered the house of Zechariah and greeted Elizabeth.

When Elizabeth heard Mary's greeting, the child leaped in her womb. And Elizabeth was filled with the Holy Spirit and exclaimed with a loud cry, "Blessed are you among women, and blessed is the fruit of your womb. And why has this happened to me, that the mother of my Lord comes to me? For as soon as I heard the sound of your greeting, the child in my womb leaped for joy. And blessed is she who believed that there would be a fulfillment of what was spoken to her by the Lord" (Lk 1:39-45).

———————

Reflection: On this feast of the Visitation, celebrated as the second joyful mystery of the rosary, Our Lady states that "as I bore Jesus in my womb, so also, dear children, do I wish to bear you unto holiness." Here Mary draws a beautiful parallel: just as she carried the unborn Jesus to her cousin Elizabeth, so she wishes to bear each of us, safe and protected, to holiness—to intimacy with God.

Her cousin was deeply aware of the greatness of the gift that Mary bore: "blessed is the fruit of your womb." In a like fashion, Our Lady asks us today "to understand the greatness of the gift God is giving you through me"—the gift of Medjugorje: the extraordinary graces, the messages which have changed the world, and the gift of her presence among us for so many years.

Application: The spirit of gratitude is the theme of Mary's message today. In prayer, reflect on the great gifts Our Lady has given us through Medjugorje. Offer the Joyful Mysteries in thanksgiving.

To become priests and religious

Our Lady expresses her high regard for the priesthood and religious life, and for our free will:

> I would like all of you to become priests and religious, but only if you desire it. You are free. It is up to you to choose (FY 12-8-81).

And in his letter to Timothy, Paul calls for appreciation and support of the local church leaders (elders):

> Let the elders who rule well be considered worthy of the double honor especially those who labor in preaching and teaching. Never accept any accusation against an elder except on the evidence of two or three witnesses (1 Tm 5:17, 19).

Reflection: In answering questions from the visionaries about their futures, it is significant that the Virgin would first recommend the priesthood and religious life. Her esteem for these vocations is shared by St. Paul, who called on the early church to support and encourage their leaders.

It's not surprising, then, that the priesthood is a special target of the Evil One. No greater damage can be done to the church than to injure its shepherds. Add to this the apathy and secularism of many Catholics, and it is not hard to understand the discouragement of some priests and the subsequent clergy shortage.

But there are reasons for hope. Medjugorje and the Marian and charismatic movements have been producing scores of vocations and deepening the spiritual lives of many Catholics, brightening the horizon of the church as she enters the twenty-first century.

Application: Here are a few ways you can buoy the priesthood in your own area through the support and encouragement of your parish priest:

- Simply befriend your local priest; be positive and supportive rather than critical and discouraging.
- Greet your parish priest after Mass; if you liked his homily, be sure to tell him so.
- Send him a little note or greeting card at Christmas and Easter, perhaps with a gift.
- Our Lady once said, "Do not judge the priest." Gossip or slander, like any other sin, should be avoided.
- Remember that priests are human beings. Like everyone they have strengths and weaknesses, virtues and foibles. Be as accepting and supportive of them as you would of any friend.

JUNE 2

Pray and fast

In January of 1984, Jelena received the following locution:

Pray and fast. For those who want to make a special sacrifice, fast up to three times a week at the most, but do not prolong it further (LJM 1-22-84).

Jesus also advises his followers on fasting:

And whenever you fast, do not look dismal, like the hypocrites, for they disfigure their faces so as to show others that they are fasting. Truly I tell you, they have received their reward. But when you fast, put oil on your head and wash your face, so that your fasting may be seen not by others but by your Father who is in secret; and your Father who sees in secret will reward you (Mt 6:16-18).

Reflection: A fruitful fast often depends on the right attitude at the beginning. Here, then, is a condensed version of a prayer for just that purpose, written by Fr. Slavko Barbaric, spiritual director to the visionaries.

Loving Father, today I have decided to fast. I can remember that your prophets of old fasted, that Jesus our Lord fasted, as did his disciples. The Blessed Virgin also fasted and has called me as well. Eternal Father, I offer this day of fasting to you. May it draw me closer to you, teach me your ways, and open my eyes to see your many gifts. May love for you and for my neighbor fill my heart to overflowing.

Lord, may this fast help me to grow in understanding the hungry, the deprived, the poor. Let me see my possessions as gifts for the journey meant to be shared. Grant also to me the grace of humility and the strength to do your will.

Lord, may this fast cleanse me of bad habits, calm my passions, and increase your virtues within me. And may you, Mother Mary, obtain for me the grace of a joyful fast, that my heart may sing with you a song of thanksgiving. I place my decision to fast firmly in your hands. Teach me through fasting to be more and more like your Son, Jesus Christ, through the Holy Spirit. Amen.

Application: Use Fr. Slavko's prayer on the morning of your next several fast days.

Read the Bible

Today the Blessed Mother speaks of sacred scripture:

Dear children, today I ask you to read the Bible in your homes every day. Put it in a visible place where it will always remind you to read it and pray it (WM 10-18-84).

St. Paul also speaks of the value of scripture:

All scripture is inspired by God and is useful for teaching, for reproof, for correction, and for training in righteousness, so that everyone who belongs to God may be proficient, equipped for every good work (2 Tm 3:16-17).

Reflection: A record price of two million dollars was paid recently for a copy of the Latin gospels, dated 997. The book, originally printed in Germany, is 9 x 6½ inches long and consists of 168 parchment pages illustrated with colorful scenes from scripture.

Those who place such value on works of art could gain far richer treasure if they were to become as motivated to study the scriptures as were the monks who adorned them so beautifully. The original artists devoted painstaking effort to the long and arduous task of copying the gospels by hand and embellishing the margins. They were sparked by the ardent desire to glorify God and to remind their fellow men and women of the lasting beauty of his inspired word.

Application: Today let us simply take Our Lady's advice to, "read the Bible every day in your homes, and let it be in a visible place so as to always encourage you to read it and pray."

JUNE 4

I call you to humility

The Blessed Mother calls us to humility today:

> *Dear children, today I call you to humility. These days you have felt great joy because of all the people who have come here, and to whom you have spoken with love about your experiences. With humility and an open heart, continue to speak with all who are coming (WM 6-27-85).*

Jesus also speaks of humility, of becoming children in the hands of God:

> At that time the disciples came to Jesus and asked, "Who is the greatest in the kingdom of heaven?" He called a child, whom he put among them, and said, "Truly I tell you, unless you change and become like children, you will never enter the kingdom of heaven. Whoever becomes humble like this child is the greatest in the kingdom of heaven" (Mt 18:1-4).

Reflection: Christ points to the characteristics of a child to help his self-centered disciples get the message. We are not to be *childish* (like the disciples, arguing over petty issues), but rather *childlike*, with humble and sincere hearts.

The disciples had become so preoccupied with the organization of Jesus' earthly kingdom, they had lost sight of its divine purpose. Instead of seeking a place of service, they sought positions of advantage. How easy it is to lose our eternal perspective and to seek to fulfill our own ambitions. How hard it is to identify with little children, humble and dependent people with little status or influence.

Application: Thoreau once wrote, "Humility like darkness reveals the heavenly lights." Today as Our Lady asks, pray for this virtue which deepens our trust and peace.

JUNE 5

Be reconciled

The Virgin today speaks of reconciliation and unity:

> *Pray, because I need more prayers. Be reconciled, for I desire reconciliation among you and a greater love for each other, like brothers. It is my wish that prayer, peace, and love blossom within you (LJM 2-2-84).*

St. Paul calls for unity and reconciliation within the church at Corinth:

> I have applied all this to Apollos and myself for your benefit, brothers and sisters, so that you may learn through us the meaning of the saying, "Nothing beyond what is written," so that none of you will be puffed up in favor of one against another. For who sees anything different in you? What do you have that you did not receive? And if you received it, why do you boast as if it were not a gift (1 Cor 4:6-7).

Reflection: Both Paul and Our Lady call us to unity and a non-judgmental attitude toward others. We may be tempted to judge a fellow Christian, evaluating whether he or she is a worthy follower of Christ. But only God knows a person's heart, as Paul stresses today, and he is the only one who has the right to judge.

The Corinthians, to whom Paul was writing, had split into various factions, each following its own spiritual leader. Each clique believed it was the only one that had the whole truth, and was proud of it. Paul chided them for their arrogance and emphasized that they were all humble servants of the Lord, simple messengers of the gospel of Jesus Christ. His exhortation was like that of Our Lady's today: "Be reconciled, because I desire reconciliation among you, and more love for each other, like brothers."

Application: Sometimes friction or rivalries can develop among various parish groups, organizations, or individuals. Today, make a commitment to the Lord to be a peacemaker within your home parish. Pray that all will be united in the service and love of Christ.

JUNE 6

The Devil tries to impose his power

In the first months of the apparitions, Our Lady spoke of Satan:

The Devil tries to impose his power on you, but you must remain strong and persevere in your faith. You must pray and fast. I will always be close to you (FY 11-81).

And in John's gospel, Jesus also speaks of the Evil One:

You are from your father the devil, and you choose to do your father's desires. He was a murderer from the beginning and does not stand in the truth, because there is no truth in him. When he lies, he speaks according to his own nature, for he is a liar and the father of lies (Jn 8:44).

Reflection: Satan normally tries to work in a covert manner, but at times he can be clearly recognized because of the intensity of the evil. Our Lady says that he has been especially active during this century; his presence dominated the war years and such abhorrent places as concentration camps. Here he reigned supreme amid the slave labor and gas chambers.

In my visit to Dachau in 1992, I could still discern his shadow, like so many others, in the crematoriums, the watch towers, the mass graves. During the war the Dachau prisoners were hired out and full use was made of them in the armaments industry, always under strong guard. In the office of the Dachau commandant, the Allies found an incredible document that estimated the profit that could be made from each worker. It read as follows:

Average daily amount for loan of prisoner	6.00 Marks
Deduction for food	-.60
Deduction for use of clothes	<u>-.10</u>
	5.30 Marks
Average duration of life:	9 months
270 days x 5.30 Marks =	1,431 Marks
Proceeds from rational disposal of corpse:	
1. Gold teeth, 2. Clothes, 3. Valuables	202.00 Marks
Deduction for the costs of cremation	-2.00
Average net profit	<u>200.00</u>
Total profit after 9 months	1,631.00 Marks
Plus proceeds from the utilization of bones and ashes	

I would have liked to think that such evil and violence was part of history now. But on the drive back to Medjugorje, we passed through the Croatian city of Zoar, where the buildings were riddled with machine-gun and mortar fire from the federal army.

Our Lady's emphasis on the reality of Satan is not meant to frighten us, but to protect us. Our armor is the gospel and her messages.

Application: Today, pray especially for the innocent victims of evil and for the grace to recognize Satan and his works.

JUNE 7

Love each other

The Madonna speaks of loving one another:

> *Dear children, thank you for every prayer. Try to pray continuously, and do not forget that I love you and that I desire all of you to love each other (LJM 5-26-84).*

One of the fruits of love is reconciliation. In his letter to Philemon, Paul acts as a reconciler between this wealthy Christian and his runaway slave, Onesimus:

> For this reason, though I am bold enough in Christ to command you to do your duty, yet I would rather appeal to you on the basis of love—and I, Paul, do this as an old man, and now also a prisoner of Christ Jesus. I am appealing to you for my child, Onesimus, whose father I have become during my imprisonment. . . .
>
> So if you consider me your partner, welcome him as you would welcome me. If he has wronged you in any way, or owes you anything, charge that to my account (Phlm 1:8-10, 17-18).

Reflection: According to Fr. Slavko Barbaric, reconciliation is a fundamental process that God intends every soul to experience. It is a means of freeing oneself from inner ties and chains, of tearing down the walls and barriers that we have erected through sin and hate.

"Reconciliation means simply accepting oneself and others as we are," he says, "and starting where we are now to tear down the walls that separate us from God and one another."

He continues, "Reconciliation also means to let go of hasty judgments of one another and to accept that we are all weak and limited in many ways." It means to deeply experience our common origin from God, that we are truly one in him.

Application: This week, make an overture to someone you have resented or disliked in the past. Ask Our Lady to be with you during this encounter.

JUNE 8

Testify through your lives

The Gospa speaks of living the messages of Medjugorje:

> *Dear children, today I invite you to live in humility all the messages which I have given you. Do not become arrogant in living the messages and boast that, "I am living the messages."*
>
> *If you live and bear my messages with your heart, everyone will sense it so that words, which serve only those who do not obey, will not be necessary. For you, dear children, it is necessary to testify through your lives (WM 9-20-85).*

Paul also expresses concern about those who merely speak of faith, but do not live it:

> But I will come to you soon, if the Lord wills, and I will find out not the talk of these arrogant people but their power. For the kingdom of God depends not on talk but on power (1 Cor 4:19-20).

Reflection: We have all met people who have talked a lot about faith, but that was all it was—talk. They may know all the right words to say, but their lives are not examples of Christian living. Today Paul says that the kingdom of God is to be lived, not just discussed. There is a big difference between knowing the right words and living them out.

This is the message of Our Lady as well: "It is necessary to live and testify by your lives."

Application: Today, pray simply for the grace to "live in humility all the messages which I have given you."

JUNE 9

Abandon your concerns to Jesus

Today the Blessed Mother asks us to abandon our worries to her Son:

> *Why do you not put your trust in me? I know that you have been praying for a long time, but truly, surrender yourself. Abandon your concerns to Jesus. Listen to what he says in the gospel: "And who among you, through his anxiety, is able to add a single cubit to the length of his life?" (LJM 10-30-83).*

In Psalm 37, trust is seen as the remedy to anxiety:

> Trust in the Lord, and do good;
> so you will live in the land, and enjoy security.
> Take delight in the Lord,
> and he will give you the desires of your heart.
> Our steps are made firm by the Lord,
> when he delights in our way;
> Though we stumble, we shall not fall headlong,
> for the Lord holds us by the hand.
> —Psalm 37:3-4, 23-24

Reflection: The confident trust that the psalmist and Our Lady speak of today is a sister virtue to acceptance. For some, such as members of Alcoholics Anonymous, the spirit of acceptance can be a life and death matter, for it is an indispensable tool in their recovery.

In chapter 17 of Alcoholics Anonymous' *Big Book*, a physician in the program writes:

> At last, acceptance proved to be the key to my drinking problem . . . to *all* my problems today. When I am disturbed, it's because I find some person, place, thing, or situation—some fact of my life—unacceptable to me, and I can find no serenity *until I accept that person, place, thing, or situation as being exactly the way it is supposed to be at this moment.*
>
> Nothing, absolutely nothing happens in God's world by mistake. Until I could accept my alcoholism, I could not stay sober; unless I accept life completely on life's terms, I cannot be happy.
>
> I need to concentrate not so much on what needs to be changed in the world as on what needs to be changed in me and in my attitudes.

With hard-won insight, the doctor speaks of his peace, or serenity, as inversely proportional to his expectations. The higher his expectations of other people are, the lower his serenity. "I can watch my serenity level rise," he says, "when I discard my expectations."

Application: First, as Our Lady asks, abandon your anxieties and fear to her today, trusting in her great power. Second, as they do in A.A. meetings around the world, offer the Serenity Prayer. Keep it in mind for troubling times.

O Lord, grant me the serenity to accept the things
I cannot change; the courage to change the things
I can; and the wisdom to know the difference.

JUNE 10

The gift of love

Today Our Lady speaks of our greatest need:

*Love is a gift from God. Pray, then, that God may give
you the gift of love (LJM 5-28-84).*

St. Paul remarks on the love of the Colossians:

This you learned from Epaphras, our beloved fellow servant. He is a faithful minister of Christ on
your behalf, and he has made known to us your
love in the Spirit (Col 1:7-8).

Reflection: The Colossians had such a great love for
others because the Holy Spirit had transformed their
lives. The ability to love our neighbor as Christ loves us
comes through the grace of the Spirit. Scripture speaks
of love as an action or attitude, not just an emotion; it is
the fruit of our new life in Christ.

The Holy Spirit not only empowers us to love others,
but also to recognize how much we are loved by God
and the Blessed Mother. "You know, dear children, that
I love you immeasurably," the Madonna once said, "and
each day I pray that the Lord will help you to understand the love I give you." When we comprehend that
love, we cannot help but turn around and love others
in return.

Application: Since love is a pure gift from the Lord, the
Virgin asks us to, "pray that God may give you the gift to
love." Today, let us devote our rosary to that intention.

JUNE 11

I want you to be happy

Today Our Lady gives us her purpose in coming to Medjugorje:

Dear children, I call each of you to begin to live in God's love. Dear children, you are ready to commit sin and to place yourselves in Satan's hands without reflection. I call on each one of you to consciously choose God and to reject Satan.

I am your Mother and so I wish to lead all of you to complete holiness. I want you to be happy on earth and then to join me in heaven. This is, dear children, my purpose in coming here, and my desire (MM 5-25-87).

St. Paul also speaks of the happiness which is ours as heirs of Christ:

When we cry, "Abba! Father!" it is that very Spirit bearing witness with our spirit that we are children of God, and if children, then heirs, heirs of God and joint heirs with Christ—if, in fact we suffer with him so that we may also be glorified with him (Rom 8:16-17).

Reflection: Paul uses the term adoption to illustrate the believers' new relationship with God. In Roman culture, one who was adopted gained all the rights of a legitimate child in his new family. He became a full heir to his father's estate. Likewise, when a person becomes a Christian, he or she gains all the privileges and responsibilities of a child in God's family. As the Creator's children we are no longer slaves. This is the core of the gospel message and the messages of Our Lady in Medjugorje: we are God's heirs, sharing in the great treasures of his kingdom. Even now he has given us the greatest of gifts: his Son, forgiveness, the Holy Spirit, and eternal life.

Application: The Blessed Mother states that, "I want each one of you to be happy here on earth and to be with me in heaven." That is her purpose and her desire. She asks only that we, *"consciously* choose God and reject Satan." In your own words make this commitment today in prayer.

JUNE 12

Enter into the Mass

Today's message concerns prayer and the eucharist:

Always have God's love within you, for without this love you cannot convert yourselves completely. Let the rosary be in your hands in memory of Jesus. Dear children, strive to enter more deeply into the Mass as you should (LJM 6-1-85).

———————————

And in John's gospel, Jesus speaks of the eucharist as well:

Those who eat my flesh and drink my blood abide in me, and I in them. Just as the living Father sent me, and I live because of the Father, so whoever eats me will live because of me. This is the bread that came down from heaven, not like that which your ancestors ate, and they died. But the one who eats this bread will live forever (Jn 6:56-58).

———————————

Reflection: Fr. Slavko Barbaric offered these reflections on the eucharist in a sermon given in Medjugorje in May of 1989:

Our Lady once said, "Come to church a little early," which I would interpret to mean about twenty minutes early, to prepare for Mass by offering the rosary. Also, we should remain after Mass for at least ten minutes in order to give thanks. [The Mass] is somewhat like a beautiful banquet spread out before us; if we do not take the initiative to socialize and eat the carefully prepared food, then the event is meaningless.

In the same way, if we eat the food quickly and then hurry away without thanking our host, it would be considered rude behavior. Likewise, hurrying away from Mass is disrespectful to the Lord. We need to spend some time giving thanks and praying for our healing as well as the healing of others. Then the Mass will have a real effect on our lives.

Application: This Sunday, come to Mass early to prepare, and leave a bit later, in order to give thanks.

JUNE 13

Accept divine peace

Today Our Lady asks us to accept and live divine peace:

The attitude of the Christian toward the future should be one of hope in salvation. Those who think only of wars, evils, and punishments are ill-advised. If you dwell on evil, punishment, or wars, you are on the road to encountering them. Rather, your responsibility is to accept divine peace, to live it, and to spread it (LJM 8-84).

And in Colossians, Paul also issues a call to peace:

> Above all, clothe yourselves with love, which binds everything together in perfect harmony. And let the peace of Christ rule in your hearts, to which indeed you were called in the one body. And be thankful (Col 3:14-15).

Reflection: In the beginning of the apparitions, the Blessed Virgin said: "Through prayer and fasting, you can avert wars and suspend the laws of nature." In a sermon on peace, Fr. Slavko Barbaric stated: "The Lord of Peace enables us to understand the profound importance of peace within our own hearts—for this is how it is spread throughout the world." The more hearts that live peace, the sooner will it flourish on earth. "Let us therefore," he concludes, "be instruments of peace, for 'blessed are the peacemakers—they shall be called the children of God.'"

Application: In addition to your prayers for peace, strive to be a peacemaker wherever you are today.

JUNE 14

You will endure everything

In the second month of the apparitions, the visionaries have a vision of Christ. Our Lady says to them:

> *My angels, I send you my Son, Jesus, who was tortured for his faith, yet he endured everything. You also, my angels, will endure everything (FY 7-27-81).*

Similarly, Paul encourages the Thessalonians in their trials:

> Therefore we ourselves boast of you among the churches of God for your steadfastness and faith

during all your persecutions and the afflictions that you are enduring. This is evidence of the righteous judgment of God, and intended to make you worthy of the kingdom of God, for which you are also suffering (2 Thes 1:4-5).

Reflection: Every life includes trials and hardships. Theologians tell us it is the consequence of sin and evil in the world, which disrupts even nature and affects the innocent as well as the guilty. Today, St. Paul teaches that God can draw good out of our hardships: "for he is using your sufferings to prepare you for his kingdom."

Our problems can help us look upward and forward, rather than inward. They can help to build strong character, and they can imbue us with an extra measure of compassion for others who also struggle. Problems are unavoidable for people of faith living in a faithless world. Yet, linked to the sufferings of Christ, they have a redemptive value and meaning.

Application: Today, offer any hardships or pain you experience for a special prayer intention.

JUNE 15

Draw ever closer to the Father

The Blessed Virgin wishes to draw us close to the Father:

Dear children, today I ask you to open your hearts to God like spring flowers which yearn for the sun. I am your Mother and I wish you to draw ever closer to the Father, that he may grant abundant gifts to your hearts (WM 1-31-85).

One of these gifts is the vision to see from the perspective of heaven as God does:

> So if you have been raised with Christ, seek the things that are above, where Christ is, seated at the right hand of God. Set your minds on things that are above, not on things that are on earth, for you have died, and your life is hidden with Christ in God (Col 3:1-3).

Reflection: The believer's real home, Paul says today, is with Christ in heaven. This gives us a different perspective on our lives here on earth. To "set your minds on things that are above," as Paul says today, means simply to look at life from God's perspective. Among other things, this is an antidote to materialism, for we gain a proper perspective of material goods when we take the Lord's view of them. From his viewpoint in eternity, how would he perceive money, prestige, or power? What of family, friendships, or acts of sacrifice? The more we see the life around us as God does, the more we can live in harmony with him. As Our Lady has advised in several of her messages, we must not become too attached to what is only temporary.

Application: In prayer today, spend several minutes thinking of the priorities in your life. Then switch to God's viewpoint, and examine the same priorities. Is there a match?

The Mass

Of the Mass, Our Lady says:

Dear children, I am calling you to more attentive prayer and to greater participation in the Mass. I wish your Mass to be an experience of God (WM 5-16-85).

Jesus also speaks of the eucharist, the living bread:

I am the bread of life. Your ancestors ate the manna in the wilderness, and they died. This is the bread that comes down from heaven, so that one may eat of it and not die. I am the living bread that came down from heaven. Whoever eats of this bread will live forever; and the bread that I will give for the life of the world is my flesh (Jn 6:48-51).

Reflection: Stories continue to come out of China, from time to time, of the heroic efforts of the few remaining bishops and priests to keep the faith alive and nourish the underground church. One such story tells of a priest who lives and works as a coolie. By means of prearranged sign language, he gets messages around of where he is to be found—usually at the corner of a local market selling soap. Customers who, like the early Christians, give a secret sign, are given a piece of soap, between the wrappings of which is hidden a small consecrated host.

The Chinese Catholic takes his purchase home and usually, after a short family service, receives communion. Clearly the most exalted gift of Christ is his very body and blood in the eucharist. St. Ambrose wrote of the miracle: "Christ is food for me; Christ is drink for me; the flesh of God is food for me, the blood of God is drink for me. Christ is ministered to me daily."

Application: For reflection today: Do you prepare for the Mass? Do you participate in the responses and singing? Do you spend a few minutes in thanksgiving afterwards? How can you enter more deeply into the eucharist?

JUNE 17

Many are seeking money

The Gospa expresses a special concern to Mirjana:

> *Right now many are greatly seeking money—not only in the parish, but throughout the world. Woe to those who seek to exploit those who are coming here, and blessed are those who have been exploited (SM 3-18-85).*

And in Mark's gospel, Jesus encounters a rich young man:

> Jesus, looking at him, loved him and said, "You lack one thing; go, sell what you own, and give the money to the poor, and you will have treasure in heaven; then come, follow me." When he heard this, he was shocked and went away grieving, for he had many possessions. Then Jesus looked around and said to his disciples, "How hard it will be for those who have wealth to enter the kingdom of God!" (Mk 10:21-23).

Reflection: There was a barrier keeping the young man out of the kingdom: his love of money. Perhaps it represented his self-respect, accomplishments, or family name. Whatever the reason, money had become his first priority.

Why did Jesus feel it was hard for the rich to enter heaven? Perhaps because the wealthy have most of their basic physical needs met, and thus often become self-reliant rather than reliant on God. Perhaps Jesus knew that money can be a salve to dull the pain that was meant to draw them to God. Ironically, in their wealth, the rich can suffer the truest poverty, the absence of God in their lives.

Christ explained that in the world to come, the values of this world will be reversed. Those who seek status and importance here will have none in heaven, and vice versa. It is important, then, to begin to live heaven's values while still on earth.

Application: In prayer today give Our Lady your money and possessions, asking her to help you use them unselfishly and wisely.

JUNE 18

Now is the time

The following was given to the locutionist Marijana:

> *My angel, pray for unbelievers. People will tear their hair, brother will plead with brother, they will curse their past lives lived without God. They will repent, but it will be too late. Now is the time for conversion. I have been calling you for the past four years. Pray for them. Invite everyone to pray the rosary (SM 8-15-85).*

In equally strong language, Jesus urges readiness for his second coming:

> For as the days of Noah were, so will be the coming of the Son of Man. For as in those days before the flood they were eating and drinking, marrying and giving in marriage, until the day Noah entered the ark and they knew nothing until the flood came and swept them all away, so too will

be the coming of the Son of Man. Then two will be in the field; one will be taken and one will be left. Two women will be grinding meal together; one will be taken and one will be left. Keep awake therefore, for you do not know on what day your Lord is coming (Mt 24:37-42).

Reflection: "Now is the time of conversion," the Madonna says today, echoing the words of Jesus in the gospels. Of course the best reason for converting or deepening our faith is out of love for God, but some may need the impetus of the warnings of Christ and his Mother today. How one comes to faith is as unique as each individual.

The British educator F. H. Drinkwater tells the story of Ira Dutton, born on a farm in Vermont, a teen-age dropout from school, and an enlistee in the northern army when the Civil War broke out. Eventually promoted to officer's rank, he was twenty-two when the war ended.

From there he began the tragic downward spiral of alcoholism. For years he led a kind of double life, sober in the daytime, but drunk and carousing at night, until that time when the disease entered its final, terminal stage. At this juncture he experienced, through the grace of God, a life-changing conversion and a miraculous healing of his alcoholism.

At the age of forty, he was received into the Catholic church and changed his first name to Joseph. Two years later he read about Fr. Damien and determined to go and help him with the lepers. When he met Damien on the beach of Molokai in 1886, he told him he wanted no special treatment: "I wish only to serve my fellow man." Fr. Damien already had leprosy, and in another few months was dead. Brother Joseph lived for another forty years on Molokai, devoting himself to the care of the lepers until his own death in 1926.

Application: In prayer today, abandon yourself again to Our Lady, asking for the grace of deep conversion.

JUNE 19

Let peace rule

The Blessed Mother speaks of peace today:

> *Dear children, today I invite you to peace. As the Queen of Peace I have come to deepen within you my motherly peace. Dear children, I love you and I wish that all of you experience God's peace which enriches every heart.*
>
> *I invite you to become carriers and witnesses of my peace to this unpeaceful world. Let peace rule over all the earth, which is devoid of peace and yet longs for it. I bless you with a mother's blessing (MM 7-25-90).*

St. Peter also urges us to seek peace:

> Those who desire life and desire to see good days, let them keep their tongues from evil and their lips from speaking deceit; let them turn away from evil and do good; let them seek peace and pursue it (1 Pt 3:10-11).

Reflection: To be truly at peace we must put our lives and talents to use in serving God and our neighbor, in the service of love. The prizes that the world values— money, fame, or pleasure—never truly satisfy. God never allows even one human being whom he has created to be content with anything short of himself. As St. Augustine wrote, "Our hearts are restless until they rest in thee." And so Our Lady reminds us that peace is a gift "which only God gives and which enriches every heart." This is the peace that comes from purpose in our lives, from loving and serving God and neighbor.

Application: Today, pray that through your life, talents, and prayers, you may become, as Our Lady says, "a carrier and witness of my peace to this unpeaceful world."

JUNE 20

Give me all your problems

The anniversary of the Medjugorje apparitions (June 25) seems to be very important to Our Lady, for she begins preparing us for it days in advance. For instance, on this day in 1985, she said:

Dear children, for the coming feast day, I wish to call you to open your hearts to the Master of all hearts. Give me all your problems and worries! I want to comfort you in all your trials. Truly, I wish to fill you with peace, joy, and love for God (WM 6-20-85).

St. Peter speaks of the good fruit which trials can bear:

In this you rejoice, even if now for a little while you have had to suffer various trials, so that the genuineness of your faith—being more precious than gold that, though perishable, is tested by fire—may be found to result in praise and glory and honor when Jesus Christ is revealed (1 Pt 1:6-7).

Reflection: Problems and trials are a part of life, of course, but there are several ways of dealing with them. Rather than holding onto them through worry and fear, Our Lady asks us to, "Give me all your problems and worries," a way of saying "Let go, and let God." This trusting surrender to the Lord of our problems is the spirit behind this passage by St. Francis de Sales:

> Do not look forward to the trials and crosses of this life with dread and fear. Rather, look to them with full confidence that, as they arise, God, to whom you belong, will deliver you from them.
>
> He has guided and guarded you thus far in life. Do you but hold fast to his dear hand and he will lead you safely through all trials. Whenever you cannot stand, he will carry you lovingly in his arms.

Application: Offer this prayer by St. Francis whenever you feel burdened with problems.

JUNE 21

Surrender yourselves

In anticipation of the anniversary, the Virgin calls us to surrender ourselves to God:

> *Dear children, until the anniversary day, I call you, the parish, to pray more and to let your prayer be a sign of surrender to God. Dear children, I know that you are all tired, but you don't know how to surrender yourselves. During these days, surrender yourselves completely to me! (WM 6-13-85).*

Perhaps the greatest example of surrender was that of Job, who remained faithful in prosperity and poverty, in illness or in health, in joy and in tragedy. His simple words were:

> Naked I came from my mother's womb, and naked shall I return there; the Lord gave, and the Lord has taken away; blessed be the name of the Lord (Jb 1:21).

Reflection: Surrender to God is one of most difficult tasks of the spiritual life, for we are ingrained with a self-centeredness and egotism (original sin) that impels us to seek control not only over our own lives, but over everyone and everything around us. Left unchecked, this sometimes unconscious attitude leads inevitably to emptiness and despair.

However, turning from self to God allows us to enter a new life of God-centeredness, oneness, and joy that we were created for. Instead of moving inward, we move outward, and become free. It all begins, as Our Lady says, with a conscious choice.

Application: Today, let us make that choice—using a special prayer written by St. Thérèse of Lisieux, "The Little Flower":

> I consider that "all is vanity but to love God and serve him alone." The grace which I especially ask, O Jesus, is never to offend you. My gifts are all unworthy, and so I offer you my very soul, O most loving Savior.
>
> I fear only one thing, my God, to keep my own will. Take it, therefore, for I choose all that you choose. O my Beloved, I offer myself to you, that you may perfectly accomplish in me your holy designs, and I will not allow anything created to be an obstacle to their accomplishment.

JUNE 22

Prepare yourselves with love

As we approach the anniversary, Our Lady asks us to prepare with love:

Dear children, your Mother is happy to be with all of you. Dear children, you have helped me to realize the plans of God.

I wish to speak to you of love, and give you love. During these days, prepare yourselves for the anniversary with love, with my messages, and with joy. Your Mother will help you, dear children, and your Mother will remain with you. There is nothing more important for you than to make what I have said your first priority (VPG 6-6-89).

St. John also recognizes the primacy of love:

We love because he first loved us. Those who say, "I love God," and hate their brothers or sisters, are liars; for those who do not love a brother or sister whom they have seen, cannot love God whom they have not seen. The commandment we have from him is this; those who love God must love their brothers and sisters also (1 Jn 4:19-21).

Reflection: Some years ago the BBC sent its star journalist, Malcolm Muggeridge, to India to do a documentary on Mother Teresa. The BBC wanted to televise her and her sisters picking up the dying in the slums of Calcutta and caring for them at a shelter they ran. Here the dying are washed up and cared for, as Mother Teresa puts it, "within the sight of a loving face."

The shelter is dimly lit by tiny windows high up in the walls. The television crew had not anticipated the poor lighting inside the building, and had not brought any portable lights with them. They concluded that it was useless to try to film the sisters working with the dying inside the building. But someone suggested they do it anyway. Perhaps some of the footage would be usable. To everyone's surprise the footage turned out to be absolutely spectacular. The whole interior was bathed in a mysterious warm light. Technically speaking, the camera crew said, the results were impossible to explain.

Muggeridge has his own theory about the mysterious light: "Mother Teresa's home for the dying is overflowing with love. . . . This love is luminous, like the haloes artists have seen and made visible round the heads of the saints. I find it not at all surprising that the luminosity should register on photographic film."

Application: Today, pray especially for this gift of luminous love, as Our Lady urges us today.

JUNE 23

Have a pure heart

On this day in 1988, the Madonna said to Ivan's prayer group:

> *Dear children, I am happy and so is my Son. Go to confession to have a pure heart for the anniversary. Come to pray on the hill tomorrow between ten and midnight, but I will not appear (VPG 6-23-88).*

St. John also speaks of confession:

> If we say that we have no sin, we deceive ourselves, and the truth is not in us. If we confess our sins, he who is faithful and just will forgive us our sins and cleanse us from all unrighteousness. If we say that we have not sinned, we make him a liar, and his word is not in us (1 Jn 1:8-10).

Reflection: John's words speak to our times. Today there is a growing tendency to joke about sin, to downplay it, or to deny it. For example, people nowadays no longer lie; they merely juggle the facts or stretch the truth. People no longer steal; they rip-off, lift, or "borrow." People no longer commit adultery; they fool around or live in the fast lane. People no longer cheat; they pad expenses or fudge figures. People no longer kill unborn children; they terminate a pregnancy or remove an unwanted fetus.

Downplaying or denying sin inevitably leads to downplaying or denying one's need for Christ. For if we have no sins that need forgiving, we have no need for Jesus Christ. Thus the worst evil is not to commit sin, but to commit sin and then to deny it. Theologian Louis Evely once said: "It is better to sin with sincerity than to lie to oneself in order to stay virtuous."

Concretely, as Our Lady asks of us today, this means using the sacrament of reconciliation: admitting our sin, seeking forgiveness, and receiving absolution. For it was for this gift that Jesus Christ, the Lamb of God, offered himself for us on Calvary. Its fruit is new life.

Application: This week, if you have not done so for a while, receive the sacrament of reconciliation so as, "to have a pure heart for the anniversary," as Our Lady urges.

JUNE 24

Anniversary of the Medjugorje apparitions

On the sixth anniversary of the apparitions, Marija invited the pilgrims to climb Krizevac at 11:30 p.m. A crowd of thousands climbed the rocky footpath. After reciting the rosary, toward midnight, Marija told the pilgrims the content of the apparition.

"The Blessed Virgin was joyful. First of all, she prayed over all of us. We asked her to bless us. She did. Then she gave us, in substance, this message":

> *Dear children, I want to lead you on the road to conversion. I desire that you convert the world and that your life be a conversion for others. Do not fall into infidelity. Let each one of you be completely submitted to my will and to the will of God. Beginning this day, I give you special graces, and in particular the gift of conversion. Let each one of you take home my blessing, and motivate others to a real conversion (SM).*

Also speaking of conversion, Psalm 51 relates:

> Restore to me the joy of your salvation,
> and sustain in me a willing spirit.
> Then I will teach transgressors your ways,
> and sinners will return to you.
> Deliver me from bloodshed, O God,
> O God of my salvation,
> and my tongue will sing aloud of
> your deliverance.
>
> —Psalm 51:12-14

Reflection: Appropriately, on this anniversary of the apparitions of Medjugorje, which is also the feast of St. John the Baptist, Our Lady speaks of conversion, the primary reason for her coming. The world was in darkness, careening blindly toward catastrophe in its sin. But the Virgin again came to earth to save humanity by calling it back to God; in her words: "I want to lead you to the road of conversion."

This call to conversion, to change, to transformation, is uppermost in the plans of the Blessed Mother, and she gives us the tools to achieve it: prayer, fasting, confession, Mass, sacred scripture, and peace. It is important then to reflect on these core messages as we celebrate this anniversary. It calls us to a renewed commitment to our *ongoing* conversion, to an ever deeper relationship with God.

Lastly, in her message today she asks us "to convert the world, that your life be *conversion for others*." We are to be her partners in bringing the world back to God, chiefly through prayer and a living faith that invites others to experience the peace of Christ as we have. It is a "ministry of attraction."

Application: At church or at home this week, light five votive candles symbolizing the five core messages of Medjugorje: prayer, peace, fasting, the sacraments, and sacred scripture. Ask Our Lady to help you live each of these messages, these "tools of conversion," more fully in the months ahead.

JUNE 25

The Queen of Peace

To the question, "When should the feast of the Queen of Peace be celebrated?" Mary smiled and said:

> *I would prefer that it take place June 25. The faithful have come for the first time on that day, on the hill (FY 2-2-82).*

And on this feast day in 1989 she said:

> *Dear children, today I call you to live the messages which I have been giving you during the past eight years. This is a time of grace and I desire that the grace of God overflow in each of you. I bless you, and I love you with a special love (MM 6-25-89).*

St. James also speaks of living our faith in a concrete way:

> What good is it, my brothers and sisters, if you say you have faith but do not have works? Can faith

save you? If a brother or sister is naked and lacks daily food, and one of you says to them, "Go in peace; keep warm and eat your fill," and yet you do not supply their bodily needs, what is the good of that? So faith by itself, if it has no works, is dead (Jas 2:14-17).

Reflection: The messages given on the feast of the Queen of Peace in previous years are beautiful confirmations of Our Lady's love. It is in her profound love for us that Mary intercedes to gain us "a time of grace," and desires that, "the grace of God overflow in each of you." She has gathered all graces together to enable us to live her messages, to live a Christian life that will bring us to eternal joy.

Note that the Blessed Virgin calls us today to *live* her messages, for simply hearing them is not enough. St. James reminds us of the same thing when he calls us to express our faith in works. Our greatest motivation to live the messages, to live our faith, is the boundless love of God and the constant encouragement of our Mother who said, "If you knew how much I loved you, you would weep for joy."

Application: How can you put your faith and love of God into action this week? Check your church bulletin for opportunities, or contact your parish office.

JUNE 26

The prayer group

On this day after the anniversary, Our Lady said to Ivan's prayer group:

> Dear children, your Mother told you yesterday (the anniversary) to renew the messages from now on. Your Mother asks, especially from the prayer group, that you

live my messages in prayer from this time forward. If you want your Mother to give other and new messages, you have to first live the messages I have already given (VPG 6-26-89).

In the Acts of the Apostles, we find that Our Lady too was part of a very special prayer group:

When they had entered the city, they went to the room upstairs where they were staying, Peter, and John and James, and Andrew, Philip and Thomas, Bartholomew and Matthew, James son of Alphaeus, and Simon the Zealot, and Judas son of James. All these were constantly devoting themselves to prayer, together with certain women, including Mary the mother of Jesus, as well as his brothers (Acts 1:13-14).

Reflection: Prayer groups have played a major role in Medjugorje. At the request of Our Lady, Ivan and Marija formed a group, as did Jelena and Marijana, the locutionists. Among the prayer guidelines the Madonna gave them are the following:

Pray in deep meditation. Do not look at your watch all the time, but allow yourself to be led by the grace of God. Do not concern yourself too much with the things of this world, but entrust all that in prayer to the Heavenly Father.

If one is greatly preoccupied, he will not be able to pray well because internal serenity is lacking. God will contribute to bring a successful end to the things of here below, if one strives to work for the things of God.

Those who attend school or go to work must pray half an hour in the morning and in the evening and, if possible, participate in the eucharist. It is necessary to extend the spirit of prayer to daily work, that is to say, to accompany work with prayer.

Application: Consider attending a prayer group meeting in your local Catholic community in the next week or two. If there are not any, would you consider organizing a group with the help of your parish priest?

JUNE 27

May your prayer be joyful

Today Our Lady speaks of joy in prayer:

Dear children, may your prayer be a joyful encounter with the Lord. But know that I cannot guide you as long as you do not experience joy in prayer. From day to day I wish to lead you more deeply into prayer, but I cannot force you (WM 8-14-86).

Psalm 34 is a prayer of rejoicing:

I will bless the Lord at all times:
his praise shall continually be in my mouth.
My soul makes its boast in the Lord;
let the humble hear and be glad.
O magnify the Lord with me,
and let us exalt his name together.

—Psalm 34:1-3

Reflection: Our Lady of Medjugorje emphasizes that it is the *quality* of our prayer which is most important. It is to be an intimate encounter with God, a touching of our heart to his. The story is told by the English journalist William Aitken of a certain priest who was disturbed to see a shabby old man go into his church at noon every day and come out again after a few minutes. What could he be doing? He informed the caretaker and bade him question the old man. After all, the place contained valuable furnishings.

"I go to pray," the old man said in reply to the caretaker's questioning.

"Come, come now," said the other, "you are never long enough in the church to pray."

"Well, you see," the shabby old man went on, "I cannot pray a long prayer, but every day at twelve o'clock, I just comes and says, 'Jesus, it's Jim' and waits a minute and then comes away. It's just a little prayer, but I guess he hears me."

When Jim was injured some time later and taken to the hospital, he had a wonderful influence on others in the ward. Grumbling patients became cheerful and often the ward would ring with laughter.

"Well, Jim," said the sister to him one day, "the men say you are responsible for this change in the ward. They say you are always happy."

"Aye, sister, that I am. I can't help being happy. You see, it's my visitor. Every day he makes me happy."

"Your visitor?" The sister was puzzled. She always noticed that Jim's chair was empty on visiting days, for he was a lonely old man, with no relations. "But when does he come?"

"Every day," Jim replied, the light in his eyes growing brighter. "Yes, every day at twelve o'clock he comes and stands at the foot of my bed. I see him and he smiles and says, 'Jim, it's Jesus.'"

Application: Today seek to make your prayer a meeting of hearts, an encounter with love.

Fast

In a special apparition to Ivan in 1984, the Blessed Mother asked him to convey the following message:

I would like the people to pray with me as much as they can during these days. Fast strictly on Wednesdays and Fridays and each day pray at least one full rosary, the Joyful, Sorrowful, and Glorious Mysteries (SM 8-14-84).

In Acts we see the infant church engaged in fasting and prayer:

While they were worshipping the Lord and fasting, the Holy Spirit said, "Set apart for me Barnabas and Saul for the work to which I have called them." Then after fasting and praying they laid their hands on them and sent them off (Acts 13:2-3).

Reflection: Although fasting may seem to be a difficult teaching, the rewards far outweigh its inconvenience. Our Lady wants us to be aware of its power, especially when combined with prayer. It is by prayer, of course, that we *attach* ourselves to God, but it is by fasting that we *detach* ourselves from the world. Thus fasting leads to a new freedom of mind and heart.

"Fasting," says Fr. Slavko Barbaric, "is a call to conversion directed to our body. And as we free ourselves from things *outside* of ourselves, we also free ourselves from the passions *within* us that are keeping our interior life in chains."

This new freedom allows us to embrace spiritual values through which we can experience true happiness. In this way fasting liberates us from bondage and sets us free to live the joyous life for which we were created.

Application: On your next fast day, pray especially for freedom from the material.

JUNE 29

Sts. Peter and Paul

Jelena received the following message intended for the Pope:

> *In my messages, I recommend to everyone, and to the Holy Father in particular, to spread the messages which I have received from my Son here at Medjugorje. I wish to entrust to the Pope, the word with which I came here: "mir" (peace), which he must spread everywhere.*
>
> *And here is a message which is especially for him: that he bring together the Christian people through his word and his preaching; that he spread, particularly among the young people, the messages which he has received from the Father in his prayer, with which God inspires him (LJM 9-16-83).*

St. Paul charges Timothy with preaching the word:

> Proclaim the message; be persistent whether the time is favorable or unfavorable; convince, rebuke, and encourage, with the utmost patience in teaching (2 Tm 4:2).

Reflection: Peter and Paul no doubt were the greatest evangelists of the church, converting in turn the Jews and Gentiles of their age. In his second letter to Timothy, Paul charges him to, "preach the word . . . put up with hardship, perform your work as an evangelist, fulfilling your ministry."

In a similar way, today Our Lady charges the successor of Peter, and all of us really, to evangelize as well by carrying her messages to others. She entrusts to us the message of peace.

As Paul exhorts Timothy, so the Blessed Virgin encourages the Holy Father to "bring together the Christian people through his word and preaching. . . ."

On this feast of two great evangelists, the Mother of God urges us again to spread her messages by our words and by our lives. May the example of Peter and Paul inspire us to active roles in this great work.

Application: Reflect today on the ways you can spread Our Lady's messages. Possibilities include word-of-mouth, printed material and audio/video cassettes, a program in your home or parish hall, and volunteer work or financial assistance for your nearest Medjugorje center.

JUNE 30

The miraculous

Concerning the miracle of a fire that several hundred people saw burning on Mt. Podbrdo, but which did not consume anything, the Gospa said:

The fire seen by the faithful was miraculous. It is one of the signs—a forerunner of the great sign (FY 10-28-81).

In the gospel of Luke, we see the miraculous healing of a crippled woman:

Now he was teaching in one of the synagogues on the sabbath. And just then there appeared a woman with a spirit that had crippled her for eighteen years. She was bent over and was quite unable to stand up straight. When Jesus saw her, he called her over and said, "Woman, you are set free from your ailment." When he laid his hands on her, immediately she stood up straight and began praising God (Lk 13:10-13).

Reflection: A striking miracle occurred in Medjugorje involving a forty-three-year-old Italian secretary and mother of three, Diana Basile. Multiple sclerosis had been diagnosed in 1972, along with total urinary incontinence, perineal dermatitis, blindness in one eye, difficulty in walking and, to compound matters, a severe clinical depression. In May of 1984, a friend persuaded Diana to join a pilgrimage group going from Milan to Medjugorje.

On the evening of May 23, she was in the church and a friend helped her to climb the steps to the side chapel where the apparitions were then occurring. From the records kept at the parish in Medjugorje, here are her own words:

> At that point I no longer wanted to enter the chapel . . . but the door was opened and I went in. I knelt just behind the door. When the children came in and knelt down. . . . I heard a loud noise. After that I remember nothing, except an indescribable joy and certain episodes of my life passing before my eyes as though on film.
>
> When it was all over, I followed the children, who went straight to the main altar in the church. I was walking just like everybody else, and I knelt down just as they did. It didn't actually occur to me that anything extraordinary had happened, until my friend came up to me in tears.

Diana's cure had been instantaneous. Later that night she found that she was no longer incontinent, and the dermatitis had completely disappeared. Her right eye, useless for twelve years, had regained perfect vision. The following day she walked the six miles from her hotel in Ljubuski to the church in Medjugorje, and later climbed Mt. Podbrdo.

Application: Today, offer a prayer of thanksgiving for the miracles at Medjugorje, which give witness to the world of the love of Christ and the Blessed Mother.

Mt. Podbrdo

A special gift

Our Lady speaks of talents to Jelena's prayer group:

Each of you has a special gift which is your own, and can alone understand it interiorly (LJM 7-85).

And in Romans, Paul urges the people to utilize their gifts:

We have gifts that differ according to the grace given to us: prophecy, in proportion to faith; ministry, in ministering; the teacher, in teaching; the exhorter, in exhortation; the giver, in generosity; the leader, in diligence; the compassionate, in cheerfulness (Rom 12:6-8).

Reflection: Looking at Paul's list of talents, we can imagine the kinds of people who would have each gift. For instance, prophets are often bold and articulate; servers are faithful and loyal; teachers are clear thinkers; preachers know how to motivate others. Givers are generous and trusting, while administrators are good organizers and managers. Comforters are sympathetic and have a natural ability to listen. It would be impossible for one person to embody all these gifts. An assertive prophet would not usually make a good counselor, and a generous giver might fail as an administrator.

Once you have identified your own gifts (and Paul's list is far from complete), ask yourself how you can use them to God's glory. Aware that your gifts cannot do the work of your local church alone, give thanks for the people whose gifts are completely different from your own. Let your strengths balance their deficiencies, and vice versa, so that we can all build up Christ's church together.

Application: Identify at least one talent that you can use in the Lord's service.

JULY 2

A song of love

The foundation of the Medjugorje messages, and of the Christian life itself, is love:

> *Dear children, today I call you to a love which is loyal and pleasing to God. Little children, your love should bear all that is bitter and difficult for the sake of Jesus, who is love. And so, dear children, pray that God may come to your aid—but not according to your wishes, but in accord with his loving plans for you.*
>
> *Surrender yourselves to God so that he may heal you, console you, and forgive everything inside of you which hinders you on the way of love. In this way, God can mold your life and you will grow in love. Dear children, glorify God with a song of love so that his love may grow in you day by day to its fullness (MM 6-25-88).*

Paul also emphasizes love as the one thing necessary:

> Love is patient; love is kind; love is not envious or boastful or arrogant or rude. It does not insist on its own way; it is not irritable or resentful, it does not rejoice in wrongdoing, but rejoices in the truth. It bears all things, hopes all things, endures all things (1 Cor 13:4-7).

Reflection: Having discussed spiritual gifts earlier in his letter, Paul now focuses on the core of spirituality: love. No matter what gift a person has, if he or she does not express love in using that gift, then whatever is done is empty.

The greatest measure of spirituality is the extent to which Christlike love fills our lives. This is not a love that we can muster up within ourselves; it is a supernatural love given by the Holy Spirit. In this context, the Virgin could say to Jelena: "Pray unceasingly to Jesus, that he fill your heart with love." For Paul, our love is central to all that we do, for it is the foundation of spirituality. The more intimately we know and love Christ, the more love will grow in our hearts.

Application: In her message today, the Madonna equates growth in love with surrender to God. This day, then, surrender yourself again to God (for surrender is an ongoing process, like conversion), so his love will take deeper root in your heart.

JULY 3

Learn to be grateful

The Blessed Mother speaks of gratitude today:

Dear children, I wish to tell you to thank God for all the graces he has given you. For the many fruits of his grace, praise the Lord and thank him. Dear children, learn to be grateful for all the little things, and then you will be able to give thanks for the great things as well (MM 10-3-85).

From Ephesians, more on gratitude:

Sing psalms and hymns and spiritual songs among yourselves, singing and making melody to the Lord in your hearts, giving thanks to God the Father at all times and for everything, in the name of our Lord Jesus Christ (Eph 5:19-20).

Reflection: Many years ago a wealthy family in England took their children for a holiday in the country. When the children went swimming in a pool, one of the boys began to drown. The other boys screamed for help and the son of the gardener jumped in and rescued the drowning one. Later, the grateful parents asked the gardener what they could do for the youthful hero. The gardener said his son wanted to go to college. "He wants to be a doctor," he said. The visitors shook hands on that. "We'd be glad to pay his way through," they told him.

When Winston Churchill was stricken with pneumonia after the Teheran conference, the King of England instructed that the best doctor be found to save the Prime Minister. The doctor turned out to be Dr. Fleming, the developer of penicillin. "Rarely," said Churchill to Fleming, "has one man owed his life twice to the same rescuer." It was Fleming who saved Churchill in that pool.

Application: Today, give thanks in your own words for the Lord's saving grace, which rescues us continually from sin and despondency, freeing us to live in hope and freedom.

JULY 4

Independence Day

Appropriately, Our Lady speaks of freedom today—a great gift of God to his people:

Therefore, little children, I desire that your decisions be free before God, because he has given you freedom. Therefore, pray so that, free from any influence of Satan, you may decide only for God (MM 11-25-89).

And in John's gospel, words of freedom from Christ:

> Then Jesus said to the Jews who had believed in him, "If you continue in my word, you are truly my disciples; and you will know the truth, and the truth will make you free" (Jn 8:31-32).

Reflection: As we see in the words of Christ and Our Lady today, freedom is first and foremost a gift from God. In its fundamental form, it is an intrinsic and inalienable right of every human being.

Since gaining its own freedom, America has had both the honor and the cross of defending it throughout the world, notably during the two World Wars and the Cold War. These were moments of glory for the United States, and we pray that its influence in the future will continue to be one of justice, liberty, and the inalienable rights of all people.

Application: Today, simply offer this Prayer on Independence Day:

> Heavenly Father, like the Israelites of old, our ancestors in the faith, our country has struggled long and hard to be free and to keep its freedom as a nation. It too has met with success and failure in trying to achieve its goals. As we ponder the strengths of America, may we also strive to eliminate her weaknesses, whether they be social, political, or economic.
>
> Today we reflect on the teachings of your Son who brought us a message of peace and freedom and taught us to love as brothers and sisters. His message took form in the vision of our founders as they fashioned a nation where people might live as one with the rights to life, liberty, and the pursuit of happiness.

May this legacy live on in our midst as a task for people today and a promise for tomorrow. Thank you for all your past blessings and, with your help, for all that we will achieve in the future. Amen.

JULY 5

I offer you happiness

Our Lady speaks of joy today:

Dear children, tonight your Mother joins you in your happiness and joy. I would like to offer you happiness. I would like to give you love, so that you can extend this love to others. I would like to give you peace, so that you can give this peace to others, so you can extend it especially to families where hatred exists.

Dear children, I would like all of you to renew family prayer. I would like you yourselves to encourage others to renew this prayer. Your Mother will help you (VPG 10-17-88).

In Luke's gospel, Jesus brings great joy to a widow:

When the Lord saw her, he had compassion for her and said to her, "Do not weep." Then he came forward and touched the bier, and the bearers stood still. And he said, "Young man, I say to you, rise!" The dead man sat up and began to speak, and Jesus gave him to his mother (Lk 7:13-15).

Reflection: The widow's situation was serious. She had lost her husband, and now her only son, her last means of support, was dead. The crowd of mourners would go home, and she would be left penniless and friendless.

She was probably past the age of childbearing and would not marry again. Unless a relative came to her aid, her future was bleak. She would be an easy prey for swindlers, and she would likely be reduced to begging for food. In fact, as Luke repeatedly emphasizes, she was just the kind of person Jesus came to help—and help her he did. Christ has the power to bring hope and even joy out of tragedy.

Application: Like the widow whose son was raised to life, Our Lady also wishes us to experience deep joy in Christ. Today, pray that you may live the Virgin's messages so as to realize in your life the happiness and peace the world cannot give, but only the Son of God.

JULY 6

Fear nothing

Our Lady calls us to safe harbor, to fear not:

> *I am your Mother and Jesus is your great friend. Fear nothing in his presence. Give him your heart. Tell him of your sufferings from the bottom of your heart, for this way you will be strengthened in prayer. Your heart will be free, at peace and without fear (LJM 11-29-83).*

And in Luke's gospel, Jesus quiets the fear of his disciples:

> A windstorm swept down on the lake, and the boat was filling with water, and they were in danger. They went to him and woke him up, shouting, "Master, Master, we are perishing!" And he woke up and rebuked the wind and the raging waves; they ceased, and there was a calm. He said to them, "Where is your faith?" They were afraid and amazed, and said to one another, "Who then is this, that he commands even the winds and the water, and they obey him?" (Lk 8:22-25).

Reflection: The Sea of Galilee is still the scene of fierce storms, sometimes with waves as high as 20 feet. Christ's disciples were not frightened without cause. Even though several of them were expert fishermen and knew how to handle a boat, their peril was real.

We, like the disciples, are called to experience awe at the immense power of Christ, who calms a fierce storm with a word. Jesus demonstrates his power over creation in a way that only the Creator could. Through this story we recognize that Jesus the Messiah is the Creator of the universe, the most high God. As John writes: "All things came into being through him, and without him, nothing came to be" (Jn 1:3).

Application: Mary tells us that "Jesus is your great friend. Do not fear anything in his presence." Today, briefly call to mind any fears, lifting them up to Christ so that he can calm and release them from your heart.

JULY 7

Be the carriers of my peace

Our Lady gave the following message to Vicka for the prayer group:

> *Dear children, I give you my motherly blessing and ask you to be the carriers of my peace, and to pray for peace in the world (VPG 11-14-88).*

In Colossians, Paul also speaks of peace:

> And let the peace of Christ rule in your hearts, to which indeed you were called in the one body (Col 3:15).

Reflection: One of the great passages on peace was engraved on a monument dated 1629 in a Baltimore church. It has come down to us known as the Desiderata. The following excerpt is an appropriate reflection today with our readings on peace:

Go placidly amid the noise and haste, and remember what peace there may be in silence. As far as possible, without surrender, be on good terms with all persons. Speak your truth quietly and clearly; and listen to others, even the dull and ignorant; they too have their story. . . .

You are a child of the Universe, no less than the trees and the stars. You have a right to be here. And whether or not it is clear to you, no doubt the universe is unfolding as it should.

Therefore, be at peace with God, however you conceive him to be, and whatever your labors and aspirations in the noisy confusion of life, keep peace with your soul. With all its sham, drudgery, and broken dreams, it is still a beautiful world. Be careful. Strive to be happy.

Application: Explore the wisdom of the Desiderata by reflecting on it again during your prayer time today.

JULY 8

Abandon yourselves to God

From Our Lady's weekly message of August 9, 1984:

Dear children, Satan continues to hinder my plans. Pray, pray, pray! Abandon yourselves to God in prayer. Pray with the heart (WM 8-9-84).

Christ asks us to present our needs to the Father in prayer:

If you abide in me, and my words abide in you, ask for whatever you wish, and it will be done for you. My Father is glorified by this, that you bear much fruit and become my disciples (Jn 15:7-8).

Reflection: One of the fruits of prayer is trust in God; he becomes our refuge and safe harbor. "All things work together," writes the English poet R. H. Benson, "if one will but trust God." Trusting, confident prayer is the fruit of a fervent faith that believes the Lord hears every request. From the Shepherd of Hermas:

Cast off indecision and doubt not in the least, when asking anything from God. . . . Those who are divided in purpose are they who waver before the Lord and altogether fail to obtain any of their requests. But those who are wholly perfect in the faith ask everything with reliance on the Lord and they receive.

Application: After your prayers of petition today, confidently thank the Lord for hearing and answering your requests.

JULY 9

Sing more joyfully

To Jelena's prayer group, a message of happiness:

I wish only that you would be happy, that you would be filled with joy. May you be filled with peace and announce this joy (LJM 86).

And to the visionaries in 1981, when leading them in a song about Jesus:

Come on, sing more joyfully. Why are you so pensive?

From the song of Deborah:

> Hear, O kings; give ear, O princes;
> to the Lord I will sing,
> I will make melody to the Lord, the God of Israel.
> —Judges 5:3

Reflection: "Come, Love! Sing On! Let me hear you sing this song—sing for joy and laugh, for I the Creator am truly subject to all creatures," sings the mystic Mechtild of Magdeburg. Truly life without joy and song and playfulness is incomplete. The beauty of music uplifts our spirits and shows us the face of our Creator.

For many, music is also a means of meditation and contact with God. When we experience the creativity of a musical piece, as it speaks to us, we take a step beyond the practical world, into the profound level of creation.

Some might say, "How can you celebrate when there is so much suffering, so much to grieve about?" Yet we have all grieved: we continue to grieve alongside our joy. But we need not pour all our energies into the painful and sad. Life is also wonderful. Music and dance and the joy of love enrich our lives and strengthen us to go on.

Application: Today heed Our Lady's advice: "Come on, sing more joyfully. Why are you so pensive?"

JULY 10

Jesus gives himself at the Mass

Speaking of the Mass, the Blessed Virgin said to Jelena,

> *My children, I wish that the holy Mass would be the day's gift to you. Attend it, wish for it to begin. Jesus gives himself to you at the Mass. Therefore, look forward to that moment, for then you are cleansed.*

> *Pray a great deal that the Holy Spirit will renew your parish, for if people attend Mass with lukewarmness, they will return to their homes cold, with an empty heart (LJM 3-30-84).*

St. Mark offers us this account of Jesus' institution of the eucharist:

> While they were eating, he took a loaf of bread, and after blessing it he broke it, gave it to them, and said, "Take; this my body." Then he took a cup, and after giving thanks he gave it to them, and all of them drank from it. He said to them, "This is my blood of the covenant, which is poured out for many" (Mk 14:22-24).

Reflection: The Mass is by far the most precious gift of God to his people, for it is the gift of himself. St. Augustine wrote that, "Although God is all powerful, he is unable to give more; though supremely wise, he knows not how to give more; though vastly rich, he has no more to give."

St. Thomas Aquinas, one of the great theologians of the church wrote that, "The celebration of holy Mass is as valuable as the death of Jesus on the cross."

Padre Pio, the contemplative friar who carried the wounds of Christ, made the remarkable statement that, "It would be easier for the world to survive without the sun than to do so without the holy Mass."

And last, from Pope Pius X, who allowed children to receive communion: "If the angels could envy, they would envy us holy communion."

Application: Today, reflect prayerfully on these lines from St. Anthony Claret:

> When we go to holy communion, all of us receive the same Lord Jesus, but not all receive the same

grace. . . . Our differences in disposition are the reason. When a branch is grafted on a tree, the more similar the branch is to the tree, the better the graft will succeed. Likewise, the more the one going to holy communion resembles Jesus, the better will the fruits of holy communion be.

JULY 11

St. Benedict, Abbot

The Blessed Mother gave Jelena this explanation after she saw a beautiful pearl divide itself. Each half sparkled and then faded away:

Jelena, everyone's heart is like this lovely pearl. When one belongs completely to the Lord, one shines even in the darkness. But when one is divided—a little to Satan, a little to sin, a little to everything—one's heart fades away and becomes worthless (LJM 6-15-85).

And from the Book of Revelation:

I know your works; you are neither hot nor cold. I wish you were either cold or hot. So, because you are lukewarm, and neither cold nor hot, I will spit you out of my mouth (Rv 3:15-16).

Reflection: St. Benedict, the father of Western monasticism, was known for his steadfast loyalty and love of the Lord, and he carefully inculcated these virtues in his friars. Born in 480 and educated in Rome, he began the monastic life at Subiaco where he gathered disciples, and then departed for Monte Cassino. There he established the famous monastery and composed the Benedictine Rule, which spread throughout Europe.

His undivided faith, which Our Lady calls us to today, can be easily discerned in his writings. From the Rule of St. Benedict:

> What could be more delightful, dearest brothers, than the voice of our Lord's invitation to us? In his loving kindness he reveals to us the way of life. And so, girded with faith and the performance of good works, let us follow in his paths by the guidance of the gospel; then we shall deserve to see him who has called us unto his kingdom. If we wish to attain a dwelling-place in his kingdom we shall not reach it unless we hasten there by our good deeds.

Application: Today, pray for an undivided heart that expresses itself in good deeds for others.

JULY 12

Pray the rosary

To the prayer group on Mt. Podbrdo, the Blessed Mother speaks of the rosary:

> *Dear children, your Mother is so happy tonight to see you all. I wish to call you again to pray the rosary, and to pray this month especially, because I am in need of your prayers (VPG 5-7-90).*

Jesus speaks of persevering prayer in this passage from Luke:

> Then Jesus told them a parable about their need to pray always and not to lose heart. He said, "In a certain city there was a judge who neither feared God nor had respect for people. In that city there was a widow who kept coming to him and saying, 'Grant me justice against my opponent.' For a

while he refused; but later he said to himself, 'Though I have no fear of God and no respect for anyone, yet because this widow keeps bothering me, I will grant her justice, so that she may not wear me out by continually coming.'"

And the Lord said, "Listen to what the unjust judge says. And will not God grant justice to his chosen ones who cry to him day and night? Will he delay long in helping them?" (Lk 18:1-8).

Reflection: Fr. Albert Shamon tells the story of Austria's great Rosary Crusade that liberated the country from Soviet control. At the end of World War II, the victorious allies pulled out of Austria and left it in Soviet hands. After three years of tyranny the Austrian people could no longer bear the communist yoke, but they were helpless to do anything. Then a certain priest named Pater Petrus was put in mind of a revered Austrian hero, Don John, who credited the rosary with his miraculous defeat of the Ottoman turks at Lepanto in 1591, though he was outnumbered three to one.

And so Fr. Peurus called for a Rosary Crusade against the occupying Soviets. He asked for a tithe: that ten percent of the Austrians, 700,000, would pledge to offer a daily rosary for the withdrawal of Russian forces from their country.

The needed ten percent, 700,000 Austrians, made the pledge, and the Rosary Crusade continued for seven years. And then, on May 13, 1955, the anniversary of the Fatima apparitions, the Russians withdrew from Austria. Their evacuation made no sense. Austria was a war prize, industrialized, strategically located, and rich in natural resources. To this day historians are baffled by the pullout.

Application: Do not hesitate to offer the rosary for great intentions: world peace, an end to abortion, the conversion of sinners, and the special intentions of the Blessed Mother. It was for such intentions as these that Our Lady came to Medjugorje to seek our help.

JULY 13

Do not worry about material things

From Our Lady's weekly message of April 17, 1986:

Dear children, you are so preoccupied with material things that you lose everything God wants to give you. Pray, then, dear children, for the gifts of the Holy Spirit. They are necessary so that you can give witness to my presence here, and to all that I give you. Dear children, abandon yourselves to me so that I can guide you completely. Do not worry so much about material things (WM 4-17-86).

Jesus also asks us not to worry about the material:

Consider the lilies, how they grow: they neither toil nor spin; yet I tell you, even Solomon in all his glory was not clothed like one of these. But if God so clothes the grass of the field, which is alive today and tomorrow is thrown into the fire, how much more will he clothe you—you of little faith!

And do not keep striving for what you are to eat and what you are to drink, and do not keep worrying. For it is the nations of the world that strive after all these things, and your Father knows that you need them. Instead, strive for his kingdom, and these things will be given to you as well (Lk 12:27-31).

Reflection: The psychiatrist Erich Fromm once wrote, "In the sphere of material things, giving means being rich. Not he who has much is rich, but he who gives much." Material possessions have great significance in our world. Not only do we strive to own a special car, an expensive watch, and far more clothes than we need, but we also think in terms of possessing our spouse, or our health, or happiness, or things that cannot be owned. Some of us have become addicted to buying and owning things.

Rather than enriching us, this possessive mentality impoverishes us. Tangible things enrich us only when we use and share them to improve our lives and the lives of others. Wise people have known for thousands of years that an individual's spirituality is deeply affected by his relationship to his possessions. When we respect what we own as a gift from God and share it with others, we open the door to a much deeper spirituality.

Application: Today, pray that you will hold your possessions loosely and with respect, so they can be used well and shared.

JULY 14

God comes to help everyone

Questioned about curing the sick, the Virgin responded:

> *I cannot cure. God alone cures. Pray! I will pray with you. Believe firmly. Fast and do penance. I will help you as long as it is in my power to do so. God comes to help everyone. I am not God. I need your sacrifices and your prayers to help me (FY 12-83).*

And in Matthew's gospel, the cure of a leper:

> When Jesus had come down from the mountain, great crowds followed him; and there was a leper who came to him and knelt before him, saying, "Lord, if you choose, you can make me clean." He stretched out his hand and touched him, saying, "I do choose. Be made clean!" Immediately his leprosy was cleansed. Then Jesus said to him, "See that you say nothing to anyone; but go, show yourself to the priest, and offer the gift that Moses commanded, as a testimony to them" (Mt 8:1-4).

Reflection: In ancient Israel, leprosy was a feared disease since there was no known cure. The term was used for a variety of similar diseases, and some forms were contagious. If a person contracted the contagious type, a priest declared him a leper and banished him from his home and city. He was sent to live in a community with other lepers until he either got better or died.

Yet when the leper begged Jesus to heal him, Jesus reached out and touched him, even though his skin was covered with the dread disease. Through a single touch, Jesus heals; when he speaks a single word, demons flee his presence. As Our Lady affirms today, her Son has authority over all earthly disease and every form of evil. In the future, when God cleanses the earth from sin, there will be no more sickness and death. Jesus' healing miracles, in scripture as well as in Medjugorje, are a foretaste of what will one day be experienced in the kingdom of God.

Application: Today, lift up to God in prayer those who are sick in body, mind, or spirit. Remember them especially on your next fast day.

Live in mutual love

Today the Blessed Mother speaks of love:

> Dear children, today I call you to live and practice love
> in your life—love for God and for your neighbor.
> Without love, dear children, you can do nothing. There-
> fore I call you to live in mutual love. Only in that way
> can you love and accept me, as well as all those around
> you who are coming to the parish.
>
> Then everyone will sense my love through you. And
> so I beseech you, dear children, to start loving from
> today with an ardent, powerful love—the same love
> with which I love each one of you (WM 5-29-86).

St. John speaks of love casting out all fear:

> God is love, and those who abide in love abide in
> God, and God abides in them. Love has been
> perfected among us in this: that we may have
> boldness on the day of judgment, because as he is,
> so are we in this world. There is no fear in love, but
> perfect love casts out fear; for fear has to do with
> punishment, and whoever fears has not reached
> perfection in love (1 Jn 4:16-18).

Reflection: In this passage from John's first letter, we
are assured that, "there is no fear in love." This is
illustrated in a story set in Nazi Germany. An order had
gone out that incurables and the insane were no longer
to be a burden on the Reich.

Three high officials descended upon the Bethel institution (a huge hospital for epileptics and the mentally
ill). "Herr Pastor," they said, "the Fuehrer has decided
that all these people must be gassed." Dr. Von
Bodelschwingh, the administrator, looked at them

calmly. "You can put me into a concentration camp, if you want; that is your affair. But as long as I am free, you do not touch one of my patients. I cannot change to fit the times or the wishes of the Fuehrer. I stand under orders from our Lord Jesus Christ."

Application: Can you remember a time when, out of love, you chose to stand up for the right thing? Today, pray for the love that casts out all fear, and for the courage of faith.

JULY 16

Our Lady of Mt. Carmel

Our Lady speaks of consecration today:

> *Dear children, I call you daily to live the messages which I am giving you because I want to draw you closer to the heart of Jesus. Therefore, little children, I am calling you today to the prayer of consecration to Jesus, my dear Son, so that each of your hearts may be his. And then I am calling you to consecration to my immaculate heart. I want you to consecrate yourselves as persons, families, and parishes so that all belongs to God through my hands (MM 10-25-88).*

Consecration is a way of confirming our total dedication to the Lord. As Peter writes:

> Therefore, brothers and sisters, be all the more eager to confirm your call and election, for if you do this, you will never stumble. For in this way, entry into the eternal kingdom of our Lord and Savior Jesus Christ will be richly provided for you (2 Pt 1:10-11).

Reflection: The feast of Our Lady of Mt. Carmel speaks of profound dedication or consecration to the loving hearts of Jesus and Mary, as Carmelite religious have done for centuries. This is an act of love that links us to them forever.

Today the Virgin asks to help us on this path of love: ". . . I want to draw you closer to the heart of Jesus." And so she calls us to the prayers of consecration to the heart of Jesus and to her immaculate heart, "so that all belongs to God through my hands." To *consecrate* means to completely dedicate ourselves. It means to irrevocably decide for God, to commit ourselves body and soul. It puts us in mind of the inscription on the papal coat of arms: "*totus tuus,*" or "totally yours."

It is in regard to this act of profound dedication that Mary exhorts us: "pray that you may comprehend the greatness of this message (of consecration) which I am giving you." Consecration must be taken very seriously, for it is a radical commitment, a vow to the Lord himself.

Application: On this feast of Our Lady of Mt. Carmel, let us again reverently consecrate ourselves to Jesus and Mary (prayers on November 24 and 25) and, as she says, "by constant prayer press tightly to my motherly heart."

JULY 17

Prevent Satan from entering

The Virgin speaks of Satan to Ivan's prayer group:

Dear children, again today your Mother wants to warn you that Satan, by every means possible, wants to ruin everything in you, but your prayers prevent him from succeeding. When you fill up all the empty space in your soul with prayer, you prevent Satan from enter-

ing. Pray, dear children, and your Mother will pray with you to defeat Satan.

May this be a time when all of us convey peace to others. And so please spread peace within your homes, in your families, in the streets, and everywhere (VPG 3-21-88).

In strong, clear language, Paul identifies and warns the Ephesians of Satan and the powers of evil:

Put on the whole armor of God, so that you may be able to stand against the wiles of the devil. For our struggle is not against enemies of blood and flesh, but against the rulers, against the authorities, against the cosmic powers of this present darkness, against the spiritual forces of evil in the heavenly places. Therefore take up the whole armor of God, so that you may be able to withstand on that evil day, and having done everything, to stand firm (Eph 6:11-13).

Reflection: Both St. Paul and Our Lady wish us to recognize the reality and danger of Satan and the demonic, that we might be prepared and armed to defeat him. This is of such consequence to Mary that she has given over twenty-five messages on Lucifer.

Obviously Satan is not to be taken lightly. The trouble is that he usually works undercover, subtly plying us with temptations and eroding our faith. He can also be overt and dramatic, as in some of the exorcisms that have occurred in Medjugorje, but this is rare behavior for him, for he does not like to show his face.

Our defense? Our Lady gives us five weapons: Prayer, fasting, scripture reading, monthly confession, and the Mass. She asks that we wear blessed objects, make use of holy water, and "to let the rosary in your hands be a sign to Satan that you belong to me."

Application: In prayer today, call to mind those temptations that bother you the most. See these as your weakest links, and place them before God in prayer each morning, asking for his protection against the Evil One.

JULY 18

Adore the Most Blessed Sacrament

Although many of the villagers had worked hard in the fields all day, many remained after Mass for adoration. In this context Our Lady said:

> *Dear children, I am especially grateful that you are here tonight. Adore unceasingly the Most Blessed Sacrament of the altar. Know that I am always present when the faithful are adoring (SM 3-15-84).*

And in the gospel of John, Christ speaks of the bread that we adore:

> Then Jesus said to them, "Very truly, I tell you, it was not Moses who gave you the bread from heaven, but it is my Father who gives you the true bread from heaven. For the bread of God is that which comes down from heaven and gives life to the world" (Jn 6:32-33).

Reflection: Our Lady of Medjugorje urges us to adore her Son in the Blessed Sacrament, and has promised to be present herself as we do so. Special graces are received, she says, whenever we are in adoration before the eucharist.

On this subject, Fr. Albert Shamon tells the story of the Countess of Feria, whose mentor was the great Spanish mystic, St. John of the Cross. The countess, who had entered the Order of Poor Clares, had such a great devotion to eucharistic adoration that she was called the "Spouse of the Blessed Sacrament." Once, when asked what she did during all those hours before the sacrament, she responded,

> Good Lord! I'm asked what I do in his presence! What does a poor man do in the presence of a rich man? What does a sick person do in the presence of his doctor? What does a thirsty man do at the well? What does a starving person do before a table laden with food? He is rich; he is the physician; he is the fountain; he is the bread from heaven. And his love for us is so great that he died that he might dwell among us. Why? That he might enrich us, heal us, refresh and nourish us.

Application: Visit the Lord in the Blessed Sacrament at your parish church this week, perhaps before or after Mass. Can you do this on a regular basis?

JULY 19

Give thanks to God

In the fall of 1989, the Blessed Mother gave a message on gratitude:

> *Dear children, today I invite you to give thanks to God for all the gifts you have been given in the course of your life. Thank him even for the smallest gifts you have received. I give thanks with you and hope that you will experience joy in all these gifts.*
>
> *I want God to be everything to you. Then, dear children, you can continue to grow in the way of holiness (MM 9-25-89).*

Psalm 30 also speaks of giving thanks and praise to God:

You have turned my mourning into dancing;
you have taken off my sackcloth
and clothed me with joy,
so that my soul may praise you and not be silent.
O Lord my God, I will give thanks to you forever.
—Psalm 30:11-12

Reflection: Some time ago, a seventy-year-old toymaker gave his toy shop to the children of Denmark. His "house of toys," one of the biggest in the world, was started 157 years ago by his family. It was a favorite haunt of fairytale writer Hans Christian Andersen, as well as hundreds of thousands of enchanted youngsters who romped through the five-story toyland.

When he announced that the toy store would be placed in trust for needy youngsters, the owner said, "We earned all our money from children, so it comes quite naturally to us to give the money back to the children, especially to those who have never had the joy that toys can give."

God abundantly blesses those who show gratitude; thus Our Lady calls us to "give thanks to God for all the gifts you have discovered in the course of your life." This also draws us closer to him, for we begin to see the tremendous depth of his love, expressed in an endless array of gifts.

Application: Live the Madonna's message today by taking several minutes to call to mind God's gifts, and then giving thanks for them. Can you include this as part of your daily prayer?

Love your brothers

Today, a message of love:

> *Love your Serbian, Orthodox, and Muslim brothers,*
> *and even the atheists who persecute you (SM 87).*

Paul also speaks of the love and unity that marks God's family:

> For he is our peace; in his flesh he has made both groups into one and has broken down the dividing wall, that is, the hostility between us . . . that he might reconcile both groups to God in one body through the cross, thus putting to death that hostility through it (Eph 2:14-16).

Reflection: There are many barriers that can divide us from other Christians: age, appearance, intelligence, politics, economic status, race, culture. Unfortunately, we can stifle Christ's love in catering only to those for whom we have a natural affinity.

But Christ broke these barriers and unified all believers into one family. As Paul says today, "But now in Christ Jesus you who once were far off have been brought near by the blood of Christ"—the blood that was shed for all human beings without distinction. Thus the cross is the focus of our unity and our motivation for loving all God's children. As Jesus prayed to the Father at the Last Supper: "The glory that you have given me I have given them, so that they may be one, as we are one, I in them and you in me, that they may become completely one" (Jn 17:22-23).

Application: Today, pray to the Holy Spirit that he may help you look beyond the barriers of our differences, to the unity that we are all to share.

JULY 21

Your Mother gives you her love

Today the Madonna charges us with carrying her love and peace to others:

Dear children, tonight your Mother is happy to see so many of you. Your Mother wishes to give you her love tonight so that you can share it with others when you go back to your homes. Live love.

I wish to give you peace, so you can carry it to others. Realize that you cannot give peace to others if you do not have this peace within yourselves. I need you, dear children, to cooperate with me, for today there are many plans that I cannot fulfill without you. I need your cooperation. Pray, pray, pray (VPG 7-24-89).

Paul also charges the Thessalonians to build up and encourage one another:

For God has destined us not for wrath but for obtaining salvation through our Lord Jesus Christ, who died for us, so that whether we are awake or asleep we may live with him. Therefore encourage one another and build up each other, as indeed you are doing (1 Thes 5:9-11).

Reflection: When an athlete nears the end of a race, his legs ache, his throat burns, and his whole body cries out for him to quit. This is when supporters are most valuable. Their encouragement helps the runner to push through the pain to the finish.

In the same way, Christians are to encourage one another, as Our Lady and St. Paul urge us today. Encouragement offered at the right moment can make the difference between finishing well or giving up along the way.

There are plenty of nay-sayers around, those who discourage others and point to the bleak side. But to support and affirm others is a much needed ministry, and a calling of the gospel as well. Sharing enthusiasm, giving a sincere compliment, supporting another's project or new idea, are all ways of sharing in the affirming work of the Holy Spirit.

Application: Look around you today, sensitive to the need of others for encouragement; offer an affirming word or a supportive gesture.

JULY 22

St. Mary Magdalene

In answer to Ivan's question regarding reports that the Madonna was being seen at the foot of the cross on Krizevac, she responded:

> *Yes, it is true. Almost everyday I am at the foot of the cross. My Son carried the cross. He has suffered on the cross, and by it, he saved the world. Every day I pray to my Son to forgive the sins of the world (FY 12-31-81).*

In Matthew's gospel, we find Mary Magdalene at the foot of the cross:

> Many women were also there, looking on from a distance; they had followed Jesus from Galilee and had provided for him. Among them were *Mary Magdalene*, and Mary the mother of James and Joseph, and the mother of the sons of Zebedee (Mt 27:55-56).

Reflection: Mary Magdalene's faithfulness to Jesus, even at the foot of the cross, is a dramatic witness to her love. So many others had deserted him, but she remained with the Blessed Mother and the apostle John to the very end. Further, on that first Easter morning she was at the tomb of Christ as one of the first witnesses of the resurrection.

Such faithfulness also characterized Jesus himself in his relationship to his Father; during his agony in the garden, Christ asked that, if possible, the cup of suffering pass by him, but added, "Not my will, but thine be done." And nailed to the cross itself, he remained faithful to his Father and, in this redemptive act, faithful to all mankind.

In today's message, Our Lady says that she is often at the foot of the cross on Krizevac because her Son carried the cross, died on the cross, and through it saved the world. Mary's faithfulness, like that of Jesus, also extends to each of us; "Every day I pray to my Son to forgive the sins of the world." She is our eternal advocate.

Application: Take several minutes to review how faithful you have been to the Gospa's messages. In what areas can you be more constant?

JULY 23

Consecrate yourselves to me

In this message to Jelena, the Blessed Mother speaks of consecration to her heart:

> *Dear children, at this time it is especially necessary for you to consecrate yourselves to me and to my heart. Love, pray, and fast.*

Consecration is an act of deep love, of which Paul speaks in this passage from Ephesians:

I pray that, according to the riches of his glory, he may grant that you may be strengthened in your inner being with power through his Spirit, and that Christ may dwell in your hearts through faith, as you are being rooted and grounded in love (Eph 3:16-17).

———————————

Reflection: Our readings today speak eloquently of love, which motivates Our Lady to ask that we consecrate ourselves to her Immaculate Heart, the source of great love and peace. Let us do just that, using a prayer written by St. Louis de Montfort:

This day, with the whole court of heaven as witness, I choose you, Mary, as my Mother and Queen. I surrender and consecrate myself to you, body and soul, with all that I possess, both spiritual and material, even including the spiritual value of all my actions, past, present, and yet to come. I give you the full right to utilize me and all that belongs to me, without any reservations, in whatever way you please, for the greater glory of God in time and throughout eternity.

Accept, gracious Virgin, this offering of my life and service, to honor and imitate that obedience which the child Jesus chose to have towards you, his Mother. I wish to acknowledge the authority which both of you have over this poor sinner, and by my life and service, to also thank God for the privileges bestowed on you by the Blessed Trinity. I solemnly declare that for the future I will strive to honor and obey you, my Lady, in all things as your humble servant. Amen.

Application: Begin to offer this prayer, or another like it, on Saturdays, the special day of the week given by the church to honor the Blessed Virgin.

JULY 24

Pray especially for peace

In her monthly message for December, 1990, the Virgin spoke of peace:

> *Dear children, today I call you to pray especially for peace in the world. Offer sacrifices and good deeds for peace, for Satan is strong and tries with all his strength to destroy the peace which comes from God. Therefore, dear children, pray with me in a special way for peace. I am with you and I wish to help you with my prayers— and to guide you—on the path to peace. I bless you with my motherly blessing, and ask you not to forget to live the messages of peace (MM 10-25-90).*

And in Luke's gospel, the angels sing of peace:

> And suddenly there was with the angel a multitude of the heavenly host, praising God and saying, "Glory to God in the highest heaven, and on earth peace among those whom he favors!" (Lk 2:13-14).

Reflection: Prayer for peace is one of Our Lady's most frequent requests, and so let's simply take her advice, using a prayer written by Fr. Slavko Barbaric, spiritual director to the visionaries:

> O Lord of Peace, we praise and glorify you for giving us your son, Jesus Christ. Through him you have reconciled the world to yourself, showing us the deepest love.

Father, grant us your peace so that we might spread it throughout the world. We place ourselves under your protection and pray for those who are suffering wherever there is conflict. We lift up to you those who are destroying themselves through sin and evil, seeking only the happiness of this world.

Lord of Peace, we thank you for the opportunities for peace you have given us in this new age; help us, in the words of St. Francis, to be instruments of your peace.

Through the intercession of our Holy Mother, may we experience and sing within our hearts the song of the angels: "Glory to God in the highest, and peace to his people on earth." May we truly live this peace to your glory, and for the good of all our brothers and sisters. Amen.

Application: Try to offer Fr. Slavko's prayer one day each week as a family, before or after the evening meal.

JULY 25

Give me your difficulties

Today the Madonna asks that we surrender our problems and anxieties to her:

> *Dear children, tonight your Mother is happy to see you. I especially ask you tonight to give me your problems and difficulties, so that you will be able to pray with more joy and freedom—and thus your prayer will be from the heart. That is why I ask you tonight to free yourselves from your troubles through prayer. Know that I am with you, dear children, and that I need your prayers (VPG 5-11-90).*

And in Luke's gospel, the prodigal son reaches the end of his rope and surrenders to his father's care:

> So he set off and went to his father. But while he was still far off, his father saw him and was filled with compassion; he ran and put his arms around him and kissed him. Then the son said to him, "Father, I have sinned against heaven and before you; I am no longer worthy to be called your son" (Lk 15:20-21).

Reflection: Unfortunately, some of us need to hit bottom before we awaken to the real meaning and purpose of life. The prodigal son's errant attitude was based on a desire to live as selfishly as he pleased. That attitude is not so different from the desires of a great many people in our society today. It may take great sorrow and tragedy to cause them to look to God for true fulfillment and peace.

In Alcoholics Anonymous, it is said that one of the chief characteristics of the addictive personality is "self-will run riot." Unless the individual can surrender to a "higher power," and exchange self-will for God's will, the addictive disease will kill him. Alcoholism is far more than a physical addiction to alcohol; it is a degenerative disease of the mind and spirit as well as the body. A new way of living and thinking must replace the old, or there can be no recovery. In the same way, our own spiritual survival is dependent upon our surrender to the will of God. Like the prodigal son, we will find only acceptance and love at the hand of our Father.

Application: As Our Lady urges us today, surrender yourself and all your problems and anxieties to the Lord in prayer. Ask also for the grace to continue to "let go and let God."

Sts. Joachim and Ann

Of holiness and the family, Our Lady says:

*Dear children, what joy you give me; you are on the
road to holiness! I beg you, help by your witness, all
those who do not know how to live in holiness. That is
why your family must be the place where holiness is
born. Help everyone to live in holiness, especially the
members of your own family (WM 7-24-86).*

And in the Book of Proverbs, advice from wise parents
is likened to a beautiful garland:

Hear, my child, your father's instruction,
and do not reject your mother's teaching;
for they are a fair garland for your head,
and pendants for your neck.

—Proverbs 1:8-9

Reflection: On this Feast of Joachim and Ann, the
parents of Mary, it is fitting to speak of holiness and the
family, for that is where the latter is often born and
nourished. In a broad sense, to be holy is to be a reflection
of God, to possess the characteristics of the divine, especially love. In holiness, love illuminates the whole person; it becomes a living dynamism or energy within us.

Yet love cannot be isolated from the other virtues and
usually does not spring up suddenly within us. As the
Blessed Virgin said in 1985: "If you live the messages,
you are living the seeds of holiness." It is a process, a
journey.

This brings us to the family and today's message in
which Our Lady says to, "let your family be a place
where holiness is born," and "help your family to live
in holiness." In other words, families are urged to live

the messages of prayer, scripture reading, fasting and the sacraments, and then love will be born and nourished within them.

Prayer is essential to holiness and love, as Mary said in 1987: "Pray, because in prayer each one of you will be able to achieve complete love" (and its corollary, holiness).

With holiness alive in our families, we can achieve the good fruits of family life which St. Paul recommends to the Ephesians today, and which were evident in the family of Joachim, Ann, and their child Mary.

Application: Is there a holiness within your family? How can you better foster it in the future?

JULY 27

Pray without ceasing

Today the Mother of God calls us to persistent prayer:

Dear children, these days the Lord is allowing me to intercede for more graces for you. Thus I urge you once more to pray, dear children. Pray without ceasing. That way I can give you the joy which the Lord has given me. With these graces, dear children, your sufferings can be turned to joy. I am your Mother and I want to help you (WM 6-19-86).

Persistent prayer is the subject of a story Jesus once told:

Then Jesus told them a parable about their need to pray always and not to lose heart. He said, "In a certain city there was a judge who neither feared God nor had respect for people. In that city there was a widow who kept coming to him and saying, 'Grant me justice against my opponent.'

"For a while he refused; but later he said to himself, 'Though I have no fear of God and no respect for anyone, yet because this widow keeps bothering me, I will grant her justice, so that she may not wear me out by continually coming.'"

And the Lord said, "Listen to what the unjust judge says. And will not God grant justice to his chosen ones who cry to him day and night? Will he delay long in helping them?" (Lk 18:1-7).

Reflection: To repeat our prayers until the answer comes does not mean endless repetition or painfully long prayer sessions. Constant prayer means keeping our requests constantly before God as we live for him day by day, always believing he will answer. When we thus live by faith, we are not to give up; the Lord may delay answering, but his delays always have special reasons, and we must not confuse them with neglect. As we persist in prayer, we also grow in character, faith, and hope.

Application: Our Lady calls us to pray without ceasing. she promises to give us "the joy which the Lord gives to me." Call to mind the presence of God throughout this day, that you may feel the comfort of his nearness.

JULY 28

The life of heaven on earth

The kingdom of Heaven, Our Lady says, begins on earth:

If you would abandon yourselves to me, you will not even feel the passage from this life to the next. You will begin to live the life of heaven on earth (LJM 86).

Christ also speaks of the kingdom in Luke's gospel:

> On their return the apostles told Jesus all they had done. He took them with him and withdrew privately to a city called Bethsaida. When the crowds found out about it, they followed him; and he welcomed them, and spoke to them about the kingdom of God, and healed those who needed to be cured (Lk 9:10-11).

Reflection: The kingdom of God was a focal point of Christ's teachings. He explained that it was not just a future kingdom: it was among them, embodied in *him*, the Messiah.

Even though the kingdom will not be complete until Christ comes again in glory, we can experience a foretaste of it, for the kingdom begins in the hearts of those who believe in the Son of God. Thus it is as present with us today as it was with Christ's hearers two thousand years ago.

This is the meaning of Our Lady's message today: when the Spirit of God takes root in a heart that is abandoned to him, the kingdom of God is experienced within.

Application: Reflect on the following today:

> See, this kingdom of God is now found within us. The grace of the Holy Spirit shines forth and warms us, and, overflowing with many varied scents into the air around us, regales our senses with heavenly delight, as it fills our hearts with joy inexpressible (Seraphim of Sarov).

Awaken the faith

In answer to a question about the miraculous signs associated with Medjugorje, the Virgin said:

It is God who gives them. My children, have you not observed that the faith has begun to be extinguished? There are many who come to church simply through habit. It is necessary to awaken the faith, for it is a gift from God. If it is necessary, I will appear in each home (FY 5-82).

Jesus also speaks of faith to the father of a possessed boy:

Jesus asked the father, "How long has this been happening to him?" And he said, "From childhood. [The Devil] has often cast him into the fire and into the water, to destroy him; but if you are able to do anything, have pity on us and help us." "If you are able!—All things can be done for the one who believes." Immediately the father of the child cried out, "I believe; help my unbelief!" (Mk 9:21-24).

Reflection: Faith is not, of course, something tangible that can be taken like medicine. It is, rather, an *attitude* of trusting and believing. And yet even our ability to believe is a gift from God; no matter how much faith we have, we never reach the point of being self-sufficient. Faith cannot be stored away like money in the bank; growing in faith is a constant *process* of renewing daily our trust in Christ.

In the verse following today's reading from Mark's gospel, Jesus says, "This kind [of demon] can come out only by prayer." In other words, when faced with difficult situations, prayer is the answer. It is also the key that unlocks faith in our lives. Effective prayer needs both an *attitude*—complete dependence, and an *action*—asking. Prayer demonstrates our reliance on God as we humbly invite the Lord to fill us with faith and power. There is no substitute for prayer, especially in circumstances that seem unconquerable.

Application: Today Our Lady states that, "It is necessary to awaken faith." In prayer, ask for this awakening within your own family, parish, and community.

JULY 30

Follow the shepherd

Mary asks us not to fear, but to follow the Good Shepherd:

> *Dear children, sometimes you oppress your hearts with certain matters, but this is not necessary. Sometimes you are frightened by this or that, but again, why do you need that? Who is with Jesus need not fear. Do not worry or be anxious about what will happen tomorrow or a few years from now. Abandon yourselves to Jesus, for only that way can you be the faithful sheep that follow their Shepherd (LJM 3-1-87).*

And in John's gospel, Jesus also speaks of the Good Shepherd:

> I am the good shepherd. I know my own and my own know me, just as the Father knows me and I know the Father. And I lay down my life for the sheep (Jn 10:14-15).

Reflection: At night, sheep in ancient Israel were gathered into a sheepfold to protect them from thieves, weather, or wild animals. The sheepfolds were caves, sheds, or open areas surrounded by low walls made of stones or branches. The shepherd slept in the fold to protect the sheep, often at the entrance. Wild animals could not get in, nor the sheep get out, without alerting him. He was, literally, the "sheepgate."

Jesus' listeners were aware of the shepherd's role and his dedication in protecting his flock. In speaking of himself as the Good Shepherd, Christ also evoked the comforting images of Psalm 23, which he and his followers may well have known by heart.

Application: The following is a poetic version of the Twenty-Third Psalm. Pray it "with the heart," as Our Lady asks, that it may calm any anxiety:

> The Lord is my shepherd, I shall not want.
> He maketh me to lie down in green pastures;
> he leadeth me beside the still waters;
> he restoreth my soul.
> He leadeth me in the paths of righteousness
> for his name's sake.
>
> Yea, though I walk through the valley
> of the shadow of death,
> I will fear no evil,
> for thou art with me;
> thy rod and thy staff they comfort me.
>
> Thou preparest a table before me
> in the presence of my enemies;
> thou anointest my head with oil;
> my cup runneth over.
>
> Surely goodness and mercy shall follow me
> all the days of my life,
> and I will dwell in the house of the Lord
> for years without end (King James Version).

St. Ignatius of Loyola

On the anniversary of the apparitions in 1990, Our Lady gave the following message:

Dear children, today I want to thank you for all your sacrifices and prayers. I give you my special motherly blessing.

I call you to decide for God and through prayer discover his will for you day by day. I call all of you to full conversion, dear children, so that you may know joy in your hearts (MM 6-25-90).

Christ also speaks of conversion, of being born again from above:

Very truly, I tell you, no one can enter the kingdom of God without being born of water and the Spirit. What is born of flesh is flesh, and what is born of the Spirit is spirit. Do not be astonished that I said to you, "You must be born from above" (Jn 3:5-7).

Reflection: St. Ignatius of Loyola underwent a remarkable conversion to God through the written word. Born in 1491, he spent his early years at the Spanish court and as a soldier. While recuperating from injuries received in battle, he asked for books to read on his favorite subject: tales of knight-errantry. But no books of that sort could be found, and so he was given instead a life of Christ and a collection of the lives of the saints.

By constantly reading these books he began to be attracted to what he found narrated there. He began to ask such questions as, "What if I should do what St. Francis or St. Dominic did?" Finding that these reflections gave him a special joy, he resolved to dedicate his life to the Lord he had come to know so well in his borrowed books.

Clearly the grace of God can work through any medium to effect conversion. For St. Francis it was nature; for St. Martin de Porres it was the poor. Grace requires only, as Our Lady has often said in Medjugorje, an open heart.

Application: Today, pray that the process of conversion may continue in your life as your heart is kept open to God.

St. Alphonsus Liguori

Today Our Lady gives us words of hope and consolation:

> *Dear children, these days you have been experiencing how Satan is working. But do not be afraid of temptations, for I am always with you and God always watches over us. I have also given myself to you and sympathize even in your smallest temptation (WM 7-19-84).*

The letter of James gives us further encouragement:

> Blessed is anyone who endures temptation. Such a one has stood the test and will receive the crown of life that the Lord has promised to those who love him (Jas 1:12).

Reflection: In one of the prayers he composed, St. Alphonsus wrote, "My Lady, since you are so powerful with God, obtain for me the strength to overcome all temptations, until death." The founder of the Redemptorists had a deep aversion to temptation and sin, and was himself the author of many books on moral theology.

He is the author of this little-known prayer to the Virgin Mary:

> Most holy Virgin Immaculate, my Mother Mary, to you who are the Mother of my Lord, the Queen of the Universe, the advocate, the hope, the refuge of sinners: I, who am the most miserable of sinners, have recourse to you today.
>
> I venerate you, great queen, and I thank you for the many graces you have obtained for me. I love you, most dear Lady, and because of this love I

promise to serve you willingly and to do what I can to make you loved by others.

Since you are so powerful with God, obtain for me the strength to overcome all temptations, until death. Help me have a true love for your Son, Jesus Christ. Assist me always, but especially at the last moment of my life. Forsake me not then until you see me safely in heaven. Such is my hope. Amen.

Application: Perhaps the best gift you could give to St. Alphonsus on his feast day is to offer this prayer to the Virgin once more today, perhaps at the end of your rosary.

AUGUST 2

Sin has gained ground

In her weekly message for September, 1984, the Gospa said:

> *Dear children, I continually need your prayers. You wonder why all these prayers? Look around you, dear children, and you will see how much ground sin has gained in this world. Pray, therefore, that Jesus conquers (WM 9-13-84).*

But although sin abounds, forgiveness abounds all the more, as the psalmist sings:

> Gladden the soul of your servant,
> for to you, O Lord, I lift up my soul.
> For you, O Lord, are good and forgiving,
> abounding in steadfast love to all who call on you.
> —Psalm 86:4-5

Reflection: In Jesus' day, the rabbis taught that Jews should forgive those who offended them three times. Peter, in trying to be especially generous, asked Christ if seven (the "perfect" number) was enough times to forgive someone. But Jesus answered, "Seventy times seven," meaning that we should not even keep track of the number of times.

Realizing how completely Christ has forgiven us produces a free and generous attitude of forgiveness toward others. When we refuse to forgive, we set ourselves outside and above Christ's law of love.

Application: Today, reflect on these words of George Herbert:

> "He who cannot forgive others breaks the bridge over which he must pass himself."

AUGUST 3

Firmly believe

Regarding the miraculous cure of a sick young boy, the Gospa said:

> *He is suffering from a very grave illness. Let his parents firmly believe, do penance, and then the little boy will be cured (FY 8-30-81).*

In John's gospel, Christ heals a man who had been ill for thirty-eight years:

> When Jesus saw him lying there and knew that he had been there a long time, he said to him, "Do you want to be made well?" The sick man answered him, "Sir, I have no one to put me into the pool when the water is stirred up; and while I am making my way, someone else steps down ahead of me." Jesus said to him, "Stand up, take your mat and walk." At once the man was made well, and he took up his mat and began to walk (Jn 5:6-9).

Reflection: The miracles that Christ performed during his life on earth pointed to the genuineness of his ministry, just as the miracles at Medjugorje speak of its authenticity. In both cases they express the ineffable love of God and deepen the faith of believers.

The cures at Medjugorje include the case of Maria Brumec, who suffered a fractured spine. All medical treatments had failed and she had been told she would be an invalid for the rest of her life. On August 8, 1983, while on pilgrimage to Medjugorje, she was instantly and inexplicably cured.

Damir Coric, who suffered from internal hydrocephaly (water in the skull), had undergone three drainage operations, all of which resulted in cerebral hemorrhages which required even more surgery. With the added complication of extreme weakness and weight loss, his prognosis was very poor. In Medjugorje during the summer of 1981, after being prayed over by Vicka, he was completely healed and rapidly gained weight and strength.

Iva Tole, crippled from multiple sclerosis, had to be carried into St. James Church on September 13, 1981 where she experienced a total cure. Later that same day she climbed the mountain of Krizevac to attend a special Mass at the summit.

The miracles of Jesus in the gospels and of Our Lady in Medjugorje inspire in us a wonder and praise of God. Truly they need no other rationale.

Application: Today, simply offer a prayer of praise and thanksgiving to God for the miracles and wonders of his grace.

St. John Vianney

The Madonna speaks of prayer today:

> *When you pray you must feel more. Prayer is a conversation with God. To pray means to listen to God. Prayer is useful for you because after prayer everything is clear. Prayer makes one know happiness. Prayer can teach you how to cry. Prayer can teach you how to blossom. Prayer is not a joke. Prayer is a dialogue with God (FY 10-20-84).*

And from Paul's first letter to Timothy:

> I desire, then, that in every place the men should pray, lifting up holy hands without anger or argument (1 Tm 2:8).

Reflection: St. John Vianney, the Curé of Ars, was born in France in 1789. After ordination to the priesthood, he was appointed pastor of a parish in the town of Ars. He was renowned for his preaching, works of charity, and devout prayer. He died on this date in 1859.

Rather than delineate his thoughts on prayer, let us listen to one of his catechetical instructions:

> My little children, reflect on these words: the Christian's treasure is not on earth but in heaven. Our thoughts, then, ought to be directed to where our treasure is. This is the glorious duty of man: to pray and to love. If you pray and love, that is where a man's happiness lies.
>
> Prayer is nothing else but union with God. When one has a heart that is pure and united with God, he is given a kind of serenity and sweetness that makes him ecstatic, a light that surrounds him with marvelous brightness. In this intimate union,

God and the soul are fused together like two bits of wax that no one can ever pull apart. This union of God with a tiny creature is a lovely thing. It is a happiness beyond understanding.

How similar are the thoughts of St. John and Our Lady on prayer and the goodness of God. May their words become a part of our lives.

Application: Through the intercession of St. John Vianney, ask the Lord today for a deeper spirit of prayer.

AUGUST 5

Dedication of St. Mary Major

Reflection: Today we honor the Blessed Mother for two reasons: it is her birthday (as related by the visionaries in Medjugorje), and it is also the anniversary of the dedication of the Church of St. Mary Major, the oldest church in the West dedicated to the Mother of God. On her birthday in 1985, Our Lady appeared in golden splendor and said:

Praised be Jesus Christ. My children, I am joyful to be with you this evening and to see so many of you. I give you my special blessing.

Grow in holiness through the messages; I will help you. Give your utmost and we will be together, sensitive to the sweetness of life, light, and joy. Go in the peace of God, my children, my little children (SM 8-5-85).

Our Lady's happiness calls to mind her joyful words to Elizabeth at the Visitation:

My soul magnifies the Lord,
and my spirit rejoices in God my Savior,
for he has looked with favor on the
   lowliness of his servant.

Surely, from now on all generations will call
me blessed;
for the Mighty One has done great things for me,
and holy is his name.

—Luke 1:47-49

Since today is also the anniversary of the dedication of
St. Mary Major, it is fitting to close with the Virgin's
message on the reverence due to our churches:

*Dear children, God wants to make you holy. Through
me, he is inviting you to complete surrender. Let Holy
Mass be your life. Understand that the church is God's
palace, the place in which I gather you and want to show
you the way to God. Come and pray! Neither look at
others, nor slander them. Rather, let your life be a
testimony to holiness. Churches deserve respect and are
set apart as holy because God, who became man, dwells
in them day and night.*

*Little children, believe and pray that the Father will
increase your faith; then you can ask for whatever you
need. I am with you and I am rejoicing because of your
conversion. I am protecting you with my motherly
mantle (MM 4-25-88).*

Application: Today, review your conduct in church. Is
it reverent in the presence of the Blessed Sacrament?

AUGUST 6

The Transfiguration of the Lord

On this day, let us listen to St. Matthew's account of the
transfiguration:

Six days later, Jesus took with him Peter and James
and his brother John and led them up a high
mountain, by themselves. And he was trans-

figured before them, and his face shone like the sun. And his clothes became dazzling white. Suddenly there appeared to them Moses and Elijah, talking with him. Then Peter said to Jesus, "Lord, it is good for us to be here; if you wish, I will make three dwellings here, one for you, one for Moses, and one for Elijah."

While he was still speaking, suddenly a bright cloud overshadowed them, and from the cloud a voice said, "This is my Son, my Beloved; with him I am well pleased; listen to him!" When the disciples heard this, they fell to the ground and were overcome by fear. But Jesus came and touched them, saying, "Get up and do not be afraid." And when they looked up, they saw no one except Jesus himself alone (Mt 17:1-8).

Reflection: As Christians who are trying to live their faith ever more deeply, we find ourselves being gradually transfigured into the reflection of God. This process continues as long as our hearts are open to the grace of God and the promptings of the Holy Spirit.

Our dedication to the Blessed Mother and to living her messages is a special sign of the extraordinary graces we are being given in this transfiguration.

Mary is helping us through her intercessory prayer, and she asks us to be aware and open to the profound role of the Holy Spirit in this process of transformation:

Begin by calling on the Holy Spirit each day; It is vital to pray to the Spirit. When the Holy Spirit descends on earth, then all becomes clear and everything is transformed (FY 11-83).

Application: On today's feast, let us pray for openness to God's Spirit that can change us more deeply into the image of Christ:

Come Holy Spirit, Creator, come,
    from thy bright heavenly throne,
come, take possession of our souls,
    and make them all thine own . . .

O guide our minds with thy blest light,
    with love our hearts inflame;
and with thy strength, which ne'er decays,
    confirm our mortal frame.

AUGUST 7

Follow the Mass well!

Of the Mass, the Madonna once said:

Open the door wide, follow the Mass well! Go in the peace of God, my angels! If you suffer for a just cause, blessings will be even more abundant for you (FY 3-2-82).

St. Luke offers this account of Jesus' institution of the eucharist:

Then he took a loaf of bread, and when he had given thanks, he broke it and gave it to them, saying, "This is my body, which is given for you. Do this in remembrance of me." And he did the same with the cup after supper, saying, "This cup that is poured out for you is the new covenant in my blood" (Lk 22:19-20).

Reflection: During the winter of 1992, I had the opportunity to visit the Dachau concentration camp near Munich, where the Nazi's had imprisoned most of the clergymen and priests who had opposed the Third Reich. It was there that I acquired a remarkable booklet by the auxiliary bishop of Munich, Johannes Neuhausler, who had been a prisoner at Dachau himself. In chapter seven, "*Christ at Dachau*," he speaks of the incredible lengths the prisoners would go to in order to offer Mass and receive the eucharist:

> The Polish priests . . . were not permitted to practice their religion in the block, so they had to devise means to help themselves.
>
> Many worked in the plantation greenhouses. While one of them kept guard and the other comrades pretended to be working, the Polish priest who had spent the longest time in the camp knelt on the ground, with his face turned towards the greenhouse so as to give the impression that he was weeding. Indeed, the SS sentries might be spying from their watchtower.
>
> The kneeling priest had pressed a small portable altar into the ground and there he celebrated Mass. Many comrades hurried by, holding grass or plants in their hands as if they had some work to do there. They also knelt down and received holy communion from their own hands.

Application: Share this story with a family member or friend. It helps us to deepen our appreciation of the eucharist—the point of Our Lady's message today.

AUGUST 8

St. Dominic

Our Lady gave the following message on the Vigil of Pentecost:

> *Dear children, tomorrow night pray for the Spirit of truth—especially you of the parish. For you need the Spirit of truth to be able to convey the messages just the way they were given, neither adding anything to them,*

nor taking anything whatever away from them, but just as I said them (WM 6-9-84).

In John's gospel, Christ also speaks of testifying to the truth:

When the Advocate comes, whom I will send to you from the Father, the Spirit of truth who comes from the Father, he will testify on my behalf. You also are to testify because you have been with me from the beginning (Jn 15:26-27).

Reflection: This passage from St. John was the motivating force behind the life and work of St. Dominic—to preach the truth as contained in the gospels. Dominic (1170-1221) was one of the church's greatest preachers and founded, in fact, the Order of Preachers, or Dominicans.

From childhood he showed signs of a vocation, which was encouraged. He also gave evidence of a great concern for the poor. During a time of hunger he sold his books, precious items in his day, to feed the poor. Like St. Francis of Assisi, he saw poverty in practice as a remedy for many of the ills that afflicted the church in the late twelfth and early thirteenth centuries.

St. Dominic's ideal was to combine prayer and asceticism with study and the ministry of preaching. What one preached is learned in prayer and contemplation. "Bring to others what you contemplate," is the motto he gave to the order he founded. It could well be the motto of every Christian.

Application: "You need the Spirit of truth," Our Lady says today, "to be able to convey the messages just the way they were given." In the spirit of St. Dominic, seek to share your faith with at least one other person this week.

Abandon yourselves to God

Our Lady calls us to abandonment today:

> *Dear children, your Mother calls you to completely abandon yourselves to God. Dear children, this is a time of grace. Pray as you can and renew yourself through prayer. Form yourself spiritually. This formation will last all your life. Continue to pray as much as you can, for by your prayers you will help me (VPG 3-27-89).*

And Paul speaks of courage in God:

> You yourselves know, brothers and sisters, that our coming to you was not in vain, but though we had already suffered and been shamefully mistreated at Philippi, as you know, we had *courage* in our God to declare to you the gospel of God in spite of great opposition (1 Thes 2:1-2).

Reflection: Hemingway wrote that "Courage is grace under pressure." Eddie Rickenbacker, the highly decorated flyer of the First World War, concluded: "Courage is doing what you're afraid to do. There can be no courage unless you're scared." Courage is also a vital quality in following Christ—an almost reckless trust in the Lord, which Our Lady calls "abandonment to God."

A striking example is that of Edith Stein. Born of a Jewish family in 1891, she was raised and educated in Germany. A brilliant student, she received her Doctorate in Philosophy *cum laude* from the University of Freiburg, where she later became assistant to Professor Edmund Husserl, the eminent philosopher. In 1922 she entered the Catholic church and thereafter devoted her time to teaching, lecturing, and writing. In 1932, she was offered a professorship at the University of Muenster.

A year later, as the Nazis came to power, her varied activities were curtailed. She was, however, permitted to enter the cloistered Carmelite convent in Cologne, taking the name Terese Benedicta of the Cross. She prayed that God would accept her life and her death in expiation for the sins of unbelievers, the salvation of Germany, and for peace in the world. Her Calvary was Auschwitz. She died there in the gas chambers on August 9, 1942. On May 1, 1987 she was beatified by Pope John Paul II at Cologne, Germany. The process of her canonization is now in its final stage.

Application: In prayer today, heeding Our Lady's advice, abandon yourself completely to the Lord, asking for that radical trust that marks the life of the committed Christian.

AUGUST 10

False prophets

Regarding catastrophic predictions, Our Lady said:

> *That comes from false prophets. They say, "such a day, on such a date, there will be a catastrophe," I have always said that evil will come if the world does not convert itself. Call the world to conversion. Everything depends on your conversion (LJM 12-15-83).*

Jesus also speaks of false prophets in Matthew's gospel:

Jesus answered them, "Beware that no one leads you astray. For many will come in my name, saying, 'I am the Messiah!' and they will lead many astray" (Mt 24:4-5).

Reflection: "But not everyone who speaks on the spirit is a prophet, but only if he follows the conduct of the Lord." This excerpt from the apocryphal Teaching of the Twelve Apostles is another way of putting the old adage, "actions speak louder than words," or "by their fruit you shall know them."

The gauge of a teacher, prophet, or any Christian lies in his behavior rather than his words. Does he *live* the spirit of the scriptures? Does he help others in concrete ways? Do his words and actions promote peace or dissention? Before placing any trust in would-be prophets, preachers, or evangelists, look carefully at their lives.

As Catholics, we are guided by the magisterium, or teaching arm, of the church, which has preserved the body of faith in its essential form since the time of Christ. Indeed, one of the chief responsibilities of the Pope and bishops is to teach and preserve this faith, passed down within the church by each succeeding generation. The Holy Spirit remains with us always, guiding and protecting the church's beliefs and teachings until the advent of the kingdom.

Application: Today, recite the Apostles' Creed slowly and prayerfully, reflecting on the meaning of each phrase. The visionaries of Medjugorje report that it is the Virgin's favorite prayer.

AUGUST 11

St. Clare of Assisi

The following was given to Vicka one day when she was away from Medjugorje:

I bless you with the benediction of a Mother. Pray every day and confide yourselves to my son, Jesus. In this way you will understand what God asks of each of you (SM 3-21-87).

St. Clare discovered in prayer the will of God for her, and this enabled her not only to live a holy life, but one marked by miracles as well. From John's gospel:

> Very truly, I tell you, the one who believes in me will also do the works that I do and, in fact, will do greater works than these, because I am going to the Father. I will do whatever you ask in my name, so that the Father may be glorified in the Son. If in my name you ask me for anything, I will do it (Jn 14:12-14).

Reflection: Next to St. Francis of Assisi, St. Clare (1193-1253) was most responsible for the growth and spread of the Franciscan ideal which changed the face of the church in the thirteenth century.

Born in Assisi of wealthy parents, Clare heard a sermon by St. Francis when she was a teen-ager. It affected her to such a degree that she left home to join him and his followers, and to live the life of gospel poverty. Francis gave her the veil when she was nineteen years old, and she was shortly joined by her two sisters and, later, her mother. Living at the convent at the church of San Damiano, Francis charged her under obedience to accept the office of abbess, which she then held for nearly forty years until her death.

Clare's understanding of poverty, embodied in the Rule of Poor Clare Nuns, was designed to bring the individual into intimate union with Christ and away from all earthly attachments. She founded monasteries for her nuns in Italy, France, Germany, and Hungary, and was credited with many miracles throughout her life, notably the saving of her convent and the town of Assisi from the Saracen invaders.

St. Clare endured an illness for thirty years that confined her to the convent, yet she was known to be a spirited, energetic leader, always loving and kind toward her sisters. She was motivated always by her love of the gospel ideal of simplicity after the example of Christ. She died in 1253 and was canonized just two years later.

Application: "Pray every day," the Virgin says. "In this way you will understand what God asks of each of you." Today, simply pray for this knowledge of God's will, as St. Clare did throughout her life.

AUGUST 12

Prepare yourselves in prayer

On this day in 1988, in anticipation of the Assumption, Our Lady gave the following message to Ivan's prayer group:

> *Dear children, your Mother asks you to pray as much as you can during these two days. Prepare yourselves in prayer for the feast to come.*
>
> *Dear children, I would like to tell you to bring peace to others during these days. Encourage others to change. You cannot, dear children, give peace if you, yourselves, are not at inner peace. Tonight I give you peace. Give peace to others! Dear children, be a light that shines.*
>
> *I ask you pray the Glorious Mysteries when you go back to your homes tonight. Pray them in front of the cross (VPGM 12-12-88).*

The peace of prayer often comes in times of quiet and solitude. From Psalm 131:

O Lord, my heart is not lifted up,
my eyes are not raised too high;

I do not occupy myself with things
too great and too marvelous for me.
But I have calmed and quieted my soul,
like a weaned child with its mother;
my soul is like the weaned child that is with me.
—Psalm 131:1-2

Reflection: As the Madonna says today, prayer is the means to great love and peace. But it often requires solitude and quiet so that the tranquil presence of God's Spirit can be felt. From a poem by James Dillet Freeman:

Prayer is a state of being, like snowfall
At night. As in the silence of yourself you pray,
All things particular, familiar, small
Or large, dissolve and slowly melt away.
Only the white perfection of your prayer
Is there, enveloping all things, until
The oneness of the One is everywhere.
Nothing remains the same—only the still,
Only the peace of being, not so much
Filling space as obliterating space,
An emptiness and allness, like the touch
Of snowfall in the night upon your face.
But when your prayer ends and you rise and go,
Your world shines new around you, like
   new snow.

Application: Today, as the Virgin asks, begin preparing for the Assumption through quiet time in prayer; seek a place of solitude and rest in God's peace.

There are souls in purgatory

To the visionary Mirjana, regarding purgatory:

There are souls in purgatory who pray ardently to God, but for whom no relative or friend prays on earth. But God allows them to benefit from the prayers of other people (FY 1-10-83).

And in Psalm 73, the author expresses confidence in God, both now and in the hereafter:

Nevertheless I am continually with you;
you hold my right hand.
You guide me with your counsel,
and afterward you will receive me with honor.
Whom have I in heaven but you?
And there is nothing on earth that I desire
    other than you.
My flesh and my heart may fail,
but God is the strength of my heart and my
    portion forever.

—Psalm 73:23-26

Reflection: Through the dogma of the communion of saints, the church teaches that the living can actively help those who have died through prayer, sacrifice, and especially the Mass, "the greatest prayer," as Mary says elsewhere.

It is common practice to arrange for Masses to be offered for loved ones, often on the anniversary of their death, but any time is appropriate. Your parish secretary or priest can assist you in this; Mass intentions are normally announced in the church bulletin, unless you wish otherwise (it is customary, though not required, to give an offering).

Application: Today, pray for the souls in purgatory, especially the forgotten dead.

AUGUST 14

Do works of mercy

The Virgin calls us to good works today:

> *Dear children, today I invite you to do works of mercy out of love for me and your brothers and sisters. May all that you do for others be done with great joy and humility before God. I am with you and day after day I offer your sacrifices and prayers to God for the salvation of the world (MM 11-25-90).*

In Matthew's gospel, Jesus reveals how we will be judged:

> Then the king will say to those at his right hand, "Come, you that are blessed by my Father, inherit the kingdom prepared for you from the foundation of the world; for I was hungry and you gave me food, I was thirsty and you gave me something to drink, I was a stranger and you welcomed me, I was naked and you gave me clothing. I was sick and you took care of me, I was in prison and you visited me" (Mt 25:34-36).

Reflection: These words from the Second Vatican Council ring with the same urgency as those in today's gospel.

> Since there are so many people in this world afflicted with hunger, this sacred Council urges all, both individuals and governments, to remember the saying of the Fathers: "Feed the man dying of

hunger, because if you have not fed him, you have killed him."

To be our brother's keeper is not optional for the Christian, but a mandate from Christ.

We are further challenged by Pope Paul VI in his encyclical, *The Progress of Peoples*:

Am I really doing all I can to help the poor and hungry? Am I prepared to pay more taxes in order that the government can do more for development? Am I prepared to pay more in the shops for goods imported from abroad so that the people who produce these goods are paid a decent wage?

Application: This week, make an extra effort to help those in need, either through personal service or material support. Also, check your parish bulletin and diocesan newspaper for opportunities to help with service projects or social justice activities that need volunteer assistance.

AUGUST 15

The Assumption of Our Lady

On this feast day in 1985, Our Lady said:

Dear children, today I am blessing you and I wish to tell you that I love you and that I urge you to live my messages. Today I am blessing you with the solemn blessing that the Almighty grants me (WM 8-15-85).

And from the prophet Isaiah, almost as if he were speaking of the Assumption:

Arise, shine; for your light has come,
and the glory of the Lord has risen upon you.
For darkness shall cover the earth,

and thick darkness the peoples;
but the Lord will arise upon you,
and his glory will appear over you.

—Isaiah 60:1-2

Reflection: Today we celebrate the Assumption of Our Lady, body and soul, into heaven. Jesus preserved his mother's body from the corruption of death, for it was the temple of his conception and the crowning glory of the human race.

In honoring the Blessed Virgin the Lord honors us all, for she too was human; her glory is reflected upon all her children. Our oneness with Mary is indicative of our awesome and mysterious unity with all people of all ages. Fr. Jozo teaches that we are not "beside" each other, but rather are "inside" one another. Our unity even embraces God himself, who became one with us through the incarnation:

> I do not pray for them alone. I pray also for those who will believe in me through their word, that all may be one as you, Father, are in me, and I in you; I pray that they may be one in us, that the world may believe that you sent me (Jn 17:20-21).

In the mystery of our oneness we can perceive how our actions and prayer have a ripple effect on the entire Body of Christ; how our virtue as well as our sin has an effect far beyond ourselves.

Today we rejoice in the reflected glory of our Mother's Assumption. May the solemn blessing that she imparts to us on this feast bring us to a new awareness of our sacred communion with God and with one another.

Application: As a gift to Our Lady today, offer her your rosary for her special intentions.

Love your neighbor

Today the Queen of Peace urges us to love:

Dear children, I call you to love your neighbor, especially those who do you harm. In this way you will be able to discern the intentions of hearts with love. Pray and love, dear children. It is with the strength of love that you will be able to accomplish what seems impossible to you (WM 11-7-85).

Paul also speaks of love to the church at Rome:

Owe no one anything, except to love one another; for the one who loves another has fulfilled the law. The commandments, "You shall not commit adultery; You shall not murder; You shall not steal; You shall not covet," and any other commandment, are summed up in this word, "Love your neighbor as yourself." Love does no wrong to a neighbor; therefore, love is the fulfilling of the law (Rom 13:8-10).

Reflection: Many people struggle with the idea that self-love is wrong, yet if this were the case, it would be pointless to love our neighbors as ourselves. In our second reading today, Paul explains what he means by self-love. Even if we have low self-esteem, we do not willingly let ourselves go hungry. We clothe ourselves reasonably well and make sure we have a roof over our heads. We try to avoid being injured or cheated. This is the kind of love we are asked to have for our neighbors as well.

When we have the opportunity, do we help others to be fed, clothed, and housed as well as they can be? Are we careful to never injure, defraud, or in any way hurt another? Loving others as ourselves means to be alert to their needs, helping whenever we can. Not surprisingly, when we focus on others rather than on ourselves, we will rarely suffer from low self-esteem.

Application: Today, pray that the Father will give you a deep and abiding love for others. This week, be especially alert to those who can use your help.

AUGUST 17

The spirit of faith

In the first months of the apparitions, the Madonna gave this message on faith:

> It is necessary for the world to be saved while there is still time—that it pray ardently and have the spirit of faith (FY 11-29-81).

For Paul, faith is the source of righteousness:

> But now, apart from law, the righteousness of God has been disclosed, and is attested by the law and the prophets, the righteousness of God through faith in Jesus Christ for all who believe. For there is not distinction, since all have sinned and fall short of the glory of God (Rom 3:21-23).

Reflection: Faith is one of the five core messages of Medjugorje. It is also the greatest gift of God, from which all others flow.

For addicted people, faith is not an option, but a matter of life and death. In this "age of psychology," it is significant that in the treatment of alcohol and drug addition, a degenerative disease of body, mind, and spirit, only faith can unlock the door to recovery and a new life. We can learn a great deal from these treatment methods, especially the Twelve-Step program of Alcoholics Anonymous. Its major tenent is that, although one is powerless over alcohol or another addiction, God has all power, and in turning to him, his power will conquer what the individual cannot.

Application: Today, confide to God your powerlessness over some weakness or vice (such as anger, overeating, anxiety, smoking, etc.). In faith, ask that his power control what for you is uncontrollable.

AUGUST 18

Act with love

The Blessed Mother speaks of love today:

Dear children, hatred gives rise to division and blinds one to everything and everybody. I call you, then, to spread harmony and peace, especially where you live. Dear children, act with love. May love be your only tool. With love, change into good all that Satan is trying to destroy and take for himself. In this way you will be completely mine and I will be able to help you (WM 7-31-86).

In his first letter, St. John takes up the theme of love:

For this is the message you have heard from the beginning, that we should love one another. We know love by this, that he laid down his life for us and we ought to lay down our lives for one another.

How does God's love abide in anyone who has the world's goods and sees a brother or sister in need and yet refuses help? Little children, let us love, not in word or speech, but in truth and action (1 Jn 3:11, 16-18).

Reflection: St. Bede once wrote: "To love our neighbor in charity is to love God in man." This story from T. A. Beetham's *Christianity and the New Africa* might illustrate.

In 1964 in the Congo there was widespread rebellion against the central government, which was to bring persecution and death to many Congo Christians. The actions of the Simbas, or Lions, were usually unpredictable.

"Why did you shelter a white woman?" asked the Simba military court of one pastor. "Because she is my sister in Christ, the child of my own heavenly Father," was the reply.

Although he was condemned by the court to be shot, the effect of his bearing on the major was such that he set him free.

Love is spread not so much by what we say, but by what we do, by our example. To live the messages of Our Lady, to praise God with our lives, means first to love.

Application: How can you express your love in a concrete way today?

AUGUST 19

St. John Eudes

Today Our Lady explains why she has been with us so long in Medjugorje:

Dear children, this is the reason for my presence among you for such a long time: to lead you to Jesus. I want to save you and, through you, to save the whole world.

Many people now live without faith; some don't even want to hear about Jesus, and yet they still want peace and fulfillment! Children, this is the reason why I need your prayer: Prayer is the only way to save the human race (LJM 7-30-87).

In John's gospel, Christ prays to the Father for the salvation of souls:

And for their sakes I sanctify myself, so that they may also be sanctified in truth. I ask not only on behalf of these, but also on behalf of those who will believe in me through their word. . .(Jn 17:19-20).

Reflection: The salvation of souls was also the chief concern of St. John Eudes, a seventeenth century French priest who founded two religious orders and was noted for his tireless work for the poor. He was especially devoted to the Blessed Mother, and wrote a litany of praise in her honor.

Application: It would be appropriate to offer this litany today, our intention being the same as that of Our Lady—the salvation of souls:

Hail Mary, daughter of God the Father.
Hail Mary, Mother of God the Son.
Hail Mary, Spouse of God the Holy Spirit.
Hail Mary, Temple of the most Blessed Trinity.
Hail Mary, pure lily of the effulgent Trinity.
Hail Mary, celestial rose of the ineffable love
   of God.
Hail Mary, Virgin pure and humble, of whom
   the God of heaven willed to be born and with
   your milk to be nourished.
Hail Mary, Virgin of virgins.
Hail Mary, Queen of martyrs, whose soul
   was transfixed by a sword
Hail Mary, Lady most blessed! Unto whom
   all power in heaven and earth is given.

Hail Mary, my Queen and my mother! my life, my
 sweetness and my hope.
Hail Mary, Mother most amiable.
Hail Mary, Mother most admirable.
Hail Mary, Mother of divine Love.
Hail Mary, Immaculate; conceived without sin.
Hail Mary full of grace . . . .

Blessed be your spouse, St. Joseph.
Blessed be your father, St. Joachim.
Blessed be your mother, St. Ann.
Blessed be your guardian, St. John.
Blessed be the holy angel, St. Gabriel.
Glory be to God the Father who chose you.
Glory be to God the Son who loved you.
Glory be to the Holy Spirit who espoused you.
O Glorious Virgin Mary, may all love and
 praise you.
Holy Mary, Mother of God, pray for us and
 bless us, now, and at death in the name of Jesus,
 your divine Son.
Amen.

AUGUST 20

St. Bernard

In a message on love in 1986, the Blessed Mother said:

*Dear children, again today I wish to show you how
much I love you. But I regret that not everyone under-
stands my love. I call you, then, to prayer and complete
surrender to God so that you will be able to comprehend
how very much I love you.*

*Be aware that Satan wants to affect you in everyday
affairs and wants to claim first place in your lives.*

Therefore, dear children, pray without ceasing! (WM 10-16-86).

———————————

And from Psalm 118:

O give thanks to the Lord, for he is good;
his steadfast love endures forever!
Let Israel say,
"His steadfast love endures forever."
Let the house of Aaron say,
"His steadfast love endures forever."
Let those who hold the Lord in awe, say,
"His steadfast love endures forever."

—Psalm 118:1-4

Reflection: Born in 1090 in France, St. Bernard joined the Cistercian order and later served as abbot. Renowned for his many theological and spiritual works, his words on God's love are just as pertinent today: "Love is sufficient of itself. It gives pleasure by itself and because of itself. It is its own merit, its own reward."

Application: St. Bernard also had a great devotion to the Blessed Mother and wrote this Prayer in Praise of the Mother of God. Let us offer it today for Our Lady's intentions of peace:

Mary, our Mother,
the whole world reveres you
as the holiest shrine of the living God,
for in you the salvation of the world dawned.
The Son of God was pleased
to take human form from you.
You have broken down the wall of hatred,
the barrier between heaven and earth
which was set up by man's first disobedience.
In you heaven met earth

when divinity and humanity were joined in one
person,
the Man-God.
Mother of God, we sing your praises,
but we must praise you even more.
Our speech is too feeble to honor you
as we ought,
for no tongue is eloquent enough
to express your wonders and beauty.
Mary, most powerful, most holy,
and worthy of all love!
Your name brings new life,
and the thought of you inspires love
in the hearts of those devoted to you. Amen.

AUGUST 21

It is indispensable

Today the Madonna makes her most frequent request:

Pray! I wish to purify your hearts. Pray. It is indispensable, for God gives the greatest graces when you pray (LJM 1-30-84).

In the Book of Daniel, we see a man devoted to prayer:

Daniel . . . continued to go to his house . . . and to get down on his knees three times a day to pray to his God and praise him, just as he had done previously (Dn 6:10).

Reflection: Our Lady gave one of her most beautiful messages on prayer to Jelena's prayer group in January of 1986. It is quoted here in its entirety:

Each moment of prayer is like a drop of dew in the morning which refreshes each flower, each blade of grass, the whole earth.

In the same way, prayer refreshes man. Just as he must rest when tired, seek peace when troubled, so he must pray and listen to the Spirit of God to renew himself.

How beautiful the scenery is when we look at nature in the morning, in all its freshness! But how much more beautiful is someone who conveys peace, love, and happiness to others. Children, if only you knew what prayer does to human beings, especially prayer from the heart! In this way, you can become a beautiful, fresh flower for God. See how long the drops of dew linger on the flowers before the first rays of sunlight.

In this way, nature is refreshed and renewed. For nature to remain beautiful, it requires a daily renewal and refreshment. In the same way, prayer refreshes man, renewing and strengthening him. Because temptations afflict him again and again, weakening him, he must pray so as to be renewed and empowered to love. Therefore, pray and rejoice in the refreshment God gives you!

Application: Today, enter into prayer deeply and calmly, asking especially for the grace of renewal and peace.

AUGUST 22

The Queenship of Mary

Our Lady speaks of her queenship to Jelena:

I have come to tell the world that God is truth; he exists. True happiness and the fullness of life are in him. I have come here as Queen of Peace to tell the world that peace is necessary for the salvation of the world. In God, one finds true joy from which true peace is derived (LJM 6-16-83).

And from a monthly message in 1988:

I am your mother and the Queen of Peace. I give you blessings of joy that God may be everything in your life (MM 7-25-88).

———————

From Revelation:

A great portent appeared in heaven: A woman clothed with the sun, with the moon under her feet, and on her head a crown of twelve stars (Rv 12:1).

———————

Reflection: The crowning glory of Mary's life was her coronation as Queen of Heaven and Earth. The description of her above from the Book of Revelation has inspired artists and poets for centuries.

As Queen of Heaven, Our Lady continues to direct us to the King. In her message of July 25, 1988, she calls us "to a complete surrender to God." "Everything you do," she says, "and everything you possess, give over to God so that he can take control in your life, as King of all that you possess." In this way, God can then lead us into the depths of the spiritual life.

Our Lady's own surrender to God, as exemplified by the Annunciation and her presence at the cross, inspires us to imitate her dependence on the Father. This trusting dependence harbors a strength, a courage, and peace that belies any power the world can give. As St. Paul says, it is through our "weakness" that the power of God himself bursts forth. And so it is that what the world saw as a lowly maiden was, in the reality of God's power, the Queen of Heaven and Earth.

Application: Today, pray that you may not rely on your own strength and wisdom, but on the Lord's.

The Spirit is always willing

Our Lady speaks of prayer and the Holy Spirit to Ivan's prayer group:

Dear children, tonight your Mother calls you to pray as much as you can during these days for this is a time of grace. Abandon yourselves to the Holy Spirit that he may renew you. Prayer renews your body, soul, and heart. Do not let your body be weak, for the Spirit is always willing (VPG 5-5-89).

John the Baptist foretells baptism with the Holy Spirit at the hands of the Messiah:

I baptize you with water for repentance, but one who is more powerful than I is coming after me; I am not worthy to carry his sandals. He will baptize you with the Holy Spirit and fire (Mt 3:11).

Reflection: "Abandon yourselves to the Spirit," the Madonna says, "that he may renew you." This is a frequent call of Our Lady, and rather than speak of it, let us simply invoke the Holy Spirit as she asks, using the following Prayer of Invocation to the Holy Spirit:

Eternal Father, in the name of Jesus Christ, and through the intercession of the Immaculate Virgin Mary, send upon me the Holy Spirit.

Come, Holy Spirit, into my heart and sanctify it.
Come, Father of the poor, and bring me relief.
Come, Author of all good, and console me.
Come, Light of our minds, and enlighten me.
Come, consoler of souls and comfort me.
Come, sweet guest of our hearts, and never
    depart from me.

Come, true repose of my life, and restore me.

Pause. Then three Glory Bes.
Holy Spirit, Eternal Love,
Fountain of heavenly light,
Come, inflame our hearts.

(Continued tomorrow)

Application: Simply spend a few quiet moments with this prayer, reflecting on the role of the Holy Spirit in your life.

AUGUST 24

That the Spirit may descend on you

Our Lady addresses Jelena's prayer group:

> *Why have you stopped saying the prayer to the Holy Spirit? Remember that I have asked you to pray always and at all times that the Holy Spirit may descend upon you. Begin again to pray for this (LJM 1-2-84).*

And in John's gospel, Christ asks us to drink of the Spirit:

> On the last day of the festival, the great day, while Jesus was standing there, he cried out, "Let anyone who is thirsty come to me, and let the one who believes in me drink. As the scripture has said, 'Out of the believer's heart shall flow rivers of living water.'" Now he said this about the Spirit, which believers in him were to receive; for as yet there was no Spirit, because Jesus was not yet glorified (Jn 7:37-39).

Reflection: Today the Blessed Mother calls us to "pray always and at all times so that the Holy Spirit may descend upon you." Yesterday we began a special prayer to the Spirit. Today, taking Our Lady's advice, let us conclude the Prayer of Invocation to the Holy Spirit:

Eternal Father, in the name of Jesus Christ, and through the intercession of the Immaculate Virgin Mary, send to me your Holy Spirit.

Come, Holy Spirit, and grant me the gift of wisdom.

Come, Holy Spirit, and grant me the gift of understanding.

Come, Holy Spirit, and grant me the gift of counsel.

Come, Holy Spirit, and grant me the gift of fortitude.

Come, Holy Spirit, and grant me the gift of knowledge.

Come, Holy Spirit, and grant me the gift of piety.

Come, Holy Spirit, and grant me the gift of fear of the Lord.

Pause. Then three Glory Bes.

Holy Spirit, Eternal Love,
Fountain of heavenly light,
Come, inflame our hearts.

Application: Thank God for the gifts of the Spirit which you have received. Reflect on how you are using these gifts for the sake of others.

AUGUST 25

St. Joseph Calasanctius

We are called to evangelize through the Madonna's words and miracles at Medjugorje:

I am anxious for people to know what is happening in Medjugorje. Speak about it so that everyone will be converted (SM 85).

And in Matthew's gospel, the risen Christ also gives his disciples a special charge:

Go therefore and make disciples of all the nations, baptizing them in the name of the Father and of the Son and of the Holy Spirit, teaching them to obey everything that I have commanded you (Mt 28:19-20).

Reflection: St. John Calasanctius took this commission of Christ to heart in his evangelization and teaching of the young. Born in 1557, he was ordained a priest and later dedicated himself to caring for poor children, founding a religious order pledged to that work. "This ministry," he once wrote, "is directed to the well-being of body and soul. At the same time that it shapes behavior, it also fosters devotion and Christian doctrine."

Application: Deeply devoted to the Blessed Virgin, St. Joseph Calasanctius wrote this Trinitarian Prayer of Praise to Mary. Let us offer it now for all children that live in poverty:

Let us offer praise and thanksgiving to the Most Holy Trinity who has shown us the Virgin Mary, clothed with the sun, the moon beneath her feet, and on her head a mystic crown of twelve stars.
Let us praise and thank the divine Father who
　　elected her for his daughter. Our Father. . . .
Praised be the divine Father who predestined her
　　to be the Mother of his divine Son.
　　Hail Mary. . . .
Praised be the divine Father who preserved
　　her from all stain in her conception.
　　Hail Mary. . . .

Praised be the divine Father who adorned her at her birth with his most beautiful gifts.
Hail Mary. . . .

Praised be the divine Father who gave her
St. Joseph to be her companion and
chaste spouse.
Hail Mary. . . . Glory be. . . .

Let us praise and thank the divine Son who chose her for his Mother. Our Father. . . .

Praised be the divine Son who became incarnate in her bosom and there abode for nine months.
Hail Mary. . . .

Praised be the divine Son who was born of her and was nourished by her. Hail Mary. . . .

Praised be the divine Son who in his childhood was taught by her. Hail Mary. . . .

Praised be the divine Son who revealed to her the mystery of the redemption of the world.
Hail Mary. . . . Glory be. . . .

Let us praise and thank the Holy Spirit who took her for his spouse. Our Father. . . .

Praised be the Holy Spirit who revealed first to her his name of Holy Spirit. Hail Mary. . . .

Praised be the Holy Spirit by whose miracle she was at once Virgin and Mother. Hail Mary. . . .

Praised be the Holy Spirit by whose power she was the living temple of the ever blessed Trinity.
Hail Mary. . . .

Praised be the Holy Spirit by whom she was exalted in heaven above every living creature.
Hail Mary. . . . Glory be. . . .

Fasting with the heart

Today Our Lady speaks of fasting "with the heart":

Dear children, today I call you to begin fasting with the heart. There are many people who fast only because everyone else is fasting. It has become an empty practice. And so I ask the parish to fast out of gratitude to God for allowing me to remain so long with you. Dear children, fast and pray with the heart (WM 9-20-84).

In Luke's gospel, Jesus fasts in the wilderness:

Jesus, full of the Holy Spirit, returned from the Jordan and was led by the Spirit in the wilderness, where for forty days he was tempted by the Devil. He ate nothing at all during those days, and when they were over, he was famished (Lk 4:1-2).

Reflection: At times, Our Lady of Medjugorje speaks of "fasting with the heart," a term meaning, first of all, accepting the invitation to fast with confidence in God, who will bring forth beautiful fruits from our efforts.

Second, it means to anticipate and welcome the spiritual dynamic that will begin to reshape our lives; this includes a deeper sense of repentance, a joyous realization of God's forgiveness, and a growing love, faith, and hope.

Fasting with the heart also means experiencing a new freedom from material things, for we will begin to see the essential in life and not be mired in the superfluous. It means growing in a profound love for God and neighbor, a deepening joy in Christ, and new eyes to see as the Lord sees. Ultimately, to fast with the heart is a gift of grace, not a penance, from the heavenly Father.

Application: Can you identify any changes that have happened to you since you began fasting? What changes would you like to see?

AUGUST 27

St. Monica

Today the Blessed Mother speaks of faith as the foundation of our lives:

From the very beginning I have been conveying the messages of God to the world. It is a great pity not to believe it. Faith is essential, but one cannot compel a person to believe. Faith is the foundation from which everything else flows (FY 12-31-81).

In his letter to the Hebrews, Paul defines faith:

Now faith is the assurance of things hoped for, the conviction of things not seen. Indeed, by faith our ancestors received approval. By faith we understand that the worlds were prepared by the word of God, so that what is seen was made from things that are not visible (Heb 11:1-3).

Reflection: Today we honor one of the great women of faith, St. Monica, the patroness of Christian mothers. Born in 331, she married and had children, one of whom was Augustine. She poured forth many tears and prayers for his conversion, which she witnessed in her lifetime. He later went on to become a priest, bishop, and one of the church's greatest theologians. It is appropriate that our readings today deal with faith, for this was the foundation of Monica's life and her legacy to her children.

Application: Faith is a gift. Today, pray in thanksgiving for this most precious of gifts, and ask the Lord to deepen it.

AUGUST 28

St. Augustine

The following is Our Lady's monthly message for May, 1990:

Dear children, I wish to help you grow in renunciation and mortification. In this way you will be able to understand the beautiful life of those who especially give themselves to me. Dear children, God blesses you day after day and wishes to change your life. Therefore, pray that you may have the strength to change it (MM 5-25-90).

John the Baptist also called the people to change their lives by turning from sin:

In those days John the Baptist appeared in the wilderness of Judea, proclaiming, "Repent, for the kingdom of heaven has come near" (Mt 3:1-2).

Reflection: St. Augustine was born in Africa in 354. His young adulthood was a stormy period, including fathering a child out of wedlock. In his twenties he moved to Milan, Italy, where he became a professor of rhetoric, but his personal life continued to be stormy and wayward.

While in Milan, two things happened to him. First, he became increasingly unhappy with his personal life, and second, he became attracted to Christianity. It was in this frame of mind that he sat down one day and began to ponder his life. Suddenly he broke into tears and began to cry out to God: "and you, Lord! How long will you be angry with me? Forever? Why not at this very hour put an end to my life?"

Augustine said later:

I was crying out like this when, suddenly, I heard the voice of a child. It seemed to say, "Take and read! Take and read!" I stood up, for now the voice seemed like a command to read the Bible. I got a Bible and opened it, and the first words my eyes fell upon were from the letter of Paul to the Romans. They read: "Throw off the works of darkness and put on the armor of light; let us conduct ourselves properly as in the day, not in orgies and drunkenness . . . not in rivalry and jealousy. But put on the Lord Jesus Christ, and make no provision for the desires of the flesh" (Rom 13:12-14).

When Augustine read this, he stopped. There was not need to go on. He says: "My heart was suddenly flooded with a light that erased all my doubts. And my soul was filled with a deep peace."

Application: Today, as Our Lady asks, pray for the strength to continue your ongoing conversion.

AUGUST 29

Pray for the young

Our Lady speaks of young people today:

My dear children, your prayers have helped me to fulfill my plans. Praised be Jesus, my dear children! Dear children, tonight I especially ask you to pray for the young. I would like to recommend to my priests that they organize groups where young people can be taught and given good advice for their lives.

To all of you who are here tonight, I ask that you be the messengers of peace to others, especially to young people. Your Mother is praying for you tonight (VPG 8-22-88).

Paul's words to the people of Thessalonica can be applied to young people:

> As you know, we dealt with each one of you like a father with his children, urging and encouraging you and pleading that you lead a life worthy of God, who calls you into his own kingdom and glory (1 Thes 2:11-12).

Reflection: Some time ago a quick thinking ten-year-old boy saved the life of a nine-year-old girl who had fallen through the ice on a river near Toledo, Ohio. Spotting Janet Rospert struggling in the cold waters of the ice-crusted river, young Richard Dicken wasted no time in putting his ax to the best use he ever made of it. He quickly climbed a nearby tree and chopped off a sturdy branch. Then, hurrying to the shore, he reached out with the branch to Janet, who was precariously hanging onto a thin piece of ice. In a matter of moments he had pulled her to safety.

In these days much is said and written about the shortcomings of young people. But there are countless instances like this that reflect the unselfishness and courage that God has instilled in his youth. For our part, the Blessed Mother asks us to be "the messengers of peace to others, to young people especially."

Application: Today simply put into practice the Gospa's message: "Pray especially for the young."

Deeds of love and mercy

In her monthly message for March, 1987, the Virgin said:

> Dear children, today I thank you for your presence here where I am giving you special graces. I call each of you to begin to live, starting today, the life which God desires of you, and to begin doing good deeds of love and mercy. But, dear children, I do not want you to live this message and, at the same time, sadden me by committing sin.
>
> Dear children, I also want each of you to begin living a new life, being careful not to ruin all that God has done in you and has given to you. As I give you my special blessing, know that I am constantly with you on your road to conversion (MM 3-25-87).

At the Last Supper, Jesus also spoke of love and service:

> After he had washed their feet, had put on his robe, and had returned to the table, he said to them, "Do you know what I have done to you? You call me teacher and Lord—and you are right, for that is what I am. So if I, your Lord and teacher, have washed your feet, you also ought to wash one another's feet. For I have set you an example, that you also should do as I have done to you" (Jn 13:12-15).

Reflection: Loving service to others was a major theme of Christ's ministry on earth, and a repeated message at Medjugorje as well. The example of love has drawn countless numbers to the faith over the ages. One famous example:

When Sir Henry Stanley went out to Africa in 1871 and found the missionary Dr. Livingstone, he spent months in his company. Livingstone never spoke to Stanley about spiritual things. Throughout those months, Stanley watched the old man. Livingstone's habits were beyond his comprehension, and so was his patience. He could not understand Livingstone's sympathy for the Africans. For the sake of Christ and his gospel, the missionary doctor was patient, untiring, and eager. Stanley wrote, "When I saw that unwearied patience, that unflagging zeal, those enlightened sons of Africa, I became a Christian at his side, though he never spoke to me about it."

Application: Call to mind someone who has inspired you by their example of faith. Has your own faith had an effect on others?

AUGUST 31

What to say in prayer

To Jelena, concerning prayer, Our Lady said:

I know that I speak to you very often about prayer, but know that there are many people in the world who do not pray, who do not even know what to say in prayer (LJM 1-15-84).

And in Psalm 81, the Lord himself speaks in answer to a prayer:

I relieved your shoulder of the burden;
your hands were freed from the basket.
In distress you called, and I rescued you.
—Psalm 81:6-7

Reflection: In a conversation with Marija Pavlovic on February 2, 1992, as we were discussing this book, she asked that I especially emphasize Our Lady's call to prayer.

> It is the most important thing. There is nothing the Gospa wants more. She calls everyone to three hours of prayer—which is only one-eighth of our day. She asks for prayer in the morning, at noon, and in the evening. Her favorite prayer, of course, is the rosary, and the greatest of all prayer is holy Mass.

Marija has been invited to many Medjugorje conferences in America and elsewhere, but they pose a problem for her: "They should follow the idea of a retreat rather than a convention. Our Lady calls us to actually pray and live her messages, but sometimes we get caught up in just talking about them."

It is significant that when Marija travels abroad with Fr. Slavko to give presentations on Medjugorje, the format they use is that of a retreat. Marija speaks only briefly and then leads the participants in the rosary. Such a conference retreat would still bring together Medjugorje's friends in camaraderie and support, with the emphasis on prayer and spiritual growth.

Application: Today, reflect on the priority and time you give to prayer. Can you expand your private prayer a bit at a time? This was the approach Our Lady used with the seers and villagers of Medjugorje.

Everything is unfolding

On the anniversary of the apparitions in 1982, the Blessed Virgin said:

Thank the people in my name for their prayers, sacrifices, and acts of penance. Have them persevere in prayer, fasting, and conversion, and ask them to wait patiently for the realization of my promise. Everything is unfolding according to God's plan (FY 6-24-82).

Matthew's gospel portrays Jesus himself fasting:

Then Jesus was led up by the Spirit into the wilderness to be tempted by the devil. He fasted forty days and forty nights, and afterwards he was famished. The tempter came and said to him, "If you are the Son of God, command these stones to become loaves of bread." But he answered, "It is written, 'One does not live by bread alone, but by every word that comes from the mouth of God'" (Mt 4:1-4).

Reflection: Our Lady has often said that fasting and prayer are essential in achieving peace. Fr. Slavko Barbaric writes:

Those who are assiduous in their prayer and fasting will attain absolute confidence in God; they will obtain the gifts of reconciliation and forgiveness, and thus serve the cause of peace; for peace originates in our heats and from there spreads to our neighbors, and ultimately to the entire world.

Peace is not static; it is dynamic, flowing; therefore it can prosper only in the hearts of those who live the faith, who can love and forgive as a way of living.

The Lord wishes that we fast and pray so that we can find our joy in him and in our neighbor, so that we can live in harmony with others and so create peace in ever widening circles.

Application: Today, simply reflect on the following: "Peace is not made at the council tables or by treaties, but in the hearts of men" (Woodrow Wilson).

SEPTEMBER 2

Satan wants you

To Ivan's prayer group, regarding Satan:

My dear children, tonight your Mother warns you that during these times Satan wants you and is looking for you! It takes only a little spiritual emptiness to allow Satan to work in you. For this reason your Mother wishes you to begin to pray, for your weapon against Satan is prayer. In prayer with the heart you will overcome him (VPG 9-5-88).

In Mark's gospel, Jesus confronts the Evil One:

Then Jesus asked him, "What is your name?" He replied, "My name is Legion; for we are many." He begged him earnestly not to send them out of the country. Now there on the hillside a great herd of swine was feeding; and the unclean spirits begged him, "Send us into the swine; let us enter them." So he gave them permission. And the unclean spirits came out and entered the swine; and the herd, numbering about two thousand, rushed down the steep bank into the sea, and were drowned in the sea (Mk 5:9-13).

Reflection: As we see, Jesus brings about the healing of this demon-possessed man by commanding the legion of demons to come out. By this action, Christ revealed his identity as the Son of God, with authority even over the powers of evil. Later, through his cross and resurrection, he would win the eternal victory over these powers, establishing a kingdom free of sin, evil, and death.

Through prayer and discernment, we can often recognize activities in which the demonic is involved. Besides the raw occult, the Evil One can subtly use a number of channels to influence us, including spiritism, horoscopes, mediums, ouija boards, the New Age movement, and the like. Out of concern and love for her children, the church has always condemned such practices as contrary to the teaching and spirit of Christ, who alone is our way, truth, and life.

Application: In what areas of your life are you most susceptible to the power of the Evil One? Pray for discernment and strength.

SEPTEMBER 3

St. Gregory the Great

Regarding the similarity of the third secret of Fatima and the secrets given at Medjugorje, the Virgin said:

Do not fear anything. You must forget what is behind you in your life. From now on, I want only that you be new people. Do not fear anything when I am near you, for I love you (LJM 1986).

And from St. John's first letter:

There is no fear in love, but perfect love casts out fear; for fear has to do with punishment, and whoever fears has not reached perfection in love (1 Jn 4:18).

Reflection: St. Gregory the Great was a fearless champion of the faith, practicing the love and sacrifice that he preached so eloquently. After a career in civil and political service, Gregory became a monk and rigorously observed the Benedictine Rule the rest of his life, even after becoming Pope in 590 (a position he tried to avoid).

As Pope he continued his work on behalf of the poor of the city, and was a competent administrator of the early church. He gave his fellow bishops a model and was an outstanding moral teacher of his time. His writings are very pastoral and in one of them, a homily on Ezekiel, he gives advice to other church leaders:

> Note that a man whom the Lord sends forth as a preacher is called a watchman. A watchman always stands on a height so that he can see from afar what is coming. Anyone appointed to be a watchman for the people must stand on a height for all his life to help them by his foresight.

Gregory was a Pope of great determination, immense ability and tireless energy. Although he was ill throughout the years of his pontificate, he did not spare himself.

Application: "Do not fear anything," the Madonna says today, "for I love you." Taking these words to heart, give over to Our Lady any fears or anxieties that are burdening you, for she truly wants us to experience the peace of God, that same peace which sustained St. Gregory in his heavy responsibilities.

The kingdom of love

The Queen of Peace speaks of love today:

I wish to engrave in every heart the sign of love. If you love all mankind, then there will be peace within you. When you are at peace with all men, it is the kingdom of love (LJM 1-18-84).

And out of love, Jesus heals the blind beggar Bartimaeus:

Bartimaeus, son of Timaeus, a blind beggar, was sitting by the roadside. When he heard that it was Jesus of Nazareth, he began to shout out and say, "Jesus, Son of David, have mercy on me!" Many sternly ordered him to be quiet, but he cried out even more loudly, "Son of David, have mercy on me!" Jesus stood still and said, "Call him here," and they called the blind man, saying to him "Take heart; get up, he is calling you." So throwing off his cloak, he sprang up and came to Jesus. Then Jesus said to him, "What do you want me to do for you?" The blind man said to him, "My teacher, let me see again," Jesus said to him "Go; your faith has made you well." Immediately he regained his sight and followed him on the way (Mk 10:46-52).

Reflection: Beggars were a common sight in most towns in first-century Israel. Since most occupations of that day required physical labor, anyone with a crippling disease or handicap was at a severe disadvantage and was usually forced to beg, even though the law of Moses commanded care for such needy people.

Blindness was considered a curse from God due to sin; but Christ refuted this idea when he reached out in love to heal those who were blind. It was to the ignored, oppressed, and despised of society that Christ went to proclaim—in both word and deed—the kingdom of love. He charges us with the same mission, as does Our Lady of Medjugorje: to bring God's love to the ignored, oppressed, and despised of our own community.

Application: Today, look about to see those in special need of your care and attention. Pray for a deeper measure of God's love to help the needy.

SEPTEMBER 5

The Lord's Prayer

From Luke's gospel, the gift of the Lord's Prayer:

> [Jesus] was praying in a certain place, and after he had finished, one of his disciples said to him, "Lord, teach us to pray, as John taught his disciples." He said to them, "When you pray, say:
> 'Father, hallowed be your name.
> Your kingdom come.
> Give us each day our daily bread,
> And forgive us our sins,
> for we ourselves forgive everyone indebted to us.
> And do not bring us to the time of trial.'"
>
> —Luke 11:1-4

Reflection: For the next three days, let us reflect on the Lord's Prayer, using the commentary that Our Lady herself dictated to Jelena, the young locutionist:

Our: This is *your* Father. Do not be afraid—hold out your hands to him (pause a moment). *Our Father* means that God has given himself to you truly as a Father, and when you possess him, you possess everything. Just as your earthly father would do anything good for you, so would your heavenly Father, but infinitely so. My child, *Our Father* means that the Lord offers you everything.

Father: Reflect on who the Father is. Whose Father is he? Where is this Father?

Who art in heaven: (Pause for a moment.) Just as your earthly father loves you, so your heavenly Father loves you beyond imagining. A human father may get angry, but God the Father does not; he offers only love.

Hallowed be thy name: For your part, deeply respect your Father, for he has given you everything; he deserves and wants your love. Glorify and praise his name. Say to those who sin, "He is truly your Father, as he is my Father. So let us serve him and glorify his name." This is the meaning of *Hallowed be thy name.*

Application: Today simply meditate on God's name, "Father," for several minutes.

SEPTEMBER 6

The Lord's Prayer

Yesterday we read Luke's passage on the Lord's Prayer; today, let us review Matthew's account:

Pray then in this way:
Our Father in heaven,
hallowed be your name.
Your kingdom come.
Your will be done,
on earth as it is in heaven.
Give us this day our daily bread.
And forgive us our debts,
as we also have forgiven our debtors.
And do not bring us to the time of trial,
but rescue us from the Evil One.

For if you forgive others their trespasses, your heavenly Father will also forgive you; but if you do not forgive others, neither will your Father forgive your trespasses (Mt 6:9-15).

———————

Reflection: We continue today with Our Lady's commentary on the Lord's Prayer as given to Jelena:

Thy kingdom come: These are words of gratitude to Christ; we are telling him: "Truly, Lord, we know nothing. Without your kingdom, without your presence among us, we are weak and empty. Help us to realize that our earthly kingdom soon passes away, but that the kingdom of heaven remains eternally. O Lord, re-establish your kingdom among us!"

Thy will be done: "O Lord, help us to realize the futility of our kingdoms of materialism and vanity; may they fade to nothing in the presence of your kingdom of light and truth. At this moment, and forever, may thy will be done."

On earth as it is in heaven: "In heaven, Lord, the glorious angels revere and adore you; may our spirits be joined to theirs, that we may also revere and obey you. And through your power, may the holiness of heaven touch the earth, making it holy and bright with your love and peace."

Give us this day our daily bread: "Give us, Lord, your peace, your love, your mercy, as our spiritual bread. Nourish us today and always with this bread, your divine spirit within us. O Lord, we pray for this food, for it is life; help us to understand how to open our hearts to receive this precious gift, the fruit of grace and prayer."

Application: Today, pray the Our Father slowly and reverently, reflecting on each phrase.

The Lord's Prayer

Having given his disciples the Lord's Prayer, Jesus then encourages them to pray perseveringly to the Father:

So I say to you, ask, and it will be given you; search, and you will find; knock, and the door will be opened for you. For everyone who asks, receives; and everyone who searches, finds; and for everyone who knocks, the door will be opened (Lk 11:9-10).

Reflection: Today we conclude Our Lady's commentary on the Lord's Prayer, as dictated to Jelena:

And forgive us our trespasses: "Forgive us, Lord, our sins. Forgive us for not being faithful, for not being better than we are."

As we forgive those who trespass against us: "Forgive us our sins, Lord, and help us to forgive those whom we have been unable to forgive. O Jesus, we beseech you to forgive all our sins."

Dear children, I, your Mother, call you to genuine forgiveness. Although you pray that your sins be forgiven to the extent that you forgive those of others, if this truly came to pass, you would be forgiven little. Therefore, forgive one another from the heart. This is what your heavenly Father expects when you pray the words: "as we forgive those who trespass against us."

And lead us not into temptation: "Lord, deliver us from severe trials, for we are weak. Guard us so that temptations may not lead us to ruin."

But deliver us from evil: "Lord, deliver us from every evil. Help us so that only good comes out of our trials and temptations, that we may move forward in our spiritual journey."

Amen: "So be it, Lord; thy will be done."

Application: Today, pray the Our Father again as a meditation, using Our Lady's thoughts as given over the last three days. You may wish to use this reflection several more times this month, for it gives a freshness and added meaning to this greatest of prayers.

SEPTEMBER 8

Love

Given to Ivan's prayer group in June, 1986:

Love. If you do not love, you will not be able to give your testimony. You will not be able to witness for either me or for Jesus (6-6-86).

And for Paul, love creates our unity in Christ:

There is one body and one Spirit, just as you were called to the one hope of your calling, one Lord, one faith, one baptism, one God and Father of all, who is above all and through all and in all. But each of us was given grace according to the measure of Christ's gift (Eph 4:4-7).

Reflection: "We are all parts of one body," Paul says, and we have been given many gifts and abilities. Unity does not just happen; we have to work at it. Often differences among people can lead to division, but this should not be true in the church. Instead of concentrating on what divides us, we are called to remember what unites us: one body, one Spirit, one Lord, one faith, one baptism, one God.

Have we grown in appreciating those who are different from us? Are we able to see how their differing gifts and viewpoints can help the church as it strives to serve God and his people? With a little effort, we may learn to enjoy the way members of Christ's body complement one another.

Application: This week, consciously try to be a bridgebuilder between people at your workplace, in your parish, and in your local community. This is ministry you can practice your whole life long.

SEPTEMBER 9

Surrender all your problems

The Virgin speaks of surrender and prayer today:

> *Dear children, today I am calling you to renew your heart. Open yourself to God and surrender to him all your problems and crosses, so that God may transform everything into joy.*
>
> *Little children, you cannot open yourselves to God if you do not pray. From today, then, decide to consecrate a time and a day solely for an encounter with God in silence. In that way, you will be able, with God's help, to witness my presence here. Little children, I do not wish to force you; rather, freely give God your time—as the children of God (MM 7-25-89).*

Psalm 125 also urges us to trust in God:

> Those who trust in the Lord are like Mount Zion
> which cannot be moved, but abides forever.
> As the mountains surround Jerusalem,
> so the Lord surrounds his people,
> from this time on and forevermore.

—Psalm 125:1-2

Reflection: Our Lady of Medjugorje often speaks of trust, of surrendering ourselves completely to the Lord, as an essential step in our spiritual journey. For members of Alcoholics Anonymous, this surrender is a matter of life and death. Suffering from an incurable addiction that ruthlessly destroys the body, mind, and soul, the only way to arrest the disease is by spiritual means, for simple willpower is useless. The alcoholic must surrender himself and his disease to God, who has the power to do for him what he cannot.

Thus step three of the twelve steps of A.A. states: "We made a decision to turn our will and our lives over to the care of God as we understood him." From Alcoholics Anonymous:

> At the third step, many of us said to our Maker, as we understood him: "God, I offer myself to thee— to build with me and to do with me as Thou wilt. Relieve me of the bondage of self, that I may better do Thy will. Take away my difficulties, that victory over them may bear witness to those I would help by Thy Power, Thy Love, and Thy Way of life. May I do Thy will always!"

With this surrender, a new life opens up for the alcoholic. Our Lady knows that this would also be the case with us, that we too would know a new freedom, peace, and joy in life, if we could but surrender and trust in God.

Application: Today, abandon yourself to God using the above prayer from A.A.

SEPTEMBER 10

Let prayer be life for you

In this monthly message, Our Lady encourages us to pray:

Dear children, today I wish to call all of you to prayer. Let prayer be life for you. Dear children, devote your time only to Jesus and he will give you everything that you are seeking. He will reveal himself to you fully.

Dear children, Satan is strong and he watches each of you in order to tempt you. Pray, and then he will neither be able to injure you nor block you on the way to holiness. Dear children, grow closer to God day by day through prayer (MM 9-25-87).

And in Psalm 61, a prayer for refuge:

Hear my cry, O God;
listen to my prayer.
From the end of the earth I call to you,
when my heart is faint.

—Psalm 61:1

Reflection: The church has a great treasury of prayer, the subject of our readings today. One little known prayer is The Crown of Twelve Stars of the Blessed Virgin, sometimes called The Little Crown of Mary, referring to the image of Mary in Revelation, the woman clothed with the sun and crowned with twelve stars. It was a favorite prayer of St. Louis de Montfort, the tireless supporter of Marian devotion. It is presented here in three parts, over the next three days:

1. The Crown of Excellence: To honor the divine motherhood of the Blessed Virgin, her ineffable virginity, eternal purity, and perfection in virtue.

First star: Our Father . . . . Hail Mary . . . .
Blessed are you, Queen of Peace, who bore the Lord, the Creator of the world; you gave birth to him who made you and yet remain a virgin forever.

Rejoice, O Virgin Mary, rejoice with us a thousand times!

Second star: Hail Mary . . . .

O holy and immaculate Virgin, I know not with what praise to extol thee, since you bore in your womb the One whom even the heavens cannot contain.

Rejoice, O Virgin Mary, rejoice with us a thousand times!

Third star: Hail Mary . . . .

You are beautiful, O Mother of God, with no stain upon you.

Rejoice, O Virgin Mary, rejoice with us a thousand times!

Fourth star: Hail Mary . . . .

Your virtues, O Queen of Heaven, surpass the number of stars in the sky.

Rejoice, O Virgin Mary, rejoice with us a thousand times!

Glory be . . . .

Application: Offer this prayer during your quiet time today.

SEPTEMBER 11

Be united to Jesus

Our Lady desires us to be united with Christ through prayer:

Dear children, today I am calling you to pray with the heart. Throughout this season of grace, I wish each of you to be united to Jesus. But without unceasing prayer you will not be able to experience the beauty and greatness of the grace which God is offering you.

Therefore, little children, always fill your hearts with even the smallest prayers. Know that I am with you and that I keep constant watch over every heart that is given to me (MM 2-25-89).

And in Psalm 66, the author praises God for hearing his prayers:

Come and hear, all you who fear God,
and I will tell what he has done for me.
I cried aloud to him,
and he was extolled with my tongue.
If I had cherished iniquity in my heart,
the Lord would not have listened.
But truly God has listened;
he has given heed to the words of my prayer.
Blessed be God,
because he has not rejected my prayer
or removed his steadfast love from me.

—Psalm 66:16-20

Reflection: "Little children," the Madonna says today, "at all times fill your heart with even the smallest prayers." Let us do just that, as we continue with The Little Crown of Mary:

2. *The Crown of Power:* To honor the Queenship of Mary, her magnificence, her universal mediation and the power of her love.

Fifth star: Our Father . . . . Hail Mary . . . .
Glory to you, Empress of the World! Bring us with you to the joys of heaven.

Rejoice, O Virgin Mary, rejoice with us a thousand times!

Sixth star: Hail Mary . . . .

Glory to you, O treasure house of the Lord's graces! Grant us a share in thy riches.

Rejoice, O Virgin Mary, rejoice with us a thousand times!

Seventh star: Hail Mary . . . .

Glory to you, O Mediatrix between God and man! Through you may the Almighty show us favor.

Rejoice, O Virgin Mary, rejoice with us a thousand times!

Eighth star: Hail Mary . . . .

Glory to you who forever guards truth, who steps upon the serpent's head! Be thou our loving guide.

Rejoice, O Virgin Mary, rejoice with us a thousand times!

Glory be . . . .

Application: Meditate on the prayers of the Second Crown today.

SEPTEMBER 12

Dedicate yourselves to prayer

The Blessed Virgin asks us to consecrate ourselves to prayer "with special love":

Dear children, again today I call you to pray. You do not realize, dear children, the value of prayer, as long as you refuse to say: "Now is the time for prayer; now nothing else is important to me; now no one is important to me but God alone."

Dear children, dedicate yourselves to prayer with special love. In this way, God will be able to give you his graces (WM 10-2-86).

And in Psalm 84, a prayer of joy to the Lord:

> O Lord God of hosts, hear my prayer;
> give ear, O God of Jacob!
> Behold our shield, O God;
> look on the face of your anointed. . . .
> For the Lord God is a sun and shield;
> he bestows favor and honor.
> No good thing does the Lord withhold
> from those who walk uprightly.
>
> —Psalm 84:8-9, 11

Reflection: In a number of her messages, the Virgin has urged us to set aside a special time for prayer each day, forgetting our worries and resting in God, who takes care of all the rest. We conclude today with part three of The Little Crown of Mary.

3. The Crown of Goodness: To honor the love and mercy of the Blessed Mother toward sinners, the poor, the just, and the dying.

Ninth star: Our Father . . . . Hail Mary . . . .
Blessed are you, O Refuge of Sinners! Intercede for us with God.

Rejoice, O Virgin Mary, rejoice with us a thousand times!

Tenth star: Hail Mary . . . .
Blessed are you, Mother of Orphans! Seek the Lord's favor to us.

Rejoice, O Virgin Mary, rejoice with us a thousand times!

Eleventh star: Hail Mary . . . .
Blessed are you, Queen of Angels! Lead us with you to the peace of heaven.

Rejoice, O Virgin Mary, rejoice with us a thousand times!

Twelfth star: Hail Mary . . . .

Blessed are you, Our Mother, who comes to our aid in life and in death! Lead us with you to the kingdom of Heaven.

Rejoice, O Virgin Mary, rejoice with us a thousand times!

Glory be . . . .

Application: Simply offer The Little Crown of Mary once more this week, to familiarize yourself with its structure, rhythm, and message.

SEPTEMBER 13

Rejoice in the Mass

Our Lady speaks of the Mass today:

Dear children, I call you to live the holy Mass. There are many of you who have experienced the beauty of the Mass, but there are others who go unwillingly. I have chosen you, dear children, and Jesus gives you his graces in the Mass. And so let everyone who comes to Mass be joyful. Come with love and rejoice in the Mass (WM 4-3-86).

And in John's gospel, the Lord says:

Those who eat my flesh and drink my blood abide in me, and I in them (Jn 6:56).

Reflection: When we receive communion at Mass, we receive the living Christ and, in a real sense, embrace him. But in communion Jesus also receives us and embraces us.

Fr. Albert Shamon uses the analogy of a child running to embrace his father. But because of his size, he cannot do it until his father first picks him up and hugs him. "In the same way," Fr. Shamon says, "at holy communion we rush to meet Christ, but we can do little more. He must pick us up, embrace us, love us, pour his life and love into us."

Not only does Christ embrace us, but he is *in* us and we are *in* him. St. Cyril of Alexandria compared this union in holy communion to two pieces of wax melted together. St. Thérèse of Lisieux described her first communion as a *fusion* with Christ. Just as food becomes one with the eater (some say "you are what you eat"), so communion makes us one with Christ. We become God-like, divinized, eternal, like him. It is the greatest gift in the world.

Application: Reflect today on Christ's profound "bread of life" discourse, found in John 6:25-59.

SEPTEMBER 14

The Triumph of the Cross

The following are two messages the Madonna gave on the feast of the Holy Cross:

Dear children, during these days, when you joyfully celebrate the feast of the cross, I wish that your own cross become a source of joy.

Especially, dear children, pray in order to be able to accept sickness and suffering with love, as Jesus did. It is only in this way, that I can experience the joy of giving you the graces and the cures, which Jesus permits me to grant you (WM 9-11-86).

Dear children! I wish to tell you these days to put the cross at the center of your life. Pray especially before the cross which is the origin of great graces. In your homes make a special consecration to the cross of the Lord. Promise that you will not offend Jesus nor the cross (WM 9-12-85).

And from Paul's Letter to the Philippians:

And being found in human form, he humbled himself and became obedient to the point of death—even death on a cross. Therefore God also highly exalted him and gave him the name that is above every name (Phil 2:7-9).

Reflection: To the secular world, the triumph of the cross is a contradiction in terms. How can life and victory come from death and defeat? Yet to believers, the Lord can and does transform evil into good, tragedy into victory, death into life. In this perspective Our Lady can say, "I desire that your cross also would be a joy for you." For our crosses are not dead-ends. When linked to the passion and cross of Christ, they become grace-filled and redemptive for ourselves and others.

The key to unlocking the redemptive power of our crosses is, first of all, our acceptance of them. The Blessed Virgin asks us to, "pray that you may be able to accept sickness and suffering with love, the way Jesus accepted them." As the Serenity Prayer says,

O God, grant me the serenity to accept the things I cannot change,
    the courage to change the things I can,
    and the wisdom to know the difference.

Secondly, to consciously offer our suffering to Christ, to link our cross to his, is to give it a redemptive power. "Only that way," Our Lady says, "shall I be able, with joy, to give out to you the graces and healings which Jesus is permitting me."

Application: At one point in his talks before pilgrims, Fr. Jozo asks them to kiss the picture of Mary he has just given them, for "she is your Mother." Today take down your household cross and reverently kiss it, for this is our Brother. Then offer the Serenity Prayer.

SEPTEMBER 15

Our Lady of Sorrows

Our Lady said to Jelena in sorrow:

> *Where are the prayers which you addressed to me? My clothes were sparkling. Behold them soaked with tears. Oh, if you would know how the world today is plunged into sin. It seems to you that the world sins no longer, because here you live in a peaceful world where there is no confusion or perversity.*
>
> *If you knew how lukewarm they are in their faith, how many do not listen to Jesus. Oh, if you knew how much I suffer, you would sin no more. Oh, how I need your prayers. Pray! (LJM 11-6-83).*

From Psalm 51:

> For I know my transgressions,
> and my sin is ever before me.
> Against you, you alone, have I sinned,
> and done what is evil in your sight,
> so that you are justified in your sentence
> and blameless when you pass judgment.
>
> —Psalm 51:3-4

Reflection: On this feast of Our Lady of Sorrows, it is important to recall why the Blessed Virgin came to Medjugorje in the first place: "The world today," she said, "is plunged into sin." Mary does not want to discourage us in her description of the modern world.

But she wants us to be aware of the situation so we can help in changing it.

Our Lady of Sorrows gives us five weapons to combat the darkness of sin and hate, and it is fitting to review them once again:

1) *Prayer:* "Pray, and let the rosary be in your hands as a sign to Satan that you belong to me" (2-25-88);

2) *Fasting:* "The Devil is trying to conquer you. Do not permit him. Keep faith, fast, and pray" (11-16-81);

3) *Scripture reading:* "I call you to read the Bible every day in your home" (10-18-84);

4) *Confession:* "It is necessary to believe firmly, to go to confession regularly, and, likewise, to receive Holy Communion. It is the only salvation" (2-10-82);

5) *Holy Mass:* "Mass is the greatest prayer of God. You will never be able to understand its greatness" (1983).

Application: In praying the Sorrowful Mysteries today, use as your intention for each mystery one of the five messages Our Lady gives us, asking that she help us live it more fully.

SEPTEMBER 16

Satan plans to work even more

From a message on Satan in 1985:

Dear children, during these days you have savored the sweetness of God through the renewal in your parish. But Satan plans to work even more fiercely to take away your joy. Through prayer, however, you can completely disarm him and ensure your happiness (WM 1-24-85).

Paul tells the Thessalonians that the Lord will protect them from the Evil One:

> Finally, brothers and sisters, pray for us, so that the word of the Lord may spread rapidly and be glorified everywhere, just as it is among you, and that we may be rescued from wicked and evil people; for not all have faith. But the Lord is faithful; he will strengthen you and guard you from the Evil One (2 Thes 3:1-3).

Reflection: Both St. Paul and Our Lady speak of the reality of Satan. Beneath the surface of the routine of daily life, a fierce struggle among spiritual powers is being waged. The Virgin has said the stakes are high: human souls. Like wildfire, the power of evil forces can be devastating, often because it is disguised and its slow rot is not dramatic.

Our main defense, the Madonna says today, is prayer with the heart, and an awareness that the Evil One really does exist—for to be forewarned is to be forearmed. In another message, she recommended that we wear a blessed object. "Let the rosary in your hand be a sign to Satan that you belong to me."

Application: Today, pray for the gift of discernment, that you can recognize the presence of the Evil One when he is near. Remember that he takes flight at the first word of prayer.

SEPTEMBER 17

St. Robert Bellarmine

Our Lady gave this message of joy on Good Friday in 1984:

You should be filled with joy. Today, Jesus died for your salvation. He descends into hell and opens the gates of paradise. Let joy reign in your hearts! (LJM 4-20-84).

The promise of eternal life also marks this passage from John's gospel:

Do not let your hearts be troubled. Believe in God, believe also in me. In my Father's house there are many dwelling places. If it were not so, would I have told you that I go to prepare a place for you? And if I go and prepare a place for you, I will come again and will take you to myself, so that where I am, there you may be also (Jn 14:1-3).

Reflection: In his treatise "On the Ascent of the Mind to God," St. Robert Bellarmine (1542-1621) wrote:

Is it not true that you promise those who keep your commandments a reward more desirable than great wealth and sweeter than honey? You promise a most abundant reward, for as your apostle James says: "The Lord has prepared a crown of life for those who love him."

What is this crown of life? It is surely a greater good than we can conceive of or desire, as St. Paul says, quoting Isaiah: "Eye has not seen, ear has not heard, nor has it so much as dawned on man what God has prepared for those who love him."

These three readings all bear witness to the greatest promise of Christianity: eternal life. It is from this perspective that we are called to view life, a journey that culminates in sharing the life of God.

This certainly was the motivating force behind the life and work of Robert Bellarmine. Recognized as a brilliant scholar and preacher, he was named cardinal and bishop by Pope Clement VIII. Living in the stormy times following the Council of Trent, he became one of the church's greatest teachers. Thomas Jefferson in writing the Declaration of Independence incorporated his teaching on the inalienable rights of man.

In his personal life he was an austere ascetic, and tried always to live as closely as possible like the poor of his day. He died on this day in 1621, was canonized in 1930, and the following year declared a Doctor of the Church.

Application: The Mother of God reminds us: "[Christ] opens the gates of paradise. Let joy reign in your hearts!" Today reflect on your own experience of loss or death and take comfort in the words of Christ and the Virgin.

SEPTEMBER 18

Observe the complete fasts

In August of 1985, Our Lady told Ivan:

Observe the complete fasts, Wednesdays and Fridays. Pray at least the full rosary, the Joyful, Sorrowful, and the Glorious Mysteries (SM 8-14-85).

St. John the Baptist is seen fasting in Mark's gospel, but not in the usual way.

John the baptizer appeared in the wilderness, proclaiming a baptism of repentance for the forgiveness of sins. And the people from the whole Judean countryside and all the people of Jerusalem were going out to him, and were baptized by him in the river Jordan, confessing their sins. Now John was clothed with camel's hair, with a leather belt around his waist, and he ate locusts and wild honey (Mk 1:4-6).

Reflection: In Medjugorje, of course, Our Lady has asked for a return to the ancient practice of fasting. Once, in response to the question, "What is the best kind of fast?" the Virgin responded, "Bread and water."

Fr. Slavko Barbaric, who has been in Medjugorje since the apparitions began, states that, "We recognize that bread and water is not the *only* way to fast, but it is the 'best' way, according to the Madonna." Fr. Slavko suggests that most people need to grow into this kind of fasting. If someone has never fasted at all, it could be very discouraging to fast on bread and water only, unless he has received a special call from the Lord.

"There are other ways of fasting," he says, "which will accomplish the same objectives in us and, at the same time, help us to move toward the best fast." As examples, he mentions fasting from certain foods, eating foods without seasoning, eating what we normally dislike, foregoing desserts, or simply eating considerably less at each meal. "These are just a few ways of fasting related to food. The important thing is that we *begin* to fast in some way."

Application: St. John the Baptist fasted on locusts and wild honey, something that would probably kill us, but which suited his own spirituality. We have the freedom to choose our way of fasting. Today, then, while in prayer choose your fast for the next several weeks.

SEPTEMBER 19

Love with all your heart

The Queen of Peace speaks of love today:

If you love with all your heart, you will receive so much. If you hate, you will lose every thing. Dear children, love makes great things. The more love you have within you, the more you can love the people around you. That is why I ask you to pray unceasingly to Jesus that he fill your hearts with love (LJM 4-12-87).

Christ also speaks of the great commandment:

This is my commandment, that you love one another as I have loved you. No one has greater love than this, to lay down one's life for one's friends (Jn 15:12-13).

Reflection: Captain George Grant gives us a unique example of love in action. Several years ago he was given an extraordinary award for saving 106 lives during his fifty years at sea. His rescues included two men on a sinking fishing boat in the Gulf Stream, three others on a raft off the west coast of Mexico, seventeen sailors from a navel vessel that sank outside of San Francisco harbor, as well as eighty-three survivors of a collision between a tanker and an icebreaker.

The most unique rescue involved one of his own sailors who fell overboard and was not missed until several hours later. The captain immediately turned his ship about and retraced the exact course. After a careful search the seaman was eventually picked up unharmed.

Few of us can duplicate such dramatic feats of love, but in our own lives we have countless opportunities to love others by showing a Christlike concern and alertness for those in distress.

Application: As Our Lady says today, "Pray to Jesus that he may fill your hearts with love," and be on the lookout for those in trouble.

Pray to the Holy Spirit

Our Lady speaks today of the Holy Spirit:

The important thing is to pray to the Holy Spirit that he may descend upon you. When you have him, you have everything (FY 10-21-83).

In John's gospel, Jesus also speaks of the Holy Spirit:

And I will ask the Father, and he will give you another Advocate, to be with you forever. This is the Spirit of truth, whom the world cannot receive, because it neither sees him nor knows him, because he abides with you, and he will be in you (Jn 14:16-17).

Reflection: "Pray to the Holy Spirit," the Blessed Mother tells us today; and Jesus assures us that the Spirit "abides with you and is in you."

Let us then use this time to pray to the Spirit, using St. Augustine's Prayer for the Indwelling of the Spirit:

Holy Spirit, powerful Consoler, sacred Bond of the Father and the Son, Hope of the afflicted, descend into my heart and establish in it your loving dominion. Enkindle in my tepid soul the fire of your Love so that I may be wholly subject to you.

We believe that when you dwell in us, you also prepare a dwelling for the Father and the Son. Deign, therefore, to come to me, Consoler of abandoned souls, and Protector of the needy. Help the afflicted, strengthen the weak, and support the wavering.

Come and purify me. Let no evil desire take possession of me. You love the humble and resist the proud. Come to me, glory of the living, and hope of the dying. Lead me by your grace that I may always be pleasing to you.

Application: Continue to use this prayer throughout the week to deepen your devotion to the Spirit of God.

SEPTEMBER 21

St. Matthew

The virgin gives an appropriate message for this feast of Matthew, author of the first gospel:

> *Dear children, today I ask you to read the Bible in your homes everyday. Place it in a visible place there, where it will always remind you to read it and to pray (WM 10-18-84).*

And, of course, the call of Matthew:

> As Jesus was walking along, he saw a man called Matthew sitting at the tax booth; and he said to him, "Follow me." And he got up and followed him.
>
> And as he sat at dinner in the house, many tax collectors and sinners came and were sitting with him and his disciples. When the Pharisees saw this, they said to his disciples, "Why does your teacher eat with tax collectors and sinners?" But when he heard this, he said, "Those who are well have no need of a physician, but those who are sick. Go and learn what this means, 'I desire mercy, not sacrifice.' For I have come to call not the righteous but sinners" (Mt 9:9-13).

Reflection: One of the hallmarks of Christ's teaching was to love impartially all of God's children, to "hate the sin but love the sinner," to "judge not lest you be judged." This is especially clear in today's gospel passage. Having scandalized the Pharisees by associating with tax collectors and known sinners, Jesus responds to their accusations by saying simply, "People who are in good health do not need a doctor; sick people do."

The reasons for this impartial or unconditional love are several: 1) Our Lord requests this of us, reserving judgment to himself. Again from Matthew's gospel: "his sun rises on the bad and the good, he rains on the just and the unjust" (Mt 5:45). 2) We cannot see deeply or clearly into the heart of another person; only God has this ability and so only he can judge fairly. We are put in mind of Jesus' remarks about the speck in our neighbor's eye, and the plank in our own. 3) In judging others we run the risk of pride, one of the seven deadly sins. 4) Christ calls us to love others unconditionally like the Father, even our enemies and persecutors: "I give you a new commandment: Love one another. Such as my love has been for you, so must your love be for each other. This is how all will know you are my disciples: your love for one another" (Jn 13:34-35).

Application: On this feast, let us pray for the grace to love unconditionally, and for the serenity which is its fruit.

SEPTEMBER 22

Prolong your personal prayer

The following was a message given to Jelena's prayer group:

> *Pray! But when I always ask you to pray, it does not mean that your prayers are not good. But I call you to prolong your personal prayer, and to pray more intensely for others (LJM 11-17-83).*

In Luke's gospel, Jesus speaks of persistence in prayer:

And he said to them, "Suppose one of you has a friend, and you go to him at midnight and say to him, 'Friend, lend me three loaves of bread, for a friend of mine has arrived, and I have nothing to set before him.' And he answers from within, 'Do not bother me; the door has already been locked, and my children are with me in bed; I cannot get up and give you anything.' I tell you, even though he will not get up and give him anything because he is his friend, at least because of his persistence he will get up and give him whatever he needs.

"So I say to you, ask and it will be given you; search, and you will find; knock, and the door will be opened for you. For everyone who asks receives, and everyone who searches finds, and for everyone who knocks, the door will be opened" (Lk 11:5-10).

Reflection: One little beaver caused a dike to collapse in England several years ago. After the animal had burrowed through the embankment of a canal, water began seeping through. Slowly but surely the original trickle became a sizable stream. Soon one bank collapsed and a forty-foot breakthrough let the water pour out in torrents.

Three million gallons of water escaped; the canal was drained for seven miles; more than one million fish were swept away and a twenty-foot gorge was channeled through a nearby field. It took sixty men with bulldozers three weeks to shift 30,000 tons of soil and repair the damages.

As one small beaver caused tremendous harm, so can one individual in prayer start a chain reaction that will benefit all of God's people.

We may never be aware in this life of the far-reaching effects of our prayer, but gathered by Mary to the prayers of countless others, they have clearly changed the world since that first June day in 1981. What she will accomplish in the future with this steady stream of prayers we can only imagine!

Application: Today simply heed Our Lady's advice: "I invite you to prolong your personal prayer, and to pray more intensely for others."

SEPTEMBER 23

Have a firm faith

Of faith, the Virgin once said:

You are, and you will always be, my children. You have followed the path of Jesus, and no one shall stop you from spreading faith in him. You must have a firm faith (FY-9-2-81).

Paul also speaks of faith:

For I am longing to see you so that I may share with you some spiritual gift to strengthen you—or rather so that we may be mutually encouraged by each other's faith, both yours and mine (Rom 1:11-12).

Reflection: It has been said that, "Faith is caught, not taught." Certainly the people closest to us have had a profound influence on our faith, beginning with our parents. As a child I remember, for instance, the great importance my mother placed on Sunday Mass, preparations for which began early in the morning. Somehow she got the five of us groomed, dressed in our good clothes, and transported to the church (how she got herself ready as well I can't say).

Once at Mass, we saw her in prayer, of course; after communion, I remember my mother kneeling in thanksgiving, her hands covering her face so as not to be distracted (as the nuns had taught her as a girl). These things along with our parents' moral code, sacrifices, and faithfulness to us and to each other made a lifelong impression on us kids. Even such seemingly minor things as grace before meals, the rosary on our mother's night stand, and the crucifix on the living room wall, had a lasting effect. Taken all together we could not help but catch the faith, for its evidence was all around us.

Application: How can you, without words, pass on the faith to your family? Is there more that you could do?

SEPTEMBER 24

I especially thank the young

The Blessed Virgin commends the young today:

Dear children, today I thank you for all of your prayers. Continue to pray all the more so that Satan will remain far from here. Dear children, Satan's plan has failed. Pray for the fulfillment of God's plans for the parish. I especially thank the young people for the sacrifices they have offered (WM 9-5-85).

And in the Book of Proverbs, the author addresses the young:

My child, be attentive to my words;
incline your ear to my sayings.
Do not let them escape from your sight;
keep them within your heart.

> For they are life to those who find them,
> and healing to all their flesh.
>
> —Proverbs 4:20-22

Reflection: A fifteen-year-old girl pulled a driver from his burning truck recently near Washington, D.C., saving his life. The girl had been riding in a car with her mother when the 13-ton truck passed by. Moments later it overturned and burst into flames when its steering wheel broke.

Seeing the driver unconscious, the young lady leaped out of her car, dragged the driver through the truck window, and quickly beat out the flames, which were rapidly spreading over his body.

An emergency such as this provides eloquent proof of the love and courage that God has instilled in our youth. Today Our Lady thanks them for the sacrifices they have made in living her messages, and asks us to continue to encourage and pray for her young people.

Application: This week, make a special effort to befriend and encourage any young people who cross your path. If the occasion permits, share with them the story of Medjugorje.

SEPTEMBER 25

With love overcome every sin

The Queen of Peace speaks of love today:

Dear children, today I call you to holiness. Without holiness you cannot live. Therefore, with love overcome every sin and difficulty which comes to you. Dear children, I beseech you to live love in your lives (WM 7-10-86).

In Luke's gospel, Zacchaeus is converted through Christ's love.

> When Jesus came to the place, he looked up and said to him, "Zacchaeus, hurry and come down; for I must stay at your house today." So he hurried down and was happy to welcome him. All who saw it began to grumble and said, "He has gone to be the guest of one who is a sinner."
>
> Zacchaeus stood there and said to the Lord, "Look, half of my possessions, Lord, I will give to the poor; and if I have defrauded anyone of anything, I will pay back four times as much." Then Jesus said to him, "Today salvation has come to this house, because he too is a son of Abraham. For the Son of Man came to seek out and to save the lost" (Lk 19:5-10).

Reflection: To finance their great world empire, the Romans levied heavy taxes against all nations under their control. The Jews opposed these taxes because they supported a secular government and its pagan gods, but they were still forced to pay. The tax collectors—Jews by birth who chose to work for Rome—were considered traitors among the people of Israel. Further, it was common knowledge that they enriched themselves by gouging their fellow Jews of extra tax money which they kept for themselves.

No wonder the crowds were displeased when Jesus went home with the tax collector Zacchaeus. But despite the fact that Zacchaeus was a turncoat, Christ loved him. In response, the little tax collector was converted.

In every society certain groups of people are considered "untouchable" because of their politics, their immoral behavior, or their lifestyle. It is important not to give in to social pressure to avoid these people, for they are still loved by Christ and his Mother. Like Jesus, we are called to reach out to them and convey a love and concern that will help them on the road to conversion. As Our Lady says today, "With love, overcome every sin and every difficulty that confronts you."

Application: Today, pray for the tolerance and love to help the sinners and outcasts of your own community.

SEPTEMBER 26

Listen to the voice of God

Our Lady speaks to Jelena with great seriousness today:

Dear children, you must understand that a person has to pray. Prayer is no laughing matter, but a conversation with God himself. In every prayer, then, you must listen to the voice of God. Truly, without prayer a person cannot live. Prayer is life (LJM 9-10-84).

And in Luke's gospel, Jesus also urges us to pray:

So I say to you, ask and it will be given you; search, and you will find; knock, and the door will be opened for you. For everyone who asks receives, and everyone who searches finds, and for everyone who knocks, the door will be opened (Lk 11:9-10).

Reflection: Prayer is by far the most frequent message given in Medjugorje, since from it flows a fountain of graces that are obtainable in no other way. For example:

Peace: "In prayer, you will find peace" (WM 7-5-84).

Joy: "By means of prayer . . . you will obtain joy" (MM 8-25-89).

Love: "Pray, because in prayer each one of you will be able to achieve complete love."

Holiness: "By prayer and sacrifice you will begin to live in holiness" (WM 11-13-86).

Grace: "Without prayer, dear children, you cannot experience . . . the graces which I offer to you" (WM 7-3-86).

Happiness: "Prayer makes one know happiness" (FY 10-20-84).

We can see why Our Lady calls us so urgently to prayer, for there are so many gifts she wishes to give us. "Before all, pray," she once told Jelena. "I say it again, pray! Know that in your life the most important thing is prayer."

Application: Today, spend some extra time in prayer, opening your heart to receive the graces of the Holy Spirit.

SEPTEMBER 27

St. Vincent de Paul

Speaking of her plans for us, the Blessed Virgin said:

Dear children, today I want to call all of you to start living a new life from this day on. Dear children, I want you to understand that God has chosen each of you to participate in his great plan for the salvation of mankind. You cannot comprehend how great your role is in God's design (MM 1-25-87).

St. Paul also speaks of God's plan of salvation and our responsibility to participate in it:

Therefore we must pay greater attention to what we have heard, so that we do not drift away from it. For if the message declared through angels was valid, and every transgression or disobedience received a just penalty, how can we escape if we neglect so great a salvation? It was declared at first through the Lord, and it was attested to us by those who heard him, while God added his testimony by signs and wonders and various miracles, and by gifts of the Holy Spirit, distributed according to his will (Heb 2:1-4).

Reflection: Proclaiming the salvation of God through word and deed was the primary motivation of the life and work of St. Vincent de Paul (1581-1660). Ordained a priest in 1600, his work with the poor and his preaching attracted widespread attention. In 1625 he founded his own community, the Congregation of the Mission, dedicated to the care of the poor and the formation of priests. Eight years later, together with St. Louise de Marillac, he founded the Sisters of Charity, whose main work was care of the sick, of orphans, and children in need.

He once said to his priests:

> Do the good that presents itself to be done. I do not say we should go out indiscriminately and take on everything, but rather those things God lets us know he wants of us. We belong to him and not to ourselves. If he increases our work, he will add to our strength as well.

To all his religious he wrote, "It is our duty to prefer the service of the poor to everything else and to offer such service as quickly as possible."

Application: In her message today, the Virgin calls us to pray to discern our role in God's plan. Today, simply pray for this grace of understanding and for the compassion to serve Christ in the poor.

Satan lies in wait

Our Lady speaks of the ancient serpent:

Dear children, Satan lies in wait for each of you. Every day he tries to plant doubts in you. Therefore, dear children, each day pray and abandon yourself to God (WM 9-4-86).

And in Luke's gospel, Jesus confronts the Evil One:

In the synagogue there was a man who had the spirit of an unclean demon, and he cried out with a loud voice, "Let us alone! What have you to do with us, Jesus of Nazareth? Have you come to destroy us? I know who you are, the Holy One of God."

But Jesus rebuked him, saying, "Be silent, and come out of him!" When the demon had thrown him down before them, he came out of him without having done him any harm. They were all amazed and kept saying to one another, "What kind of utterance is this? For with authority and power he commands the unclean spirits, and out they come!" And a report about him began to reach every place in the region (Lk 4:33-37).

Reflection: The people were amazed at Christ's authority to cast out demons, those evil spirits ruled by Satan and sent to tempt people to sin. Like their master, demons are fallen angels who have joined him in rebellion against God. Christ faced many of them during his time on earth; yet his power over them was absolute.

In today's reading, not only does Jesus expel the demon, but Luke records that it left the man unhurt. Through this exorcism, Christ was demonstrating the advent of the kingdom of God, that he himself was Emmanuel, or "God with us," able to subject even the powers of hell.

Application: In her message today, Our Lady warns us that Satan wants to plant doubts in us. But she also gives us the weapons to defend ourselves: Prayer from the heart and surrender to God. Today, take up these weapons.

SEPTEMBER 29

The Archangels Michael, Gabriel, and Raphael

With the angels, Our Lady is exultant over the conversion of many souls:

> *Rejoice with me and with my angels because part of my plan has already been realized! Many have been converted—but many are not willing—and so pray (SM 3-25-84).*

And from Revelation, the famous passage on the Archangel Michael:

> And war broke out in heaven; Michael and his angels fought against the dragon. The dragon and his angels fought back, and they were defeated, and there was no longer any place for them in heaven (Rv 12:7-8).

Reflection: During the next several days we will celebrate two great feasts of the angels—today's feast of Michael, Gabriel, and Raphael, and on October 2nd, the feast of the guardian angels.

Speaking of today's feast, St. Gregory the Great wrote: "Some angels are given proper names to denote the service they are empowered to perform. Thus, Michael means 'Who is like God,' Gabriel is 'The strength of God,' and Raphael is 'God's remedy.'"

Application: Today, let us offer this special Michaelmas Prayer (based on an ancient Gaelic hymn):

Michael of the Sword,
Michael of the Victories,
Save the human way
Save the human countenance;
Help sweet Mary's Son,
Dying still in agony;
In the final dark
Of a new Gethsemane.
Strike the dragon down;
Michael of the Victories,
Michael of the Sword,
Help sweet Mary's Son
Towards a new nativity.

Verse: Blessed Michael, Archangel, defend us
Refrain: Against the spirits of wickedness.

V. Blessed Michael, Archangel, be with us
R. Now and in the time of travail.

V. Blessed Michael, Archangel, lead us on
R. To the fullness of Christ in the glory of the Spirit
To the fullness of Christ in the glory of the Father.
Amen.

—Noel D. O'Donoghue

Say, rather, that it is God's

Speaking of humility, the Blessed Mother once said:

> If you have received a gift from God, you must be grateful and not credit it to yourself. Say, rather, that it is God's (SM 9-10-85).

> Pray that Satan does not entice you with his pride and deceptive strength (MM 11-25-87).

Paul also advises that we be wary of pride and boastfulness:

> We do not dare to classify or compare ourselves with some of those who commend themselves. But when they measure themselves by one another, and compare themselves with one another, they do not show good sense. . . . "Let the one who boasts, boast in the Lord." For it is not those who commend themselves that are approved, but those whom the Lord commends (2 Cor 10:12, 17-18).

Reflection: Although the Blessed Mother has stressed the virtue of humility in her messages, it is unfortunate that some adherents of Medjugorje engage in what might be called "spiritual one-up-manship," a form of pride in which one seeks to elevate oneself in the minds of others by boasting of spiritual experiences or accomplishments, often in comparison to others.

There is a great difference between this and sharing one's experience of Medjugorje as a form of evangelization or witness. The former is self-serving while the latter is in the service of God.

The effects of this spiritual pride is not only harmful to the individual (it is first among the seven deadly sins) but also to the image of Medjugorje that others have. It is easy for people to see through boasting and simply dismiss the person as immature. Regrettably, they are also likely to dismiss Medjugorje as well. The Madonna may have been referring to this danger when she told the visionaries to, "continue in humility . . . to speak to all who are coming [here]" (WM 6-28-85).

Application: Today, simply reflect on these words of the Blessed Mother: "In humility live all the messages which I am giving you" (WM 2-27-86).

Statue of Our Lady in St. James Church

The Month of Mary

The Blessed Mother speaks of grace today:

Dear children, pray during this month. God has allowed me to help you everyday with graces, in order to protect you from evil. This month is mine. I would like to give it to you. Pray and God will give you the graces that you ask for. I will support your requests (WM 10-25-84).

St. Paul also speaks of grace:

But the free gift is not like the trespass. For if the many died through the one man's trespass, much more surely have the grace of God and the free gift in the grace of the one man, Jesus Christ, abounded for the many (Rom 5:15).

Reflection: The month of October is traditionally dedicated to the Mother of God, and parishes often honor her with votive Masses, community rosaries, and other special devotions. We are thankful that the effect or merit of these prayers are her special gift to us, for she says, "This is my month—I want to give it to you."

In today's message she speaks several times of "grace," meaning the "favor," the love, or the magnanimity of God. Mary herself is often the mediator of this grace: "God allows me every day to help you with graces. . . ." These cannot be earned, but are pure gifts: "But if the choice is by grace, it is not because of their works—otherwise grace would not be grace" (Rom 11:6).

Although a gift, God always chooses to give his grace to all who ask. Our Lady says, "You just pray and God will give you the graces you are seeking."

Other than this, the most important thing is to respond to the graces given: "As your fellow workers," St. Paul writes, "we beg you not to receive the grace of God in vain" (2 Cor 6:1).

Indeed, grace and works of charity are the heavenly treasure we are asked to store up instead of earthly wealth; in this task, we have the Blessed Virgin's words: "I will help along with it."

Application: Let us pray that this Marian month of October will be a time of special grace for us as we honor the Queen of Peace, the bearer of God's grace.

OCTOBER 2

The Guardian Angels

With reference to angels, the Blessed Mother once said to Jelena:

Today I rejoice with all my angels! The first part of my plan has been realized (LJM 3-21-84).

The Book of Exodus refers to angels as guardians:

I am going to send an angel in front of you, to guard you on the way and to bring you to the place that I have prepared. Be attentive to him and listen to his voice (Ex 23:20-21).

Reflection: The Queen of Peace refers to angels a great deal in Medjugorje, and is even more often seen with them by the visionaries. They are always with her on Christmas, Easter, and other feast days.

That we each have a guardian angel has been a belief of the church for centuries, going back as far as the Old Testament, as our readings today indicate. St. Bernard, the great scholar and Doctor of the Church, said the following of them: "The angels are here; they are at your side, they are with you, present on your behalf. They are here to protect you and to serve you."

Application: Today, let us honor our guardian angels on their feast with the following prayer:

O most faithful companion,
appointed by God to be my guardian,
and who never leaves my side,
how shall I thank you for your faithfulness
    and love
and for the benefits which you have obtained
    for me!
You watch over me when I sleep;
you comfort me when I am sad;
you avert the dangers that threaten me
and warn me of those to come;
you withdraw me from sin and inspire me to good;
you exhort me to penance when I fall
and reconcile me to God.

I beg you not to leave me.
Comfort me in adversity,
restrain me in prosperity,
defend me in danger,
and assist me in temptations.
Offer up in the sight of the Divine Majesty
my prayers and petitions,
and all my works of piety,
and help me to persevere in grace
until I come to everlasting life. Amen.

Grow in love

The Queen of Peace speaks of love today:

Dear children, I desire that you grow in love. Just as a flower cannot grow without water, so you cannot grow without God's grace. Everyday, then, you should ask God for his blessing so that you can grow normally and that your actions will be in union with his will (WM 4-10-86).

In Luke's gospel, Christ extends his love to a leper:

Once, when he was in one of the cities, there was a man covered with leprosy. When he saw Jesus, he bowed with his face to the ground and begged him, "Lord, if you choose, you can make me clean." Then Jesus stretched out his hand, touched him, and said, "I do choose. Be made clean." Immediately the leprosy left him (Lk 5:12-13).

Reflection: Because it was often highly contagious and there was no known cure, leprosy was a feared disease. (Sometimes called Hansen's disease, leprosy still exists today in a less contagious, treatable form.) To prevent the spread of infection, the priests monitored the disease, banishing from the community those persons whose leprosy was active and readmitting lepers whose disease was in remission. Lepers were considered untouchable since people feared contracting their disease. Yet Jesus reached out and touched this leper out of love, and the man was healed.

We may consider certain people untouchable or repulsive, yet Christ and his Mother call us to reach out and touch them with God's love—so that we may both be healed.

Application: Look about today for those who are in special need of your care and concern, even "the least of God's children." Keep before Christ a prayer intention for the most rejected and despised of his people.

OCTOBER 4

St. Francis of Assisi

In an early message in 1981, Our Lady said:

> God has chosen St. Francis as his elected one. It would be good to imitate his life. In the meantime, we must realize what God ordains us to do (FY 10-7-81).

The life of Francis was itself a hymn of praise to God; as the psalmist sings:

> Kings of the earth and all peoples,
> princes and all rulers of the earth!
> Young men and women alike,
> old and young together!
> Let them praise the name of the Lord,
> for his name alone is exalted;
> his glory is above earth and heaven.
>
> —Psalm 148:11-13

Reflection: The Franciscans of Medjugorje are deeply devoted to their founder and patron, St. Francis of Assisi. His simplicity, poverty, and holiness are the ideals that have guided them for centuries. The vibrant faith of the Catholics of Yugoslavia has been nourished and protected by the Franciscans, even in times of great persecution under the Ottoman Turks and, more recently, under a Communist regime. Many gave their lives in service to God and his people.

Let us listen to Francis' own words which give us a glimpse of his personality. Let us pray with him:

The Prayer of St. Francis

Lord, make me an instrument of your peace; where there is hatred, let me sow love; where there is injury, pardon; where there is doubt, faith; where there is despair, hope; where there is darkness, light; and where there is sadness, joy.

O Divine Master, grant that I may not so much seek to be consoled as to console; to be understood as to understand; to be loved, as to love; for it is in giving that we receive, it is in pardoning that we are pardoned, and it is in dying that we are born to eternal life.

Application: On this feast day, let us pray for the gentle spirit of St. Francis, and also for his heroic courage, which his followers have imitated so well over the centuries.

OCTOBER 5

Draw close to God

Our Lady's monthly message for February, 1992:

Dear children, today I invite you to draw still closer to God through prayer. Only that way will I be able to help you and to protect you from every attack of Satan.

I am with you and I intercede for you with God, that he protect you. But I need your prayers and your "Yes."

You get lost easily in material and human things and forget that God is your greatest friend. Therefore, my dear little children, draw close to God so that he can protect you and guard you from every evil (MM 2-25-92).

And in Matthew's gospel, Jesus instructs his disciples in prayer:

But whenever you pray, go into your room and shut the door and pray to your Father who is in secret; and your Father who sees in secret will reward you (Mt 6:6).

Reflection: It is a striking statement that Our Lady makes today—that *only through prayer* can she help us. It is a reiteration of previous messages in which she has pleaded for our prayer, for it seems to be imperative to her. So much is at stake: personal peace, Our Lady's help in our lives, protection from the Evil One, the healing of mind or body; and more generally, the realization of Mary's plans in Medjugorje: the mitigation of the secrets, peace among nations, and the salvation of souls.

The Madonna has said that she is powerless without our prayer! Just think of it: we have it within our power to bring peace not only to our own hearts, but to the nations of the world. It is as if Our Lady magnifies our prayer a million-fold through her intercession, and so works miracles. But she *must* have our prayer; our free will in this regard either binds or frees her hands, either opens or closes the tabernacles of grace.

Application: It has been said that, "More things are wrought by prayer than this world dreams of." Today, pray to understand more fully the power of your prayer and Our Lady's dependence upon it.

OCTOBER 6

Pray and renew yourselves

Today the Blessed Mother speaks of prayer, love, and the rosary:

> *The rosary is not an ornament for the home, as some often times limit themselves to using it. Tell everyone to pray it (FY 3-18-85).*

All your prayers touch me very much, especially your daily rosary (SM 3-18-87).

Dear children, I thank you because by your coming here you have helped to fulfill the plan of God. During this time, pray and renew yourselves. Tonight when you go home, pray the Joyful Mysteries in front of the cross (VPG 3-3-89).

And in Ephesians, Paul prays for his people:

I have heard of your faith in the Lord Jesus and your love toward all the saints, and for this reason I do not cease to give thanks for you as I remember you in my prayers. I pray that the God of our Lord Jesus Christ, the Father of glory, may give you a spirit of wisdom and revelation as you come to know him (Eph 1:15-17).

Reflection: It has been said that prayer is the most exalted action of which man is capable. In Medjugorje, the Madonna speaks especially of the prayer of the rosary: "Pray, and let the rosary always be in your hands as a sign to Satan that you belong to me." Of the rosary, Fr. Slavko Barbaric once said in a sermon:

Why these one hundred and fifty Hail Mary's? It is simple, really. In the rosary, Our Lady calls us to a form of prayer which is very suitable to the present time—repetitive, meditative, and biblical.

When you start praying the rosary with your heart, you start learning from Our Lady how you should behave in this life: for example, accepting the Lord's will, as Mary did herself at the Annunciation; or thinking of others, as she did when she visited Elizabeth. The rosary is a means of living with Jesus and his Mother, teaching us about the Christian life.

Application: Today, pray the rosary which the Mother of God so ardently recommends.

OCTOBER 7

Our Lady of the Rosary

Of the rosary, Our Lady said:

> *Dear children, today I invite you to begin to pray the rosary with a living faith. Only in that way will I be able to help you. You wish to receive graces, but you do not pray. I am not able to help you if you do not decide to begin.*
>
> *I invite you, dear children, to pray the rosary in such a way that it will be a commitment for you, achieved in joy. In this way, you will understand the reason why I have been with you for such a long time. I want to teach you to pray (WM 6-12-86).*

In Luke's gospel, the risen Christ joins his disciples on the road to Emmaus:

> Then he said to them, "Oh, how foolish you are, and how slow of heart to believe all that the prophets have declared! Was it not necessary that the Messiah should suffer these things and then enter into his glory?" Then beginning with Moses and all the prophets, he interpreted to them the things about himself in all the scriptures.
>
> As they came near the village to which they were going, he walked ahead as if he were going on. But they urged him strongly, saying, "Stay with us, because it is almost evening and the day is now nearly over." So he went in to stay with them.
>
> When he was at the table with them he took bread, blessed and broke it, and gave it to them.

Then their eyes were opened, and they recognized him; and he vanished from their sight. They said to each other, "Were not our hearts burning within us while he was talking to us on the road, while he was opening the scriptures to us?" That same hour they got up and returned to Jerusalem; and they found the eleven and their companions gathered together (Lk 24:25-33).

Reflection: In this story we find that the risen Christ "interpreted for them every passage of scripture which referred to him," so that his disciples would understand the meaning of his life, death, and resurrection.

In meditating on the mysteries of the rosary, Jesus also helps us to interpret and understand the meaning of his life and death. And today Our Lady as well says to, "let the faithful meditate each day on the life of Jesus while praying the rosary." It is not necessary to concentrate on the repetitive prayers of the rosary (which serve as a type of mantra), but to let the quiet rhythm of the prayers keep us centered on the particular mystery on which we are meditating.

The more we reflect on the lives of Jesus and Mary through the mysteries, the more we become like them in mind and heart. By means of the rosary, the Spirit of God gradually transfigures our hearts and minds to resemble those of Christ and his Mother.

Application: Pray the scriptural rosary if you have a book with the verses, or if not, pray the traditional rosary truly from the heart, "meditating on the life of Jesus," as Mary asks of us.

Discover his will for you

Today the Virgin speaks of conversion and the will of God:

> *Dear children, today I want to thank you for all your sacrifices and prayers. I give you my special motherly blessing.*
>
> *I call each of you to decide for God. From day to day, discover his will for you in prayer. I wish, dear children, to call all of you to full conversion so that there may be joy in your hearts ((MM 6-25-90).*

And in John's gospel, Jesus also speaks of doing the will of God:

> Everything that the Father gives me will come to me, and anyone who comes to me I will never drive away; for I have come down from heaven, not to do my own will, but the will of him who sent me (Jn 6:37-38).

Reflection: G. Gordon Liddy was one of the men convicted in the Watergate affair that forced President Nixon to resign in 1973. After his release from prison in 1977, Liddy wrote an autobiography entitled *Will*. It was a fitting title, for since childhood Liddy has been a man of tremendous will power.

In his book he describes how he used to perform painful and distasteful acts in order to strengthen his will. For example, as a youngster he ate part of a rat. On other occasions he held his hand steady in a burning flame.

In the 1960s, Liddy abandoned his Catholic faith. But twenty years later, in the 1980s, he underwent a religious conversion. It came about as a result of attending Bible-study meetings with his former FBI colleagues. Commenting of the experience, Liddy says that he resolved to spend the rest of his life seeking and doing God's will rather than his own.

The hardest thing I have to do now, each day, is to decide what is God's will rather than what is my will. So the prayer I say most often is, first of all, "God, please tell me what you want." And second, "Give me the strength to do your will."

Application: In our gospel reading today, Christ said, "I have come down from heaven not to do my own will, but the will of him who sent me." And the Blessed Mother has urged us to "discover God's will for you in prayer." To this end, offer the following prayer today by St. Jane Frances de Chantal:

Lord, what is your will that I do? I am completely open to your plan for me. I desire to live only in you and to be guided by you forever. Grant that your holy will may be carried out perfectly in me.

OCTOBER 9

Many have begun but they forget

Decrying the lack of perseverance of some, the Madonna once said:

Many have begun to pray for healing here at Medjugorje, but when they return to their homes, they abandon prayer, forget, and also lose many graces (SM 9-12-86).

Paul also exhorts us to persevere:

Pray in the Spirit at all times in every prayer and supplication. To that end, keep alert and always persevere in supplication for all the holy ones (Eph 6:18).

———————

Reflection: The virtue of perseverance is exemplified in the life of a man who went blind at the age of three, in the year 1812. When he was old enough, he was sent to a school for the blind in Paris, which was near to his village. There Louis was taught to read by touching large raised letters of the alphabet with his fingers. He was so successful that he soon found himself teaching others to read by the same method.

But it was not easy. Some people just could not do it, so he determined to invent another method by which blind people could read. He worked and persevered for many a long hour to try to perfect a special alphabet for the blind. When Louis Braille was twenty years old he succeeded.

Application: "Great works are performed not by strength," wrote Samuel Johnson, "but by perseverance." It is a great Christian virtue, as both Christ and Our Lady attest in our readings.

Today, and especially when you feel drained or weakened, pray for perseverance.

OCTOBER 10

Pray that your lives benefit all

Today Our Lady asks that our lives be an example of good for others:

Dear children, I invite you to pray with the heart so that your prayer may be a true conversation with God. I ask that each one of you dedicate more time to God, for Satan is strong and wants to deceive you in many ways.

> *Therefore, dear children, pray every day that your lives be a source of goodness not only for your own benefit, but also for all those you meet.*
>
> *I am with you and I am protecting you even though Satan wants to destroy my plans and all that the heavenly Father wishes to accomplish here (MM 9-25-90).*

And at the Last Supper, Jesus sets an example for his apostles:

> After he had washed their feet, had put on his robe, and had returned to the table, he said to them, "Do you know what I have done to you? You call me teacher and Lord—and you are right, for that is what I am. So if I, your Lord and teacher, have washed your feet, you also ought to wash one another's feet. For I have set you an example, that you also should do as I have done to you" (Jn 13:12-15).

Reflection: *Tom Brown's School Days* was a famous British novel and was later made into a popular movie. Tom Brown was a popular boy who attended a boarding school in England. He lived with about a dozen other boys in one of the dormitories. Whatever Tom said or did always had a big impact on others at the school.

One day a new boy came to the school. When it came time for bed that night, the new boy innocently knelt down beside his bed to say his prayers. A few of the boys began to snicker; a couple of others began to laugh and joke. One even threw a shoe at the kneeling boy.

That night Tom didn't go to sleep right away. He lay awake thinking about what had happened to the newcomer. He also began to think about his mother and the

prayers she taught him to say each night before bed—
prayers he had not said since coming to the school.

The next night several of the boys in the dormitory
were looking forward to poking fun at the new boy
again. When bedtime came, however, something totally
unexpected happened. When the boy knelt down to say
his night prayers, Tom knelt down also. When the other
boys saw this, there was a hush in the dormitory.

Application: Today, try to be especially aware of your
influence on others, and the kind of influence Our Lord
and his Mother would like you to be.

OCTOBER 11

When sufferings come

The Blessed Mother urges us today to offer our sufferings to God:

> *Dear children, this evening I especially call you to*
> *perseverance in trials. Reflect on how the Almighty is*
> *still suffering today on account of your sins. So when*
> *sufferings come, offer them up as a sacrifice to God*
> *(WM 3-29-84).*

In his first letter, Peter speaks of victory over suffering:

> Beloved, do not be surprised at the fiery ordeal
> that is taking place among you to test you, as
> though something strange were happening to
> you. But rejoice insofar as you are sharing Christ's
> sufferings, so that you may be glad and shout for
> joy when his glory is revealed (1 Pt 4:12-13).

Reflection: Viktor Frankl, one of the great
psychotherapists of our time, addresses the question of
the meaning of suffering in his best-selling book *Man's*

Search for Meaning. Frankl was a prisoner of the Nazis during World War II and experienced firsthand the brutal climate in concentration camps, which turned some prisoners into animals and others into saints.

He experienced firsthand the evil that drove some prisoners to despair and hatred and others to hope and love. Frankl says the deciding difference was faith. It was faith that gave their lives—and thus their suffering—ultimate meaning. This faith put them in touch with a power that helped them maintain their humanity even in the face of incredible inhumanity.

Application: Our Lady says to us today, "When sufferings come, offer them up as a sacrifice to God." The following prayer, An Offering of Suffering, was written in that spirit:

> O my Lord Jesus Christ, I lift up my heart to you in my suffering and ask for your comforting help. I know that you would withhold the thorns of this life if I could attain eternal life without them. And so I commend myself to your loving mercy, accepting this suffering in your name.
>
> Grant me the grace to bear it and to offer it in union with your sufferings. Regardless of the suffering that may come my way, let me trust you always, for you are my Lord, my God, and my All. Amen.

OCTOBER 12

I love you all

In this weekly message during May, the Madonna spoke of love:

> *Dear children, I have told you already that I have especially chosen you just the way you are. I am your Mother and I love you all. During times that are*

*difficult, do not be afraid, for I love you even when you
are far from my Son and me.*

*Please, do not let my heart weep with tears of blood
for the souls that are being lost in sin. Therefore, dear
children, pray, pray, pray! (WM 5-24-84).*

In Romans, Paul speaks of the love that has been poured
out into our hearts:

And not only that, but we also boast in our sufferings, knowing that suffering produces endurance,
and endurance produces character, and character
produces hope, and hope does not disappoint us,
because God's love has been poured into our
hearts through the Holy Spirit that has been given
to us (Rom 5:3-5).

Reflection: One of the shows in the television series
"Highway to Heaven" dealt with children with cancer.
The late Michael Landon, who himself died of cancer,
got the idea to have real-life victims play the parts.

One victim was a boy named Josh Wood. His case was
especially tragic because he had already lost a leg to
cancer. But what bothered little Josh even more was the
fact that he had a speech defect that caused him to
stammer badly. People avoided talking to him, and the
more they did this the more he stammered.

Michael Landon surprised everybody by asking Josh
to audition for one of the parts, saying to the boy: "The
important thing about acting is to be a good actor. If you
stammer, that's all right. You're just a good actor who
stammers." To everyone's amazement, when the boy
read for the part, his stammer disappeared completely.
Josh's cancer is in remission—and his stammer has
never come back.

Josh Wood is a living example of the tremendous
power that loving kindness has, of the great power that

is contained in a little assurance, a little affirmation. He is a living example of how kindness can work miracles.

Application: Today, simply offer this Prayer for Kindness and Love:

> Lord Jesus Christ, help us to realize the power of kindness and love. Help us to use this power the way you intended us to use it when you created us. Help us to use it to bring happiness to those around us. Help us to use it to work miracles, healing people in our time, just as you healed them through love in your time. Amen.

OCTOBER 13

Sing, be full of joy!

The following was given to Jelena, the locutionist:

> *In difficulties, when you carry the cross, sing, be full of joy! (LJM 86).*

The psalmist also urges us to sing:

> O sing to the Lord a new song;
> sing to the Lord, all the earth.
> Sing to the Lord, bless his name;
> tell of his salvation from day to day.
> Declare his glory among the nations,
> his marvelous works among all the peoples.
> For great is the Lord, and greatly to be praised;
> he is to be revered among all gods.

—Psalm 96:1-4

Reflection: Joy and song are two of God's most beautiful gifts to mankind. Needless to say, the greatest joy is found in God himself, as we see from Psalm 96 today.

The following hymn is one of the most ancient in the church. Composed by St. Nicetas, it dates from A.D. 370. It is still used regularly in the Divine Office on Sundays, feasts, and solemnities. Let us offer the *Te Deum* (You Are God) with joy:

You are God: we praise you;
You are the Lord: we acclaim you;
You are the eternal Father:
All creation worships you.

To you all angels, all the powers of heaven,
Cherubim and Seraphim, sing in endless praise:
Holy, holy, holy, Lord, God of power and might,
heaven and earth are full of your glory.

The glorious company of apostles praise you.
The noble fellowship of prophets praise you.
The white-robed army of martyrs praise you.
Throughout the world the holy church
acclaims you:
Father, of majesty unbounded,
your true and only Son, worthy of all worship,
and the Holy Spirit, advocate and guide.
You, O Christ, are the king of glory,
the eternal Son of the Father.
When you became man to set us free
you did not spurn the Virgin's womb.
You overcame the sting of death,
and opened the kingdom of heaven to
all believers.
You are seated at God's right hand in glory.
We believe that you will come, and be our judge.

Come then, Lord, and help your people,
bought with the price of your own blood,
and bring us with your saints
to everlasting glory.
Amen.

Application: Joyfully pray the *Te Deum* on the next several Sundays, as priests and religious do throughout the world.

OCTOBER 14

Do not give up on meditation

Speaking again of her most crucial message, Our Lady says:

> *Pray and fast. Do not give up on meditation. At home meditate at least half an hour (LJM 1-21-84).*

And in Colossians, Paul also stresses prayer:

> Devote yourselves to prayer, keeping alert in it with thanksgiving. At the same time pray for us as well that God will open for us a door for the word. . . (Col 4:2-3).

Reflection: Fr. Mark Link tells the story of a young prince who was very handsome except for one thing: he had a crooked back. This birth defect caused him great sorrow and kept him from being the kind of prince that he really wanted to be.

One day the prince's father asked the best sculptor in his kingdom to make a statue of the prince. However, it should portray him with a straight back. The king wanted his son to see himself as he could be. When the sculptor finished the statue, it was truly magnificent. It was so lifelike that you could mistake it for the prince. The king placed the statue in the prince's private garden.

Each day when the prince went to his garden to study, he looked longingly at the statue. Then one day he noticed that when he did this, his heart beat faster and his body tingled. Months passed. Soon the people began to say to one another, "The prince's back doesn't seem as crooked as it once did." When the prince heard this, his heart beat even faster and his body tingled even more. Now he began to go to the garden more often. He spent hours standing before the statue, studying it closely, and meditating on it. Then one day a remarkable thing happened. The prince found himself standing as straight as the statue.

This story is a kind of parable of each of us. We see Jesus as the perfect image of what we were born to be. He stands spiritually straight and beautiful. And just as the prince studied and pondered the statue, so we must study and ponder Christ so that we can become his image.

Application: Today, let us simply take the Madonna's advice and meditate on the life of Christ through scriptural prayer, the rosary, or quiet contemplation.

OCTOBER 15

St. Teresa of Avila

The following was given to Ivan for the prayer group and pilgrims:

> *Dear children, tonight your mother wants to encourage you to start praying with the heart. This prayer is essential to people living in today's world. And so do not pray just with your lips or without knowing what you pray.*
>
> *Dear children, I also need your prayers during this time to accomplish the great plans I have. I wish us to work together. I have repeated that many times in my messages. I need you. And so pray, pray with the heart! (VPG 10-31-88).*

It was heartfelt prayer that sustained the early church in the power of the Holy Spirit. From the Acts of the Apostles:

> When they had prayed, the place in which they were gathered together was shaken; and they were all filled with the Holy Spirit and spoke the word of God with boldness (Acts 4:31).

Reflection: One of the greatest masters of prayer in the Catholic church was St. Teresa of Avila. Her classic writings *The Way of Perfection*, *Foundations*, and *The Interior Castle* continue to be studied even today.

Born in Avila, Spain, on March 28, 1515, Teresa was one of the most down-to-earth mystics that the church has ever known. She was described as "intelligent, hardheaded, charming, and deeply spiritual." Another described her as "talented, outgoing, affectionate, courageous . . . totally human. She is wise, yet practical; intelligent, yet much in tune with her experience; mystical, yet an energetic reformer."

Other than her writings, St. Teresa is best known for the reforms she initiated in the Carmelite Order. In 1562 she founded her first convent of Discalced (reformed) Carmelites, established for nuns who wished a more cloistered and contemplative observance rather than the relaxed discipline of her time. She went on to found sixteen more, travelling throughout Spain.

She once wrote:

> Christ has no body now on earth, but yours,
>> No hands but yours,
>> No feet but yours.
>
> Yours are the eyes through which the
>> compassion of
> Christ must look out on the world.

Yours are the feet with which he is to go about
doing good.

Yours are the hands with which he is to bless
his people.

Application: "Your mother wants to encourage you," the Virgin says today, "to start praying with the heart. This prayer is essential to people living in today's world." Today, as both Our Lady and St. Teresa advise, pray with special meaning and concentration.

OCTOBER 16

St. Margaret Mary Alacoque

The following was given to Jelena, the locutionist:

I wish that all families consecrate themselves to the Sacred Heart each day, for I am very happy when the whole family comes together to pray. In the morning, pray for half an hour (LJM 10-20-83).

The Sacred Heart is the powerful symbol of Christ's love for us. He asks us to extend that love to others:

"I give you a new commandment, that you love one another. Just as I have loved you, you also should love one another" (Jn 13:34).

Reflection: St. Margaret Mary was born in France in 1647. She joined the Sisters of the Visitation and was later graced with mystical revelations from Christ, who charged her with spreading devotion to his Sacred Heart. Our Lady has referred to this devotion a number of times in Medjugorje, as we see in today's message.

Application: You may wish to place an image of the Sacred Heart in your home, as well as offer a prayer to the Heart of Jesus each day. One short prayer that was written by Sr. Margaret herself:

O Heart of love, I put all my trust in you; for I fear all things from my own weakness, but I hope for all things from your goodness.

OCTOBER 17

The Secrets

During one apparition, Our Lady showed Mirjana the first secret, and she saw the earth desolate. The Virgin said:

It is the upheaval of a region of the world. In the world there is so much sin. What can I do, if you do not help me?

Remember that I love you. God does not have a hard heart. But look around you and see what men do, for then you will no longer say that God's heart is hard. How many people come to church, to the house of God, with respect, strong faith, and a love for God? Very few! Now you have a time of grace and conversion. It is necessary to use it well (SM 10-25-85).

And from Luke's gospel, Christ says:

There will be signs in the sun, the moon, and the stars, and on the earth distress among nations confused by the roaring of the sea and the waves. People will faint from fear and foreboding of what is coming upon the world, for the powers of the heavens will be shaken. Then they will see the Son of Man coming in a cloud with power and great glory. Now when these things begin to take place, stand up and raise your heads, because your redemption is drawing near (Lk 21:25-28).

Reflection: In November of 1988, the *Dallas Morning News* ran a front-page story about a house that burned down, killing five people. What made it especially tragic was that Sonny Simpson, the house's owner, had been planning for two weeks to install a smoke alarm. Simpson told reporters that it was something that he kept putting off because he was too busy with other things.

That tragic story hits close to home. There are so many things we want to do, but we keep putting them off. But there is one thing we must not put off—preparation for the Lord's final coming. For some it will be a time of "fear and foreboding," yet others are to "stand up and raise your heads, because your redemption is at hand." It all depends on one's spiritual preparedness.

The chastisements spoken of in the Medjugorje secrets are not planned punishments from an angry God, but the final consequences of sin and evil in the world. Like a defective boiler building up with steam, it will eventually blow. Spiritual laws cannot be continuously violated any more than the laws of nature. It is the love and mercy of God that has sent the Blessed Virgin into the world to release the building pressure of sin. But, as she has said many times, she cannot do it alone. She must have our prayers and sacrifices. "What can I do," she says today, "if you do not help me?"

Application: Today, review the priorities of your life. In what place have you put spirituality and prayer?

St. Luke

Since Luke was a physician, it is appropriate that the Madonna speaks of the sick today:

Pray for all the sick. Believe firmly. I will come to help, according to that which is in my power. I will ask my Son, Jesus, to help them. The most important thing, in the meantime, is a strong faith. Many who are sick think that it is sufficient to come here in order to be quickly healed. Some of them do not even believe in God, and even less in the apparitions, and then they ask for help from the Gospa! (FY 2-9-82).

In answer to questions about the sick in 1981, the Gospa responded:

Without faith, nothing is possible. All those who will believe firmly will be cured (FY 7-24-81).

And last, from the Acts of the Apostles:

Yet more than ever believers were added to the Lord, great numbers of both men and women, so that they even carried out the sick into the streets, and laid them on cots and mats, in order that Peter's shadow might fall on some of them as he came by. A great number of people would also gather from the towns around Jerusalem, bringing the sick and those tormented by unclean spirits, and they were all cured (Acts 5:14-16).

Reflection: On this feast of St. Luke, the physician, we cannot help but be aware of the central role that faith plays in healing, for it is mentioned throughout scripture and Our Lady's messages as the one thing necessary.

As we see in her message, Mary asks us to "pray for the sick. Believe firmly . . . the most important thing is a strong faith." Again, on July 24, 1981: "Without faith, nothing is possible. All those who will believe firmly will be cured." When asked about a sick person on July 29, 1981, the Gospa responded, "Praise be Jesus! She will be cured. She must believe firmly."

Sacred scripture bears out the great healing power of faith. From today's passage from St. James: "This prayer uttered in faith will reclaim the one who is ill, and the Lord will restore him to health" (Jas 5:15).

Taken together, both Our Lady's messages and scripture emphasize that a firm, expectant faith is needed for healing at the hands of God. And this faith, in turn, is deepened and strengthened through prayer, the foundational message of Medjugorje.

On this his feast day, let us pray to St. Luke the physician to help us grow in faith and in prayer, that we may experience healing where it is most needed in our lives today, whether it be physical, mental, or spiritual.

Application: In prayer, call to mind someone who is ill and offer the Prayer for the Sick for them (January 14), which was given by Our Lady in Medjugorje for just such a purpose.

OCTOBER 19

Love your enemies

The following is one of Our Lady's directives to Jelena's prayer group:

Love your enemies. Banish from your heart hatred, bitterness, and preconceived judgments. Pray for your enemies and call the divine blessing upon them (LJM 6-16-83).

And from Matthew's gospel:

> If anyone strikes you on the right cheek, turn the other also; and if anyone wants to sue you and take your coat, give him your cloak as well; and if anyone forces you to go one mile, go also the second mile (Mt 5:39-41).

Reflection: Corrie ten Boom was a prisoner in the Nazi concentration camp at Ravensbruck. After the war she traveled about Europe, giving talks and urging citizens of rival nations to forgive one another.

One night a man approached her and held out his hand. When Corrie saw who it was, she was shocked, for it was one of the most hated guards of the camp.

Corrie froze. Try as she may, she couldn't reach out and take his hand. As she stood there she began to pray, saying, "Jesus, I cannot forgive this man. Help me to forgive him." At that moment some mysterious power helped her reach out and grasp the guard's hand.

That episode taught Corrie an important truth. The same Jesus who gave us the command to love our enemies gives us the grace to obey the command. All we need do is ask for it.

Application: When caught in hatred or resentment of another, offer this Prayer for Love of Enemies:

> Lord Jesus Christ,
> Today I ask for the grace
> to love my enemies
> or those who have caused me harm, (Name).
> I am helpless when left to my own recourse,
> and so I rely on your miraculous grace
> that will empower me to do what I cannot.
> Bless my enemies, for whom I now pray.
> Help them to develop into the persons

you saw they could become
when you created them.
May you bless them with all the good graces
that I would wish for myself,
and lead us all to reconciliation.
Amen.

OCTOBER 20

Do not fear injustice

During the first week of the apparitions, Mirjana and Jakov were upset because people were treating them like liars. The Blessed Mother told them:

My angels, do not be afraid of injustices. They have always existed (FY 6-27-81).

And from 1 Corinthians:

Therefore do not pronounce judgment before the time, before the Lord comes, who will bring to light the things now hidden in darkness, and will disclose the purposes of the heart (1 Cor 4:5).

Reflection: Our Lady has discouraged the visionaries from seeing the world through rose-colored glasses. Rather, she has helped them to recognize both the beautiful and the ugly, the moral and the immoral, the just and the unjust. But she has also taught them that love is stronger than hate and that the ultimate victory is Christ's. Their task is to help bring about this victory through living and spreading the Medjugorje messages.

Nonetheless it is painful for us, as it was for Jesus, to witness injustice. But it is a blessing just to recognize it and thus help remedy the situation, for many are morally blind.

Application: Today, begin to look about your own community with the eyes of Christ, to see those unjust situations that need your help, prayers, and support.

OCTOBER 21

Fall asleep in prayer

The following advice was given to Jelena on prayer:

In the evening, if you fall asleep in prayer and in peace, you will wake up in the morning thinking of Jesus. Then you will be able to pray for peace. But if you fall asleep in distraction, the day after will be clouded and you will even forget to pray that day (LJM 10-30-83).

In this passage, the psalmist speaks with confidence that the Lord will hear his earnest prayer:

But I call upon God,
and the Lord will save me.
Evening and morning and at noon
I utter my complaints and moan,
and he will hear my voice.

—Psalm 55:16-17

Reflection: As we see, Our Lady stresses the importance of prayer throughout the day, especially in the morning and at night. These have always been traditional prayer times for the church, and the Divine Office is structured in this way. It has the effect of sanctifying the entire day.

The following are two prayers composed by St. Alphonsus Liguori especially for the morning and evening hours:

A Morning Prayer

Most holy and divine Trinity, one God in three Persons, I praise you and give you thanks for all the favors you have bestowed on me. Your goodness has preserved me until now.

I offer you my whole being and in particular all my thoughts, works, and deeds, together with all the trials I may undergo today. Give them your blessing. May your divine Love animate them and may they serve your greater glory.

I make this morning offering in union with the divine intentions of Jesus Christ who offers himself daily in the sacrifice of the Mass and in union with Mary, his Virgin Mother and our Mother, who was always the faithful handmaid of the Lord.

An Evening Prayer

Jesus Christ my God, I adore you and I thank you for all the graces you have given me this day. I offer you my sleep and all the moments of this night, and I implore you to keep me safe from sin.

To this end I take refuge in your Sacred Heart and under the mantle of Our Lady, my Mother. Let your holy angels surround me and keep me in peace; and let your blessing be upon me.

Application: Tomorrow, begin and end your day with these prayers, or a prayer of your own, as Our Lady asks.

Pray for peace

The following message was given to Marija for the prayer group and pilgrims who had gathered on Mt. Podbrdo:

> Dear children, I thank you for having come up here tonight to pray. At this time your Mother asks you to pray for peace in the world. Therefore, I ask you to come up often on Mt. Krizevac and Apparition Hill in order to pray for peace. I also ask you to gather as families to pray for peace and the salvation of the world (VPG 11-16-90).

When he wrote his epistle, James was also thinking of peace:

> But the wisdom from above is first pure, then peaceable, gentle, willing to yield, full of mercy and good fruits, without a trace of partiality or hypocrisy. And a harvest of righteousness is sown in peace for those who make peace (Jas 3:17-18).

Reflection: The Blessed Mother urges us strongly to pray for peace, more than any other intention. Today, then, let us do exactly that, using the following prayer:

God the Father, origin of divinity, good beyond all good, and fair beyond all fair, you are the abode of calmness, peace, and concord. Put an end to the discord that separates us from one another, and lead us back to a unity of love that may be a reflection of your divine nature.

As you are above all things, unite us by the unanimity of a good mind, so that through the embrace of love and the bonds of affection we may become spiritually one—

both in ourselves and in each other—by means of your peace which renders all things peaceful (St. Dionysius).

Application: Because of Our Lady's strong desire that we pray for peace, make this one of your major prayer intentions each day.

OCTOBER 23

I wanted to rouse the faith

During this apparition on a Monday, Marija asks the Gospa why she failed to give her regular weekly message:

I do not wish to force anyone to do what they neither feel or desire, even though I had a special message for the parish in which I wanted to rouse the faith of each believer. But truly, only a small number have accepted my Thursday messages, when in the beginning there were many. It's become a routine affair for them. And lately some are asking for the message only out of curiosity, and not out of faith and devotion to my Son and me (SM 4-30-84).

Also concerned that the people persevere in their faith, Christ said:

Be faithful until death, and I will give you the crown of life (Rev 2:10).

Reflection: A missionary named Noreen Towers had worked for years among the poor in Nigeria. In spite of all her efforts, she saw absolutely no progress. She says: "I became despondent. I finally reached the breaking point one night . . . I was beaten. When I went to bed, I didn't know how I could continue."

The next morning, shortly after she awoke, something strange happened to Noreen. It was as though Jesus himself said to her, "Can you not trust my plan for you?" She writes:

Then I realized that I did not have to see the plan; I only had to trust him. I arose from my bed a different person. My encounter with the living Christ changed me from a broken, defeated person into a person with unshakable hope and faith.

Today, the woman's work among the poor is bearing remarkable fruit.

Like all the virtues, perseverance is a gift of grace, yet Christ never fails to bestow it on those who ask. This is the primary challenge—to rely not on our own strength and endurance, but on the Lord's. It was summarized once in a small prayer: "O Lord, I can't. You can. Please."

Application: Today, let us pray to Our Lady for perseverance under one of her most revered titles, Our Lady of Perpetual Help.

OCTOBER 24

You have to be prepared

Regarding preparation for prayer, Our Lady once said:

You have to be prepared. If there are some sins, you must pull them out, otherwise you will not be able to enter into prayer. If you have worries, you should submit them to God (FY 3-85).

And in John's gospel, Christ promises to answer all prayers:

I will do whatever you ask in my name, so that the Father may be glorified in the Son. If in my name you ask for anything, I will do it (Jn 14:13-14).

Reflection: If our prayer is to be attentive and from the heart, we must prepare for this encounter with the Lord, as Our Lady asks of us today. This would include a place of quiet, a relaxed position, and a few deep breaths. Sins and worries should be given over to God so that the mind is untroubled. Last, a prayer of preparation would be appropriate, such as the following Dedication of a Prayer Time:

Gracious and beloved Lord,
at the beginning of this time of prayer,
I lift up to you
my heart overflowing with gratitude
for the many gifts and blessings
that you have given me.

I dedicate this time of worship and prayer,
and the graceful energy that shall flow
outward from the altar of my heart
as an offering for the welfare of all your children.
May your Holy Spirit take me by the hand
and lead me deep into the center of my heart,
into your Holy of Holies.
Amen.

Application: Simply use this prayer of preparation, or one of your own, before your next prayer time.

OCTOBER 25

Discover me in the poor

Our Lady advises Jelena's prayer group:

Continue to help the poor and the sick, and to pray for the dead. Do not have any fear. Completely free yourselves and abandon your hearts to me so that I can be with you. Listen to me and discover me in the poor and in all people (LJM 1-31-84).

And in the gospel, Jesus says:

> Give to everyone who begs from you, and do not refuse anyone who wants to borrow from you (Mt 5:42).

Reflection: The Jewish Talmud says, "He who gives alms is greater than Moses." But money was not the only kind of alms people gave to the needy. The Talmud also says, "Whoever gives a small coin to a poor person will receive six blessings, but whoever gives a kind word to a poor person will receive eleven blessings." Even if we can't always give money, we can give much more: forgiveness to our enemies, kindness to the elderly, example to the young, and love to all.

Application: How generous are we in our giving? The following is a Prayer for Generosity:

Father of the poor and needy, teach us to understand that generosity consists not only in providing material help but in every act of helpfulness toward those who stand in need of it, and that every human being stands in need of friendliness, sympathy, and understanding. Teach us to be generous in thought as well as in act.

Teach us to know that in the measure in which we give we also receive, that every worthy thing we do brings its own reward, and that in seeking any other kind of reward we spoil the grace of what we do. We ask this through Christ our Lord. Amen.

Sacred Heart of Jesus

Given to Jelena during an interior locution:

> *Pray! You can do anything, yes, you can do it through prayer! Place an image of the hearts of Jesus and Mary in your homes (LJM 11-11-83).*

The Sacred Heart is a symbol of God's unfathomable love. As St. John writes:

> Beloved, let us love one another, because love is from God; everyone who loves is born of God and knows God. Whoever does not love does not know God, for God is love (1 Jn 4:7-8).

Reflection: A Valentine might be considered a pale reflection of the Sacred Heart—it symbolizes human love, while the Heart of Jesus represents the infinite, divine love of Christ himself. Devotion to the Sacred Heart, then, is devotion to God's love, which we strive to imitate. This contemporary Sacred Heart Psalm by Fr. Edward Hays expresses this longing:

> O Divine Beloved,
> so often I am casual and halfhearted
> in my love for you, my God.
> Come and set my heart ablaze
> with the fire of your love.
> Inflame my heart and prayers
> as you did for your chosen son Jesus.
> His holy heart was constantly on fire
> with a consuming love for you, his God.
> Envelop me in your flaming Spirit,
> that my lukewarm prayers and acts
> may spring alive with the fire of faith.

Make my heart, like the heart of Christ,
burn with compassion for the outcast,
with comfort for the lonely
and all who are in need.

Application: Today, spend part of your prayer time reflecting on the love of Christ. When you have an opportunity, place an image of the hearts of Jesus and Mary in your home, as Our Lady asks.

OCTOBER 27

Grow in your work for the church

In this weekly message, Our Lady issues a special call:

Dear children, today I wish to call you to work within the church. I love each of you equally and desire that you do this work as much as possible. I know that you can, dear children, but you feel small and inadequate in these things. You need to be courageous and, like little flowers, grow in your work for the church and for Jesus. This will be good for everyone (WM 10-31-85).

In 1 Corinthians, Paul also calls the people to ministry:

Now, brothers and sisters, you know that members of the household of Stephanas were the first converts in Achaia, and they have devoted themselves to the service of the saints; I urge you to put yourselves at the service of such people, and of everyone who works and toils with them (1 Cor 16:15-16).

Reflection: At our confirmation, we were commissioned to assume an active role in the church as adult Christians. Today St. Paul and Our Lady remind us of that role, asking that we translate it into concrete action.

An illustration:

In the 1930s a young traveler was exploring the French Alps when he came upon a vast stretch of barren, desolate land. In the middle of this vast wasteland was a stooped old man with a sack of acorns on his back and a four-foot-long iron pipe in his hand.

The man was using the iron pipe to punch holes in the ground. Then from the sack he would take an acorn and put it in the hole. The old man told the traveler, "I've planted over 100,000 acorns. Maybe only a tenth of them will grow." The old man's wife and son had died, and this was how he spent his final years.

Twenty-five years later the traveler returned to the same desolate spot. What he saw amazed him—the land was covered with a beautiful forest two miles wide and five miles long. Birds were singing, animals were playing, and wildflowers perfumed the air—all because someone cared.

The Blessed Virgin calls us to action as well, to do our part to spread God's kingdom on earth. We may not be able to change the whole world, but we can change part of it, just as the old man did. Today St. Paul and Our Lady remind us of that role, asking that we translate it into concrete action. We received our sack of acorns and our iron pipe when we were confirmed. Now it's up to us to do something with them.

Application: What needs are there within your parish church and community? How can you actively meet some of those needs with your own gifts and talents, as Our Lady recommends today?

I give you strength

In this message to the prayer group, the Blessed Virgin speaks of giving strength:

Dear children, your Mother loves you all. I'm happy to see you here, dear children. I give you love and ask you to give this love to others. Be peacemakers and help others to change their lives.

I give you strength, dear children. With this strength, you can bear anything. May this strength make you strong in all things. Because you need it, I give you strength (VPG 6-27-88).

The prophet Isaiah also promises strength to God's people:

He gives power to the faint,
and strengthens the powerless.
Even youths will faint and be weary,
and the young will fall exhausted;
but those who wait for the Lord
will renew their strength,
they shall mount up with wings like eagles,
they shall run and not be weary,
they shall walk and not faint.

—Isaiah 40:29-31

Reflection: Cardinal John Henry Newman (1801-1890) was one of the great pastors and scholars of the Catholic church in England. His writings included this prayer for strength:

May the Lord strengthen us all the day long.
Till the shades lengthen and the evening comes,
And the busy world is hushed

and the fever of life is over,
And our work is done.

Then in his mercy may he give us
A safe lodging,
A holy rest,
And peace at the last. Amen.

One of the blessings of our faith is that we need not rely solely on our own strength, for we have an inexhaustible reservoir in God himself. Further, as Our Lady says today, we are urged to draw from this reservoir whenever we are in need.

Application: "With this strength," the Virgin says, "you can bear anything." Today, commit to memory the promise that when we are in need, the strength of Christ and Our Lady is available for the asking.

OCTOBER 29

Thank you for opening your hearts

Our Lady speaks of her joy in hearts open to God:

Dear children, today I thank you for opening your hearts. I am overwhelmed with joy for every heart that opens to God, especially in the parish. Rejoice with me! Continue to say all the prayers for the opening of sinful hearts, for not only do I desire it, but it is God's wish as well (WM 4-18-85).

And from the Book of Revelation:

Listen! I am standing at the door, knocking; if you hear my voice and open the door, I will come in to you and eat with you, and you with me (Rev 3:20).

Reflection: There is a legend along the Rhine that on a dark and cold night a thinly clad, half-starved man was toiling along one of its rugged paths. He looked with wistful eyes at the bright light that shone from the windows of a great mansion, and listened to the sounds of feasting and joyful music.

He had left the home of his youth in early life, and heard nothing from there for many years. He knew not that the magnificent property was his father's, and that he was the heir. Desperate, he asked for shelter there. At the gate he found an old servant who discovered who he was. Instantly he was ushered into the gaiety. His robes were changed to those of the heir. He had discovered a heritage he did not know existed.

In the same way, one with a closed heart is unaware of all that belongs to him as a son of God. But once the heart is opened and the grace of God enlightens the soul, he discovers he is heir to the kingdom of God.

Application: Today, pray for an ever greater openness to the Lord, and especially that sinful hearts may open to God's grace, as Our Lady asks of us.

OCTOBER 30

I want to support you

In a supportive message to Jelena, Our Lady said:

I see that you are tired. I want to support you in all your efforts, to take you in my arms so that you may be close to me. To all those who wish to ask me questions, I will answer: there is only one response—prayer, strong faith, intense prayer, and fasting (LJM 10-28-83).

And in the gospel, Christ also promises rest:

Come to me, all of you who are weary and heavily burdened, and I will give you rest. Take my yoke upon you, and learn from me; for I am gentle and humble of heart. Your souls will find rest, for my yoke is easy and my burden is light (Mt 11:28-30).

Reflection: One of the joys of Christianity is that Christ not only offers us his strength when we are weary, but also his rest and peace when we are tired. But our attitude plays an important part in this, as the following story illustrates.

A company of pilgrims were on a road, all carrying a burden of some sort. Yet they bore them cheerfully, thinking more of the purpose of their journey than of its hardships, as they went along together singing. An angel joined the little band, and passing from one to another, threw into each of the burdens a couple of little white seeds. Soon the seeds began to sprout, until they became a pair of glorious wings which carried each traveller, burden and all, along the dusty road.

Later on, a similar party was travelling on the same road, with downcast faces, and greatly complaining of the heavy burdens they carried. The angel passed again, but left them with no gift of wings. "Why did you not give them wings?" he was asked. "They look so downcast and gloomy, surely they need them more than the others." "I have only the seeds," replied the angel, "and the seeds will not grow unless they have the right soil. They will flourish only in cheerfulness and helpfulness, but will perish at once in that atmosphere of grumbling."

Application: When next you feel weary and exhausted, ask the Lord with confidence and joy for his rest and peace. Let the words of Our Lady in today's message refresh you.

You will discover a new path to joy

In this message the Blessed Virgin shows the way to happiness:

> *Dear children, today I wish to gather you under my mantle and lead you along the way to conversion. I beseech you, dear children, to surrender all of your past to the Lord, as well as all the evil that has accumulated in your hearts.*
>
> *I want each one of you to be happy, but happiness is not possible in sin. Therefore, dear children, I ask you to pray, for in prayer you will discover a new path to joy. Joy will shine forth from your hearts and thus you will be joyful witnesses of what my Son and I wish to accomplish in each of you. I bless you! (MM 2-25-87).*

And in John's gospel, Christ wishes to give all of us his joy:

> As my Father has loved me, so I have loved you; abide in my love. If you keep my commandments, you will abide in my love, just as I have kept my Father's commandments and abide in his love. I have said these things to you so that my joy may be in you, and that your joy may be complete (Jn 15:9-11).

Reflection: People have searched for happiness in many ways, often oblivious to the fact that it can only truly be found in the heart of God. One amusing story illustrates:

An Englishman, a Frenchman, and a Cuban were trying to define true happiness. "True happiness," said the Englishman, "is when you return home tired after work and find a gin and tonic waiting for you."

"You English have no romance," countered the Frenchman. "True happiness is when you go on a business trip, find a pretty girl who entertains you, and then you part without regrets."

"You are both wrong," said the Cuban. "Real happiness is when you are home in bed at four o'clock in the morning and there is a hammering at the front door and there stand members of the Secret Police, who say to you, 'Pedro Gonzalez, you are under arrest,' and you are able to reply, 'Sorry! Pedro Gonzalez lives next door!'"

Application: We often seek God in times of sorrow, but not so often when we are happy. Today offer a joyful prayer of thanksgiving for the Lord's many gifts.

Recent photo (1990) of (l. to r.) Jakov, Ivan, and Marija during an apparition

All Saints' Day

The saints of heaven wish us to share their joy:

Raise your hands, yearn for Jesus because in his resurrection he wants to fill you with grace. Be enthusiastic about the resurrection. All of us in heaven are happy, but we seek the joy of your hearts (LJM 4-21-84).

In Revelation, the great company of saints stand before the throne of God:

After this I looked, and there was a great multitude that no one could count, from every nation, from all tribes and peoples and languages, standing before the throne and before the Lamb, robed in white, with palm branches in their hands. They cried out in a loud voice, saying, "Salvation belongs to our God who is seated on the throne, and to the Lamb!" (Rv 7:9-10).

Reflection: Today is a great feast in honor of God's saints, but it is also a reminder of great promise to us, the living, that one day we shall join them in glory.

In one sense, we are united with them already in the communion of saints (which we refer to whenever we say the creed). This is the union of the living, the saints in heaven, and the souls in purgatory, all joined together as the Mystical Body of Christ. More, we are able to help each other: the living can help the souls in purgatory, and they can pray for us who are living on earth. The saints in heaven, in turn, pray for both.

This beautiful communion, the Body of Christ, remains unfulfilled until we all come to the fullness of eternal life in God. Thus Our Lady can say, "All of us in heaven are happy, but we seek the joy of your hearts."

Most of the saints are unknown to us—simple, humble people who have loved God and neighbor to the best of their ability. We are called to join them, as we see in this prayer that the Blessed Virgin gave to Jelena's prayer group: "My soul is full of love like the sea. My heart is full of peace like the river. I am not a saint, but I am invited to be one" (LJM 9-85).

Application: If you have a patron saint by virtue of your baptismal or confirmation name, offer a prayer of thanksgiving to him or her for favors past, and ask for his or her intercessory prayer for your most pressing needs. Or choose a patron saint this week if you have none, asking in prayer for his or her special help and protection.

NOVEMBER 2

All Souls' Day

In this message from 1986, Our Lady speaks of purgatory and our role in helping those who have gone before us:

Dear children, today I invite you to pray every day for the souls in purgatory. Every soul needs prayer and grace in order to reach God and his love. By this way, dear children, you will gain new intercessors, who will help you during your life to discern that nothing on earth is more important for you, than longing for heaven.

For that, dear children, pray without respite, so that you may be able to help yourselves and others, to whom your prayers will bring joy (WM 11-6-86).

The Book of Revelation also speaks of life after death:

Then I saw a great white throne and the one who sat on it; the earth and the heaven fled from his presence, and no place was found for them. And I saw the dead, great and small, standing before the throne, and books were opened. Also another book was opened, the book of life.

And the dead were judged according to their works, as recorded in the books. And the sea gave up the dead that were in it, Death and Hades gave up the dead that were in them, and all were judged according to what they had done (Rv 20:11-13).

Reflection: Especially on All Souls' Day, the church calls us to remember and pray for the souls in purgatory, including our loved ones who have gone before us.

The church's doctrine of purgatory is too often misunderstood. It is not a *place* where the residue of sin is remitted through suffering; it is rather a *process* in which we are perfected until that point when we can unite in harmony with the fullness of love and life, which is God. Just as oil and water cannot mix, so too we must resemble the Spirit of God, free from sin, before entering into his life—a state called heaven.

This process is veiled in mystery, but it is without doubt a benevolent concept, a gift from God who allows us time even after death to gain heaven. It also allows us, the living, to help those who have already died: "For every soul," Our Lady says, "prayer and grace are necessary to reach God and the love of God."

Further, those whom we have helped to obtain paradise will in turn help us: "You obtain new intercessors," Mary says, "who will help you in this life to realize that earthly things are not important, that it is necessary to strive only for heaven."

Application: All Souls' Day is an appropriate time to arrange for masses to be offered for the dead, which the Blessed Mother recommends. Your parish office can inform you of the procedure and suggested offering. Mary also asks us to pray for the forgotten dead and those in most need of God's mercy, to whom, Our Lady says, "your prayers will bring great joy."

NOVEMBER 3

St. Martin de Porres

The life of St. Martin de Porres was characterized by two great virtues: love of neighbor and service to the poor. In the following two messages, Our Lady speaks of both:

Dear children, during these days people from every nation will be coming into the parish. And so I now call you to love. First of all, love the members of your own family and in this way you will be capable of accepting and loving all who come here (WM 6-6-85).

Dear children, tonight I call you to pray for all the poor and hungry people throughout the world. I especially thank you because you have helped me to fulfill my plans (VPG 9-12-88).

And from the Beatitudes:

Blessed are you who are poor,
for yours is the kingdom of God.
Blessed are you who are hungry now,
for you will be filled.
Blessed are you who weep now,
for you will laugh.

—Luke 6:20-21

Reflection: St. Martin, patron of the poor, was born in Peru in 1579, the son of a Spanish knight and a Negro mother. During his youth he was apprenticed to a barber-surgeon and became very knowledgeable of medicines and herbs, which he later used in his care for the poor. He became a lay brother of the Dominican Order and is most remembered for his care of the slaves who were brought to Peru from Africa. He once said, "I wish to be the slave of the slaves of God." Upon his death in 1639, he was carried to his grave by bishops and noblemen. He is also, appropriately, the patron of social justice.

At his canonization in 1962, Pope John XXIII said of him:

> Saint Martin, always obedient and inspired by his divine Teacher, dealt with his brothers with that profound love which comes from pure faith and humility of service. He loved men because he honestly looked upon them as God's children and as his own brothers and sisters.

Application: Today, let us put into practice Our Lady's message: "I call you to pray for all the poor and hungry people throughout the world."

NOVEMBER 4

Open your hearts

Today the Madonna asks that we follow the lead of her Son:

> *Dear children, open your hearts and let Jesus guide you. To many people this seems to be hard, but it is really so easy! You need not be afraid for you know that Jesus*

will never leave you—and you know that he leads you to salvation (LJM 8-11-86).

In John's gospel, we are also called to follow the Shepherd:

> The gatekeeper opens the gate for him, and the sheep hear his voice. He calls his own sheep by name and leads them out. When he has brought out all his own, he goes ahead of them, and the sheep follow him because they know his voice (Jn 10:3-4).

Reflection: When in Florence every visitor seeks out Michelangelo's statue of David, the shepherd lad. It is a masterpiece in marble. It stands nine feet high, alert with all the wonderful expressiveness of artistic genius. The statue has a history that is remarkable and splendidly suggestive of today's readings. A hundred years or more before the time of Michelangelo, a magnificent block of Carrara marble was brought to Florence by an now unknown sculptor. He worked on it, blocking out the figure which was in his mind, but suddenly bungled his work by cutting a great slice out of the side, which made it useless to him, and so it was cast aside.

There it lay for a century until the trained eye of Michelangelo rested on it. Immediately he caught the possibility that lay in the stone, and soon it was taking on form under his hand. Outlining and fashioning, carving and chiselling, a majestic figure was soon seen stepping from the marble, and even the mutilation which had rendered it useless to the original workman became part of the majesty of the new design.

"Open your hearts," the Virgin says today, "and let Jesus guide you." Like marble in the hands of a sculptor, we will be formed into his very image, regardless of our former sins and flaws.

Application: Simply open your heart to Christ today, asking that he fashion it into the image of his own.

NOVEMBER 5

Those in hell

In the early months of the apparitions, the Blessed Mother gave this message on hell:

> *Today many persons go to hell. God allows his children to suffer in hell due to the fact that they have committed grave, unpardonable sins. Those in hell no longer have a chance to know a better lot (FY 7-25-82).*

And from the Book of Revelation:

> But as for the cowardly, the faithless, the polluted, the murderers, the fornicators, the sorcerers, the idolaters, and all liars, their place will be in the lake that burns with fire and sulfur, which is the second death (Rev 21:8).

Reflection: Pope John Paul I used to teach about heaven and hell through the story of a Korean general. He died, was judged, and assigned to paradise. But when he came up before St. Peter he thought of something he would like to do. He wanted to peep into hell for a moment, just to have an idea of it. "Right you are," said St. Peter.

So the general peeped in at the door of hell and saw an enormous banquet hall. In it were a number of long tables with bowls of rice and delicacies on them, well flavored, smelling delicious, inviting. The guests were sitting there hungrily, opposite one another, each with a plate of food.

What was happening? The guests all had chopsticks—which they had to use—but these were so long that, however hard they tried, not a grain of rice could they get into their mouths. And this was their torment, this was hell. "I've seen it, that's more than enough for me," said the general and went back to the gates of heaven, where he went in.

Inside, he saw the same banquet hall, the same tables, the same food, and the same long chopsticks. But the guests were cheerful, all of them smiling and laughing. Each one, having put the food onto his chopsticks, held it out to the mouth of his companion opposite, and so they managed to eat to their fill.

"Thinking of others instead of oneself," the Pope said, "had solved the problem and transformed hell into heaven."

Application: A verse for reflection today: "Hell is in heaven and heaven is in hell. But angels see only the light, and devils only the darkness" (Jacob Boehme).

NOVEMBER 6

Venerate the heart of my Son

Today Our Lady speaks of reparation to the heart of her Son:

Dear children, this evening I pray that you especially venerate the heart of my Son, Jesus. Make reparation for the wounds inflicted on my Son's sacred heart, for it is offended by all kinds of sin (WM 4-5-84).

And from John's gospel, the scene on Calvary:

But when they came to Jesus and saw that he was already dead, they did not break his legs. Instead one of the soldiers pierced his side with a spear, and at once blood and water came out (Jn 19:33-34).

Reflection: Devotion to the Sacred Heart of Jesus is associated with St. Margaret Mary Alacoque (1647-1690) to whom Our Lord appeared a number of times during her life as a nun in the Visitation Order. Christ charged her with instituting the feast of the Sacred Heart and to spread its devotion throughout the world. Reparation through prayer and sacrifice was also to be made to the Heart of Jesus for the many sins that had offended it.

As Our Lady asks today, let us make reparation to Christ's heart using the following Prayer of Reparation:

Lord Jesus Christ, we look at the cross and we, your pilgrim church, can see what sin has done to the Son of Mary, to the Son of God.

But now you are risen and glorified. You suffer no more in the flesh. The scourging, the crown of thorns, your death on the cross have now passed.

But you suffer greatly through your Sacred Heart and through your Mystical Body, the universal church, which still feels the agony of sin. For this we make our act of reparation (The Apostleship of Prayer).

Application: Mark your calendar to remember to offer the *Prayer of Reparation* on the First Friday of each month, a day that has special significance in Sacred Heart devotion. Make a special effort to receive communion on nine consecutive First Fridays as well, as this devotion carries with it great promises and graces from the Savior.

NOVEMBER 7

May true prayer fill your hearts

The Blessed Mother speaks of prayer in the following message:

Dear children, today I call you to prayer with the heart, and not just through habit. Some come here but do not want to make progress in prayer. Therefore, as your Mother, I want to warn you: pray that true prayer may fill your hearts at every moment (WM 5-2-85).

———————

And from Psalm 141:

I call upon you, O Lord; come quickly to me;
give ear to my voice when I call to you.
Let my prayer be as incense before you,
and the lifting up of my hands as an evening
    sacrifice.

—Psalm 141:1-2

———————

Reflection: Again Our Lady speaks of prayer with the heart and the tremendous grace it gives. Perhaps the highest form of this prayer is the "prayer of quiet" or "centering prayer," in which we experience God in the very depths of our being. To experience this prayer, the following guidelines will be helpful:

A. Choose a place where you can be alone without distraction. Take a comfortable bodily position, close your eyes, and put everything out of your mind.

B. Physically relax and let all tensions leave you. Deep, deliberate breathing will aid this process. Let your total being, mind and body, arrive at a gentle silence.

C. Center all your attention on God and let a word or phrase form in your consciousness. You can use "Jesus," or "Jesus, have mercy," or "Come Holy Spirit," or whatever else will relate you to the Lord.

D. The word or phrase may be repeated often or interspersed with periods of complete silence. This is your way of reaching out for and receiving the Lord.

E. Your prayer should end slowly and quietly. You may wish to recite an Our Father or Hail Mary meditatively. On occasion the Lord may invite you to a deeper silence or listening and you will come to know the joy of his Spirit in fullest measure, even in ecstasy.

Application: Practice the prayer of quiet within the next several days. For a fuller explanation, consult the books by Fr. Basil Pennington on centering prayer.

NOVEMBER 8

Do not judge yourselves

Speaking to the prayer group that Ivan and Marija had formed, the Virgin said:

> *You will be happy if you do not judge yourselves according to your faults, but understand that graces are offered to you even in your faults (VPG 5-12-86).*

And of judging, Christ said in the gospel of Luke:

> Do not judge, and you will not be judged; do not condemn, and you will not be condemned. Forgive, and you will be forgiven (Lk 6:37).

Reflection: Christ and Our Lady wish us to be truly free, but this is contingent upon our forgiveness of both ourselves and others, as our readings illustrate today.

This freedom means release from the prisons of our own minds and hearts—the capacity to receive the gift of peace. But we cannot receive this grace while bitterness and resentment toward others tears at our souls, doing more damage than any past transgressor could.

And so the Blessed Mother calls us to release the bitter past, to let go of these old resentments, and to allow God to dispense justice in his own way and in his own time. She urges us to be cleansed and healed from the pain of the past so that it cannot poison the present and the future. She calls us to allow old injustices to be purged on the funeral pyre of Christ's redeeming love. This love is Christ's own presence, the gift of himself. It comes through surrender to the Lord of Peace who makes all things new.

Application: In prayer today, surrender the pain of the past to Christ and Our Lady, asking that they heal the wounds of bitterness and hurt.

NOVEMBER 9

Withstand the days of temptation

In a weekly message from 1985, the Mother of God said:

Dear children, these days Satan is working underhandedly against the parish. You, dear children, have fallen asleep in prayer and only some of you are going to Mass. Withstand the days of temptation! (WM, 1985).

And from John's gospel:

When they kept on questioning him, he straightened up and said to them, "Let anyone among you who is without sin be the first to throw a stone at her." And once again he bent down and wrote on the ground. When they heard it, they went away, one by one, beginning with the elders; and Jesus was left alone with the woman standing before him.

Jesus straightened up and said to her, "Woman, where are they? Has no one condemned you?" She said, "No one, sir." And Jesus said, "Neither do I condemn you. Go your way, and from now on do not sin again" (Jn 8:7-11).

Reflection: As we see from this passage from St. John, no stone was thrown at the woman who had committed the sin of adultery. Under the ancient law of Moses, she deserved the punishment, but Christ brought a new law into the world, a law measured by mercy, not justice. If we receive what we deserve, and if justice is served, no one is safe. We would all be lost.

There is a story about a saintly person who had lived a life of prayer and good deeds, had been active in church and community affairs, and was an outstanding citizen. When he died and appeared before St. Peter, the entrance requirements were laid out: "You need two thousand points to get in." After relating all the achievements of his entire life, the applicant was told, "Fine, that's worth three points!" "In that case," said the man, "only the grace of God will get me in!" "That's right," answered Saint Peter, "that's worth 1,997 points. Come on in!"

Application: A prayer for today:
O, Christ, my savior, help me to seek and serve mercy before justice, to forgive before I condemn. Let me be an instrument of your love in myself and for others, and live more by grace than by law. Amen.

NOVEMBER 10

St. Leo the Great

Concerning the Pope, Our Lady once said:

> *Have him consider himself the father of all mankind and not only of Christians. Have him spread untiringly and with courage the message of peace and love to all mankind (FY 9-26-82).*

Pope or bishop, lay or religious we are all part of one church and one Lord, all sharing in the manifold graces of God for the good of one another. As Paul writes:

> Now you are the body of Christ and individually members of it. And God appointed in the church first apostles, second prophets, third teachers; then deeds of power, then gifts of healing, forms of assistance, forms of leadership, various kinds of tongues (1 Cor 12:27-28).

Reflection: Taking up this theme of many members yet one body, St. Leo wrote:

> Although the universal church of God is constituted of distinct orders of members, still, in spite of the many parts of its holy body, the church subsists as an integral whole, just as the Apostle says: "We are all one in Christ," nor is anyone separated from the office of another in such a way that a lower group has no connection with the head. In the unity of faith and baptism, our community is then undivided.

Leo the Great was elected Pope in the year 440 and guided the church through a very difficult period of its history. We know little of his personal life, but through his writing and preaching he made many lasting contributions. The introductory note in the *Liturgy of the Hours* states: "He was a true pastor and father of souls. He labored strenuously to safeguard the integrity of the faith and vigorously defended the unity of the church. He pushed back or at least softened the onrush of the barbarians. He has deservedly won the title 'the Great.'"

Application: Our Lady often asks for prayers for the Pope and all the leaders of the church. Make this, then, one of your daily prayer intentions.

NOVEMBER 11

Open yourselves more to God

Today Our Lady invites us to a special openness:

Dear children, today I call you to open yourselves more to God so that he can work through you. The more you open yourselves, the more abundantly you will receive of his fruits. I also wish to call you again to prayer (WM 3-6-86).

And in Luke's gospel, an invitation from Christ:

Then Jesus said to him, "Someone gave a great dinner and invited many. At the time for the dinner he sent his slave to say to those who had been invited, 'Come; for everything is ready now'" (Lk 14:16-17).

Reflection: We are those whom Jesus has invited to come to his banquet. The feast he beckons us to is the Kingdom, and all is ready: the table is set and the food is prepared. "Come to the table, dine!" we are urged. To wait or hold back is needless.

The call of Christ is to come to a festive and joyous feast, and Our Lady echoes that call in her message to open ourselves. But what is it that keeps us from such a celebration? Perhaps somewhere we didn't hear or receive the invitation. Perhaps we did not really believe that the Kingdom would be joyous. Whatever the reason, we have a new invitation now. Medjugorje has helped us to feel our hunger and thirst. Surely we now know we need to be fed, and most surely we could use some joy and celebration.

God is patient and tireless in summoning us, and his call is forever in the present. The feast never grows cold; he is never unprepared. If we hold back out of fear, guilt, or indifference, we can miss out entirely.

But we need not keep missing out. All we need to do is stop excusing ourselves and enter the banquet hall.

Application: A prayer for today:
Gracious Lord, rouse me to accept your invitation. Remove my laziness, dissolve my excuses, calm my fear. With a new openness to you and Our Lady, I shall take my place at your table. Amen.

NOVEMBER 12

Withstand every trial

Speaking of trials, the Madonna once said in a weekly message:

> *Dear children, today I wish to tell you that God wants to send you trials which you can overcome by prayer. God is testing you through daily difficulties. Thus, pray to peacefully withstand every trial. From God's testing you will emerge more open and loving (WM 8-22-85).*

And from Peter's first letter:

> Yet if any of you suffers as a Christian, do not consider it a disgrace, but glorify God because you bear this name (1 Pt 4:16).

Reflection: There is a legend about a monk who was walking in a monastery garden alone, thinking of the Passion of Christ. It was Holy Week. As he slowly paced along, he saw something lying in the path, and picked it up. The voice of Christ told him it was the crown of thorns that he had worn. He reverently picked it up and carried it to the chapel, where he placed it on the altar. Needless to say, never had Holy Week been so meaningful, for the sight of that crown of thorns made the monks realize the sufferings and love of Christ more than they had ever done before.

As Easter Sunday dawned, the monk rose early for his Easter prayers of thanksgiving, and came into the chapel. As the sun shone through the window, it played upon the altar and rested on the crown of thorns, but something miraculous had happened. There in the Easter sunlight the thorns had blossomed into a rainbow of budding flowers.

There are thorns of sufferings and trials in every life, and it seems that only a spirit of acceptance can bring peace in these situations—acceptance, and turning to Christ for solutions and healing, as the Virgin recommends today. Running in circles or complaining rarely helps. But recourse to the Lord of Peace always will.

Application: Today, offer this prayer for times of trial: Dear Lord, please help me to accept my trials and seek the serenity of your grace so that I might triumph over them, and not wear myself out by straining or complaining. Amen.

NOVEMBER 13

St. Frances Xavier Cabrini

The Blessed Virgin speaks of humility today:

> *Your humility must be proud. Your pride should be humble. If you have received a gift from God, you must be proud but do not say that it is yours. Say, rather, that it is God's.*

Our example of humility is Christ himself; as St. Paul writes:

Let the same mind be in you that was in Christ Jesus, who, though he was in the form of God, did not regard equality with God as something to be exploited, but emptied himself (Phil 2:5-7).

Reflection: The American saint, Frances Xavier Cabrini, was originally from Italy; she founded the Missionary Sisters of the Sacred Heart in 1880, and in the United States established schools, hospitals, and orphanages for the care especially of immigrants and children. She died in 1917 and was canonized by Pope Pius XII in 1946.

Her life and writings exemplified the humility of which Our Lady and St. Paul speak of in today's readings.

Application: The following Prayer for Humility, written by St. Frances Cabrini, would be appropriate to offer today:

Lord Jesus Christ, I pray that you may fortify me with the grace of your Holy Spirit, and give your peace to my soul, that I may be free from all needless anxiety and worry. Help me to desire always that which is pleasing and acceptable to you, so that your will may be my will.

Grant that I may be free of unholy desires and that, for your love, I may remain obscure and unknown in this world, to be known only to you.

Do not permit me to attribute to myself the good that you perform in me and through me, but rather, referring all honor to you, may I admit only to my infirmities, so that renouncing sincerely all vainglory which comes from the world, I may aspire to that true and lasting glory which comes from you. Amen.

NOVEMBER 14

They adore idols

The following was given to Jelena, the locutionist:

Pray, pray! So many have followed other beliefs or sects and have abandoned Jesus Christ! They create their own gods, they adore idols. How that hurts me! If only they could be converted! There are so many unbelievers! But that can change only if you help me with your prayers (LJM 2-9-84).

And from Paul's letter to the Romans:

I appeal to you therefore, brothers and sisters, by the mercies of God, to present your bodies as a living sacrifice, holy and acceptable to God, which is your spiritual worship. Do not be conformed to this world, but be transformed by the renewing of your minds, so that you may discern what is the will of God—what is good and acceptable and perfect (Rom 12:1-2).

Reflection: Human beings instinctively worship. We bow down and devote our energy and loyalty to something. It is our nature to believe in some important cause, ideal, or person. The tragedy is that we sometimes choose such false and unreliable gods. The first commandment of the law is: "Thou shalt have no other gods before me." Only the God of Abraham, Isaac, and Jacob, only the God and Father of our Lord Jesus Christ is worthy of worship. Only the creator, redeemer, and sanctifier—the only God—is worthy of our devotion.

Only he can heal us. Wealth, fame, pleasure, power, or knowledge cannot substitute for Christ. These things may come our way, but not by worshiping any of them. Christ has said: "Seek first his kingdom and his righteousness, and all these things shall be yours besides" (Mt 6:33).

Application: Our Lady has said that some of her children "create their own gods, they adore idols. How that hurts me!" She also gives the means to help: "That can change only if you help me with your prayers." Today, then, dedicate your prayer to this intention.

NOVEMBER 15

Every barrier will disappear

In this weekly message from 1986, the Blessed Mother spoke of conversion and reconciliation:

Dear children, again I call you to prayer with the heart. If you pray with the heart, dear children, the ice of your brothers' hearts will melt and every barrier will disappear. Conversion will be easy for all who want to accept it. You must obtain this gift for your neighbor through prayer (WM 1-23-86).

And from Paul's second letter to the Corinthians:

We have spoken frankly to you Corinthians; our heart is wide open to you. There is no restriction in our affections, but only in yours. In return—I speak as to children—open wide your hearts also (2 Cor 6:11-13).

Reflection: In the second century, a Christian priest of Antioch, named Sulpicius, had steadfastly refused to sacrifice to the pagan gods, even under torture, and was being led away to be beheaded. This was the age of relentless persecution of Christians.

On the way, a secret Christian named Nicephorus ran up to him. He had quarrelled bitterly with Sulpicius and now sought reconciliation. "Martyr of Christ!" he said, on his knees, "Forgive me, for I have wronged thee."

But Sulpicius refused to speak to him, even at the place of execution. But when the moment came to kneel under the executioner's sword, he turned pale. "No, no! I will obey the Emperor. I will sacrifice to the gods." Again Nicephorus ran up to him and implored him not to lose his martyr's crown at this last moment. But it was in vain, and Sulpicius went off to sacrifice. "Then I will take his place," said Nicephorus. "Tell the Governor I am a Christian." And so Nicephorus won the martyr's crown and Sulpicius turned coward, and all the Christians said it was because he would not forgive.

It is hard to know Christ if we cannot forgive and let go of the hatred and resentment we hold toward others. Pardon and peace go hand in hand. In life, little serenity is possible without the beauty of forgiveness.

Application: Today, pray that Our Lady may teach you to forgive and forget the hurts and bitterness of the past, that you may experience the fullness of Christ's peace.

NOVEMBER 16

Here you receive blessings

The following was given to Marija and Ivan when they were on Mt. Krizevac with their prayer group:

You are on a [Mt.] Tabor. Here you receive blessings, strength, and love. Carry them into your families and into your homes. To each one of you, I grant a special blessing. Continue in joy, prayer, and reconciliation (VPG 6-24-86).

And from John's gospel:

> Abide in me as I abide in you. Just as the branch cannot bear fruit by itself unless it abides in the vine, neither can you unless you abide in me. I am the vine, you are the branches. Those who abide in me and I in them bear much fruit, because apart from me you can do nothing (Jn 15:4-5).

Reflection: The great Russian novelist, Leo Tolstoy, told the story of a man who stopped to give alms to a beggar. To his dismay he found that he had left his money at home. Stammering his explanation, he said, "I'm sorry, brother, but I don't have anything." "Never mind, brother," was the beggar's answer, "that too was a gift." It seems that the word "brother" meant even more to him than money.

One of the finest things about our church is the care and concern we often have for one another. In a real sense, we are all brothers and sisters. We have a stake in each other's salvation, and we have learned from the gospel to value and strengthen each other. Our church becomes our family, our fortress, and our refuge.

There is a wedding prayer that says, "Now our joys are doubled, because the happiness of one is also the happiness of the other. Now our burdens are cut in half, since when we share them we divide the load." As members of the universal as well as the local church, we double our joys and cut our burdens in half. We become a family, the Body of Christ, instead of isolated individuals.

Application: Today, resolve in prayer to do what Our Lady asks of us in her message: to bring blessings, strength, and love into our families, homes, and church.

NOVEMBER 17

Give me all your hardships

The following was given to Ivan's prayer group in 1990:

Dear children, your Mother invites you to joy. Your Mother asks you to begin to live tonight's message. Again tonight, your Mother asks you to give me all your problems and all your hardships. Thank you, dear children, for continuing to live in prayer all that I have said to you (VPG 6-25-90).

And from Paul's second letter to the Corinthians:

But he said to me, "My grace is sufficient for you, for power is made perfect in weakness." So, I will boast all the more gladly of my weaknesses, so that the power of Christ may dwell in me. Therefore I am content with weaknesses, insults, hardships, persecutions, and calamities for the sake of Christ; for whenever I am weak, then I am strong (2 Cor 12:9-10).

Reflection: Abraham Lincoln once said, "I have been driven many times to my knees by the overwhelming conviction that I had nowhere else to go." Most of us know the truth of Lincoln's words. There is hope in the fact that when we do sink to our knees, we then have something to support us. When we finally exhaust our own power, we can depend on the power of God.

We know that one of the best things that could happen to us, in experiencing a low point in life, is to reach out like St. Paul, who found God most powerfully when he was the weakest.

Application: A prayer for today:
Most loving Lord, thank you for being there at the lowest points in my life. Continue to take my hand and pull me up. Amen.

NOVEMBER 18

Do not give in

Early in the apparitions, the Virgin spoke to the visionaries of endurance:

Do not give in. Keep your faith. I will accompany you at every step (FY 11-10-81).

Paul also speaks of endurance:

Therefore I endure everything for the sake of the elect, so that they also may obtain the salvation that is in Christ Jesus, with eternal glory. The saying is sure:

If we have died with him,
we will also live with him;
if we endure, we will
also reign with him (2 Tm 2:10-12).

Reflection: Many years ago two men were on board a sailing ship, going back to their home on a far-off Pacific island, when one of them noticed a little grain of corn at his feet. He picked it up and examined it. "It's a grain of corn," he said. "If it were a sackful it might be of some use!" and he threw it away again carelessly.

But the other man picked it up, put it in his pocket, and treasured it until they reached their island home. Then he sowed it. It grew into a plant, and yielded a tiny crop, so small as to be laughable. But he planted that in turn, and the next time the result was enough to fill a cup. This he sowed again, and there was enough to give a few grains to each of his many friends. So the crop grew, and in the end it yielded an abundant harvest. The little seed was the means of introducing corn to the Pacific islands.

When the seed of faith first comes into our lives with its love and power and we feel its great energy, we treat it with great reverence. As time goes by, however, we may begin to take it for granted. We can get lazy, tired, and careless. When that begins to happen, we are in danger of sliding into lukewarmness. And so Our Lady says today, "Do not give in. Keep your faith;" and in Revelation: "[This] is a call for endurance and the faith of the saints."

One of the great values of the Medjugorje messages is that they renew and energize our faith, guarding us from lethargy. As long as we heed them, our faith cannot help but deepen and bear an abundant harvest.

Application: Simply offer the following prayer today: Mother Mary, your messages have meant new life to me. They have given me healing and hope, deepening my faith. Please keep me attentive and truly careful about what I hold most dear. Amen.

NOVEMBER 19

When you need me, call me

In the first weeks of the apparitions, the Blessed Mother told the visionaries:

Pray, my angels, for these people. My children, I give you strength. I will always give it to you. When you need me, call me (FY 8-23-81).

And from Luke's gospel:

> When he has found it, he lays it on his shoulders and rejoices. And when he comes home, he calls together his friends and neighbors, saying to them, "Rejoice with me, for I have found my sheep that was lost" (Lk 15:5-6).

Reflection: One of the most popular stories of recent years is called "Footprints in the Sand." It is the reflection of a person who is puzzled that, although Christ's footprints normally appear next to his own in the sand, as they walk together through life, yet when he is in special need or trouble only one set of prints can be seen. And so he asks, "Where were you, Lord, when I needed you most?" To which Jesus replies: "Ah, but there were only one set of footprints because it was then that I carried you!"

This is a thought of great comfort, and yet to be picked up and carried is difficult for many of us to accept. Thoughts like, "I'm too heavy," "I'm too embarrassed," "I'm not helpless," or "I'm not worthy," fill our minds. But eventually we have to admit: "I am too tired; I am too sick," or "I am too scared." To surrender and submit to the strong arms of a Savior humiliates the proud but brings joy to the weary. What keeps us from being helped is our fierce self-sufficiency.

Application: Today, surrender yourself to the Good Shepherd in prayer. Be alert to others around you that need to be carried for a while in your own arms.

When my Son was dying

On Good Friday in 1990, the Virgin gave this message to the visionary's prayer group:

Dear children, I am happy to see you tonight. You know, dear children, that when my Son was dying I was alone with him with only a few other women, but tonight I am happy that so many of you are with me. Tonight, when you return home, pray a rosary in front of your crucifix and be thankful (VPG 4-13-90).

Speaking of the crucifixion, St. Luke writes:

And when all the crowds who had gathered there for this spectacle saw what had taken place, they returned home, beating their breasts. But all his acquaintances, including the women who had followed him from Galilee, stood at a distance, watching these things (Lk 23:48-49).

Reflection: When the H. M. S. Birkenhead sank, Alexander Russell, a young officer age seventeen, was ordered to command one of the boats which carried the women and children. As they were pushing off, a sailor who was drowning clasped the side of the boat, but there was no room for even one more. A woman in the boat cried, "Save him! He's my husband."

Alexander Russell rose, and in a quick movement jumped clear of the boat. He sank in the water, which was full of sharks, and was seen no more as the sailor he had saved was then pulled aboard to safety.

In the end, nothing is more beautiful than love. Yet as beautiful as it is, love is more practical than pretty. Real love deals with the real world, where there's no prettiness. Yet there is beauty.

The sight of Jesus bowing under the weight of the cross—his stumbling, bruising falls on the road, his cries from the cross, his sweat, his blood, his dying breath—none is a pretty sight. Yet how beautiful! Men have tried for centuries to capture the beauty in that ugliness. Some of the greatest works of art have tried to portray the crucified yet beautiful Savior.

Here is God in our flesh, cruelly betrayed, tortured, and nailed to the cross—what could be uglier? Nothing. Unless something more beautiful than beauty was there on that hill. Unless the ugly horror was transcended and transformed, made holy.

And it was. Each time we kneel at the foot of the cross, as we gaze in wonder upon the suffering Servant, no beauty can compare. The glory is overwhelming.

Application: Today, simply heed Our Lady's request in her message: "Pray the rosary in front of your crucifix with great thankfulness."

NOVEMBER 21

The Presentation of Mary

On this day when Mary was presented, or consecrated, to God at the Temple in Jerusalem, she calls each of us to a consecration as well:

> *Dear children, today I am happy because many of you want to consecrate yourselves to me. Thank you. You are not mistaken. My Son, Jesus Christ wishes, through my intercession, to bestow very special graces on you. He rejoices in your consecration to him (WM 5-17-84).*

When we are consecrated to God and Our Lady, we are given a mission as well. From Isaiah:

> The spirit of the Lord God is upon me,
> because the Lord has anointed me;

He has sent me to bring good news
to the oppressed,
to bind up the brokenhearted,
to proclaim liberty to the captives,
and release to the prisoners;
to proclaim the year of the Lord's favor,
and the day of vengeance of our God;
to comfort all who mourn.

—Isaiah 61:1-2

Reflection: Our Lady once recommended to the visionaries that they read an account of her life entitled *The Poem of the Man-God* by the mystical writer Maria Valtorta (1897-1961). In chapter 8 of this work, Valtorta describes her vision of Mary's presentation at the age of three.

As background: Having been childless, Joachim and Ann had vowed that if they were blessed with a child, they would consecrate her to God at childhood, when she would then reside at the Temple with other consecrated souls, to pray and glorify the Lord in a cloistered setting, until she reached maturity.

In this scene from the book, the child Mary and her parents are at the entrance of the Temple, where the high priest has come to receive her:

The high priest looks at the little girl and smiles. . . . Then, he beckons to Mary. And she departs from her mother and father, and as if fascinated, climbs the steps. And she smiles. She smiles in the shade of the Temple, where the precious veil is hanging. . . . She is now at the top of the steps, at the feet of the high priest, who imposes his hand on her head. The victim has been accepted. Which purer victim had the Temple ever received?

Then he turns around and holding his hand on her shoulder as if he were leading the immaculate little lamb to the altar, he takes her to the Temple door. Before letting her in, he asks her: "Mary of David, are you aware of your vow?" When she replies "Yes" in her silvery voice, he cries out: "Go in, then. Walk in my presence and be perfect."

Application: "Today I am very happy," Our Lady says, "because there are many who want to consecrate themselves to me. Thank you." Today, in the spirit of the Presentation, consecrate yourself again to the Blessed Mother, using either your own words or the prayer found for November 24.

NOVEMBER 22

Continue to grow

The following was given to the young locutionists for their prayer group:

> *Each member of the group is like a flower; and if someone tries to crush you, you will grow and continue to grow even more. If someone puts you down even a little, you will recover. And if someone pulls a petal, continue to grow as though you were complete (LJM 6-21-84).*

And from Paul's letter to the Galatians:

> So let us not grow weary in doing what is right, for we will reap at harvest time, if we do not give up (Gal 6:9).

Reflection: Sometimes we are lamps without light, extinguished, but with possibilities not realized. Well, I have come to light a flame in your hearts, should the disappointments you have suffered, the expectations that have not come true, have put it out. I want to say to each of you that you have capacities, often unsuspected, sometimes made even greater and more vigorous by hard experience.

These words of hope from Pope John Paul II speak of a great truth—that hope, far from being some vague, ethereal virtue, is instead a product of practical, learned experience.

Experience is not just the best teacher; it is the only teacher. As we look back at our trials and hardships, we realize that, rather than being tragic and destructive, our difficulties have given us endurance, resilience, and patience. This is the direct outcome of going through trials. This is where hope comes from. This is where God sheds his love right where we always need him the most. It is why we have "unsuspected capacities," as the Holy Father says, why we have hope.

Application: Today the Mother of God gives us a message of profound hope: in times of trial or suffering, we will not be crushed, but will recover even stronger "and continue to grow more and more." Today, give over to her any present difficulties, trusting in her help.

NOVEMBER 23

I call you to offer sacrifices

Today Our Lady speaks of one of the core virtues of Christian life:

> *Dear children, today I thank you again for everything that you have accomplished for me during these past days. I thank you especially, dear children, for the sacrifices you have offered this last week.*
>
> *Dear children, do not forget that I desire sacrifices from you so I can help you and keep Satan at a distance. And so I call you again to offer sacrifices in special reverence toward God (WM 9-18-86).*

In Hebrews, Paul speaks of the effects of the greatest sacrifice:

> But when Christ had offered for all time a single sacrifice for sins, "he sat down at the right hand of God," and since then has been waiting "until his enemies would be made a footstool for his feet." For by a single offering he has perfected for all time those who are sanctified (Heb 10:12-14).

Reflection: In Pompeii the body of a crippled boy was found with his lame foot. Round his body was a woman's arm, bejewelled. The great stream of fire suddenly issuing from the volcano had driven a terror-stricken crowd for refuge. The woman had evidently taken pity on the cripple. Only the arm outstretched to save was saved itself.

The arm of the Lord protects his people. He draws us to himself to save all of us. We are never too insignificant for his rescue. A saying goes: "If you were the only person left on earth, Christ would die for you alone." Every soul is priceless in the sight of God.

Each of us belongs to the creator, we are his flesh and blood. His salvation is directed to every one of us. No one is left out. As St. Paul writes: "For as all die in Adam, so all will be made alive in Christ" (1 Cor 15:22).

Application: With the sacrifice of Christ as our great example, let us try to live Our Lady's message today: "And so I call you again to offer your sacrifices in special reverence to God."

Consecration to the Immaculate Heart of Mary

Given to the young locutionists, Jelena and Marijana:

> *I give you my heart. Accept it! I do not wish to distress you, nor to stop talking to you, but know that I cannot stay always with you. You must realize this. In the meantime, I wish to be constantly with you, with the heart. It is necessary to pray a great deal, and not to say, "If we have not prayed today, it is nothing serious" (LJM 10-29-83).*

And from Luke's gospel:

> But Mary treasured all these words and pondered them in her heart (Lk 2:19).

Reflection: Our Lady has spoken of her heart and her love for us many times in Medjugorje. "Consecrate yourself to the Immaculate Heart," she said in August of 1983. And in December of the same year: "Tomorrow [Feast of the Immaculate Conception] will be a truly blessed day for you, if every moment is consecrated to my Immaculate Heart." "My heart is full of grace and love. My heart is the gift I give you," she said in June of 1987. There is great peace as well as great power in this consecration, for as we give our hearts and lives to the Blessed Mother, she gives her own life—and all that this entails—to us.

Application: Putting Our Lady's words into action, let us now consecrate ourselves to her Immaculate Heart, using the prayer she dictated to Jelena for that purpose:

O Immaculate Heart of Mary, overflowing
with goodness, show us your love.
May the flame of your heart, O Mary,
Descend upon all people.
We love you so very much.
Impress true love in our hearts.
May our hearts yearn for you.
O Mary, sweet and humble of heart,
Remember us even when we sin.
You know that we are all sinners.
Through your most sacred and motherly heart,
Heal us of every spiritual illness.
Make us capable of realizing the beauty
of your maternal heart,
And in this way, may we be converted
by the flame of your heart.
Amen.

NOVEMBER 25

Consecration to the Heart of Jesus

The following message was given to Jelena for the
parish:

*Devote five minutes to the Sacred Heart. Each family
is an image of it (LJM 7-2-83).*

And from John's gospel, a prayer of Jesus to the Father:

Righteous Father, the world does not know you,
but I know you; and these know that you have sent
me. I made your name known to them, and I will
make it known, so that the love with which you
have loved me may be in them, and I in them" (Jn
17:25-26).

Reflection: The love of Christ is symbolized by his heart. To be consecrated to the Sacred Heart is to be consecrated to the Lord's love, pledged and dedicated to it. Our Lady emphasizes this in her messages. From October, 1988: "I am calling you today to the prayer of consecration to Jesus, my dear Son, so that each of your hearts may be his." And in November of 1983: "Place an image of the hearts of Jesus and Mary in your homes." In April, 1984: "I pray that you especially venerate the Heart of my Son." And last, in October of 1983: "May all families consecrate themselves to the Sacred Heart each day."

Application: Today, let us live these messages of the Blessed Virgin by consecrating ourselves to the Sacred Heart, using the prayer she dictated to Jelena for that purpose:

O Jesus, we know that you are gentle,
that you have given your heart for us,
crowned with the thorns of our sins.
We know well that today you still pray for us
so that we will not be lost.

Jesus, remember us if we fall into sin.
Through your most Sacred Heart,
enable us to love one another,
that hatred may disappear from among men.
Show us your love.
We love you
and wish that you protect us
with the heart of the Good Shepherd.

Enter into each heart, Lord Jesus!
Knock on the door of our hearts
with patience and persistence.
We are still locked within ourselves
for we have not understood your will.
O Jesus, continue to knock,

that our hearts may open to you,
especially when we remember the passion
which you suffered for us.
Amen.

NOVEMBER 26

Surrender yourselves to me

Today Our Lady speaks of one of the primary messages
of Medjugorje:

> Dear children, I wish to tell you that I have chosen this
> parish. I guard it in my hands like a little flower that
> does not want to die.
>
> I beseech you to surrender yourselves to me so that I
> can present you as a gift to God, fresh and without sin.
> Satan has destroyed part of my plan and wants to
> possess all of it. Pray that he does not succeed, for I wish
> you for myself so that I may continue offering you to
> God (WM 8-1-85).

And from Paul's first letter to the Corinthians:

> For whoever was called in the Lord as a slave is a
> freed person belonging to the Lord, just as
> whoever was free when called is a slave of Christ
> (1 Cor 7:22).

Reflection: There is glory and joy in surrender to God.
When we surrender to other masters we are crushed,
shamed, and defeated. But when we give our lives over
to God, we are glorified and find victory. An unknown
poet knew the honor in this submission: "Make me a
captive, Lord, and then I shall be free."

When we abandon ourselves totally to God, we stand
before him with nothing: nothing more, nothing less,

and nothing other than his divine will. Richard Baxter, a great religious writer, died with these words on his lips: "Lord, what you will, where you will, and when you will."

When we submit to God's complete and total control, we become "God-intoxicated," filled with his own life. There is no other way but the way of abandonment and surrender, as the Virgin emphasizes today. It can be hard, but it is essential to a fulfilled life.

Application: In prayer today, live Our Lady's message: "I beseech you to surrender yourselves to me, so that I can present you as a gift to God."

NOVEMBER 27

You are mine

Our Lady gave this message of warmth to the two young locutionists:

> *I hold all of you in my arms. You are mine. I need your prayers so that you may be all mine. I desire to be all yours and for you to be all mine. I receive all your prayers. I receive them with joy (LJM 2-23-84).*

And from Psalm 4:

> I will both lie down and sleep in peace;
> for you alone, O Lord, make me lie down in safety.
> —Psalm 4:8

Reflection: Right after World War II, Europe was flooded with homeless, hungry children. Thousands of scared and frightened kids were housed in refugee camps. They were lovingly cared for and adequately housed and fed. But they could not sleep; they were restless and unable to relax.

A psychologist had an idea. After the children were put to bed, they were each given a loaf of bread to hold. If they wanted more to eat, more was provided, but this particular "bedtime bread" was not to be eaten, it was just to hold. The bread produced a miracle: the children dozed off, assured that they would have something to eat tomorrow. That assurance provided calm and restful sleep.

The Blessed Mother gives such assurance. She will place bread in our hands tonight. It will be there tomorrow. What we have to hold onto is her Son. We can be at peace.

In Psalm 23 we hear, "The Lord is my shepherd, I shall not want." Other translations say, "The Lord is my shepherd, therefore I shall lack nothing." Our faith is based upon trusting the Shepherd, resting in his arms, and knowing that we will be nourished and fed. We are safe with the bread of trust in our hands.

Application: "I hold all of you in my arms," the Mother of God says today. "You are mine. I need your prayers so that you may be all mine." Today, offer all your prayers to Mary for her intentions.

NOVEMBER 28

Find solace in prayer

A message to Jelena and Marijana:

> *Pray! It may seem strange to you that I always speak of prayer, and yet I say again, pray! Why do you hesitate? In sacred scripture you have heard it said: "Do not worry about tomorrow, for each day has worries enough of its own." And so do not worry about other days. Find solace in prayer. I, your Mother, will take care of the rest (LJM 2-29-84).*

And in John's gospel, assurance from Christ:

> I have said this to you, so that in me you may have peace. In the world you face persecution. But take courage; I have conquered the world! (Jn 16:33).

Reflection: One summer a young woman had been rehearsing some songs, leaving her harp before an open window. Suddenly she heard the sound of distant and very lovely music. It lasted only a few seconds and left her very puzzled. When it happened again she noticed that the sound came from the instrument and was caused by the gentle breeze from the open window playing on the harp strings.

At times of prayer we can be like that harp, by allowing sufficient calm to gather round us so that the Holy Spirit, the Breath of God, may play his music in us. But remember, it was a gentle breeze, and the music could be heard only because of the surrounding stillness.

Application: Today, spend several minutes in silence, repeating only the names of Jesus and Mary. Let every anxiety be calmed by their power.

NOVEMBER 29

Do not be preoccupied

Our Lady asks us to empty ourselves before we begin to pray:

> *You must not be preoccupied during prayer. In praying, do not concern yourselves with your sins. Sins must be left behind (FY 3-85).*

And from Jesus:

> "Peace! Be still!" . . . and there was a dead calm (Mk 4:39).

Reflection: At the foot of a cliff, under the windows of the Castle of Miramar, at a depth of eighty feet below the surface of the clear waters of the Adriatic, there was, years ago, a kind of cage fashioned by divers in the face of the rock. In that cage were some of the most magnificent pearls in existence. They belonged to the Archduchess Rainer.

Having been unworn for a long time, the gems lost their color and the experts were unanimous in declaring that the only means by which they could be restored to their original brilliancy was by submitting them to a prolonged immersion in the depths of the sea. For some years they were kept lying in the crystal depths, and gradually regained their unrivalled beauty and splendor.

The only secret of regaining the lost lustre of the inner life, of spirituality and faith, is to get back again to those blessed depths from which the soul first received its bright touch of the divine and holy.

Application: Today, spend some time being still, silent, and sensitive to the soft voice of the Spirit within.

NOVEMBER 30

A great whirlpool

Given to the locutionists, Jelena and Marijana:

> *My children, pray! The world has been drawn into a great whirlpool. It does not know what it is doing. It does not realize in what sin it is sinking. It needs your prayers so that I can pull it out of this danger (LJM 2-17-84).*

In Luke's gospel, Peter is confronted with a miracle at the hands of Christ:

But when Simon Peter saw it, he fell down at Jesus' knees, saying, "Go away from me, Lord, for I am a sinful man!" (Lk 5:8).

Reflection: We sometimes hear that we need to get rid of our hang-ups, or guilt; we hear that guilt and shame are wrong and destructive. But this is not entirely true. Only false guilt arising from mistaken and misplaced judgment is wrong. Only imposed shame and coercive put-downs that are unjust and unfair are destructive. True guilt and honest shame are essential to our moral fiber. Guilt is an acknowledgment of sin, while shame is what we feel when we know the judgment of guilt is correct. Guilt tells us we were wrong; shame is what makes us blush by appealing to our conscience. In the end, without acknowledging our guilt and confessing our sin we cannot receive the Lord's forgiveness and the grace of healing.

Application: A simple prayer for today:
O Lord, when the occasion warrants, help me to realize my sin and guilt, that I may amend my life through your healing forgiveness. Amen.

Village street in Medjugorje

Sacrifice

Today the Blessed Mother advises us on how to begin Advent:

Prepare yourselves spiritually and mentally for Christmas. In your prayers, offer one especially for my intentions. Sacrifice something that you like the most (VPG 12-15-89).

St. Peter also speaks of spiritual preparations:

Rid yourselves, therefore, of all malice, and all guile, insincerity, envy, and all slander. Like newborn infants, long for the pure, spiritual milk, so that by it you may grow into salvation (1 Pt 2:1-2).

Reflection: During Advent of 1989, Our Lady asked Jelena's prayer group (and by extension all of us), to prepare spiritually for Christmas through prayer and sacrifice.

These two activities build on one another in several ways. First, sacrifice amplifies the power of prayer many times over. Second, Mary knows well that actions speak louder than words. She calls us to the specific action of making a special sacrifice for Advent, which will demonstrate our love for God in a concrete manner. Third, sacrifice will help us to develop a healthy self-discipline, so that we will not jump at every stray impulse that comes our way. And last, the spiritual merit of any act of self-denial will last for eternity.

The spiritual preparation for Christmas will clearly help in our growth toward holiness. This is a special time when we can sort out virtues from vices, as Peter recommends today: "Strip away everything deceitful;

pretenses, jealousies, and disparaging remarks of any kind."

In the end, of course, Christmas will be meaningful and joyous for us to the extent that we have prepared ourselves spiritually for it, as Mary encourages us today.

Application: With reference to Our Lady's message decide today what sacrifice you can offer to God during Advent. In what ways can you deepen your prayer life during these four weeks?

DECEMBER 2

Live the messages

In October of 1990, Our Lady gave the following message to Ivan and Marija's prayer group:

> *Dear children, tonight I invite you to pray for peace. Dear children, I want to give you new messages. I am your Mother. I wish always to teach you something new, but first of all you must live the messages I have already given you. Then I can give you new messages (VPG 10-15-90).*

And from John's gospel:

> When the Spirit of truth comes, he will guide you into all the truth; for he will not speak on his own, but will speak whatever he hears, and he will declare to you the things that are to come (Jn 16:13).

Reflection: One of the most beautiful and inspiring hymns ever written is a source of constant faith for many. "Lead, Kindly Light" was composed by Cardinal John Henry Newman, and was the favorite of both

Franklin Roosevelt and Mahatma Gandhi. The words
go like this:

> Lead, kindly light, amid the encircling gloom,
> Lead thou me on;
> The night is dark, and I am far from home;
> Lead thou me on.
> Keep thou my feet, I do not ask to see
> The distant scene; one step enough for me.

As we live Our Lady's messages, our spiritual journey depends on taking one step at a time, one day at a
time. This hymn could very well be our daily prayer.
We don't need to do everything at once. The visionaries
themselves were gradually led by the Virgin in living
her messages. For instance, she initially asked them to
pray the Creed and five Our Fathers, Hail Marys, and
Glory Bes. Years later they graduated to three hours of
prayer daily, including the Mass and full rosary.

What we need most is to keep our feet on the path,
trust God, and keep making one step, and then another,
as Our Lady leads us.

Application: Today, pray that you may not become
stymied in living the Virgin's messages, but continue to
heed her urgings to move ahead one step at a time.

DECEMBER 3

Their own creators

The following was given to the visionaries in the first
weeks of the apparitions:

> *The Russian people will be the people who will glorify
> God the most. The West has made civilization progress,
> but without God, as if they were their own creators (FY
> 10-81).*

Of the persecuted and the humble, Christ said:

> Blessed are you when people hate you, and when they exclude you, revile you, and defame you. . . . Rejoice in that day and leap for joy, for surely your reward is great in heaven (Lk 6:22-23).

Reflection: We have all heard statements like: "He's only a jail-bird," or "She's only a waitress." Some people have a bag full of "onlys"—those who live in slums, maids, street cleaners, the foreigners in our land. All can be looked upon as being "only" or "just" or "merely." It is an arrogance that goes against the grain of a lived faith, and it sadly marks not only individuals but even nations.

As followers of Christ and Our Lady, who especially love the poor and the humble, we are called to eliminate the tendency to see any human being as "only" anything. If we need to label or tag anyone, let it be as brother or sister, friend or colleague. The gospel does not recognize rank. We are all equally important to God and to each other.

Application: In your prayer today, reflect on whether you have the tendency to put down certain people or groups as "only" or "merely"—including yourself. Ask for the heart of Christ to see all people as belonging to the family of God.

DECEMBER 4

I seek to guide you

Today the Virgin wants to imbue us with the virtues of faith:

> *Dear children, day by day I wish to clothe you with holiness, goodness, obedience, and the love of God, so*

that day by day you become more beautiful and more prepared for your God. Dear children, listen to my messages and live them. I seek to guide you (WM 10-24-85).

And from Paul's letter to the church at Rome:

But you are not in the flesh; you are in the Spirit, since the Spirit of God dwells in you. Anyone who does not have the Spirit of Christ does not belong to him. But if Christ is in you, though the body is dead because of sin, the Spirit is life because of righteousness (Rom 8:9-10).

Reflection: The word *church* used in most of the North European languages comes from the Greek *Kyriake-oikia*, "the family of the Lord." It is significant that when people sought a word to describe the reality of what it means to be church, the word they chose meant "family of the Lord."

As Christians, the blood of Christ flows through all of our veins, for we are his body. We belong to him and live under his protection. St. Paul speaks of our being "sealed" into the Lord's family: "But it is God who establishes us with you in Christ and has anointed us, by putting his seal on us and giving us his Spirit in our hearts as a pledge" (2 Cor 1:21-22).

Application: Today, pray for the indelible marks of faith that the Blessed Virgin speaks of in her message: holiness, goodness, obedience, and love of God.

Maintain confidence

On the fifth day of the apparitions, in response to the seer's question, "What do you expect of us?" the Virgin said:

That you have a solid faith and that you maintain confidence (FY 6-29-81).

And from Matthew's gospel:

Everyone then who hears these words of mine and acts on them will be like a wise man who built his house on rock (Mt 7:24).

Reflection: Psychologists maintain that a mentally healthy person can tolerate uncertainty and change. Our ability to adapt and live with the unknown and unexpected is our strongest survival tool. Many of those in mental hospitals cannot bear to live with unanswered questions. They must have the correct answers for everything, even if they have to create their own world to provide those answers.

Living with uncertainty is the hallmark of spiritual health as well. This is called "faith," what Our Lady continually calls us to in Medjugorje. In his letter to the Hebrews, Paul defines faith "as the assurance of things hoped for, the conviction of things not seen" (Heb 11:1). Faith is trust in God's providence and care. It's an attitude that declares, "I don't know what God is doing, but I do believe that whatever it is, it's good."

Christians do not need the answer to every question because they have the presence and love of Christ. Why do we need every answer when God is with us to comfort and assure us in the midst of our ignorance and confusion? We are like infants held in the strong, safe arms of our parent. We don't have to know it all. We're O.K. We can be content in the providence of God.

Application: A prayer for today:
Lord Jesus, you have so many surprises in store for me. I'm ready for them as long as you are with me. Amen.

DECEMBER 6

Give all your difficulties to Jesus

The following was given to Ivan's prayer group:

> *Dear children, give all your problems and difficulties to Jesus and pray. Pray, pray, pray! Every evening during this month, pray in front of the cross in thanksgiving for the death of Jesus (VPG 2-29-88).*

And from the first letter of Peter:

> Cast all your anxiety on him, because he cares for you (1 Pt 5:7).

Reflection: In the earliest Christian art, that of the Catacombs, Christ is represented as the Greek Orpheus, with the lyre in his hand, drawing everything to him by his magic spell.

These early Christians, standing near to Greek civilization, chose this out of all the figures of Greek mythology, to express their ideas of the Lord whom they loved and worshipped. And this story of Orpheus is one of the noblest which has come down to us from the ancient land of Greece. Orpheus was the greatest of all musicians, for Apollo had bestowed upon him the lyre, which Hermes had invented. So wonderfully did he play that when his fingers touched the instrument, the beasts of the field drew near, and the birds were arrested in their flight, and even the things of nature gathered spellbound around him. He could make the strings wail so pitiful a lament that tears trickled down the scarred cheeks of the rocks. When he sang of love, the world was filled with sudden sunlight, and even the wildest beast became tame and gentle.

It was thus the early Christians thought of Christ. They felt his drawing-power, the strange spell which he had over everything. Possessed in their hearts, he transfigured nature, but most of all he transfigured them. His music banished anxieties, doubts, and suffering. In his presence there could only be hope and peace.

 Application: Today, as Our Lady asks, "give all your problems and difficulties to Jesus, the Prince of Peace."

DECEMBER 7

Vigil of the Immaculate Conception

On the eve of the Immaculate Conception in 1983, Our Lady gave this message:

> *Tomorrow will really be a blessed day for you, if every moment is consecrated to my immaculate heart. Abandon yourselves to me. Strive to make your joy grow, to live in faith, to change your hearts (LJM 12-7-83).*

Psalm 27 also speaks of trust:

The Lord is my light and my salvation;
whom shall I fear?
The Lord is the stronghold of my life;
of whom shall I be afraid?
When evildoers assail me
to devour my flesh—
my adversaries and foes—
they shall stumble and fall.

Though an army encamp against me,
my heart shall not fear;
though war rise up against me,
yet I will be confident.

—Psalm 27:1-3

Reflection: On this vigil of the Immaculate Conception, Our Lady promises that "tomorrow will really be a blessed day for you, if every moment is consecrated to my immaculate heart." Further, she strikes a cord of trust in her vigil messages. On this day in 1985: "Entrust your problems to me. No one will understand you, as I do." And on this vigil in 1983: "Abandon yourselves to me."

A trusting relationship with God and Our Lady does not always come easy to our human nature; we tend to seek self-sufficiency and self-reliance, proud that we carry our own weight. And yet trust and dependence on God actually liberates our spirits and frees us from much fear, anxiety, and doubt. Perhaps our greatest human need is to be taken care of, loved, made safe. And this is exactly what Christ and his Mother offer us.

What proceeds from this trust and confidence is the very strength, courage and peace that our hearts so desire. St. Paul writes, "Therefore I am content with weakness . . . for the sake of Christ; for when I am powerless, it is then that I am strong" (2 Cor 12:10).

On this vigil, let us take Our Lady's words of trust to heart, "Entrust your problems to me." Let us confide ourselves to Christ and Our Lady, so that our trust will grow stronger, and Mary's peace may abide in our hearts.

Application: Today Our Lady asks that we set aside at least fifteen minutes to entrust our problems to her. In confidence let us do exactly that, using her title "Virgin Most Powerful."

The Immaculate Conception

The following message was given to Jelena in 1983:

Pray, pray! Have the parish pray each day to the hearts of Jesus and Mary during the Novena of the Immaculate Conception (MJM, 1983).

And the following was given to St. Bernadette at Lourdes on March 25, 1858: "I am the Immaculate Conception."

Reflection: On this great feast, we rejoice that Our Lady, as the new Eve, was conceived without original sin and, unlike the first Eve, remained sinless and faithful ever after—the immaculate temple of God.

The Blessed Virgin was thus consecrated to God at her very conception, and lived this consecration each day of her life. We too were consecrated, or dedicated, to the Lord at our baptism and given the promise of immortality. And so St. Paul exhorts us:

For we are the temple of the living God; as God said, ". . . I will be your father, and you shall be my sons and daughters, says the Lord Almighty." Since we have these promises, beloved, let us cleanse ourselves from every defilement of body and of spirit, making holiness perfect in the fear of God (2 Cor 6:16—7:1).

The Blessed Mother will help us to live out our consecration through her intercessory prayer, if we but ask. She gives us all the tools we need in her messages.

Let us close with one of those messages, the following given on this feast day in 1983:

Thank you, my children, for coming in such large numbers. Thank you! Continue your efforts and be persevering and tenacious. Pray without ceasing.

Application: Since Our Lady and St. Paul both speak of our consecration or dedication to God, let us today once again consecrate ourselves to the Sacred Hearts of Jesus and Mary, but this time, rather than using the formal prayers, create a spontaneous prayer of dedication from the heart.

DECEMBER 9

You know what you have to do

The following message on renunciation, the key to purity, was also given on the feast of the Immaculate Conception:

> *If you do not have the strength to fast on bread and water, you can give up a number of things. It would be good to give up television for after seeing some programs, you are distracted and unable to pray. You can give up alcohol, cigarettes, and other pleasures. You yourselves know what you have to do (FY 12-8-81).*

Paul discusses another dimension of purification:

> Finally, beloved, whatever is true, whatever is honorable, whatever is just, whatever is pure, whatever is pleasing, whatever is commendable, if there is any excellence and if there is anything worthy of praise, think about these things (Phil 4:8).

Reflection: What we put into our minds determines what comes out in our words and actions. Today Paul tells us to fill them with thoughts that are good and spiritually healthy, that we might express this same goodness in our lives. This is behind the Virgin's request to reduce or eliminate television viewing, for again, what you put in, is what will come out. For instance, it is easy to discount the effect of violence and immoral behavior as seen in some movies and T.V. shows, yet there will definitely be an effect.

Consequently, if we have problems with, say, impure thoughts or dishonesty, it would be wise to examine what we are putting in our minds through magazines, books, and the media. It is our responsibility to replace harmful input with healthy material, that the Spirit of God can live and breathe within us.

Application: In prayer today, reflect on how you can eliminate, or at least cut down, on harmful messages to your mind and heart. *Do not listen to gossip.*

DECEMBER 10

I give you a great love

The following was given to Jelena's prayer group:

> I wish that you would become like a flower in spring. I give you a great love but at times you reject it, and then it diminishes. And so always accept immediately all the gifts that I give you so that they can benefit you (LJM 6-11-84).

And from Psalm 91:

> Those who love me, I will deliver;
> I will protect those who know my name.
> When they call to me, I will answer them;
> I will be with them in trouble,
> I will rescue them and honor them.
>
> —Psalm 91:14-15

Reflection: A little boy visiting his grandmother was intrigued by a handstitched pillow bearing the scripture verse, "Thou, God, seest me." Noticing her grandchild's interest, she picked up the pillow and began to explain it to him.

"Some people will tell you," she said, "that God is always watching to see if you do something wrong, so he can punish you. I don't want you to think of it like that. Every time you read the words, 'Thou God, seest me,' I would rather have you remember that God loves you so much that he cannot take his eyes off you."

This is the message of Our Lady and sacred scripture today: the ineffable love of God that transcends all human understanding. It is the foundation and meaning of our lives and our faith, for the gift of love is the gift of God's very self.

Application: St. Augustine wrote that, "One loving heart sets another on fire." As God inflames our hearts, we are called in turn to inflame others through our care, compassion, and works of love. Today, simply reflect on these lines by an unknown poet:

It has hands to help others.
It has the feet to hasten to the poor and needy.
It has the eyes to see misery and want.
It has the ears to hear the sighs and sorrows
    of men.
That is what love looks like.

DECEMBER 11

Confession should invigorate your faith

Part of our Advent preparation includes the sacrament of penance, of which Mary speaks today:

Do not go to confession only through habit, to remain the same afterwards. No, that is not good. Confession should invigorate your faith; it should refresh you and bring you closer to Jesus. If confession does not mean anything to you, truly, you will be converted with great difficulty (LJM 11-7-83).

Psalm 32 also speaks of the confession of sins and the freedom it produces:

> Then I acknowledged my sin to you,
> and I did not hide my iniquity;
> I said, "I will confess my transgressions
>   to the Lord,"
> and you forgave the guilt of my sin.
> You are a hiding place for me;
> you preserve me from trouble;
> you surround me with glad cries of deliverance.
>
> —Psalm 32:5, 7

Reflection: There is a story of a Russian prince who, through the indulgence of Napoleon, was permitted to bring pardon to one convict in a French prison. Every person he interviewed professed innocence and said he was unjustly punished. At last he found one who, with sorrow, confessed his guilt and acknowledged himself as deserving of punishment. To him he said, "I have brought you pardon. In the name of the Emperor, I pronounce you a free man."

To confess our sins before the Lord always brings forth his compassion and mercy, for he desires to forgive sinners. Forgiveness has always been part of his divine nature. He revealed it to David (our psalm today), and he dramatically showed it to the world through Jesus Christ.

And so Our Lady urges us to seek forgiveness through the sacrament of penance, for it is the gateway to inner peace, to freedom, and to a closer relationship with Christ.

Application: Mark your calendar today for your Advent confession. Remember Our Lady's words, "Confession should give an impulse to your faith. It should stimulate you and bring you closer to Jesus."

DECEMBER 12

Our Lady of Guadalupe

On this feast of Our Lady of Guadalupe, patroness of the Americas, it is fitting that we reflect on a message that was actually given in America, to Marija, in January of 1989:

> *Dear children, today I am calling you to the way of holiness. Pray that you may comprehend the beauty and the greatness of this way. Pray that you may be open to everything that God is doing through you, and that in your life, you may be moved to give thanks to God, and to rejoice over everything that he is doing through each one of you. I give you my blessing (MM 1-25-89).*

St. Paul takes up the theme of holiness as well in his letter to the Thessalonians:

> For this is the will of God, your sanctification: that you abstain from fornication; that each one of you know how to control your own body in holiness and honor, not with lustful passion, like the Gentiles who do not know God; that no one wrong or exploit a brother or sister in this matter, because the Lord is an avenger in all these things, just as we have already told you beforehand and solemnly warned you. For God did not call us to impurity but in holiness (1 Thes 4:3-7).

Reflection: Today Our Lady strikes a familiar theme, that of holiness, or godliness. She calls us to "the way of holiness," and advises us to pray "so that [we] may comprehend the beauty and the greatness of this way," which is, of course, the living of her messages, the living of the gospel.

"It is God's will," St. Paul writes today, "that you grow in holiness: that you abstain from immorality, each of you guarding himself in sanctity and honor." Holiness, then, is attainable; it is truly God's will for us, and it is the fruit of deep faith. As we see in Guadalupe's visionary, Juan Diego, holiness is often the great virtue of the humble and the poor.

On this feast day, let us pray that Our Lady of the Americas will guide us down this path, and that we might take to heart the advice of St. Paul: "Strive for peace with all men, and for that holiness without which no one can see the Lord" (Heb 12:14).

Application: Holiness is not understood so much in reading about it as in actually seeing it in another person. Today call to mind a person you feel to be holy. What qualities do you admire in him or her? Which can you imitate?

DECEMBER 13

Prepare your hearts

During Advent of 1986, the Blessed Virgin spoke of purifying our hearts:

> *Dear children, today I invite you to prepare your hearts, for in these days the Lord wants above all to purify you from all the sins of your past. You cannot do it alone, dear children, and for that reason I am here to help you.*

Pray, dear children, for this is the only way in which you can know all the evil that dwells in you, and can then abandon it to the Lord. Then he can purify your hearts completely. So, dear children, pray constantly and prepare your hearts through penance and fasting (WM 12-4-86).

The Gospa's message of purification and repentance is echoed in the Book of Daniel:

I prayed to the Lord my God and made confession, saying, "Ah, Lord, great and awesome God, keeping covenant and steadfast love with those who love you and keep your commandments, we have sinned and done wrong, acted wickedly and rebelled, turning aside from your commandments and ordinances" (Dn 9:4-5).

Reflection: Both of our readings today speak of sin and repentance, appropriate topics for Advent, when we seek to prepare ourselves in a special way for the birth of Christ. However, Our Lady makes a distinction between what we can do and what we cannot. It is our responsibility to prepare our hearts for purification through prayer, fasting, and penance; but it is in the work of Christ to actually purify the hearts that have opened to him.

The process is similar to the sacrament of penance; we are the ones who acknowledge our sins, express sorrow, and atone for them through penance. However, Jesus Christ is the one who actually forgives the sins. We can only dispose ourselves to receive his gift. As we prepare our hearts for God's purification, we can be assured of the help of Our Lady, who promises to do just that in today's message.

Application: Simply put into practice the Madonna's message today on how to prepare your heart for Christ's purifying touch.

DECEMBER 14

Learning to love

During Advent of 1984 Our Lady gave the following message:

> *Dear children, you know that the day of joy is approaching but without love you will receive little. First, then, start loving your family and everyone in the parish; then you will be able to love and accept all those who come here. Let these seven days be a week of learning to love.*
>
> *This Christmas will be unforgettable if you follow me. Disconnect your television sets and radios, and begin God's programs: meditation, prayer, reading the Gospels. Prepare yourselves with faith; then, having understood love, your life will be filled with happiness (WM 12-13-84).*

Reflection: The Blessed Virgin says, not surprisingly, that love is the whole context of Christmas, "the season of joy," and it is prepared for simply by *loving*—first our own family, and then our neighbor. "Learn to love," she urges us. But how? Today's reading from John's gospel is telling:

"They who have my commandments and keep them are those who love me; and those who love me will be loved by my Father, and I will love them and reveal myself to them."

Judas (not Iscariot) said to him, "Lord, how is it that you will reveal yourself to us, and not to the world?" Jesus answered him, "Those who love me will keep my word, and my Father will love them, and we will come to them and make our home with them" (Jn 14:21-23).

How then "to learn to love"? Christ first speaks to us of keeping his commandments, of being fair and decent with all people. Second, his appeal to "love one another as I have loved you" (Jn 15:12) means that Jesus' own life is our primary example for learning to love. Like him, loving means to help, to heal, to enlighten, and above all, to love even sacrificially, as his own life testifies.

The gospels, then, which relate the life of Christ, are a canvas on which is painted the many hues and shades of his love. Our Lady asks that we carefully examine that portrait, and with her messages to help us, to live out her Son's love in our own lives.

Application: Spend some time today reflecting on how you see Jesus loving in the gospels. What were his actions of love? his words of love? How can I imitate his love in my own life? What action or word of love can I give to another today?

DECEMBER 15

I want to show you this joy

Our Lady speaks of joy in this Advent message:

Dear children, I invite you to pray during this special time, so that you may experience the joy of meeting with the newborn Jesus.

Dear children, I wish that you live these days as I lived them. I want to guide you and show you this joy, to which I want to bring all of you. That is why I ask you, dear children, to pray and abandon yourselves totally to me (WM 12-11-86).

Joy also resounds in these verses from Philippians:

> Rejoice in the Lord always; again I will say, Rejoice. Let your gentleness be known to everyone. The Lord is near. Do not worry about anything, but in everything by prayer and supplication with thanksgiving let your requests be made known to God. And the peace of God, which surpasses all understanding, will guard your hearts and your minds in Christ Jesus (Phil 4:4-7).

Reflection: Not surprisingly, the Blessed Mother equates joy with prayer, in which we encounter the living God. "I am calling you to pray," she says, "in order that you experience the joy of meeting with the newborn Jesus." Prayerful encounters with the Lord are often joyous, for that is the divine nature.

Samuel Gordon has written that joy is a distinctly Christian word and a Christian experience. "It is the reverse of happiness," he says; "Happiness is the result of what happens of an agreeable sort. Joy has its spring deep down inside, and that spring never runs dry, no matter what happens. Only Jesus gives that joy. He had joy, singing its music within, even under the shadow of the cross."

Joy, then, is the echo of God's life within us. May our prayer this Advent give rise to this joy in all our hearts.

Application: Today, put into action the advice Our Lady gives in her message: "I want to guide you to joy. Therefore, pray and abandon yourselves totally to me."

Love your neighbor

During Advent of 1981, Our Lady said:

> *Celebrate the days which are coming. Rejoice with my Son! Love your neighbor. May harmony reign among you (FY 12-24-81).*

In his second letter, St. John echoes the Virgin's call to love:

> But now, dear lady, I ask you, not as though I were writing you a new commandment, but one we have had from the beginning, let us love one another. And this is love, that we walk according to his commandments; this is the commandment just as you have heard it from the beginning—you must walk in it (2 Jn 5-6).

Reflection: In Medjugorje, adoration of the Blessed Sacrament takes place on two evenings each week, and it is conducted with great reverence and even awe. At one of these it struck me with new meaning that, since everyone present had received communion earlier in the day, they too were vessels of the sacrament of Christ's Body, and in that sense were also worthy of a comparable love and respect.

C.S. Lewis had this in mind when he wrote, "Next to the Blessed Sacrament itself, your neighbor is the holiest object presented to your senses. If he is your Christian neighbor, he is holy in almost the same way, for in him also Christ is *vere latitat*—truly hidden."

In this sense the love of neighbor is parallel to the love of God; we cannot love one without the other since they are inseparable—the vine and the branches, the Mystical Body of Christ.

Application: Reflect today on these words of St. Teresa of Avila: "Though we do not have Our Lord with us in bodily presence, we have our neighbor, who, for the ends of love and loving service, is as good as Our Lord himself."

DECEMBER 17

But you have not listened

Our Lady promises an unforgettable Christmas if we accept her messages:

> *Dear children, I am calling you to prayer during these days. Many times I have given you messages in God's name, but you have not listened. This Christmas will be an unforgettable day for you, provided you accept the messages I am giving you. Dear children, do not allow that day of joy to be a day of deep sorrow for me (WM 12-6-84).*

The Book of Daniel speaks of that sorrowful day:

> Open shame, O Lord, falls on us . . . because we have sinned against you. To the Lord our God belong mercy and forgiveness, for we have rebelled against him, and have not obeyed the voice of the Lord our God by following his laws, which he set before us by his servants the prophets (Dn 9:8-10).

Reflection: Both readings today call us to repentance, to a change of heart. The Gospa asks that we truly accept her messages, that we take them seriously and live them. This is the ancient call of Advent, to prepare one's heart for the coming of the Lord.

It was in this context that Fr. Slavko Barbaric once gave a sermon in Medjugorje that called the people to conversion:

Our Lady wants us to abandon ourselves totally to God, our hearts belonging only to him, so that we may lose nothing and gain everything. It is the same process as when Our Lady invited us to pray the creed back in 1981; "I believe" means to give with one's heart, to entrust oneself to someone, to give oneself to someone. All of the events here at Medjugorje urge us to give ourselves totally, to give our hand to Our Lady, the Mother who calls us to peace each day.

Application: In prayer today, ask the Blessed Mother to plant her messages deeply within your heart so that, in her words, "this Christmas will be unforgettable for you."

DECEMBER 18

You are like flowers

On this Advent day in 1986, Our Lady spoke of "prayer and flowers":

Dear children, today I call you again to prayer. When you pray, you are so much more beautiful. You are like flowers which, after the snows, are bursting with beauty in their indescribable colors. In the same way, dear children, after prayer, be beautiful before God to please him.

Therefore, dear children, pray and open your life to the Lord, so that he may make of you a beautiful and harmonious flower for paradise (WM 12-18-86).

And from the Song of Solomon:

The flowers appear on the earth;
the time of singing has come,
and the voice of the turtledove

is heard in our land.
The fig tree puts forth its figs,
and the vines are in blossom;
they give forth fragrance.

—Song of Solomon 2:12-13

Reflection: In her beautiful message today, the Queen of Peace draws us gently to prayer and to an inner openness to God. This openness invites the Lord to enter and transform our hearts into luminous reflections of his own.

St. Ignatius of Loyola once wrote that, "If you prepare within your heart a fitting dwelling place, Christ will come to you and console you. His glory and beauty are within you, and he delights in dwelling there."

The one essential for preparing our hearts is quiet—both within and without. François Fenelon, a sixteenth century French theologian, writes, "How can you expect God to speak in that gentle and inward voice which melts the soul, when you are making so much noise with your rapid reflections? Be silent, and God will speak again."

May we pray with such love this Advent that the Lord may make of us those "harmonious and beautiful flowers for paradise."

Application: Today simply reflect on these lines from an anonymous poet:

I need wide spaces in my heart
Where faith and I can go apart
And grow serene.
Life gets so choked by busy living,
Kindness so lost in fussy giving
That Love slips by unseen.

DECEMBER 19

A flower by the crib

The Blessed Mother speaks of the family and dedication to Christ:

Dear children, today I would like you to do something concrete for Jesus Christ. As a sign of dedication to the Lord, I want each family member to bring a flower to him before Christmas. I wish every member of the family to have a flower by the crib of Jesus so that when he comes he will see your dedication to him! (WM 12-20-84).

In the end we are all one family for we have the same Father:

For this reason I bow my knees before the Father, from whom every family in heaven and on earth takes its name (Eph 3:14-15).

Reflection: Our Lady often speaks of the family in her messages at Medjugorje. She stresses that it is the cradle of faith and prayer, where we first learn to love.

Dietrich Bonhoeffer, a German clergyman who was imprisoned by the Nazis for his beliefs, wrote:

Most people have forgotten nowadays what a home can mean, though some of us have come to realize it as never before. It is a kingdom of its own in the midst of the world, a haven of refuge amid the turmoil of our age, nay more, a sanctuary.

It is not founded on the shifting sands of private and public life, but has its peace in God. For it is God who gave it its special meaning and dignity, its nature and privilege, its destiny and worth.

Let us pray, as Our Lady asks, that our families be bright flowers of love as we prepare to celebrate the birth of the Messiah.

Application: At Christmas, as a family, plan to bring a flower or poinsettia to Mass and place it at the crib or nativity scene "as a sign of dedication to Jesus."

DECEMBER 20

I call you to love of neighbor

Our Lady speaks of love today:

Dear children, today I wish to call you to love of neighbor. The more you will to love your neighbor, the more you shall experience Jesus especially on Christmas Day. God will bestow great gifts on you if you surrender yourselves to him.

I wish in a special way on Christmas Day to give mothers my own special motherly blessing and Jesus will bless the rest with his own blessing (WM 12-19-85).

And from Mark's gospel, the two greatest commandments:

One of the scribes came near and heard them disputing with one another, and seeing that [Jesus] answered them well, he asked him, "Which commandment is the first of all?" Jesus answered, "The first is, 'Hear, O Israel: the Lord our God, the Lord is one; you shall love the Lord your God with all your heart, and with all your soul, and with all your mind, and with all your strength.' The second is this, 'You shall love your neighbor as yourself.' There is no other commandment greater than these" (Mk 12:28-31).

Reflection: "The love of neighbor," George MacDonald wrote, "is the only door out of the dungeon of self."

Both Christ and the Blessed Mother emphasize the love of neighbor as the highest Christian calling save the love of God himself. Indeed, one is not possible without the other. "He alone loves the creator perfectly," wrote St. Bede, "who manifests a pure love for his neighbor."

The Second Vatican Council speaks of this love:

> In our times a special obligation binds us to make ourselves the neighbor of absolutely every person, and of actively helping him when he comes across our path, whether he be an old person abandoned by all, or a foreign laborer unjustly looked down upon, a refugee, a child born of an unlawful union and wrongly suffering for a sin he did not commit, or a hungry person who disturbs our conscience (*The Church Today*, 27).

"The more you will to love your neighbor," the Virgin says today, "the more you shall experience Jesus especially on Christmas Day." May we make a special effort to show our love for others during this Christmas season.

Application: Check your local newspaper and parish bulletin for charitable projects that you can help with in the next few days, such as Christmas gifts or food baskets for the poor, nursing home visitation programs, ministry to the homebound, etc. Choose one actively as a special gift to the Blessed Mother.

Do not look toward material things

During Advent in 1985, Our Lady said:

Dear children, I am calling you to prepare yourselves for Christmas by means of penance, prayer, and works of charity. Dear children, do not look toward material things, because then you will not be able to experience Christmas (WM 12-5-85).

St. Paul also warns of materialism or "worldly desires":

For the grace of God has appeared, bringing salvation to all, training us to renounce impiety and worldly passions, and in the present age to live lives that are self-controlled, upright, and godly, while we wait for the blessed hope and the manifestation of the glory of our great God and Savior, Jesus Christ (Ti 2:11-13).

Reflection: Many of us are aware of the hollowness of a materialistic attitude during the Christmas season, of how it can smother the spiritual message of Christ's birth. In this vein, the Second Vatican Council stated:

Since in our times, variations of materialism are rampant everywhere, even among Catholics, the laity should not only learn doctrine more carefully, especially those main points which are the subjects of controversy, but should also provide the witness of an evangelical life in contrast to all forms of materialism (*The Laity*, 31).

We are called, then, not just to avoid materialism in our own lives, but to serve as an example to others of simplicity of lifestyle and the priority of spiritual values over the material.

Application: Let us simply take Our Lady's advice today to, "prepare . . . for Christmas by means of penance, prayer, and works of charity . . . do not look toward material things because then you will not be able to experience Christmas."

DECEMBER 22

Do something concrete

On this day in Advent, the Madonna called her children to prayer and to works of charity:

Dear children, tonight your Mother calls you to prayer during these two days before Christmas. Open your hearts through your prayer and let us keep vigil together for the day of great joy. Dear children, I wish you to decide to do something concrete during these two days (VPG 12-22-89).

And in Luke's gospel, the Good Samaritan puts his faith into concrete action:

But a Samaritan while traveling came near him; and when he saw him, he was moved with pity. He went to him and bandaged his wounds, having poured oil and wine on them. Then he put him on his own animal, brought him to an inn, and took care of him (Lk 10:33-34).

Reflection: Faith and works of charity go hand in hand in the Christian life. "As the flower is before the fruit," writes Richard Whately, "so is faith before good works." Indeed, Christ emphasizes that they will be the criteria for the last judgment: "Come . . . inherit the kingdom prepared for you; for I was hungry and you gave me food, I was thirsty and you gave me drink, I was a stranger and you welcomed me, I was naked and you gave me clothing . . ." (Mt 25:34-35).

Application: "Dear children," Our Lady says today, "I wish you to decide to do something concrete during these two days." In compliance with this message, plan several works of charity you can accomplish in the near future.

DECEMBER 23

To be like flowers

Today Our Lady gives a short but profound message:

Dear children, I would like all of you to be like flowers, which will open at Christmas for Jesus, flowers which will not cease to blossom after Christmas. Be the good shepherds of Jesus (FY 12-21-84).

The Blessed Mother uses the beautiful analogy of a flower to express the blossoming of virtues and good works in the life of the believer.

St. Paul, too, takes up this theme in his letter to the Church of Rome; he urges his people to blossom in fraternal love and the kindness this implies:

Contribute to the needs of the saints; extend hospitality to strangers. Bless those who persecute you; bless and do not curse them. Rejoice with those who rejoice, weep with those who weep. Live in harmony with one another; do not be haughty, but associate with the lowly; do not claim to be wiser than you are.

Do not repay anymore evil for evil, but take thought for what is noble in the sight of all. If it is possible, so far as it depends on you, live peaceable with all (Rom 12:13-18).

Reflection: The virtues that Paul speaks of are of course the fruits of the Holy Spirit, poured forth by God on all who ask with sincere and open hearts. These same gifts are the very qualities that enable us to be, as Our Lady says today, "the good shepherds of Jesus." And as shepherds, we are called to use the Spirit's gifts in the service of others. The gifts we have received are many. To acknowledge them, to pray for their increase, and to share them with others, is the challenge and promise of our readings today.

Application: In prayer, acknowledge a gift or virtue you have been given, and actually use it for the benefit of someone today. For example, the gift of compassion can be expressed in a visit or phone call to one who is lonely or sick.

DECEMBER 24

The Vigil of Christmas

On this vigil of Christmas, the Blessed Mother calls us to glorify Jesus and his Nativity:

Dear children, for Christmas my invitation is that together we glorify Jesus. I present him to you in a special way on that day and my invitation to you is that we glorify Jesus and his nativity. Dear children, on that day pray still more and think more about Jesus (WM 12-12-85).

And on this vigil in 1990:

Dear children, tonight your Mother invites you to give her all your problems. My dear children, Rejoice! (VPGM 12-24-90).

The following is Matthew's passage on the birth of Christ:

Now the birth of Jesus the Messiah took place in this way. When his mother Mary had been engaged to Joseph, but before they lived together, she was found to be with child from the Holy Spirit. Her husband Joseph, being a righteous man and unwilling to expose her to public disgrace, planned to dismiss her quietly. But just when he had resolved to do this, an angel of the Lord appeared to him in a dream and said, "Joseph, son of David, do not be afraid to take Mary as your wife, for the child conceived in her is from the Holy Spirit. She will bear a son, and you are to name him Jesus, for he will save his people from their sins."

All this took place to fulfill what had been spoken by the Lord through the prophet: "Look, the virgin shall conceive and bear a son, and they shall name him Emmanuel," which means, "God is with us." When Joseph awoke from sleep, he did as the angel of the Lord commanded him; he took her as his wife, but had no marital relations with her. She bore a son, and he named him Jesus (Mt 1:18-25).

Reflection: Tonight we celebrate the greatest event of all time—the birth of the Messiah—the divine God taking on human flesh. For ages the Jewish people had waited for him, and when the miracle finally occurred, the first to hear of it were not the nobility or Temple hierarchy, but simple shepherds. The birth was in a stable, not a palace. Even at the beginning, the Messiah came first to the humble, the ordinary, the poor. And he still comes to them, to all with hearts humble enough to receive him.

Application: Greet the Christ child with prayer and love this evening. Give him your heart as your gift.

DECEMBER 25

Christmas Day

On Christmas Day in 1989, Our Lady spoke of being a light for others:

> *Dear children, here is my Son in my arms! I would like to ask you to be a light for all in the year to come. I would like to call you again to live my messages—the messages of peace, conversion, prayer, penance, and faith.*
>
> *Dear children, your Mother does not seek words from you—I ask for deeds. Your Mother will help you and she will give you the strength to persevere. And tonight I would like to tell you: Rejoice! (VPG 12-25-89).*

And from Luke's gospel, the shepherds come to adore the Christ-child:

> When the angels had left them and gone into heaven, the shepherds said to one another, "Let us go now to Bethlehem and see this thing that has taken place, which the Lord has made known to us."
>
> So they went with haste and found Mary and Joseph, and the child lying in the manger. When they saw this, they made known what had been told them about this child; and all who heard it were amazed at what the shepherds told them.
>
> But Mary treasured all these things and pondered them in her heart. The shepherds returned, glorifying and praising God for all they had heard and seen, as it had been told them (Lk 2:15-20).

Reflection: Christmas is a season of light—the light of angels among shepherds, the light of a great star beckoning wise men, and in our own day, the multicolored lights of Christmas trees, outdoor decorations, and the bright glow from the windows of homes where families are gathered to celebrate.

Appropriately, today the Blessed Mother calls each of us to be, "a light for all in the year to come." Through living her messages, we have become changed people. The new peace and kindness in our lives attracts others who wish to share in these gifts of grace. In such a way, we have become beacons of hope and joy drawing others to Christ.

Although our characters differ, and our personalities are unique, yet our many colors form a harmony as Christmas lights on an evergreen. In the darkness, the glow of the shining lights is truly beautiful.

Application: As Our Lady calls us to be a light for others by living her messages, let us pray for her special help today in doing just that.

DECEMBER 26

Rejoice with me!

On Christmas in 1988, the Blessed Mother asked us to rejoice with her:

Dear children, I call you to peace. Live this peace in your heart and in your surroundings, so that everyone will recognize this peace which comes not from you, but from God.

Little children, today is a great day. Rejoice with me! Celebrate the birth of Jesus with my peace, the peace with which I have come as your Mother, the Queen of Peace.

Today I am giving you my special blessing. Carry it to every creature so that all my have peace (MM 12-25-88).

And from Luke's gospel, the birth of the Messiah:

While they were there, the time came for her to deliver her child. And she gave birth to her first-born son and wrapped him in bands of cloth, and laid him in a manger, because there was no place for them in the inn (Lk 2:6-7).

Reflection: On this day after Christmas, let us experience the birth of Jesus through the eyes of the great mystical writer, Maria Valtorta. From *The Poem of the God-Man*:

I see Mary with the newborn son in her arms. A little baby, flushed, bustling with his little hands and kicking with his small feet: and crying with a thin trembling voice just like a newborn lamb. And he moves his small head that is so blond that it seems without any hair, a little round head that his mother holds in the hollow of her hand, while she looks at her baby and adores him weeping and smiling at the same time, and she bends down to kiss him not on his head, but on the center of his chest, where underneath there is his small heart beating for us . . . where one day there will be the Wound. . . .

"Come, let us offer Jesus to the Father," says Mary. And she lifts her baby in her arms and says: "Here I am. On his behalf, O God, I speak these words to you: Here I am to do your will. And I, Mary, and my spouse, Joseph, with him. Here are your servants, O Lord. May your will always be done by us, in every hour, in every event, for your glory and your love."

Application: Today, let us simply live the Gospa's message: "Rejoice with me! Celebrate the birth of Jesus with my peace. . . ."

DECEMBER 27

I wish to deepen your love

In this Christmas season, Our Lady seeks to lead us further in love:

Dear children, I wish to thank all of you who have heeded my messages and who, on Christmas Day, have put into practice what I asked of you. Undefiled by sin from now on, I wish to deepen your love even further. And so, abandon your hearts to me! (WM 12-26-85).

The story of the Magi speaks of love expressing itself in giving:

When they had heard the king, they set out; and there, ahead of them, went the star that they had seen at its rising, until it stopped over the place where the child was. When they saw that the star had stopped, they were overwhelmed with joy. On entering the house, they saw the child with Mary his mother; and they knelt down and paid him homage. Then, opening their treasure chests, they offered him gifts of gold, frankincense, and myrrh (Mt 2:9-12).

Reflection: As our readings illustrate today, Christmas is the great season of love and giving. The Magi, awed by the miracle of God coming into the world as a helpless infant, responded by offering him their most precious gifts.

This spirit of giving is captured in this passage from Frank O'Connor's, *An Only Child*:

> One Christmas, Santa Claus brought me a toy engine. I took it with me to the convent, and played with it while mother and the nuns discussed old times. But it was a young nun who brought us in to see the crib.
>
> When I saw the Holy Child in the manger, I was distressed because little as I had, he had nothing at all. For me it was fresh proof of the incompetence of Santa Claus.
>
> I asked the young nun politely if the Holy Child didn't like toys, and she replied composedly enough, "Oh, he does, but his mother is too poor to afford them." That settled it. My mother was poor too, but at Christmas she at least managed to buy me something even if it was only a box of crayons.
>
> I distinctly remember getting into the crib and putting the engine between his outstretched arms. I probably showed him how to wind it as well, because a small baby like that would not be clever enough to know. I remember too the tearful feeling of reckless generosity with which I left him there in the nightly darkness of the chapel, clutching my toy to his chest.

Application: Today, simply reflect in prayer on the gifts you have received from the Lord. In what way can you share them?

DECEMBER 28

I am presenting you to God

Our Lady's monthly message for Christmas, 1987:

Dear children, rejoice with me! My heart is rejoicing because of Jesus and today I want to give him to you. Dear children, I want each one of you to open your hearts to Jesus and I will give him to you with love.

Dear children, I want him to change you, to teach you, and to protect you. Today I am praying in a special way for each one of you and I am presenting you to God so he will manifest himself in you.

I am calling you to sincere prayer with the heart so that every prayer of yours may be an encounter with God. In your work and in your everyday life, put God in the first place.

I call you today with great seriousness to obey me and to do as I am calling you (MM 12-25-87).

The Christmas narrative continues with the flight into Egypt:

Now after they had left, an angel of the Lord appeared to Joseph in a dream and said, "Get up, take the child and his mother, and flee to Egypt, and remain there until I tell you; for Herod is about to search for the child, to destroy him."

Then Joseph got up, took the child and his mother by night, and went to Egypt, and remained there until the death of Herod. This was to fulfill what had been spoken by the Lord through the prophet, "Out of Egypt I have called my son" (Mt 2:13-15).

Reflection: Mary says to us today, "My heart is rejoicing because of Jesus and today I want to offer him to you."

Faced with the love of Christ and his Mother, we are inspired in turn to be loving and generous ourselves. To love is catching, especially in this holy season. One example:

A report from an elementary school near Chicago tells about a Christmas pageant held in the school. A third grader was the inn keeper. He had only one line to say: "Sorry. There is no room in the inn." But the little boy entered into the spirit of the play and said his part with real feeling. And then, as Mary and Joseph turned away to leave, the little fellow called out, "Come back, Joseph. I'll give you my room!" (Anonymous).

Application: Like the little boy, allow yourself to be swept away by love during these days.

DECEMBER 29

A shepherd's heart

During Christmas of 1983, Our Lady said to Jelena:

I desire that you be a flower which blossoms for Jesus at Christmas—a flower which continues to bloom after Christmas has passed. I so wish that your heart be a shepherd's heart, for Jesus (LJM 1983).

St. John speaks of the miracle of the Incarnation:

And the Word became flesh and lived among us, and we have seen his glory, the glory as of a father's only son, full of grace and truth (Jn 1:14).

Reflection: The enduring love of Christ touches us in a special way during Christmas. At the same time it also inspires us to be shepherds after his own heart, a vocation to which the Mother of God also calls us.

To have a shepherd's heart means to look around us, even search for, those in need. A story might illustrate:

Chad Varah was an Anglican priest. In 1953, he buried a girl of eighteen who had killed herself. The coroner, at the inquest, suggested that she might not have done this desperate act if someone had been around who would have listened to her troubles.

Chad Varah decided to use his London church and a telephone to listen to people who were in despair. He put a small advertisement in the local paper, and during the first week he had twenty-seven calls.

Soon he was listening and advising people twelve hours each day. There were so many people waiting in his outer office to see him that he asked some of his congregation to come and provide cups of tea for them.

Then he found that often people who had come into the outer office in great distress had become different people by the time they reached him, and some did not even wait to see him because one of the helpers had befriended them. So he decided to train a group of his congregation so that they could be more helpful in the way they befriended the clients. That is how the Order of Samaritans was formed (Patricia Curley).

Application: Let us answer the Madonna's call today by helping those who are needful in our own family and community—the aged, the handicapped, the bereaved. Ask Our Lady to point out to you the person(s) in need whom she wishes you to help.

Let your hearts continue to be happy

Today Our Lady speaks of happiness and the retreat of Satan:

Dear children, this Christmas Satan especially wanted to spoil God's plans, but you, dear children, discerned Satan even on Christmas Day itself. God is winning in all your hearts—so let your hearts continue to be happy (WM 12-27-84).

St. Paul also speaks of joy and the defeat of Satan:

For while your obedience is known to all, so that I rejoice over you, I want you to be wise in what is good and guileless in what is evil. The God of peace will shortly crush Satan under your feet. The grace of our Lord Jesus Christ be with you (Rom 16:19-20).

Reflection: Happiness, according to many philosophers, is a state of being that nobody recognizes while they are happy, but can recollect all too clearly when they are unhappy. But the happiness that St. Paul and Our Lady refer to today is the inner joy that is born of God's love in our hearts. It is the fruit of a personal relationship with Jesus Christ based on total trust. It usually does not happen all at once, but by degrees. As our trust builds, so does our peace.

Application: Reflect today on these lines from St. Thomas á Kempis:

But true glory and holy joy is to glory in Thee, O Lord, and not in one's self; to rejoice in thy name, and not to be delighted in one's own virtue, nor in any creature, save only for thy sake.

When you hear the bells at midnight

The Mother of God speaks of peace in the new year:

Next year will be a year of peace—not because men have named it so—but because God has planned it. You will not have peace through presidents, but through prayer (LJM 12-31-85).

At the same time, to another of the little seers in Jelena's prayer group, Jesus said the following:

When you hear the bells at midnight, you shall fall on your knees, bow your head to the ground, so that the King of Peace will come. This year I will offer my peace to the world. But afterwards, I will ask where you were when I offered it (LJM 12-31-85).

Five years later, on New Year's Eve in 1990, the Gospa said to Ivan's prayer group:

Dear children, tonight your Mother invites you to go together with me to the church in joy and prayerfulness (there was a special Mass at 11:30 p.m.). In tonight's special joy, pray in church for the intention of peace (VPG 12-31-90).

And in Romans, Paul echoes the Virgin's call to peace:

For the kingdom of God is not food and drink but righteousness and peace and joy in the Holy Spirit. The one who thus serves Christ is acceptable to God and has human approval. Let us then pursue what makes for peace and for mutual upbuilding (Rom 14:17-19).

Reflection: The Queen of Peace fittingly closes the year with a call to peace. This has always been her central message, the primary reason for her apparitions in

Medjugorje. And, with the prayers of her children, what wonders she has achieved! The fall of the Berlin Wall, the liberation of Eastern Europe, the collapse of Communism, the rebirth of the Russian republics, the rise of both democracy and the philosophy of human rights.

A new age of peace has dawned "not through the presidents, but through prayer." All of us who have helped Our Lady through prayer, fasting, and sacrifice; all of us who have tried to live her messages; all of us who have believed in her and trusted her—we too have had a part in ushering in this new age.

In decades to come historians will puzzle over the cataclysmic events of the 1980s and 90s, trying to figure out how it all could have happened. And most will be unaware that it was the work of a young maiden on a hillside in Yugoslavia, who wept for peace. Gathering the faithful from every land, she worked miracles. She continues to this day.

Application: On New Year's Eve in 1985, Jesus said, "When you hear the bells at midnight, you will fall on your knees, bow your head to the ground, so that the King of Peace will come." Let us live that message tonight.

Vicka Ivankovic with the author

Fr. Richard J. Beyer is a priest of the Diocese of Davenport, Iowa. He has been to Medjugorje many times, both to lead pilgrimages and for extended stays. He has also served as a pastor and hospital chaplain for the diocese. His latest book of Marian devotions, published in 1996 by Ave Maria Press, is entitled BLESSED ART THOU, *A Treasury of Marian Prayers and Devotions.*